Latin America

PETER LANG
New York • Washington, D.C./Baltimore • Boston
Bern • Frankfurt am Main • Berlin • Vienna • Paris

Latin America

An Interdisciplinary Approach

Edited by

Julio López-Arias

and

Gladys M. Varona-Lacey

PETER LANG
New York • Washington, D.C./Baltimore • Boston
Bern • Frankfurt am Main • Berlin • Vienna • Paris

Library of Congress Cataloging-in-Publication Data

Latin America: an interdisciplinary approach / edited by
Julio López-Arias and Gladys M. Varona-Lacey.
p. cm.
Includes bibliographical references and index.
1. Latin America—Civilization. I. López-Arias, Julio. II. Varona-Lacey, Gladys M.
F1408.3.L272 980—dc21 98-38418
ISBN 0-8204-3479-5

Die Deutsche Bibliothek-CIP-Einheitsaufnahme

Latin America: an interdisciplinary approach / ed. by
Julio López-Arias and Gladys M. Varona-Lacey.
–New York; Washington, D.C./Baltimore; Boston; Bern;
Frankfurt am Main; Berlin; Vienna; Paris: Lang.
ISBN 0-8204-3479-5

Cover design by Nona Reuter.

The paper in this book meets the guidelines for permanence and durability
of the Committee on Production Guidelines for Book Longevity
of the Council of Library Resources.

275 Seventh Avenue, 28th Floor, New York, NY 10001
www.peterlangusa.com

Printed in the United States of America

To our families...

Acknowledgments

Several individuals have helped bring this book to fruition. First and foremost we owe many thanks to the contributors. Our gratitude is extended to Tina Bennett, who helped us launch the project; to David López, Jeness Ruhanen, and Karen Sunderland of Ithaca College's Office of Academic Computing for their technical assistance; and to the Office of the Provost. Dr. Heidi Burns, of Peter Lang Publishing, Inc., deserves a word of appreciation for the guidance she has given us. Finally, we would like to thank our spouses, Nancy Crane and Kevin Lacey, for their insightful comments.

Contents

Illustrations xi
Preface xiii

SOCIETY

Indians of Mesoamerica
Timothy D. Murphy 3
Either Black or White: Race Relations in Contemporary Brazil
G. Reginald Daniel 19
Language and Identity in Central America: A History of Oppression, Struggle, and Achievement
Anita Herzfeld 43
More Than Wives and Mothers: Women in Latin American History
Sarah C. Chambers 69
Malinche, Guadalupe, and La Llorona: Patriarchy and the Formation of Mexican National Consciousness
C. Alejandra Elenes 87
The Catholic Church in Latin America: From Privilege to Protest
Sarah Brooks and Christian Smith 105

POLITICS AND ECONOMICS

War in Latin America: The Peaceful Continent?
Miguel Angel Centeno 121
Development and Dependency in Latin America
Satya R. Pattnayak 137
Mixed Blessings of Foreign Capital Flows: Latin America's Record of Development Performance
Susan Randolph 159

ARTISTIC MANIFESTATIONS

Five Hundred Years of Latin American Literature
Gustavo A. Alfaro 183
The Indigenous and Neo-Indigenous Literature of Peru
Blas Puente-Baldoceda 199

Mexican Colonial Art and Architecture from the Conquest to Independence
Carol Callaway 217
The Music of Latin America
Walter Aaron Clark 233
Latin American New Song
Colleen Kattau 253
"New" Latin American Cinema, 1954–1974
John Hess 271

Contributors 293
Index 299

Illustrations

Language and Identity in Central America: A History of Oppression, Struggle, and Achievement

Figure 1. Intermediate and Mesoamerican Cultural and Linguistic Areas 56
Figure 2. English and Creole Speakers in Central America, 1978 57

Table 1. Central American Linguistic Distribution 53
Table 2. Atlantic Region: Population by Ethnic groups (1984) 62

The Peaceful Continent? War in Latin America

Figure 1. *International Wars 1816–1980* 123
Figure 2. *Civil Wars* 129
Figure 3. *Latin America in the 20th Century* 133

Table 1. *Major International Wars* 122
Table 2. *Major Civil Wars* 130

Development and Dependency in Latin America

Table 1. *Percent of Urban Households below or on the Poverty Line, 1980–1990* 146
Table 2. *Trends in Social Expenditure, Selected Countries* 149
Table 3. *Sectoral Evolution of Social Expenditures: 1990–1993 Compared to 1980–1981* 150
Table 4. *Military Expenditures as a Percentage of Central American Government Expenditure (CGE) Selected Countries* 151

Mixed Blessings of Foreign Capital Flows: Latin America's Record of Development Performance

Table 1. *Male and Female Life Expectancy: 1960–1993* 160
Table 2. *Gross Secondary School Enrollment Rate: 1960–1990* 162
Table 3. *Per Capita Gross Domestic Product: 1960–1994 Constant (1985) IPC $* 164
Table 4. *Income Share and Average Income of Poorest 20% and 40% of the Population: 1970 and 1990* 166

Table 5. *Ratio of Long-Term and Publicly Guaranteed Debt (DOD) to GNP and Ratio Resultant Debt Service Obligations to Export Earnings: (TDSDOD/XGS) 1970–1982* 171
Table 6. *Ratio of Total Debt (EDT) to GNP and Resultant Ratio Debt Service to Export Earnings (TDSEDT/XGS): 1982–1994* 176

Mexican Colonial Art and Architecture from the Conquest to Independence
Figure 1. *Augustinian Church at Acolman showing facade and open chapel* 218
Figure 2. *Angel from the Baptismal font of the Church of San Juan Evangelista.* 219
Figure 3. *Framework of a retablo at Huejotzingo* 222
Figure 4. *Bishop from the Retablo de Huejotzingo.* 223
Figure 5. *National Cathedral of Mexico showing main facade of the Sagrario.* 225
Figure 6. *Detail of the stucco decoration from the interior of the church of Santa María Tonanzintla.* 227

Preface

In 1494, as a result of the Treaty of Tordesillas (Spain), the continent to be known as America was divided between Spain and Portugal. These peoples, crossroads of western civilization, spread their Latin-derived languages (Spanish and Portuguese), their cultures, and the Roman Catholic religion throughout America, a continent already populated by indigenous cultures that had been evolving for centuries. Later on, the Dutch, the French, and particularly the English, began to make claims to Spanish and Portuguese continental territories. The Colombian José María Torres Caicedo in 1856 employed for the first time the appellative of Latin America to refer to the American region with the linguistic and cultural imprint of the Spanish and the Portuguese and thus creating a regional Latin American identity. The French soon appropriated and popularized this term to claim more of the Spanish- and Portuguese-speaking America and thus establishing the difference with Anglo-America or English speaking America.

Through cultural and racial *mestizaje*, common to the Spanish and Portuguese colonizations, the dominant Spanish and Portuguese languages and cultures incorporated linguistic and cultural elements from the pre-Columbian indigenous populations (many pre-Columbian languages are still spoken today) and from the descendants of black West Africans. In more recent periods of its history Latin America received immigrants from literally all over the world, thus diversifying even more its already varied population. This process of *mestizaje* continues. Today Latin America linguistically and culturally remains predominantly Spanish and Portuguese, although among its population, close to half a billion people, is among the most racially mixed of the world.

Latin Americans and Anglo-Americans have historically determined and will continue to shape each other's future. Since the 1820s, the relations between these two neighbors have been somewhat conflictive (the United States has intervened militarily in Latin America over 50 times), due mainly to language and cultural differences and economic interests. Today, Latin American states are still seen as politically weak and unstable. Its vulnerable governments are frequently faced with social unrest exacerbated by poverty, high unemployment, inflation, unequal distribution of wealth, and huge foreign debts. Its countries are economically dependent on the International Monetary Fund, multinational consortiums, and foreign powers, particularly the United States. In spite of their past relations, Latin Americans and Anglo-Americans are moving inevitably toward a greater continental interdependency which will bring common consequences for all the Americas. More and more Latin Americans live and will live in Anglo-America and vice versa. Consequently, learning and knowing about the diverse and vast region of Latin America seems logical and necessary in order to have a better understanding of the western hemisphere.

Latin America: An Interdisciplinary Approach offers introductory articles from various disciplines to enrich the readers with a panoramic overview and a more comprehensive and ample appraisal of Latin America. Some essays introduce the racial and ethnic *mestizaje* present in Latin America; its languages as crucial determinants of cultural identity; the role of women; and the influence of the Roman Catholic Church. A few touch upon the region's bellicose conflicts, its economic dependency, and its political susceptibility to outside powers. Other essays are devoted to artistic manifestations of the region, particularly in the fields of literature, art, cinema, and music.

The editors do not necessarily agree with all approaches, perspectives, information, and even terminologies presented in some of the contributions. The essays reflect solely the point of view of their authors. Nevertheless, it has been our aim to present a book that will promote a better understanding of the region, provoke debates among scholars and students, and foster greater respect toward Latin America. We also hope that *Latin America: An Interdisciplinary Approach* stimulates the development of interdisciplinary courses and the proliferation of Latin American studies programs.

Julio López-Arias, Ph.D.
Gladys M. Varona-Lacey, Ph.D.
Ithaca College
Ithaca, New York

SOCIETY

Indians of Mesoamerica

Timothy D. Murphy

Today there are perhaps twenty million Indians living in Mexico and Central America. There may be another one million Indians from that area living within the boundaries of the United States and Canada.

Geographically, Central America is the area between Mexico and Colombia that includes Guatemala, Belize (formerly British Honduras), Honduras, El Salvador, Nicaragua, Costa Rica, and Panamá. These countries plus Mexico (technically part of the North American continent) together comprise an area called Middle America by some scholars (Helms 1975). The indigenous population of the region is concentrated in the higher elevations of the southern half of Mexico and in Guatemala, plus the Yucatan peninsula, Belize, Honduras, and El Salvador. This more restricted region within Middle America is the culture area called Mesoamerica. It was in this culture area where the great Maya, Zapotec, Mixtec, Totonac, Tarascan (Purépecha), Aztec, and other civilizations rose to splendor prior to the arrival of the Spaniards. It is in this area also that indigenous people themselves are becoming increasingly prominent in political action and literary discourse in an ongoing process of defining what it means to be "Indian" in contemporary society.

When Spaniards, led by Hernán Cortés, invaded Mexico in the early sixteenth century, the population of Mesoamerica was perhaps twenty-seven million. One hundred years later the population of Mesoamerica had been reduced by more than ninety percent—as a result of warfare, harsh working conditions, torture, abuse, demoralization, famine, and disease—to a level of approximately 1,500,000. In the last four centuries the indigenous population of the region has rebounded in numbers and in cultural strength, even as the culture itself has experienced significant change. Today there are at least ten million speakers of one or another of some eighty distinct indigenous languages (Kaufman 1974, Valdeés 1988); perhaps another ten million or more people may be considered Indian by other cultural criteria or by self-identification. The importance of this historical trend lies not merely in rising head-counts and census figures, but also in the human, cultural, and political significance of the label "Indian" itself. Like other ethnic identities in this and other regions, "Indian" has always been a negotiated, situational, and flexible construct, neither timeless nor absolute.

In fact, it is good to remember that the idea or status "Indian" did not exist in the consciousness or social arrangements of the Mesoamericans themselves prior to the arrival of the European colonial powers. *Indígena* (or *natural*) —like other legalistic and politically potent terms such as *mestizo*, *negro*, *mulato*, *zambo*, *criollo*, *peninsular*, *gachupín*— is a concept introduced as part of the jural nomenclature of Spanish colonial administration. Colonialism, based as it is on political subjugation and an ideology legitimizing subordination of those colonized, creates and sustains racial and ethnic classification. This was the case in the colonies that Spain established in the Americas.

Before the European invasion, Mesoamerica was essentially a series of autonomous political entities engaged in commerce, intermarriage (especially among the nobility), and warfare with one another. The territorial limits of the polities tended to coincide with linguistic and cultural boundaries. The people of a particular kingdom or city-state (say, the Tlaxcalans of central Mexico, the Totonacs of the eastern lowlands of Mexico, the Tarascans of southwestern Mexico, or the Quiché of Guatemala) spoke the same language and had similar cultural practices and ideas. The evidence indicates that individuals and groups identified with particular local communities or larger political entities, not as inhabitants of the Mesoamerican culture area and certainly not as members of a population conceptualized as Indian or aboriginal. They were, much like their contemporaries in Europe, citizens of this or that state or speakers of this or that language. It was only as a consequence of contact with powerful Europeans that the people of Mesoamerica discovered what it meant—legally, politically, economically, and socially—to be Indian or non-Indian.

Despite the fact that the Mesoamericans themselves had little or no consciousness of kind, the cultures of the area shared a coherent cultural configuration or pattern. The Maya, the Zapotec, the Mixtec, the Purépecha, the Aztec, the Totonac—all had cultural patterns that incorporated traits characteristic of the region. These included material items, such as the steam bath, granaries, pyramids, ball courts; domesticated crops such as corn (maize), beans, squash, tomatoes, chiles, avocados, cotton; agricultural techniques such as slash-burn, irrigation, terracing, raised fields; social forms including classes and stratification, communal property, a high degree of craft specialization, professional merchants, well-equipped armies, full-time ritual specialists and astronomers, a highly developed priesthood, sophisticated calendrics, writing systems, states, and at least one empire (Aztec); and a religious cosmology built on a multilayered conception of a quadrilateral universe centered on an *axis mundi* linking the underworld with the world above the surface of the earth, and this universe was inhabited by a multitude of divine beings coupled with a belief in the efficacy of blood sacrifice to maintain cosmological order. There was an empirically recognizable Mesoamerican cultural pattern, a configuration of traits and complexes that made the region distinct from the adjacent culture areas of lower Central America, the Caribbean, and (to the north) the greater Southwest.

In his sensitive portrait of life in a Q'anjob'al-speaking community of the Guatemalan highlands, Mayan novelist Gaspar Pedro González conceives a conversation between two men in which the scribe, a prestigious elder in the community, reflects on the lack of salience certain state-sponsored symbolic acts have for Indians:

> What holiday is this Columbus Day, Sir?
>
> Friend Mekel, to us Mayas many things have not been revealed. Our world is not the world of the Ladinos; our holidays are not their holidays; our lives develop along different lines. We don't have the same vision of life: theirs is one way, ours another. Race, nationality or so-called national identity, means belonging to something or to a group, to be part of it, do you understand?

Yes, I understand (González 1995, 14).

Here the novelist neatly draws attention to two related issues recurrent in more than one hundred years of anthropological research in Mexico and Central America: first, the systematic opposition of, and frequent resistance to, hegemonic practices of European culture at the local level; and second, differing strategies for thinking about what it means to be Indian, an argument central to a long-standing debate on ethnicity. In their encounters with national institutions and policies, indigenous people have often adopted different strategies, from eager acceptance to strong, sometimes violent, resistance and rejection. Or the response may be indifference mixed with satirical commentary expressed through legends and the masked and costumed dancers of, say, *carnaval*, performing ribald parodies of the Spanish conquistadors and Ladinos and their ways. Whatever the strategy, it essentially amounts to recognition that Indians and non-Indians participate to some degree in two distinct cultural traditions and sets of meanings.

The second question raised by the scribe is one of definition. Is Mayan-ness delineated in terms of cultural content, by finding continuities with customs of the past, of a bygone pre-Hispanic era? Or, is being Maya not so much a matter of how one behaves, dresses, believes, or speaks in accordance with the practices of an essentialist past, but, rather, whether one is advantaged or disadvantaged by social structural arrangements and the extent and type of participation in community, regional, and national institutions (cf. Marino Flores 1967)? Yet these questions are, as the scribe's diatribe reveals, more than merely the scholarly concerns of academicians and theoreticians. They have practical import for the people themselves as, indeed, González' novel movingly elaborates. And one's response to these questions shapes one's vision of and hope for one's place, one's community, and indigenous peoples in general in the modern state-level societies of Guatemala, Mexico, and the United States of America.

The perspective that uses cultural content as ethnic marker supports an acculturation model in which a group (or individual) is portrayed as being more or less Indian by determining if traits such as language, clothing, technology, housing, social organization, and religion are of pre-Hispanic or foreign origin. This acculturation model has been the basis for a good many excellent descriptions of the direction and nature of change over the last five hundred years. Outstanding examples of this type of ethnohistorical analysis are studies of the All Saints Day ceremonial and ideological complex (Nutini 1988) and witchcraft and anthropomorphic supernaturalism (Nutini and Roberts 1993) in the rural Tlaxcala area of central Mexico.

This acculturation model seems to have provided the rationale for two different humane, yet politically loaded, twentieth-century philosophies about the fate of Indian cultures and peoples in modern society. In Mexico, at least, "state policy vis-à-vis the indigena population has either emphasized forging a strong homogeneous mestizo [blended European-Indian] culture through assimilation of indigenas (de-Indianization) or envisioned national culture in pluralistic and pluri-ethnic terms, in which nationalization of indigenas is perceived as compatible with respecting their culture, albeit with Spanish as the national language" (Cook and Joo 1995, 31).

Indigenismo, which tends to be more assimilationist than pluralistic, is "the program created specifically to promote development among the Indian peoples of the region" (Carmack, Gasco, and Gossen 1996, 266). From the point of view of the material well-being and economic circumstances of the Indians themselves, indigenismo has probably had greater success in Mexico than in Guatemala. Agricultural programs, modernization of local infrastructure (roads, potable water, electricity, sewage disposal), and school construction and literacy programs have benefited local populations and encouraged greater integration into urban labor and market systems. Nonetheless, critics in both countries have been vociferous in their concern that these policies not only devalue and stigmatize Indian culture itself but also conceal from view the process by which these very social programs make "the Indians more accessible to . . . capitalist exploitation." The flaw in the indigenismo project, according to its critics, is that

> the indigenists overvalue the importance of culture, which in their view is merely "superstructural" to the Indians' underlying class condition. That is why, the critics point out, the indigenists find it so difficult to define what the Indians are. In fact, they argue, the Indians cannot be culturally distinguished from the mestizo [ladino] peasants and rural proletariats of Mexico. Both are said to be fundamentally Western in culture, and increasingly subject to U.S. influences. (Carmack, Gasco, and Gossen 1996, 268)

Cook and Joo call attention to the recent development of "an insurgent ethnicist and neopopulist . . . movement in civil society that rejects the concept of a unified national culture. It seeks instead autonomy for the national *indígena* minority or empowerment of the indigenous minorities and redress of their social and economic grievances" (1995, 34). For these authors the problem with this insurgent ethnopopulism is not so much its political objectives as its misrepresentation of rural Mesoamerican economy and social organization. The problem with an ethnopopulism that emphasizes the uniqueness of contemporary Indian culture (as a configuration *sui generis*) is that it often "obfuscates" the similarities between the culture and social practices of mestizos and indigenes. It sees greater difference than actually exists. It imagines undiluted continuities with, and survivals from, pre-Hispanic culture, where for the most part the empirical reality is that contemporary rural culture is syncretic (Cook and Joo 1995, 35).

This emphasis on uniqueness often entails a romantic view of Indians, a view that is ultimately crippling to both society and to our historical understanding. In fact, the late Mexican anthropologist Guillermo Bonfil Batalla writes that in popular imagination the Indian is simultaneously "noble savage" and "inferior primitive" and this ambivalence colors contemporary discourse as well as social relations and political process. Both the noble savage and the inferior primitive images legitimize social and cognitive distance between mestizos and indigenes and the marginalization of the latter. "The Indian is viewed through the lens of an easy prejudice: the lazy, primitive, ignorant, perhaps picturesque, but always the dead weight that keeps us from being the country we should have been" (1996, 19).

In a similar vein, anthropologist Hugo Nutini reminds us that even those who should know better sometimes seem to be captivated by an image of Indian culture as static and unchanging, as a kind of survival from antiquity. Nutini's remonstrance is probably overstated, but nonetheless timely: "All too often anthropologists [like some other urban-based intellectuals or policy mavens, I might add] have romantically assumed a permanence of Indian culture and society that is not congruent with the historical facts" (1997, 237 n. 3). The facts are that all indigenous groups in Mexico and Central America—some more than others— have undergone significant genetic, technological, economic, social, cultural, and linguistic transformation as a result of the arrival of Europeans and Africans during the last five centuries.

The sequence of sociocultural change may be framed in two broad chronological periods: colonial (1519–1820) and republican (1820 to present). The general process has been one of acculturation, the incorporation of cultural patterns from foreign cultures by Mesoamerican people. Yet the process has not been totally one-way: European and African modes of adaptation to America have received significant and enduring influence from native cultures. The most obvious evidence of the influence of pre-Hispanic culture found at all social class levels in present-day Mesoamerican culture is in the domain of diet and cuisine, in which maize in the form of tortillas and tamales is consumed in nearly all households. Virtually all rural farmers, whether Indian or mestizo, utilize agricultural techniques that are at least partly based on pre-Hispanic knowledge and technique. The mis-named "floating gardens" of Xochimilco, the basis for a flourishing commerce in vegetables and flowers and a popular tourist stop just south of Mexico City, are not floating at all but are artificially constructed islands supporting a form of intensive agriculture called *chinampa* which was a high-yield system of food production that created an economic surplus which fueled Aztec society and its capital of Tenochtitlan (present-day Mexico City). Less obvious, perhaps, is the cross fertilization that has taken place between indigenous languages (especially Náhuatl, the language of the Aztecs) and Mexican Spanish, not only in vocabulary but also to some extent in grammar and syntax. Indeed, it was not uncommon for many members—American-born Spaniards as well as Indians and Africans—of early colonial society to be fluent in one or another Indian language. Historian Nancy Farris tells us that virtually all residents of sixteenth- and seventeenth-century Yucatan were fluent in Yucatec Maya as their *first* language and that some of the early colonists spoke a kind of halting Spanish, which they might learn only as they entered adulthood (1984, 109 ff.). During the conquest years Náhuatl became a lingua franca for large areas and certain administrators and most missionaries spoke it or another indigenous language well or fluently. It is also apparent that the folk medicine and the supernaturalism of urban mestizos probably owes as much to pre-Hispanic culture as to late Medieval Europe (Nutini 1989). In any case the process of acculturation was not straightforwardly unilineal, merely a history of substituting European patterns and ideas for Mesoamerican ones. While the main institutional structure—religion, law and politics, economy, family, medicine, language—of Mexico and Guatemala is predominantly European in origin, the highly developed Indian cultures of the region have almost inevitably left their mark.

The first decades, the years of conquest, of the colonial period were marked by violence, abrupt demographic decline, missionizing by Catholic friars, and reorganization of the political and economic life of the people. In general a kind of indirect rule was established in which surviving Indian nobility played an important administrative role. People of lesser social rank continued to reside or were resettled toward the end of the sixteenth century in what were supposed to be exclusively Indian *congregaciones* or *repúblicas de indios*. These "closed" communities (Wolf 1959) were part of the administrative machinery which provided the Indians a measure of protection—albeit not greatly effective—from rapacious colonists, while at the same time providing the Franciscan, Dominican, and Augustinian friars with a somewhat captive audience for religious conversion and for colonists and authorities of the Crown a pool of human resources from which to exact wealth in the form of tribute, taxation, and labor. For most of Mesoamerica, imposition of Spanish military, political, economic, and religious control had been accomplished by the end of the sixteenth century or in the first couple of decades of the seventeenth. In some areas, such as the highlands of Guatemala and southern Mexico (present-day state of Chiapas) and in the Yucatan, less of a Spanish presence was felt largely because of the absence in these areas of the amount and kind of economic resources (e.g., gold and silver) that were important goals of the conquest in the first place. In these areas—especially the highland Maya area of Guatemala and Mexico—one can see greater retention of certain pre-Hispanic and early colonial cultural traits than, say, in the central highlands of Mexico. The Valley of Mexico, at an altitude of about seven thousand feet above sea level, has continued to be since at least the fourteenth century, when the Aztecs established their presence there, the metropolitan hub of Mesoamerica and as such attracted a great many Spaniards from the very beginning of the colonial period.

Partly because of the catastrophic demographic collapse of the indigenous population, Africans were brought as slaves to the Americas, most of them settling in the lowlands, although some were brought to the highland urban centers as servants or even overseers in agricultural or mining operations. By the middle of the seventeenth century, miscegenation among these few Africans, the Europeans, and Indians had become widespread and the colony had become a multi-ethnic society. Sometime in the 1600s cultural definitions were displacing racial categories in the caste-like stratification system, and social status was becoming less a matter of biological inheritance (as Spaniards understood this at the time) and more a matter of culture as indicated by community of residence, occupation, clothing, religious practices, and language (Mörner 1967, Katzew 1996, Nutini 1997). By this time most of the Indian nobility had either been absorbed into the mestizo ranks or had been reduced to peasant (*macehual*, the widely used Náhuatl term for Indian farmer) status.

The eighteenth century was a period when colonial authorities relaxed control over Indian communities, and Indians were more free to create their own adaptations to colonial society. In some cases this meant reviving suppressed customs and integrating them with already introduced Spanish customs, especially in the domain of supernatural belief and ritual expression. It was during this period that the Spanish Crown formally abolished *encomienda* and *repartimiento*, the institutions by which labor and tribute had been siphoned off from Indian populations for support of the Crown itself and church and administrative personnel and activities in the colony. The Spanish relaxed control over many Indian communities "because continued exploitation was requiring greater efforts for diminishing returns," according to one anthropologist (Taylor 1989, 111). By about 1780 Indian cultures had achieved a kind of equilibrium marked by a stable integration, relatively speaking, of pre-Hispanic and foreign elements. This is what some anthropologists refer to as "Colonial Indian" culture, as opposed to its pre-contact version.

At the end of the colonial period and at the beginning of the Republican period the Crown's Bourbon reforms set in motion a kind of "second conquest" (Farris 1984) of Indian peoples. This took the form of introducing greater and more efficient control of virtually all sectors of life in the colony in an attempt to conserve Spanish institutions and dominance. The effect at the local level was for the autonomy and integrity of Indian communities to be undermined and their cultures to be further transformed. This process was intensified after the colonies achieved political independence from Spain in the 1820s with the advent of the liberal reform laws of the mid- and late-nineteenth century. Chief among these reforms was the systematic privatization of communal lands in many communities. Privatization coincided with the beginnings of industrialization of production and a renewed intervention from outside (Europeans and Americans) in the political and economic affairs of the region. Haciendas and plantations, often owned by the elite or by non-nationals, grew in size and importance as national and international markets increased demand for their products—beef, grains, cotton, coffee, sugar, sisal, and fruit. Greater premium was placed on land itself and as communal lands held by Indian communities, in some instances since pre-Hispanic times, were privatized they were sold to outsiders or illegally expropriated and devoured by the expansion of large landed estates. Indians, of course, as well as mestizos, provided most of the labor on these landed estates ("factories in the field"), and many peasants became even more entrenched in a kind of debt-peonage servitude to the *latifundistas*. In Guatemala this took the form of forced labor (the dreaded *mandamiento*) for the highland Maya on the plantations of the hot and unhealthy lowlands and coastal areas.

Ultimately, this process of modernization and capitalization of the system of production, the systematic disenfranchisement of Indian communities and families, population growth, spurts of migration, and increased urbanization, as well as various forms of oppression and abuse, set the stage for armed revolution in Mexico and then in Guatemala, in addition to other Central American republics. The Mexican Revolution, followed in the 1930s and 1940s with redistribution to peasants of parcels of land taken from many of the great estates crushed during the armed conflict, marks the emergence of "modern" or "recent" Indian culture.

Suffice it to say that at the local level many who continue to live in Indian communities and who see themselves, and are seen by outsiders, as being in some way indigenous are becoming increasingly entangled in, and influenced by, the urban-based market economy and the consumerism that almost inevitably accompanies it (Chambers and Young 1979). In my own research in Náhuatl-speaking communities of the central highlands of Mexico it is not uncommon to enter a household in which the family is engaged in traditional corn farming which is supplemented by wage work in the city of one or more members of the extended family (Nutini and Murphy 1970). Food preparation and cooking are often carried out by techniques little changed since colonial or even pre-Hispanic times, yet that same meal might be consumed in a domestic space lighted by electricity and "adorned" with the latest television model and a sophisticated audio system, with the family's automobile or pick-up truck tucked away in a corner of the patio (cf. Evon Vogt's discussion of "The Maintenance of Mayan Distinctiveness" [1993] wherein he makes similar observations for the Tzotzil of Chiapas). Some of these families experience the euphoria and frustrations of the consumer trap in the same way working class people do in, say, Chicago, St. Louis, or Pittsburgh, and so must intensify their pursuit of wages in the urban, capitalist economy. The difference is, of course, that most of the jobs to be had by people from Mesoamerican rural villages have little job security, are seasonal or episodic, don't pay well, and the working conditions are often hazardous.

Frequently these trying economic struggles get played out in the broader context of harsh state-sponsored suppression of human rights, even to the point of the massacre of whole villages, and some would even say genocide. Recent Guatemalan history (Hale 1997), from the mid-1950s up through the late 1980s, provides a particularly bloody example in which hundreds of thousands of Maya Indians as well as mestizos were killed and perhaps as many as five hundred villages were razed in a kind of scorched earth policy in the early 1980s; thousands more fled to Mexico, the United States, Canada, and other countries (Montejo 1987, Adams 1991, Lovell 1995, Arias 1990, Menchú 1984).

Nobody knows for sure how many Mexican and Central American Indians are resident in the United States and Canada. In his beautiful collection of *Tales and Legend of the Q'anjob'al Maya*, Fernando Peñalosa, a resident of California who has a close attachment with the indigenous people of Guatemala, tells us this language (also, you'll recall, the language of the people in González's novel) is "spoken by as many as 4,000 Q'anjob'ales in southern California, and thousands of others in Florida, Arizona, Colorado, and other states, and in Mexico and Canada among the refugees of the great Mayan diaspora who have fled the violence and oppression in Guatemala during the last decade and a half" (1995, 3). Undoubtedly many of these people residing outside of Mesoamerica are not only speakers of Spanish as a second language, but many have become trilingual to some extent by learning English. Other studies provide descriptions and analyses of the adaptations Maya and other groups, including mestizos, have made to living in the United States (Vigil 1980; 1997; Burns 1993; Pagan 1994; Varese 1991). Some of these studies see a kind of "ethnogenesis," a reinvigoration of Indian identity, as a way of coping with the multiculturalism of American living spaces and the economy. Among the people from Oaxaca, in the southern highlands of Mexico, many individuals choose to assert an identity based not on membership in a particular local community (as was the usual practice from conquest to the mid- or late-twentieth century), but, rather, identify themselves with a larger collectivity and way of being, as Mixtec, Zapotec, Chinantec, Trique or, if from the Mexican state of Michoacan, as Purépecha (Varese 1991, 14), thus seeming to come full circle back to the salience of cultural identities characteristic of pre-Hispanic language and political groups, a kind of political consciousness the colonial enterprise sought systematically to suppress and fragment.

In his novel, Gaspar Pedro González reminds us there is more to ethnicity than merely "objective" markers such as custom or social participation. Beyond the way in which the society at large defines, labels, and categorizes Indians, there is also the question of how these same individuals and groups see and define themselves and actively negotiate their place in the social order. This is perhaps the existential dimension, the psychic territory of an individual, an inner sense of one's identity that is not so accessible to others, especially outsiders. Inevitably this self-identification is shaped by objective political setting and process. Here we listen in as a Q'anjob'al adult tries to assuage the pain his son, Lwin, felt upon being addressed by a Ladino with the deprecatory term *Indian* (in Spanish, *indio* or even more condescendingly and paternalistically, *indito*):

> The word *Indian*, my son, can't be explained and there's nothing we can compare it to. Rather, it is a feeling that grows inside you to a greater or lesser degree, according to your own experiences. It's a thorn that most people try to avoid, preferring not to be infected by it. Those that internalize it by mixing with ladinos, prefer to exorcise it, or set it aside and struggle to free themselves from that identification. When the notion of inferiority that the word suggests grows into a monster, the desperation to flee it becomes even greater, and that's why I say there's no explanation. (González 1995, 96)

This is the dilemma faced by many who come from indigenous cultures of Mesoamerica. Space does not permit adequate discussion of various types of Indian activism, which are evident in the United States and in migrants' countries of origin, as well. The volume *Maya Cultural Activism in Guatemala* edited by Fischer and Brown (1996) gives a good idea of the scope and depth of cultural and political revitalization among the Maya. Among the topics discussed are Maya intellectuals, a renewed interest among the Maya in their own pre-Hispanic writing systems, the symbolic significance of textiles and clothing in marking identity, the role of language in revitalization, and language education policy. One could rather easily find similar examples among other indigenous groups.

In conclusion, it's worth reminding ourselves that the Indian cultures of Mesoamerica are not so many relics of the past or so many cultural curiosities, as the sentimentalists and romanticists would have us believe. Like all cultures, they have not been static, they have undergone change and readaptation to new circumstances. They have emerged from these five centuries of contact with others reconstituted, but nonetheless vibrant, alive, and engaged in helping to create the political and cultural landscape here and in their countries of origin.

References

Adams, Richard N.

1991 Strategies of Ethnic Survival in Central America. In *Nation States and Indians in Latin America*, edited by Greg Urban and Joel Sherzer. Austin: University of Texas Press, 181–206.

Arias, Arturo.

1990 Changing Indian Identity: Guatemala's Violent Transition to Modernity. In *Guatemalan Indians and the State: 1540 to 1988*, edited by Carol A. Smith with the assistance of Marilyn M. Moors. Austin: University of Texas Press.

Bonfil Batalla, Guillermo.

1996 *México Profundo: Reclaiming a Civilization.* Trans. Philip A. Dennis. Austin: University of Texas Press.

Burns, Allan F.

1993 *Maya in Exile: Guatemalans in Florida.* Philadelphia: Temple University Press.

Carmack, Robert M., Janine Gasco, and Gary H. Gossen.

1996 *The Legacy of Mesoamerica: History and Culture of a Native American Civilization.* Upper Saddle River, NJ: Prentice Hall.

Chambers, Erve J. and Philip D. Young.

1979 Mesoamerican Community Studies: The Past Decade. In *Annual Review of Anthropology*. Vol. 8, edited by Bernard J. Siegel, Alan R. Beals, and Stephen A. Tyler. Palo Alto: Annual Reviews, Inc.

Cook, Scott, and Jong-Taick Joo.

1995 Ethnicity and Economy in Rural Mexico: A Critique of the *Indigenista* Approach. *Latin American Research Review* 30, no. 2:32–59.

Farris, Nancy M.

1984 *Maya Society under Colonial Rule: The Collective Enterprise of Survival.* Princeton: Princeton University Press.

Fischer, Edward F., and R. McKenna Brown, eds.

1996 *Maya Cultural Activism in Guatemala.* Austin: University of Texas Press.

González, Gaspar Pedro.

1995 *A Mayan Life*. Rancho Palos Verdes, CA: Yax Te' press.

Hagan, Jacqueline María.
1994 *Deciding to be Legal: A Maya Community in Houston.* Philadelphia: Temple University Press.

Hale, Charles R.
1997 Consciousness, Violence, and Politics of Memory in Guatemala. *Current Anthropology* 38, no. 5: 817–838 (with comments).

Helms, Mary W.
1975 *Middle America: A Culture History of Heartland and Frontiers.* Englewood Cliffs, NJ: Prentice-Hall, Inc.

Katzew, Ilona, Curator.
1996 *New World Orders: Casta Painting and Colonial Latin America.* New York: Americas Society Art Gallery.

Kaufman, Terrence.
1974 *Idiomas de Mesoamérica.* Guatemala: Editorial "José de Pineda Ibarra" — Ministerio de Educación.

Kirchoff, Paul.
1952 Meso-America. In *Heritage of Conquest: The Ethnology of Middle America,* ed. by Sol Tax, et al. New York: Cooper Square Inc.

Lovell, W. George.
1995 *A Beauty That Hurts: Life and Death in Guatemala.* Toronto: Between the Lines.

Marino Flores, Anselmo.
1967 Indian Population and Its Identification. In *Social Anthropology.* edited by Manning Nash. Vol. 6 of *Handbook of Middle Indians,* Robert Wauchope, general editor, 12–25. Austin: University of Texas Press.

Menchú, Rigoberta.
1984 *I, Rigoberta Menchú: An Indian Woman in Guatemala.* Edited and introduced by Elisabeth Burgos-Debray, trans. by Ann Wright. London and New York: Verso.

Montejo, Victor.
1987 *Testimony: Death in a Guatemalan Village.* Willamantic, CT: Curbstone Press.

Mörner, Magnus.
1967 *Race Mixture in the History of Latin America.* Boston: Little, Brown & Co.

Nutini, Hugo G.

1988 *Todos Santos in Rural Tlaxcala: A Syncretic, Expressive, and Symbolic Analysis of the Cult of the Dead.* Princeton: Princeton University Press.

1989 Sincretismo y aculturación en la mentalidad mágico–religiosa popular mexicana. *L'Uomo: Societa Tradizione Sviluppo*: 2, no. 2: 85–124.

1997 "Class and Ethnicity in Mexico: Somatic and Racial Considerations" *Ethnology* 36, no. 3: 227–238.

Nutini, Hugo, and Timothy Murphy.

1970 "Labor Migration and Family Structure in the Tlaxcala-Puebla Valley, Mexico." in Walter Goldschmidt and Harry Hoijor, eds., *The Social Anthropology of Latin America: Papers in Honor of Ralph L. Beals*. Berkeley: University of California Press.

Nutini, Hugo G., and John M. Roberts.

1993 *Bloodsucking Witchcraft: An Epistemological Study of Anthropomorphic Supernaturalism in Rural Tlaxcala.* Tucson: University of Arizona Press.

Peñalosa, Fernando.

1995 *Tales and Legend of the Q'anjob'al Maya.* Rancho Palos Verdes, CA: Yax Te' press.

Signorini, Italo.

1989 Sobre algunos aspectos sincréticos de la medicina popular mexicana. *L'Uomo: Societa Tradizione Sviluppo* 2, no. 2:125–147.

Taylor, Robert B.

1989 *Indians of Middle America: An Introduction to the Ethnology of Mexico, Central America, and the Caribbean.* Las Cruces, NM: Lifeway Books.

Valdés, Luz María.

1988 *El perfil demográfico de los indios mexicanos.* México: Siglo Veintiuno Editores.

Varese, Stéfano.

1991 Think Locally, Act Globally. *Report on the Americas* 25, no. 3 13–17.

Vigil, James Diego.
1980 *From Indians to Chicanos: The Dynamics of Mexican American Culture*. Prospect Hts., Ill.: Waveland Press, Inc.

1997 *Personas Mexicanas: Chicano High Schoolers in a Changing Los Angeles*. Fort Worth: Harcourt Brace College Publishers.

Vogt, Evon Z.
1993 The Maintenance of Mayan Distinctiveness. In *The Indian in Latin American History Resistance,Resilience and Acculturation*, edited by John B. Kicza. Wilmington, DE: Scholarly Resources, Inc.

Wolf, Eric R.
1959 *Sons of the Shaking Earth.* Chicago: University of Chicago Press.

Selected Case Studies

Friedlander, Judith.
1975 *Being Indian in Hueyapan: A Study of Forced Identity in Contemporary Mexico.* New York: St. Martin's Press.

Greenberg, James B.
1989 *Blood Ties: Life and Violence in Rural Mexico.*Tucson: University of Arizona Press.

Hill, Jane H. and Kenneth C. Hill.
1986 *Speaking Mexicano: Dynamics of Syncretic Language in Central Mexico.*Tucson: The University of Arizona Press.

Ingham, John M.
1986 *Mary, Michael, and Lucifer: Folk Catholicism in Central Mexico.* Austin: University of Texas Press.

Martínez Saldaña, Tomás.
1997 *La diáspora Tlaxcalteca: Colonización agrícola del norte mexicano Tlaxcala*: Gobierno del Estado de Talxcala.

Murphy, Arthur D., and Alex Stepick.
1991 *Social Inequality in Oaxaca: A History of Resistance and Change* Philadelphia: Temple University Press.

Rosenbaum, Brenda.
1993 *With Our Heads Bowed: The Dynamics of Gender in a Maya Community.* Albany, NY: Institute for Mesoamerican Studies (Distributed by the University of Texas Press).

Sandstrom, Alan R.
1991 *Corn Is Our Blood: Culture and Ethnic Identity in a Contemporary Aztec Indian Village*. Norman: University of Oklahoma Press.

Schroeder, Susan, Stephanie Wood, and Robert Haskett, editors.
1997 *Indian Women of Early Mexico*. Norman: University of Oklahoma Press.

Schryer, Frans J.
1990 *Ethnicity and Class Conflict in Rural Mexico*. Princeton University Press.

Sexton, James D., trans. and ed.
1985 *Campesino: The Diary of a Guatemalan Indian*. Tucson: University of Arizona Press.

Slade, Doren L.
1992 *Making the World Safe for Existence: Celebration of the Saints among the Sierra Nahuat of Chignautla, Mexico*. Ann Arbor: University of Michigan Press.

Stephen, Lynn.
1991 *Zapotec Women*. Austin: University of Texas Press.

Taggart, James M.
1997 *The Bear and His Sons: Masculinity in Spanish and Mexican Folktales*. Austin: University of Texas Press.

Warren, Kay B.
1989 *The Symbolism of Subordination:Indian Identity in a Guatemalan Town*. Austin: University of Texas Press.

Watanabe, John M.
1992 *Maya Saints and Souls in a Changing World*. Austin: University of Texas Press.

Either Black or White: Race Relations in Contemporary Brazil

G. Reginald Daniel

Introduction

Traditionally, Brazil has been contrasted with the United States in terms of its history of pervasive racial (phenotypical, ancestral) and cultural (beliefs, values, customs, artifacts) blending.[1] Furthermore, Brazil has validated this process by implementing a ternary model of race relations that differentiates its population into Whites (*brancos*), multiracial individuals (*pardos*), and Blacks (*pretos*).[2] This in turn has led to notably fluid racial/cultural markers and been accompanied by the absence of legalized barriers to equality in both the public and private spheres. Consequently, it has been argued that class and culture, rather than race, have come to determine one's identity and status in the social hierarchy.[3]

In the United States, European Americans have sought to preserve their cultural and racial purity, as well as their dominant status, by enforcing an ironclad policy of hypodescent (the one-drop rule). This mechanism maintains a binary model of race relations that designates everyone of African descent as Black. Moreover, it has served as the underpinning for both legal and informal exclusion of individuals of African descent from having contact with Whites as equals. This has encompassed public facilities, and other areas of the secondary structural sphere (political, economic, educational), as well as the primary structural sphere (residential, associational, interpersonal), particularly the area of miscegenation. At the turn of the twentieth century, these restrictions reached drastic proportions with the institutionalization of Jim Crow segregation.

Despite the absence of legalized barriers to racial equality in Brazil, as compared to the United States, data collected over the last half century indicate that race, quite apart from questions of culture and class, is a prime variable in determining the distribution of wealth, power, privilege, and prestige. Furthermore, the divide between haves and have-nots primarily coincides, respectively, with the racial divide between Whites (*brancos*) and the African Brazilian masses (*negros*), including both the Black and multiracial populations. These findings not only have challenged Brazil's traditional image as a racial democracy, but also have moved the discussion on race relations much closer to the binary model of the United States. Consequently, racial questions are increasingly being framed in either Black or White terms.[4]

The Old Brazilian Model: Neither Black nor White

The Escape Hatch

Brazil's image as a racial democracy, and notions about the exceptional openness to miscegenation with people of African descent on the part of the

Portuguese colonizers of Brazil—as well as the altruistic motives underlying their differentiation of mulattos from Blacks—originated largely in Gilberto Freyre's monumental study of Brazilian race relations.[5] Such arguments, however, had more to do with racial romanticism than with reality. Throughout the Americas, and irrespective of the national and cultural origins of the colonizing Europeans, racial attitudes and behavior were motivated primarily by self-interest. The quantity of miscegenation was closely related to the ratio of European men to women. Social distinctions made between individuals of varying degrees of African ancestry were influenced, if not determined, by the ratio of Whites to Blacks.

In Brazil, as in other parts of Latin America, the colonizing Europeans were a minority and mostly single males. Africans comprised a majority of the colonial population. Consequently, rape, fleeting extramarital relations, as well as extended concubinage and common-law unions between White men and women of African descent were more or less approved, if not encouraged, by the prevailing unwritten moral code. There were, however, legal barriers to interracial marriages during most of the colonial period, and formidable social prejudice against these relationships that remained in place long afterwards. As slaves, the mulatto offspring of these unions were often assigned tasks that required greater skill or symbolized greater personal worth (e.g., artisans and domestics). The scarcity of White women mitigated significant opposition from the legal wife and enhanced the likelihood that these offspring would be the recipients of socially tolerated demonstrations of affection, as well as economic and educational protection. Furthermore, mulattos were given preferential liberation over Blacks, who overwhelmingly were slaves. This made it possible for them early in the colonial period to enter the free classes, where they filled interstitial roles in the economy—particularly in the artisanal and skilled trades—due to a shortage of European labor; furthermore, for these types of work the use of slave labor was generally considered to be less practical.[6]

Free Coloreds, long before abolition, readily advanced from these favored positions into the arts, letters, and liberal professions (including medicine, engineering, law, and the civil service). They were, however, barred from holding public office and from entering high-status occupations in the clergy and governmental bureaucracy, they experienced limitations on educational attainment and were denied equal rights in a variety of categories. Furthermore, Free Coloreds did not achieve their vertical mobility through direct competition in the open market. Rather, their social ascension was facilitated through the paternalistic support of patrons in the White elite who always controlled their advancement.[7] It should come as no surprise, therefore, that these mulattos proved to be valuable allies in preserving the status quo. They were not only reticent to fight against slavery, but also tended to eschew alliance with slaves. So reliable were mulattos that the planter class utilized their services in local militias as a means of protecting their property, and in the suppression of slave uprisings, as well as in the catching and returning of fugitive slaves.

European Brazilians, by granting mulattos a social status somewhat superior to that of Blacks, but significantly inferior to that of Whites, won their loyalty in efforts to exclude Blacks from power without at the same time undermining White domination and control. The process of abolition signed and sealed this social contract and made it possible for Whites to continue to rely on mulatto support long after slavery. As long as Blacks were retained in the least remunerative sectors of the secondary labor force as agricultural, industrial, and service laborers, mulattos settled for token integration into the skilled trades, the petty bourgeoisie, intelligentsia, and the primary labor force comprised of white-collar workers.[8]

The paradoxical nature of the Brazilian model has thus assured that African Brazilians, collectively speaking, are denied the privileges of Whites, but mulattos are at the same time rewarded in proportion to their cultural and phenotypical approximation to the European psychosomatic ideal.[9] This window of opportunity that Degler calls the "escape hatch" does not imply that the masses of mulattos in Brazil gain access carte blanche to the prestigious ranks of Whites by virtue of the fact that they are mulatto as opposed to Black. Rather, his argument is that the escape hatch is an informal social mechanism by which a select few "visibly" multiracial individuals, for reasons of talent, culture, or education, have been allowed token vertical socioeconomic mobility into the middle class and with it the rank of situational "whiteness." In its broadest sense, however, the escape hatch is an epistemological device that has fostered a collective state of amnesia and schizophrenia, making it possible for other millions of individuals whose ancestry has included African forebearers, but who are phenotypically White, or near-White, to become legally White.[10] This aspect of the escape hatch is indicative of a socially sanctioned "implicit passing," clearly setting apart Brazilian race relations from the explicit, but concealed and not so socially approved, "passing" of many light-skinned African–descent Americans as Whites in the United States, where the one-drop rule can transform into Black an individual who appears otherwise White.[11]

Black into White

Brazil's long history of pervasive miscegenation, and its conspicuous absence of institutionalized White supremacy and legalized barriers to equality as compared to the United States, should not, however, obscure the fact that "white" is synonymous with being superior, and inferiority is a general term that has as one of its synonyms the adjective "black." The ruling elite is overwhelmingly of European descent and European in manners. It also has implemented covert and overt forms of discrimination that have kept the African Brazilian masses in a de facto subordinate status, both before and after the abolition of slavery. Furthermore, if miscegenation has made the line between Black and White imprecise at best, and became a central tenet in the twentieth-century evolution of Brazil's concept of racial democracy, racial and cultural blending were not posited on egalitarian integration. That is to say, there was not a random blend of European, African, and by extension, indigenous traits, seeking its own "natural" equilibrium, in which equal value was attached to each of these racial and cultural constituents through a reciprocal *transracial/transcultural* process. It was rather, a process of inegalitarian integration (or *assimilation* in disguise), an unnatural contest between unequal participants artificially manipulated in order to purify the Brazilian pedigree and culture of its vast accumulation of "inferior" African (and Native American) traits with the goal of *perpetuating* only one: the European.[12]

Some of these attitudes, of course, were reflective of toxins indigenous to Brazil's own racial ecology. We cannot, however, ignore the fact that this "whitening" ideology was part of Brazil's compromised response to nineteenth-century Europeans and European Americans who expounded upon the evils of miscegenation. In order to understand the seriousness of this matter, we need only consider that by the latter half of the nineteenth century, the vast majority of Brazilians, despite official claims to the contrary, were de facto *mulato claro* (clear[light]-skinned mulatto), or *claramente mulato* (clearly mulatto) in terms of culture, ancestry, and/or phenotype.[13] Not even the most phenotypically and culturally European individuals of the elite could be certain that their genealogy had remained free of African ancestry and, therefore, insulated from the stigma of slavery and the "evils" of miscegenation.

If miscegenation was the disease, whitening through miscegenation became the prescription for a cure. In order to achieve this, the Brazilian government encouraged the immigration of Europeans, particularly those of Germanic origin, and passed waves of legislation restricting the immigration of Blacks. This was matched by the tendency of many individuals to seek a spouse more apparently European in values, beliefs, and physical appearance than themselves, plus the feverish desire to assimilate any and everything from ideas to cultural artifacts that tasted of Europe, and by extension, the United States. At the same time, the majority of Blacks and mulattos were excluded de facto from having contact with Whites as equals by virtue of their racial/cultural differences. This legacy of informal inegalitarian pluralism was envisioned as the final solution that eventually would eliminate African Brazilians through the "laissez-faire genocide" of sharply lower levels of education and higher rates of poverty, malnutrition, disease, and infant mortality.[14]

Escape Hatch or Trap Door?

Pervasive miscegenation and the escape hatch, by blurring and softening the line between Whites and Blacks, indeed helped to diminish any collective problem in post-slavery Brazil stemming from race per se. These phenomena also have served as a means of maintaining de facto White dominance and control. They have achieved this by creating the illusion that whatever prejudice and discrimination exist in Brazil are not based on ascribed, and, thus, essentially immutable characteristics such as race. Rather, discrimination is supposedly based on acquired social, economic, and cultural characteristics that are subject to alteration by individual merit and achievement during one's lifetime. In fact, however, the privilege of first-class citizenship is awarded selectively in accordance with one's approximation to European phenotypical and cultural traits, working in combination with their economic standing. Consequently, for the most part, the socioeconomic polarization between haves and have–nots, respectively, follows the racial divide between White and Black.

These dynamics indicate that Brazilian race relations are propelled by the same hierarchical valuation, if not complete dichotomization, of "blackness" and "whiteness," originating in African and European racial and cultural differences that has characterized race relations in the United States, although these restrictions were not formalized. The escape hatch in Brazil, however, has historically brought with it the expectation, if not the actual achievement, of social advantages in the larger society, and more important, a psychological edge in the pursuit of those opportunities, that have not historically been available to individuals designated as "light-skinned" African Americans in Anglo-America. By virtue of this inegalitarian integrationist dynamic, the escape hatch has assured that the majority of those few African Brazilians who are beneficiaries of this meritocracy are mulatto more so than Black.

Furthermore, this dynamic has retarded, if not prevented, political mobilization along racial lines. It has achieved this by guaranteeing that many of those individuals most likely to possess the cultural, intellectual, and social skills to unmask the reality behind the myth of racial democracy, and serve as mouthpieces of the African Brazilian masses, are neutralized or co-opted, if you will, into silence.[15] Breaking through the hardened chrysalis of second-class citizenship without also studiously avoiding the topic of racism is, therefore, a delicate balance that even the most vigilant of vertically mobile mulattos would find challenging. Not being White, yet aspiring to be first-class citizens, mulattos at any time could be classified as racial inferiors by even the most socially and culturally "inferior" Whites by simply being treated as second-class citizens racially, such that the escape hatch could easily become a "trap door."

The New Brazilian Model: Either Black or White

Race, Research, and Revisionism

Despite the absence of legalized barriers to equality in Brazil, as compared to the United States, Brazil's image as a racial democracy began to erode under the weight of massive data compiled in the 1950s by both Brazilian and foreign social scientists. These scholars, most of whom were part of a UNESCO-sponsored project, used the latest research techniques to reveal a complex web of correlations between physical appearance, culture, and class in determining social stratification. Comprehensive data were lacking, and important regional variations existed, and opinions varied on how phenotype might affect future social mobility. There was a general consensus, however, that Brazilians who were phenotypically more African were disproportionately represented at the bottom of society in terms of education and occupation.[16]

Journalists soon followed with anecdotal evidence that confirmed the existence of a subtle, yet unmistakable, pattern of racial discrimination in social relations. Discrimination was more complex than in the binary model of Anglo-American race relations, and had never been codified since the colonial era. Furthermore, Brazi lians could still tout the fact that they had avoided the United States' violent urban uprisings and escaped its distorted White supremacist ideology. Nevertheless, the growing body of evidence not only made the Brazilian elite cautious about discussing their society's contemporary race relations, much less its racial future, but paradoxically, made the myth of racial democracy an even more crucial official ideology. It was systematically and staunchly defended by Brazil's ruling elite, and reinforced by the series of military dictatorships that dominated the Brazilian political scene between 1964 to 1985.[17]

During this time period, further research and discussion on the problem of racial inequality was severely censored by claims that no such problem existed. In 1969, this resulted in the "involuntary" retirement of University faculty who were branded as subversives for doing research on Brazilian race relations. The political machinery of the state also decreed that any efforts to mobilize along racial lines were "racist," "subversive," a threat to national security, and punishable by imprisonment. Individuals who were inclined to organize to address a problem which the state declared did not in fact exist, therefore, were themselves viewed as creating a problem, and accused of having been infected with a contagion imported from the United States. Many individuals were imprisoned; others were exiled either through self-imposition or governmental decree.[18]

The intense censorship of public discussion on racial issues was paralleled by the fact that no racial data were collected on the 1970 census. The principal reason given for the decision was that previous data had been notoriously unreliable, due to the fact that definitions of racial category lacked uniformity. In actuality, government officials were seeking to promote the notion that racial criteria were insignificant in determining the distribution of societal wealth, power, privilege, and prestige—and thus meaningless statistical categories. Part of their strategy for achieving this was to deprive researchers (and therefore the public and politicians) of nationwide figures that would make it possible to document the deplorable conditions endured by African Brazilians in terms of education, jobs, income, and health.[19]

The Black Consciousness Movement

The long veil of silence on the discussion of racial inequality in Brazil was not lifted until the 1970s during the gradual liberalization of the national sociopolitical ecology—the *abertura democrática*, or democratic opening. Beginning in 1978, in several major cities (primarily in the industrialized Southeast), African Brazilian activists took advantage of the celebration of the abolition of slavery in May of 1978 to organize protests against police brutality, mistreatment at the hands of public agencies, and an overt act of discrimination in which three African Brazilian youths were barred from a yacht club. None of these events was unusual in and of themselves. Nevertheless, the growing, but covert, racial tension and the lifting of authoritarian rule in Brazil, as well as the civil rights movement in the United States, all combined to set the stage for the formation of the Unified Black Movement, the MNU (*O Movimento Negro Unificado*). African Brazilians thus made progress in rekindling the previous militancy which the MNU's predecessor, the Black Front (*A Frente Negra*), had exhibited during the 1930s before having reached its nadir during the repressive dictatorship of Getúlio Vargas (1937–1945).[20]

The MNU's vision of Brazil diverges significantly from the official assimilationist ideology. Instead, activists propose a mosaic of mutually respectful and differentiated, if not mutually exclusive, African Brazilian and European Brazilian racial/cultural centers of reference in the manner of egalitarian pluralism. Both Whites and Blacks would have equal access to all aspects of the public sphere, with the option of integrating in the private sphere—egalitarian integration. In this case, the selective pattern would be voluntary, rather than mandated by Whites, such that if and when African Brazilians choose to integrate they do so as equals. Nevertheless, the MNU has met with blatant hostility from sectors of the political and cultural establishment. At best, their goal of achieving a more equitable society by mobilizing an African Brazilian plurality to challenge the dominant assimilationist ideology has been termed as "un-Brazilian" and a mindless imitation of the United States' civil rights movement. At worst, the MNU's tactics have been described as racist in the manner of a reverse type of apartheid.[21]

African Brazilian activists have received warmer, if somewhat tentative, support from intellectuals, students, and progressive sections of the church and workers committed to political and social change. Many of these individuals, however, have socialist leanings and view African Brazilians as part of a larger transracial proletariat. They consider racism to be an epiphenomenon of class inequality and argue that by addressing the latter, one automatically addresses the former. Although they agree that the racial prejudice and discrimination directed against African Brazilians has led to gross inequalities in educational, socioeconomic, and political attainment, they have focused their attention primarily on the poor, the unemployed, and the illiterate. Consequently, they believe that singling out African Brazilians for special treatment as a racial plurality would deviate from the main course of social reform.[22]

The MNU enjoyed a significant amount of publicity in the late 1970s and early 1980s, but has gained greater attention from academics abroad than in Brazil. Since its inception it has tended to be dominated by individuals from the urban bourgeoisie and been plagued by class divisions within its ranks. These factors have prevented the MNU from garnering broad support from other urban, and particularly, rural sectors of the African Brazilian community, which remain largely unaware of its existence. Notwithstanding the MNU's conspicuous lack of success in garnering massive support for a race–specific political agenda, or organizing a large race-based electorate in governmental politics, it is, nonetheless, part of a larger Black Consciousness Movement encompassing a variety of significant social, cultural, and political organizations and activities. This can be seen in the revitalization of African–derived religious and musical expression in Brazil, as well as a surge in the writing of African Brazilian literature, much of which has been published in modest editions at the authors' expense. Furthermore, militant African Brazilian action groups have gained the support of the leading national labor confederation and among domestic employees. Prominent African Brazilians (particularly artists and entertainers) have become increasingly willing to speak out publicly about their experiences with racial discrimination.[23]

The Increasing Significance of Race

The MNU's efforts also have been aided by a new generation of social scientists. These researchers (most of whom are White) not only helped get the race question reinstated on the 1980 census, but also were funded with a grant from the Ford Foundation to provide a rigorous analysis of official data contained in such sources as the 1940, 1950, and 1980 censuses, and the National Household Surveys of the 1970s and 1980s. As a result, they verified glaring disparities in the areas of health, income, and education between African Brazilians, who make up close to 46 percent of the population and Whites, who constitute approximately 54 percent.[24] These findings underscored the significance of race, quite apart from culture or class, and its role in determining social inequality. More important, they clearly pointed to the fact that, in terms of overall socioeconomic stratification, the racial divide is primarily located between Whites and the African Brazilian masses, and only secondarily between mulattos and Blacks.

It is true that mulattos have been able to enter the primary occupational tier as schoolteachers, journalists, artists, clerks, low–level officials in municipal government and tax offices, and get promoted more easily. They also earn 42 percent more than their Black counterparts.[25] It is equally true that rates of intermarriage and residential integration among mulattos and Whites are comparatively higher than between Whites and Blacks, and that the multiracial population does occupy an intermediate position in the Brazilian racial hierarchy.[26] Also, the presence of African ancestry in one's genealogy and/or some phenotypically African traits does not preclude a self–identification or social designation as White. Consequently, the credentials distinguishing someone who is White from someone who is multiracial are ambiguous.

Nevertheless, Whites earn another 98 percent more than mulattos, and the intermediate positioning of the majority of those 40 percent of Brazilians who are considered multiracial is much closer to Blacks than to Whites. For the most part, they are excluded from professions in medicine, law, academia, upper-level government, and the officer and diplomatic corps. Even entry-level jobs in the primary labor force that require a "good appearance," such as receptionists, secretaries, bank tellers, or even minimal authority positions, such as entry-level federal employees, are effectively closed to the majority of mulattos. The multiracial population, along with the 6 percent of African Brazilians who are designated as Black, remain concentrated at the bottom of society. They make up a majority of the secondary labor force, comprised of agricultural and industrial workers, service employees, janitors, porters, laundresses, day laborers, and domestic servants, and so forth, and are over-represented in the ranks of the underemployed and unemployed.[27]

Whites and African Brazilians do experience similar disadvantages at the undermost levels of society, which gives credence to the notion that social inequality is based primarily on social class. Data indicate, however, that these disadvantages are superseded by Whites with higher rates of tangible returns in terms of wealth, power, privilege, and prestige once they have made educational gains (which have become increasingly important as a variable influencing occupational mobility in the labor market). Whites are not only seven times more likely than African Brazilians to be college graduates, but African Brazilian professionals, such as physicians, teachers, and engineers, also earn 20 to 25 percent less than their White counterparts.[28]

Furthermore, if the achievements of individual African Brazilians can be pointed to as examples of meritocracy in action, they also divert attention from the fact that Blacks and mulattos, collectively speaking, not only have a more difficult time breaking out of the proletariat, but also suffer increasing disadvantages as their vertical class mobility increases. Whites are more successful at the intergenerational transferal of their achieved status in terms of wealth, power, privilege, and prestige, given the same starting point. African Brazilians are handicapped by the cumulative disadvantages of previous, as well as persistent, racial discrimination. These factors hamper and erode, if not preclude, their ability to pass on wealth, power, privilege, and prestige from generation to generation. This is due precisely to the superordinate and subordinate ascribed racial status respectively assigned to Europeans and African Brazilians.[29]

Closing the Escape Hatch

Prior to the 1970s, discussion on Brazilian race relations relied heavily on "qualitative" data, and was primarily framed in the context of historical and anthropological discourse. Historians focused on laws, travelers' accounts, memoirs, parliamentary debates, and newspaper articles in which anecdotal accounts remained the standard source of information. They generally neglected researching police and court records, health archives, personnel files, and other sources from which they might have constructed time series. When such sources were consulted, it was generally to study slavery. Although historians did not hesitate to draw conclusions about the historical nature of race relations, they seldom studied race relations in the larger contemporary society. Anthropologists generally studied African-derived religious and linguistic systems, and creative expression in the arts. When they did examine race relations, their focus was primarily on the ambiguous and situational nature of racial/cultural markers. They provided little analysis of the extent to which race and culture were signifiers in terms of larger structural issues of education, income, occupation, and so forth.[30]

The new generation of sociologists, following in the footsteps of their predecessors in the 1960s, however, have provided activists with the necessary quantitative data to wage their struggle for social change at the level of unions, courts, employers, and the media. Nevertheless, there is no in-depth overview of the post-1976 statistics. Much more data on health, housing, education, family structure, etc., is needed, yet questions on census forms are designed to collect only the most basic information. Furthermore, researchers have had to go to great lengths to gain access to the data already gathered by virtue of the fact that most of the important information has never been published. The data that are available can only be obtained on tapes, and researchers were denied access to these sources for years. When the tapes were released they were made available only at great expense to users. A group of researchers, in response to these obstructionist procedures, has pressured the Census Bureau to release future data on a timely and accessible basis.[31]

Also, it would be premature to conclude that the Black Consciousness Movement has had a major impact on the dominant ideology. It is true that the 1988 Constitution, for the first time in Brazilian history, outlawed racism, declaring that "the practice of racism constitutes a crime that is unbailable and without statute of limitation and is subject to imprisonment according to the law."[32] Yet, the Preliminary Study Commission on the New Constitution, which was organized in 1985, omitted the names of the three African Brazilians who had been recommended by the recently deceased president Tancredo Neves. Only after vigorous protest by Black organizations was the name of one African Brazilian added. Furthermore, the antiracist article in the Constitution of 1988, like the Affonso Arinos Law of 1951 (which outlawed racial discrimination in public accommodations), is more rhetoric than a societal commitment. Even with the passage of the necessary enabling law (the *Lei Caó*), Brazilian civil rights lawyers are finding it difficult in practice to establish a legal basis for their criminal complaints.[33]

Although Geledés, a São Paulo–based nongovernmental organization focusing on the problems of African Brazilian women, has pressed at least 62 cases of racial discrimination before the courts, by 1992 only four cases had been brought to trial. Governor Franco Montoro in São Paulo (and his successor, Orestes Quércia), and Leonel Brizola during his first term as mayor in Rio de Janeiro, initiated policies to move against racial discrimination. They placed African Brazilians in prominent positions, and created the Council for the Participation and Development of the Black Community, and prohibited employers from requiring domestics to use separate stairwells and elevators. However, these initiatives have been largely undermined by their successors, sometimes blatantly. There has been some discussion of compensatory measures in the manner of affirmative action to ensure African Brazilians equal representation in the public sphere in proportion to their numbers in the population. Such tactics, nevertheless, are viewed with suspicion, or as a form of reverse discrimination, which would aggravate rather than provide a solution to the problem of racial inequality.[34]

These contradictory trends clearly indicate that the political, intellectual, and cultural establishment in Brazil has not yet been significantly affected by the new data about racial inequality. Although the myth of racial democracy has been largely discredited, it still dominates public discussion. There were no African Brazilians on the committee set up in 1984 by the Ministry of Justice to publish five books on the centennial of the abolition of slavery. Although African Brazilians mounted massive public demonstrations against racism during the centennial in the spring of 1988, a barrage of academic papers and civic ceremonies extolling Brazil's genius in having allegedly liquidated slavery without such upheavals as the Civil War in the United States, largely overshadowed their protests.[35]

Brown into Black

African Brazilian activists, however, regard their battle as only in its preliminary stages. Since 1978, one of their prime goals has been to awaken more individuals to the fact that Brazil's racial democracy ideology is more myth than reality. Contrary to its egalitarian rhetoric, this ideology has translated into inegalitarian integration (that is, assimilation), for a privileged few multiracial individuals (and some rare Blacks)—who are, thus, co-opted into an alliance as "insiders." More importantly, it has obscured the pervasive inegalitarian pluralism originating in a system of de facto, if not de jure, apartheid that perpetuates gross inequities between Whites and the African Brazilian masses in the areas of education, jobs, income, and health.

The Brazilian Institute of Geography and Statistics (IBGE), and more specifically within IBGE, the Department of Social Studies and Indicators (which is the government agency responsible for collecting census and other demographic data), fully documented these disparities between Whites (*brancos*) and the African Brazilian masses (*negros*) when it changed its policy in 1980 and began analyzing and publishing racial data in dichotomous, rather than trichotomous, form. The impetus for this quiet, seemingly routine decision by a group of government researchers and technocrats appears to have originated to some extent in the IBGE's own analysis of the 1976 and 1980 data. Yet, this change in procedure was no doubt a response in part to demands made by African Brazilian activists, and similar recommendations made by the new generation of social scientists. Consequently, it actually had broader implications. That is to say, although IBGE had not abandoned the traditional three-category concept of race (or four, if one includes the category of "yellows," *amarelos*, used to designate individuals of Asian ancestry), it had moved toward a conceptualization of Brazilian race relations similar to the binary Anglo-American model, in which both the *preto* and *pardo* populations are seen as a single racial group.[36]

Beginning in 1990, Black organizations, along with nine governmental agencies (including development groups and research centers), gained the support of IBASE (*Instituto Brasileiro de Análisis Sociais e Económicas*) in mounting a joint publicity campaign with funds from the Ford Foundation, and *Terra Nuova* (an Italian agency for cooperation), directing all Brazilians to be more "conscientious" in filling out the racial question on the 1990 census. The spirit of the campaign was captured best in its poster and brochure slogan—*"Não Deixe sua Côr Passar em Branco. Responda com Bom C/Senso," (Don't let your color be passed off as White. Respond with good [census] sense).* This slogan utilized a play on words between census (*censo*) and sense (*senso*) to address the tendency of many individuals to identify themselves on previous surveys with a lighter color (racial) category than their "actual" phenotype might warrant. Over time, this process of racial alchemy has led to a "distortion" of racial demographics. Consequently, Blacks numerically have lost a great deal and gained little; multiracial individuals have gained more than they have lost, and Whites have lost nothing and have made substantial gains.[37]

The ultimate goal of the campaign, however, was to explain the reality behind the myth of racial democracy and get African Brazilians to identify with the concept *negro*—rather than the color codings *preto* and *pardo*—in order to affirm a politicized racial identity. Furthermore, *pardo* includes all possible types of blended backgrounds and therefore was considered so general as to be meaningless. It also stirred controversy because it was a remnant of the racial divisiveness of the past. The campaign began in 1990, but the census was canceled that year because of problems between the Ministry of the Economy and the Census Bureau. The census was finally taken in 1991. Yet, strikes by census staff short-circuited dialogue between campaign organizers, the Bureau administrators and enumerators who potentially would have resulted in changing the wording on the census questionnaire from *branco* (White), *pardo* (multiracial), and *preto* (Black), to reflect instead, the *branco* (White) and *negro* (African Brazilian) designations.[38]

Conclusion

The Black Consciousness Movement has helped discredit the myth of racial democracy and awaken African Brazilians to the fact that socioeconomic gains do not automatically outweigh one's phenotype. In response to these revelations, many previously multiracial-identified (and some White-identified individuals) have embraced an identity as *negros*, that is African Brazilians, rather than as *pardos* (mulattos), and so forth. Activists were unsuccessful in getting the Census Bureau to use *negro* as an official overarching term in collecting data on the 1990 census. However, they hope that identification with this concept will increase to such an extent that Census Bureau administrators will be forced to use *negro* as the official designator on the year 2000 census. The net result of these trends has been to move Brazilian race relations closer to a binary model in which there is greater emphasis on the *branco/negro* designations, that is to say, the Black/White dichotomy—if not the absolute enforcement of the rule of hypodescent—as has so long been the case in the United States.

Notes

A special thank you to the UCLA Latin American Center for the support it provided me in the completion of this essay.

1. Other versions of this chapter were presented at the Center for African American Studies, Winter Colloquium Series (University of California, Los Angeles, 1989), the Latin American Studies Association Annual Meeting (Los Angeles, California, September 23–27, 1992), and at the Ethnicity and Multiethnicity: The Construction and Deconstruction of Ethnicity Conference (Brigham Young University, Hawaii, May 10–13, 1995).

2. In everyday parlance, *branco*, *mulato*, and *preto* are used to refer respectively to White, multiracial, and Black individuals, whereas the term *negro* is used to include both *mulatos* and *pretos*. *Pardo* (which literally means brown) is more of an official term used to refer to multiracial individuals, particularly mulattos. A vernacular term such as *moreno* (brunette), however, can be used to describe a wide variety of brunette phenotypes, including those individuals who are designated as *preto*, *pardo*, or *branco* (particularly if the latter has dark hair and eyes). Also, the issues surrounding multiracial identity are by no means limited to the experience of individuals of African and European descent. Indeed, the Native American component has contributed significantly to racial formation in Brazil, particularly from the colonial period to the first half of the twentieth century. Nevertheless, an analysis of the history of slavery and the unique legacy of attitudes and policies that have crystallized around the experience of individuals of African descent is particularly meaningful. Consequently, the words "multiracial" and "mulatto" are used interchangeably in this chapter. The terms "African Brazilian" and "African–descent Brazilian" (*negros*) generally include both Black and multiracial individuals.

3. See Carl N. Degler, *Neither Black Nor White: Slavery and Race Relations in Brazil and the United States* (New York: Macmillan Publishing Co., Inc., 1971). Also see Marvin Harris, *Patterns of Race in the Americas* (New York: W.W. Norton, 1963).

4. See I. K. Sundiata, "Late Twentieth-Century Patterns of Race Relations in Brazil and United States," *Phylon* 47 (1987): 62–76. See Howard Winant, *Racial Conditions: Politics, Theory, Comparisons* (Minneapolis: University of Minnesota Press, 1994), 130–69. Paradoxically, the emergence of the New Multiracial Consciousness Movement in the United States indicates that Anglo-American race relations may be moving toward the ternary model which traditionally has been associated with Brazil. See G. Reginald Daniel, "Beyond Black and White: The New Multiracial Consciousness," in *Racially Mixed People in America*, ed. Maria P. P. Root (Newbury Park, Cal.: Sage Publications, 1992), 333–41. See G. Reginald Daniel, "Converging Paths: Multiracial Identity in Brazil and the United States" (paper presented at the

Ethnicity and Multiethnicity: The Construction and Deconstruction of Ethnicity Conference, Brigham Young University, Hawaii, 10–13 May 1995). Also see Thomas A. Skidmore, "Bi-Racial U.S.A. vs. Multi-Racial Brazil: Is the Contrast Still Valid?" *Journal of Latin American Studies* 25 (1993): 383–86.

5. See Gilberto Freyre, *The Masters and the Slaves: A Study in the Development of Brazilian Civilization*, trans. Harriet de Onís (New York: Alfred A. Knopf, 1963); and Freyre, *The Mansions and the Shanties: The Making of Modern Brazil*, trans. Harriet de Onís (New York: Alfred A. Knopf, 1963); and also see Freyre, *Order and Progress: Brazil from Monarchy to Republic*, trans. and ed. Rod W. Horton (New York: Alfred A. Knopf, 1970).

6. See Degler, *Neither Black Nor White*, 213–16, 226–38. See G. Reginald Daniel, "Passers and Pluralists: Subverting the Racial Divide," in *Racially Mixed People in America*, ed. Maria P. P. Root (Newbury Park, Cal.: Sage Publications, 1992), 91–107. See H. Hoetink, *Slavery and Race Relations in the Americas: Comparative Notes on Their Nature and Nexus* (New York: Harper & Row, 1973), 37, 41–42, 108.

7. See Emilia Viotti da Costa, *The Brazilian Empire: Myths and Histories* (Chicago: University of Chicago Press, 1985), 239–43.

8. See H. Hoetink, *Slavery and Race Relations*, 37, 41–42, 108. See John Burbick, "The Myth of Racial Democracy," *North American Congress on Latin America: Report on the Americas* 25, no. 4 (February 1992): 40–42.

9. The escape hatch allows vertical mobility primarily in terms of phenotypical, that is, somatic approximation to the dominant European norm image as defined by Hoetink, *Slavery and Race Relations*, 197–98. However, somatic (external) characteristics of a cultural and economic nature, e.g., speech, mannerisms, attire, occupation, income, etc., and psychological (internal) factors, such as beliefs, values, and attitudes are also taken into consideration. Consequently, a few exceptional Blacks have gained vertical mobility in accordance with their socioeconomic and sociocultural, if not phenotypical, approximation to the dominant Whites.

10. See Degler, *Neither Black Nor White*, 140, 196–99. This has historically been the dominant trend in the states from Rio de Janeiro northward—particularly the state of Bahia—where individuals of African descent have always been a majority. In that region, the line between Black and White is far more illusive and has even given rise to the interesting designations *branco da terra* or *branco da Bahia*. These terms translate literally as "home grown White" and "Bahian White," and refer to individuals who clearly display some African phenotypical traits (or at least have known African ancestry), but who are regarded as Whites in Bahia, and the Northeast by extension. This is a far more liberal attitude than in the states from São Paulo southward, where Europeans have been significantly more numerous, if not always a majority. Consequently,

the markers delineating Blacks from Whites, and more specifically multiracial individuals from Whites, is far more restrictive.

11. See Daniel, "Passers and Pluralists," 91–107.

12. See Anani Dzidzienyo, *The Position of Blacks in Brazilian Society: Minority Group Rights Reports*, no. 7 (London: Minority Rights Group, 1979), 2–11. See Abdias do Nascimento, *Mixture or Massacre?Essays on the Genocide of a Black People*, trans. Elisa Larkin Nascimento (State University of New York at Buffalo, Puerto Rican Studies and Research Center, 1979), 74–80. Thomas A. Skidmore, *Black into White: Race and Nationality in Brazilian Thought* (New York: Oxford University Press, 1974), 64–77. It should be pointed out, however, that Brazilian popular culture and the physiognomy of the Brazilian people remain strongly indebted to and influenced by the African component despite attempts by the elite to ignore and disguise, if not wipe out, its presence.

13. See Afranio Coutinho, "El Fenómeno de Machado de Assis," *Brasil Kultura* XIV, 63 (Julio de 1989): 8–12.

14. See David T. Haberly, "Abolitionism in Brazil: Anti-Slavery and Anti-Slave," *Luso-Brazilian Review* 9, 2 (November 1972): 30–46.

15. See Degler, *Neither Black nor White*, 182–83.

16. See Thomas A. Skidmore, "Race Relations in Brazil," *Camões Center Quarterly* 4, 3 & 4 (autumn and winter, 1992–1993): 49–57. See Charles H. Wood and José Alberto Magno de Carvalho, *The Demography of Inequality in Brazil* (New York: Cambridge University Press, 1988), 135–53.

17. See Skidmore, "Race Relations in Brazil," 49–57.

18. Ibid.

19. See Nascimento, *Mixture or Massacre?* 79–80. See Peggy Lovell–Webster, "The Myth of Racial Equality: A Study of Race and Morality in Northeast Brazil," *Latinamericanist* 22, 2 (May 1987): 1–6.

20. See George Reid Andrews, *Blacks and Whites in São Paulo, Brazil, 1888–1988* (Madison: University of Wisconsin Press, 1991), 146–56. See Michael George Hanchard, *Orpheus and Power: The Movimento Negro of Rio de Janeiro and São Paulo, Brazil, 1945–1988* (Princeton: Princeton University Press, 1994), 104–29. See Michael Mitchell, "Blacks and the Abertura Democrática," in *Race, Class and Power in Brazil*, ed. Pierre-Michel Fontaine (Center for Afro-American Studies, University of California, Los Angeles, 1985), 95–119. Although the Black Front had several successors in the 1940s and 1950s (*Teatro Experimental do Negro, União dos Homens de Côr, Associação Cultural do Negro*), none of these organizations achieved its level of

prominence.

21. See Skidmore, "Race Relations in Brazil," 49–57.

22. See Skidmore, "Race Relations in Brazil," 49–57. See Rebecca Reichmann, "Brazil's Denial of Race," *North American Congress on Latin America: Report on the Americas* 28, 6 (May/June 1995): 35–42.

23. See Skidmore, "Race Relations in Brazil," 49–57. See Lelia González, "The Unified Black Movement: A New Stage in Black Mobilization," in *Race, Class and Power in Brazil*, ed. Pierre-Michel Fontaine, 120–34. See Andrews, *Blacks and Whites in São Paulo*, 211–44. John Burdick, "Brazil's Black Consciousness Movement," *North American Congress on Latin America: Report on the Americas* 25, no. 4 (February 1992): 23–27. See Luiz Silva, "The Black Stream in Brazilian Literature," *Conexões*. African Diaspora Research Project, Michigan State University 4, no. 2 (1992): 12–13.

24. See Mac Margolis, "The Invisible Issue: Race in Brazil," *Ford Foundation Report* 1, no. 2 (summer 1992): 3–7. See Reichmann, "Brazil's Denial of Race," 35–45. See Regina Domingues, "The Color of a Majority without Citizenship," *Conexões*. African Diaspora Research Project, Michigan State University 4, no. 2 (November 1992): 6–7. See Carlos Hasenbalg, "Race and Socioeconomic Inequalities in Brazil," in *Race, Class and Power in Brazil*, ed. Pierre-Michel Fontaine, 25–41. See Lovell-Webster, "The Myth of Racial Equality," 1–6. See Peggy Lovell-Webster and Jeffery Dwyer, "The Cost of Not Being White in Brazil," *Sociology and Social Research* 72, no. 2 (January 1988): 136–38. See Nelson do Valle Silva, "Updating the Cost of Not Being White in Brazil," in *Race, Class and Power in Brazil*, ed. Pierre-Michel Fontaine, 42–55. See Anani Dzidzienyo, "Brazil," in *International Handbook on Race and Race Relations*, ed. Jay A. Sigler (New York: Greenwood Press, 1987), 23–42.

25. See Burdick, "Brazil's Black Consciousness Movement," 23–27. See Silva, "Updating the Cost," 42–55.

26. Much as in the United States, the vast majority of marriages in Brazil (approximately 80 percent) are racially endogamous. Although multiracial individuals appear to intermarry with Blacks and Whites in about equal proportions, Black/White intermarriage is comparatively rare. See Carlos A. Hasenbalg, Nelson do Valle Silva, and Luiz Claudio Bracelos, "Notas Sobre Miscegenação Racial no Brasil," *Estudos Afro-Asiáticos* 6 (Junho de 1989): 189–97. See Edward E. Telles, "Racial Distance and Region in Brazil: Intermarriage in Brazilian Urban Areas," *Latin American Research Review* 28, no. 2 (spring 1992): 141–62.

27. See Dzidzienho, "Brazil," 23–42.

28. See Burdick, "Brazil's Black Consciousness Movement," 23–27. See

Hasenbalg, Silva, and Bracelos, "Notas Sobre Miscegenação Brasil," 189–97. See Hasenbalg, "Race and Socioeconomic Inequalities in Brazil," in *Race, Class and Power in Brazil*, ed. Pierre-Michel Fontaine, 25–41. See Laurie Goering, "Beneath Utopian Facade, Brazilians Uncover Racism," *Chicago Tribune,* 20 December 1994, 1, 11. See Marlise Simmons, "Brazil's Blacks Feel Prejudice 100 Years After Slavery's End, *New York Times,* 14 May 1988, 1, 6. See Edward E. Telles, "Residential Segregation by Skin Color in Brazil," *American Sociological Review* 57, no. 2 (April 1992): 186–97. See Lovell-Webster & Dwyer, "The Cost of Being Nonwhite," 136–38. See Silva, "Updating the Cost," 42–55.

29. See Silva, "Updating the Cost," 42–55; Hasenbalg, "Race and Socioeconomic Inequalities," 25–41.

30. See Skidmore, "Race Relations in Brazil," 49–57.

31. See Reichmann, "Brazil's Denial of Race," 35–42. See Skidmore, "Race Relations in Brazil," 49–57.

32. See Skidmore, "Race Relations in Brazil," 55.

33. See Skidmore, "Race Relations in Brazil," 49–57. See Hasenbalg, "O Negro nas Vésperas do Centenário," *Estudos Afro-Asiáticos* 13 (Março de 1987): 79–86.

34. See Andrews, *Blacks and Whites*, 218–33. See Skidmore, "Race Relations in Brazil," 49–57. See Margolis, "The Invisible Issue," 3–7. See Reichmann, "Brazil's Denial of Race," 35–42.

35. See Skidmore, "Race Relations in Brazil," 49–57. See Hasenbalg, "Race and Socioeconomic Inequalities in Brazil," 25–41. See Reichmann, "Brazil's Denial of Race," 35–42. See Burdick, "Brazil's Black Consciousness Movement," 23–27. See Andrews, *Blacks and Whites*, 218–33.

36. See Andrews, *Blacks and Whites*, 250. See Elvira Oliveira, "Dia Nacional da Consciencia Negra," *Nova Escola* (Novembro de 1993): 23–25. See Lori S. Robinson, "The Two Faces of Brazil: A Black Movement Gives Voice to an Invisible Majority," *Emerge* (October 1994): 38–42.

37. See Skidmore, *Black into White*, 64–77. See Dzidzienho, *The Position of Blacks in Brazilian Society*, 2–11. See Margolis, 64–77. "The Invisible Issue," 3–7. See Nascimento, *Mixture or Massacre?* 74–80. See Oliveira, "Dia Nacional," 3–25. See Robinson, "Two Faces of Brazil," 38–42. See Wood and Carvalho, *The Demography of Inequality*, 135–53. See Melissa Nobles, "'Responding with Good Sense': The Politics of Race and Censuses in Contemporary Brazil," (Ph.D. diss., Yale University, 1995), 133–75, 181–215. In 1890, *pardos* comprised 41.4 percent of the population. Their apparent

decline from 41.4 percent to 21.2 percent between 1890 and 1940, and the growth of the *branco* population from 43.97 to 63.5 percent during the same period is more related to the massive immigration of Europeans to Brazil than to increased miscegenation or racial self-recoding. Census figures make clear, however, that between 1940 and 1990, the *pardo* population was the country's fastest growing racial group, rising from 21.2 percent to 38.8 percent (+/– 48 million) of the national population. During the same period *brancos* declined from 63.5 percent to 54.2 percent (+/– 86 million) and *pretos* from 14.6 percent to 5.9 percent (+/– 6 million). See Hasenbalg, Silva, and Bracelos, "Notas Sobre Miscegenação," 189–97. This trend does indicate a progressive "lightening" of the population. It would be less appropriately described as a "whitening," however, and more as a "browning." If upwardly mobile African Brazilians have been moving out of the *pardo* category into the *branco* category, it, therefore, has not been in numbers sufficient to reverse this trend. See Andrews, *Black and Whites*, 252.

38. See Burdick, "Brazil's Black Consciousness Movement," 23–27. See Domingues, "The Color of a Majority without Citizenship," 6–7. See Oliveira, "Dia Nacional," 23–25. See Jerry Michael Turner, "Brown into Black: Changing Attitudes of Afro-Brazilian University Students," in *Race, Class and Power in Brazil*, ed. Pierre-Michel Fontaine, 73–94. See Nobles, "'Responding with Good Sense,'" 133–75, 181–215. A significant portion of Whites have African ancestry and display varying degrees of African phenotypical traits. If we were using the Anglo-American rule of hypodescent, multiracial individuals would completely vanish, as would a large portion of Whites. Combining the figures for the approximately 40 percent of Brazilians who are designated as *pardos* with the 6 percent designated as *pretos*, rather than counting them as separate categories, brings the total of African Brazilians (*negros*) to roughly 46 percent. This combined format, by reinforcing a dichotomous racial classification system, not only serves to counter the "whitening" ideology but also gives a more accurate picture of Brazilian racial dynamics since the primary divide in terms of social stratification is located between the *branco* and *negro* racial groups and only secondarily—and minimally—between *pardos* and *pretos*.

Literature Cited

Andrews, George Reid. *Blacks and Whites in São Paulo, Brazil, 1888–1988*. Madison: University of Wisconsin Press, 1991.

Burbick, John. "Brazil's Black Consciousness Movement." North *American Congress on Latin America: Report on the Americas* 25, no. 4 (February 1992): 23–27.

Cohen, David W., and Jack P. Greene. "Introduction." *In Neither Slave Nor Free: The Freemen of African Descent in the Slave Societies of the New World*, edited by David Cohen and Jack P. Greene, 1–23. Baltimore: Johns Hopkins University Press, 1972.

Costa, Emilia Viotti da. *The Brazilian Empire: Myths and Histories*. Chicago: University of Chicago Press, 1985.

Coutinho, Afrânio. "El Fenómeno de Machado de Assis." *Brasil Kultura* 14, no. 63 (Julio de 1989): 8–12.

Daniel, G. Reginald. "Beyond Black and White: The New Multiracial Consciousness." In *Racially Mixed People in America*, edited by Maria P. Root, 333–41. Newbury Park, Cal.: Sage Publications, 1992.

———. "Black and White Identity in the New Millennium: Unsevering the Ties That Bind." In *The Multiracial Experience: Racial Borders as the New Frontier*, edited by Maria P. Root, 121–39. Newbury Park, Cal.: Sage Publications, 1996.

———. "Converging Paths: Race Relations in Brazil and the United States." Paper presented at the Winter Colloquium Series, University of California, Los Angeles, Center for Afro-American Studies, 1989.

———. "Converging Paths: Multiracial Identity in Brazil and the United States." Paper presented at Ethnicity and Multiethnicity: The Construction and Deconstruction of Ethnicity Conference. Brigham Young University, Hawaii, l0–13 May 1995.

———. "Passers and Pluralists: Subverting the Racial Divide." *In Racially Mixed People in America*, edited by Maria P. P. Root, 91–l07. Newbury Park, Cal.: Sage Publications, 1992.

Degler, Carl N. *Neither Black Nor White: Slavery and Race Relations in Brazil and the United States*. New York: Macmillan Publishing Co., Inc., 1971.

Domingues, Regina. "The Color of a Majority without Citizenship." *Conexões*. African Diaspora Research Project, Michigan State University, 4, no. 2 (November 1992): 6–7.

Dzidzienyo, Anani. *The Position of Blacks in Brazilian Society. Minority Group Rights Reports*, no. 7. London: Minority Rights Group, 1971.

———. "Brazil." In International Handbook on Race and Race Relations, Edited by Jay A. Sigler, 23–42. New York: Greenwood Press, 1987.

Fontaine, Pierre-Michel, 120-34. Center for Afro-American Studies, University of California, Los Angeles, 1985.

Freyre, Gilberto. *The Masters and the Slaves: A Study in the Development of Brazilian Civilization*, translated by Harriet de Onís. New York: Alfred A. Knopf, 1963.

———. *Order and Progress: Brazil from Monarchy to Republic*, translated and edited by Rod W. Horton. New York: Alfred A. Knopf, 1970.

———. *The Mansions and the Shanties: The Making of Modern Brazil*, translated by Harriet de Onís. New York: Alfred A. Knopf, 1963.

Goering, Laurie. "Beneath Utopian Facade, Brazilians Uncover Racism." *Chicago Tribune*, 20 December 1994, 1, 11.

González, Lelia. "The Unified Black Movement: A New Stage in Black Mobilization." In *Race, Class and Power in Brazil*, edited by Pierre-Michael Fontaine, 120–34. Center for Afro-American Studies, University of California, Los Angeles, 1985.

Haberly, David T. "Abolitionism in Brazil: Anti-Slavery and Anti-Slave." *Luso-Brazilian Review* 9, no. 2 (November 1972): 30–46.

Hamilton, Ruth Simms. "From the Editor." *Conexões*. African Diaspora Research Project, Michigan State University, 4, no. 2 (November 1992): 2, 13.

Hanchard, Michael George. *Orpheus and Power: The Movimento Negro of Rio de Janeiro and São Paulo, Brazil, 1945–1988*. Princeton: Princeton University Press, 1994.

Harris, Marvin. *Patterns of Race in the Americas*. New York: W. W. Norton, 1963.

Hasenbalg, Carlos A. "Race and Socioeconomic Inequalities in Brazil." In *Race, Class, and Power in Brazil*, edited by Pierre-Michel Fontaine, 25–41. Center for Afro-American Studies, University of California, Los Angeles, 1985.

———. "O Negro nas Vésperas do Centenário." *Estudos Afro-Asiáticos* 13 (Marzo de 1987): 79–86.

———, Nelson do Valle Silva, and Luiz Claudio Bracelos. "Notas Sobre Miscegenação Brasil." In *Estudos Afro-Asiáticos* 16 (Junho de 1989): 189–97.

Hoetink, Hartimus. *Slavery and Race Relations in the Americas: Comparative Notes on Their Nature and Nexus*. New York: Harper & Row, 1973.

Klein, Herbert S. "Nineteenth-Century Brazil." In *Neither Slave Nor Free: The Freemen of African Descent in the Slave Societies of the New World*, edited by David Cohen and Jack P. Greene, 309–34. Baltimore: Johns Hopkins University Press, 1972.

Lovell-Webster, Peggy. "The Myth of Racial Equality: A Study of Race and Mortality in Northeast Brazil." *Latinamericanist* 22, no. 2 (May 1987): 1–6.

———, and Jeffrey Dwyer. "The Cost of Being Nonwhite in Brazil." *Sociology and Social Research* 72, no. 2 (January 1988):136–38.

Margolis, Mac. "The Invisible Issue: Race in Brazil." *Ford Foundation Report* 23, no. 2 (summer 1992): 3–7.

Mitchell, Michael. "Blacks and the Abertura Democrática." *In Race, Class and Power in Brazil*, edited by Pierre-Michel Fontaine, 120–34. Center for Afro-American Studies, University of California, Los Angeles, 1985.

Nascimento, Abdias do. *Mixture or Massacre? Essays on the Genocide of a Black People*, translated by Elisa Larkin Nascimento. Puerto Rican Studies and Research Center, State University of New York at Buffalo, 1979.

Nobles, Melissa. "'Responding with Good Sense': The Politics of Race and Censuses in Contemporary Brazil." Ph.D. diss., Yale University, 1995.

Oliveira, Elvira. "Dia Nacional da Consciencia Negra." *Nova Escola* (Novembro de 1993): 23–25.

Reichmann, Rebecca. "Brazil's Denial of Race." *North American Congress on Latin America: Report on the Americas* 28, no. 6 (May/June 1995): 35–42.

Robinson, Lori S. "The Two Faces of Brazil: A Black Movement Gives Voice to an Invisible Majority." *Emerge* (October 1994): 38–42.

Silva, Luiz. "The Black Stream in Brazilian Literature." Conexões. African Diaspora Research Project, Michigan State University, 4, no. 2 (November 1992): 12.

Silva, Nelson do Valle. "Updating the Cost of Not Being White in Brazil." In *Race, Class, and Power in Brazil*, edited by Pierre-Michel Fontaine, 25–41. Center for Afro–American Studies, University of California, Los Angeles, 1985.

Simmons, Marlise. "Brazil's Blacks Feel Prejudice l00 Years After Slavery's End." *New York Times* 14 May 1988, 1, 6.

Skidmore, Thomas *A. Black into White: Race and Nationality in Brazilian Thought*. New York: Oxford University Press, 1974.

———. "Race Relations in Brazil." *Camôes Center Quarterly* 4, nos. 3 & 4 (autumn and winter 1992–1993): 49–57.

———. "Bi-Racial U.S.A. vs. Multi–racial Brazil: Is the Contrast Still Valid?" *Journal of Latin American Studies* 25 (1993): 383–86.

Sundiata, I. K. "Late Twentieth-Century Patterns of Race Relations in Brazil and United States." *Phylon* 47, 1 (1987), 62–76.

Telles, Edward E. "Racial Distance and Region in Brazil: Intermarriage in Brazilian Urban Areas." *Latin American Research Review* 28, no. 2 (1992): 141–62.

———. "Residential Segregation by Skin Color in Brazil." *American Sociological Review* 57, no. 2 (April 1992): 186–97.

Turner, J. Michael. "Brown into Black: Changing Racial Attitudes of Afro-Brazilian University Students." In *Race, Class and Power in Brazil*, Edited by Pierre-Michel Fontaine, 73–94. Center for Afro-American Studies, University of California, Los Angeles, 1985.

Winant, Howard. *Racial Conditions: Politics, Theory, Comparisons.* Minneapolis: University of Minnesota Press, 1994.

Wood, Charles H., and José Alberto Magno de Carvalho. *The Demography of Inequality in Brazil*. New York: Cambridge University Press, 1988.

Language and Identity in Central America: A History of Oppression, Struggle, and Achievement

Anita Herzfeld

Introduction

Language is often seen as the most critical characteristic of identity for a group. Nevertheless, this essay argues that while critical, language is so embedded in history and culture that these elements cannot be viewed separately as components of identity. In a comparative analysis of the Maya in Guatemala and the Limonese Creole speakers of Costa Rica, I argue that two subordinate linguistic groups have radically diverse prospects of language survival because of the sociohistorical background of each. While many scholars (e.g., Fishman 1977, Gumperz 1982, Giles 1977) consider the possession of a given language of particular relevance—almost essential—to the maintenance of group identity, others (e.g., Edwards 1985) claim that it is important not to lose sight of its non-unique status as a marker. Of all the powerful elements of group identity (ethnicity, nationalism, and the relationship between them), Edwards (1985:22) states that "the most important ingredients are the subjective sense of groupness and the continuation of group boundaries." He considers that these two are indeed related, but since certain aspects of group culture are always subject to change, the continuing identity must depend upon elements that transcend any purely objective markers.[1] "This is not to say," he continues, "that visible markers are dispensable, but rather that the presence of any particular marker is not essential."

It is my contention that social identity and ethnicity are in large part maintained and reinforced through language. However, a subordinate people's language will either survive or become extinct as a symbol of identity because of the sociohistorical process through which a group's language is evaluated.[2] Members of a linguistic community may derive feelings of pride or shame from their perception of the degree of standardization their language has undergone. Thus the prestige value attached to the history of their language may facilitate or inhibit the vitality of a given ethnolinguistic group (Giles 1977:312), depending upon whether the language carries a sense of historical pride and identity or dislocation and shame. Nowadays, given the climate of socioeconomic distress that Central America is undergoing, power-minority speakers feel more self-conscious than ever about their linguistic background, which differs from Spanish, the officially accepted code. While for some peoples of the region, the Maya speakers for instance, language may well act as a symbol of linguistic rebellion conducive to feelings of group solidarity, for many others, such as the creole speakers of Costa Rica, their mother tongue is clearly considered a liability.

Subsequently, a linguistic panorama of Central America will be sketched, placing the indigenous languages within a basic classificatory perspective and defining the concepts of pidgins and creoles. Then, in order to analyze the relationship between language and identity, ethnicity will be explained and the danger of equating linguistic nationalism with race will be highlighted. To exemplify linguistic contact and conflict situations within multilingual nations, various outcomes are discussed, taking into account political and socioeconomic subordinate and superordinate groups. Finally, the article focuses on two particular issues: the strength of the Pan-Mayan movement of linguistic unity in Guatemala and the lack of political power exercised by the speakers of Limonese Creole in Costa Rica Both cases illustrate the possibilities of survival or endangerment of a linguistic code in the light of the sociohistorical process its speakers are living.

The Linguistic Panorama of Central America

Central America comprises the countries of Guatemala, Belize, Honduras, El Salvador, Nicaragua, Costa Rica, and Panama. Except for Belize, where English is the official language, the concept of Central America used here refers mainly to the other five independent Spanish-speaking countries.[3] As is well-known, Spanish was introduced by the Spanish conquerors in the sixteenth century and has since become the national and official language in all of these states.[4]

Less well known is the fact that, despite this process of linguistic homogenization, today there are still over fifty different Amerindian and Afro-Central American ethnic groups in Central America, each with its own language. However, while the Maya of Guatemala run into the millions, the indigenous peoples of the rest of Central America vary between a few hundred to a few thousand members each. In spite of the fact that in Guatemala the Maya actually constitute a numerical majority, in all the Central American countries indigenous ethnic groups as well as Afro-Central Americans are decidedly power minorities (Addenda, Table 1, Central American Linguistic Distribution).

Linguistically, most of the Amerindian languages of Central America form part of the so-called "Intermediate Area" that encompasses the eastern regions of Honduras; the Atlantic coast and central region of Nicaragua; all of Costa Rica, except for the Nicoya peninsula; and all of Panama.[5] The indigenous groups established in the north of Central America and in Mexico belong to the Mesoamerican families of languages[6] (Addenda, Figure 1, Intermediate and Mesoamerican Cultural and Linguistic Areas).

Afro-Central Americans arrived in the region through two waves of immigration. Originally, they came from Africa as slaves who were sold to plantation and mine owners of sixteenth-century Spanish colonies; three centuries later, many Afro-Caribbean islanders settled on the coastal areas of Central America in search of jobs and land. Today the people from this second wave of immigration still communicate in various English-based creoles all along the Atlantic coast (Addenda, Figure 2, English and Creole Speakers in Central America, 1978).

A word about these creole languages. If the European and African contact prior to the sixteenth century had proceeded along non-exploitative terms, the usual foreign language learning process would have led to some Africans speaking European languages fluently, others speaking them passably, and still others having only a smattering of knowledge (Bickerton 1975:175). The slave trade disrupted this pattern, isolating many Africans from their own speech communities and truncating their acquisition of a European language.[7] Some creolists would say that this left them with the ability to speak their own native tongue(s) along with a European language acquired incompletely.[8] The need to communicate amongst themselves produced a pidgin, which is commonly defined as "a reduced language that results from extended contact between groups of people with no language in common" (Holm 1988:5).

Usually, this makeshift language borrows vocabulary from the superordinate language, although the structure and meaning may be strongly influenced by the subordinate language(s). By definition the resulting pidgin must be easy to learn, i.e., it is a simplified language (with no inflections, for instance), it has a reduced vocabulary, and it is restricted to limited semantic domains (trade, for example, in which case it is considered a lingua franca).[9] To the inherited pidgin language, developed under the social disruption suffered by their parents, children who become creole speakers (i.e., those whose mother tongue is a pidgin) add some enlargement and organization in response to communicative needs. Due to the geographic displacement of the speakers and the broken ties with their sociocultural identity and their original language, their sociolinguistic history, and not just the structure of their language, is an important determinant of the linguistic outcome in these types of language contact situations.

As we shall see in greater detail below, when two peoples who speak different languages come into contact, one of the most common scenarios is for the subordinate group to give up its native tongue, as the superordinate group establishes its language as the means of national communication. Although this has taken place in all of Central America, certain languages have managed to survive in this contact and conflict situation. Five hundred years of concerted efforts by the superordinate group to completely annihilate indigenous diversity have failed, partly because of sheer density of population; partly because of significant ancestral cultural and religious traits, which have been difficult for national campaigns toward homogeneity to suppress; and most importantly, because of the effect, in some cases, of repression having prompted a rebellious reaction manifested in linguistic adherence as a means of defiance. How these languages help determine the identity of their speakers is discussed below.

Dimensions of Language and Ethnicity

Attempts to analyze the relationship between language and identity have focused foremost on the relationship between language and ethnicity. Language is a highly structured and sophisticated system which, with subtlety and flexibility, is crucially related to a human being's most significant capacities, thought and cognition, including the ability to categorize, classify, and symbolize. Ethnicity, on the other hand, comprises a number of concepts because of the many interrelated factors that it subsumes. At a simple level, ethnicity can be thought of as a "sense of group identity deriving from real or perceived common bonds such as language, race or religion" (Edwards 1977:254).[10]

In those general terms, ethnicity is based on a collectivity's self-recognition. It differs from other kinds of group recognition signals in that it operates basically in terms of what Fishman (1977:16) calls "paternity."[11] Through ethnicity individuals not only attain social integration, but they are also linked to social norms and values, to a certain *Weltanschauung*, to inherited and acquired, both stable and changing notions of society and the world. It is easy to see why language, one of the essential characteristics of human behavior, is associated with ethnic "paternity." Moreover, because one can exert more control over one's linguistic behavior (more than over other dimensions of ethnic identity), language is seen (and heard!) by others as "a truer reflection of one's ethnic allegiance" (Giles 1977:326). However, since the course of language is dynamic, it is also very susceptible to change as an element of identity, inextricably linked as it is to the social determinants of human life.

Indeed, in the history of humankind, nationalism records its strong link with language and identity from the moment of its modern inception. Largely a product of German romanticism of the late eighteenth and early nineteenth centuries, both Herder and Fichte, and a little later Wilhelm von Humboldt, felt that nothing was more important for national culture and continuity than possession of the ancestral tongue.[12]

On many occasions language became a tool for achieving nationalistic goals. The idea of linguistic nationalism was a dangerous one, however, when it equated language and race. Although the power of language is undoubtedly a factor in nationalism, Smith (1971:149–150) has made the useful point that emphasis upon language follows the growth of nationalist fervor; it does not create it. Thus all the Central American countries developed their national identity prior to establishing Spanish as their official language. But what has happened to the multitude of other languages spoken in the region?

Languages in Contact

Multilingual societies are found in all parts of the world; they existed in the past and they occur today; they are found in older nations as well as in the newly created states. Currently, for instance, there is more than one viable language in each Latin American country. The political and social situation created by this linguistic diversity ranges from the quasi-perfect harmony of Spanish and Guaraní in Paraguay to Guatemala or Peru, where the entire political fabric is torn into factions that often coincide with linguistic boundaries. Even in those societies where equality between linguistic groups would seem to have been achieved in official, legal, and political terms, it is rare to accomplish equality either in the social or economic sphere. To complicate matters further, linguistic differences often become associated with racial or ethnic differences, thus making the language contact situation a hopelessly entangled one (Lieberson 1981:1). Generally speaking, speakers of diverse languages do not come into contact under neutral emotional conditions; more often than not the contact situation involves some kind of dominance of one group over the other, thus always producing significant attitudinal reactions.

In studying the relationship of language and identity within a bilingual or multilingual nation, it is important to examine the history and nature of the contact situation between the peoples who speak diverse codes, whether dialects or languages. One fundamental step is to distinguish groups that are politically and economically superordinate from those that are subordinate in these institutional domains (Lieberson 1981:2), and to ascertain how such a differential power relationship was created. Likewise, one should also distinguish between migrant and indigenous populations at the time of their contact. Additionally, the migrant group can be further subdivided into the kind of group that leaves its original settlement in pursuit of economic adventure and religious glory, and the group that is coerced into departing due to dire circumstances. From these distinctions, one can develop a rudimentary theory that suggests that the course of linkage between language and identity in Central America will be different in settings where the indigenous group is subordinate as opposed to those where the migrant population is subordinate.

When two distinct linguistic groups come into contact, we may find a situation in which:

1. The indigenous group is superordinate.
2. The migrant group is superordinate.
3. The indigenous group is subordinate.
4. The migrant group is subordinate.
5. Neither group is superordinate in all domains.[13]

The languages spoken by group (1) or group (2) are not likely to shift if these speakers are dominating the political and economic spheres of a country. The superordinate group may decide in favor of keeping the languages of the groups in contact as their strategy for achieving their goals (policy which is likely to bring about multi- or bilingualism); or in favor of making their language the official language (in which case monolingualism of the dominant language obtains). Indigenous subordinate groups (3), on the other hand, may be placed in a condition where they are not permitted to maintain their language (which results in monolingualism of the dominant language), or where they are permitted to use their language solely in private domains (a situation which creates diglossia).[14] Alternatively, they may enter a self-segregation condition in which they refuse to learn the dominant language (monolingualism of the subordinate language is the consequence).[15]

Rich in diversified indigenous cultural heritages, Central America has maintained linguistic reminders of ancient civilizations; although these groups may have once been in a position of power, they have now come to exemplify the case of subordinate indigenous groups (group 3 above). The impressive Mayan ruins of Copán in Honduras, and the magnificent relics of Tikal in Guatemala, stand as silent testimony of the grandeur of yesteryear; today, however, out of a total of approximately 9 million inhabitants, the 6 million speakers of the twenty Mayan languages in Guatemala[16] constitute a political "minority" within the Spanish-speaking society, whose members comprise the superordinate group. Ever since the beginning of the nineteenth century, using nationalism as their banner, the Spanish and *criollo* elites have promoted the link between their country's nascent identity and their own native Spanish. Thus they have maintained sociopolitical and linguistic dominance with little regard for concerns of linguistic minorities, a situation that has finally caught national attention.

Speakers of migrant subordinate groups (of type 4 above), by contrast, seem to show a relatively rapid rate of linguistic and identity shift.[17] This is the case of most English-based creole speakers of Central America: Panamanian Creole speakers, Limonese Creole speakers of Costa Rica, Bay Islands English speakers of Honduras, creole speakers of Guatemala, and to a certain extent the creole speakers of the Miskito coast of Nicaragua. West Indian Creole speakers migrating from their own established social order to a subordinated situation in these Central American nations were forced by circumstances to assimilate or adapt to the new order. In a non-symmetrical culture contact situation such as this one, varying degrees of socio-structural and socio-psychological change took place under the considerable pressure exercised by the superordinate group. Language played an important role as the vehicle for acquiring the new culture; it was, in fact, the most important element secured in the quest for a new identity.

Language and Identity: Maintenance, Shift, or Extinction

Linguistic diversity constitutes a threat to the broader political order of a nation. Usually, a commonly shared tongue is seen as a vehicle for the maintenance of the perceived unity of purposes and needs shared by the country's inhabitants. Thus it is hardly surprising that in order to develop and keep the political loyalties in place, the states put forth programs to promote the use of the national language by the entire population.

Even though our social identity is established by the parameters and boundaries of our ethnicity, gender, and class, once we study language as the interactional discourse of that social identity, we find that these parameters are not constants that can be taken for granted, but are communicatively produced (Gumperz 1982:1). Therefore, to understand issues of identity and how they affect and are affected by social, political, and ethnic divisions we need to gain insight into the communicative processes through which they arise. However, communication cannot be studied in isolation; it must be analyzed in terms of its effect on people's lives. Two examples will be discussed briefly to illustrate this point, that of the Mayan speakers of Guatemala and the Afro-Limonese Creole speakers of Costa Rica.

Considered from a national perspective, Guatemala has a hierarchical social system in which a large number of people are Spanish speakers. Among the laborers and peasant farmers who usually work lands belonging to others, many have as a mother tongue one of the many mutually unintelligible Amerindian native languages. The current social hierarchy has placed Spanish as the national and official language. However, in the last two decades a diverse group of subjected linguistic minorities have made their dissenting voices heard because of a revitalization of the Maya pre-Hispanic heritage and the national acknowledgment of their dignified past, embedded in the tradition of their mother tongue.

The Guatemalan democratic governments from 1945 to 1956[18] went to great lengths to construct a national identity, but they did not manage to solve "the Indian problem," i.e., to integrate the indigenous groups into the national society in such a way that they could preserve their cultural traits. This precluded the total assimilation of these ethnic groups into Guatemalan socioeconomic and political life. With the elected governments having been overthrown by the armed forces in 1956, these various indigenous peoples were exposed to brutal violence and flagrant violations of their human rights by governmental armed forces in the long war that just ended; the twenty Mayan peoples of Guatemala became united as one, "the Maya people" of Guatemala.[19] Consequently, of late they have been trying to overcome their linguistic differences, uniting under one common revolutionary cause, that of the dispossessed and the downtrodden. Even though they have had to forcibly settle for bilingualism, at present they are making inordinate efforts to keep their native tongues alive against all odds.[20]

On the other hand, the creole languages spoken on the Atlantic "rimland"—a region of islands and coasts washed by the Caribbean—in Guatemala,[21] Honduras,[22] Nicaragua, Costa Rica,[23] and Panama are best described as linguistic continuums that stretch from a variety of a West Indian English-based creole to a variety of Standard English that differs from country to country; they are spoken by Afro-Central American minorities of mostly Caribbean origin, as mentioned earlier. For many years they were considered "foreigners" by the Spanish speakers of each country, because they kept the traits typical of sociocultural life in the Western Caribbean.[24] Presently these settlements are characterized by a sort of hybridization of Afro-Antillean and Hispanic-American cultures.

One of these groups, that of the Limonese Creole (LC) speakers, consists of approximately 40,000 Afro-Costaricans,[25] who live mostly on the Atlantic lowlands of Costa Rica, in the Province of Limon, while Costa Rican society and culture have tended to be considered as existing only in the highlands. This dichotomy has been significant throughout the entire history of the country.

At the end of the nineteenth century, since the government of the lowlands was then exercised by U.S. entrepreneurs,[26] the imported West Indian workers' process of acculturation and assimilation to Costa Rican culture and society was slowed. The workers as well as the managers introduced their languages—

Jamaican Creole and American English—as the everyday languages in their community. The Antilleans who had been acculturated to British West Indian culture (mostly in Jamaica) and were "English"-speaking Protestants found it very easy to comply with their managers' pressure to maintain both their language and their religion. Obviously they were encouraged to do so. No national ideas or Costa Rican sentiments were pressed on them; they preferred to maintain their own ethnic identity; their houses remained separate from everyone else's; and they kept in touch with their kin through Jamaican newspapers. They were hoping to go back "home" and prepared their children for that return, but that never happened.

When the United Fruit Co. folded on the Atlantic coast in 1942, the pervading picture of unity among the West Indians in Limon started to give way to a rise of native Costa Rican prestige and power groups. Once outside the plantation system, Afro-Costa Ricans began to adopt Costa Rican customs. At first the process proceeded at a slow pace, but gradually the "West Indian Antillean" was transformed into a new cultural type. The Afro-Limonese became citizens of the country, started sending their children to public schools, and though they spoke Limonese Creole at home,[27] they also learned how to speak Spanish and, in some cases, even became Catholics. Actually, there has been considerable structural change in Costa Rican society since the Revolution of 1948. In fact, the position of Afro-Limonese in that society has gone "from that of 'foreign laborer' on foreign-owned banana plantations to that of 'Costa Rican,' filling positions at the middle and bottom of the wealth, authority and prestige substructures" (Olien 1977:153). At the same time, there developed a pride of involvement in participating in national Costa Rican issues.

How does this briefly sketched socio-cultural process of change affect the linguistic minorities of Guatemala and Costa Rica? The indigenous peoples, who labored as farmers, and the Afro-Central Americans, who made their living as railroad workers, stevedores, and plantation laborers, have taken a long time to enter the middle class.[28] As a result, although in both groups there are a handful of successful professionals today, and a few have been given key managerial positions, for the most part they have of necessity remained working class members.

Interestingly enough, however, socio-historical events have led these groups into very different directions. As mentioned above, the Maya of Guatemala have become an active instrument of change in the educational policy of their country. The government of Guatemala has finally had to recognize the need for a bicultural bilingual education for the Amerindian majority. Instead of launching a literacy campaign to just teach the Maya speakers Spanish, it is now engaged in establishing a curriculum that assures a smooth transition from the children's mother tongue to the language of power.[29] In other words, instead of practicing linguistic genocide, it is providing policies to rescue the linguistic patrimony of the country.

Although Limonese Creole is still alive, its speakers have not fared quite as well. As people acquire a language, they also acquire attitudes and beliefs toward that language and toward other people's languages. As happens with most creole languages, their speakers have fallen prey to the widespread belief that they speak "dialects" but not "real languages." Proof of this, they claim, is that they speak a "broken language," that the Creoles are not written languages and consequently, that "they have no grammar." It is obvious that languages that are transmitted exclusively through the speech of individuals, without the formal frame that education gives to language variants, make their speakers develop certain feelings of their being "second-class languages" (and consequently, of their speakers being "second-class citizens"). In the case of Limonese Creole speakers, these very deeply seated prejudices against their own language are apparent, associated with what they believe is their own self-portrayal: lack of education, primitive ways, poverty, superstitious beliefs, slavery, and a general inadequacy for acquiring a high social status. Loaded with such negative baggage, Creole usage is practically reduced to the familial domain, while Spanish has taken over all others.[30]

Conclusion

Predictions on the life or death of a language are dangerous, and the conditions that bring it about cannot be generalized. The sociohistorical process of transformation that has taken place in Central America in the last 100 years has had a different impact on the various ethnic groups. In view of this, we may ask ourselves, how important is it for members of these minorities to be indigenous and speak their languages, or be Afro-Costaricans and speak Limonese Creole? And does the language express their ethnicity?

The point has been made already that few other elements involve the emotional attachment that oral communication produces in members of an ethnic group; however, the death of a language does not inevitably mean the total disappearance of a group's identity. One of the common circumstances for language death is that of the gradual disappearance of its speakers. The scenario both in Guatemala and Costa Rica is a case of languages in contact and conflict with one superordinate language actively threatening to supplant the others.

The sociolinguistic process outlined above indicates that, as was originally stated, the importance of language in the maintenance and survival of an ethnic minority's identity cannot be overestimated. However, how do we account for the difference between the Maya and the Limonese Creole experiences, since they are both linguistically subordinate to superordinate Spanish? Predictions about the future of the Mayan languages in Guatemala, as risky as they may be, would seem to bode well. They have survived hundreds of years of homogenization efforts and have finally been granted an official chance to endure. As to the Limonese Creole speakers, what is in store for them? It seems that, ultimately, the decisive factor that will determine the survival of a language rests on the embedded degree of pride and positive heritage associated with it. Thus it may very well be that the Limonese Creole speakers' underlying sense of dignity and a feeling of self-worth derived from their ancestral roots—

apparent today in a revival of their folklore—will possibly deter the decline in language usage.

As Fishman has suggested, the question to be asked is "Do they love it in their [the speakers'] hearts?" (quoted by Huffiness 1991:9). I would venture to say that if, in light of their sociohistorical background, the groups value their identity—particularly in the face of present socioeconomic pressures toward the universalization of culture—it is entirely possible that their languages will prevail. If so, and if the language potential of minority populations is granted official recognition, there may eventually ensue a recognition, not only of their human dignity and identity, but also of the worth of multiculturalism.

Addenda

Table 1

Central American Linguistic Distribution

Country	Language	Number of Speakers
Belize		
	Belizean Creole	55,051
	English	55,998
	Garífuna	12,274
	Kekchí	9,000
	Maya Yucateco	5,800
	Mopán Maya	7,750
	Plautdietsch	5,763
	Spanish	80,477
Costa Rica		
	Boruca	1,000
	Bribri	6,000
	Cabécar	3,000
	Chinese	4,500
	Chorotega	extinct
	Guatuso	365
	Plautdietsch	100
	Terraba	°5
	Spanish	3,300,000
	Limonese Creole	55,100
El Salvador		
	Cacaopera	extinct
	Kekchí	12,286
	Lenca	nearly ext.
	Pipil	°°20
	Spanish	5,900,000
Guatemala		
	Achí	°°°55,000
	Aguacateco	16,700
	Cakchiquel	°°°442,500
	Chortí	31,500
	Chuj	°°°41,588
	Garífuna	16,700
	Itzá	12
	Ixil	°°°62,000

Country	**Language**	**Number of Speakers**
	Kanjobal	°°°44,167
	Kekchí	335,800
	Mam	°°°445,800
	Mopán Maya	2,600
	Pokomam	°°°49,012
	Pokomchí	°°°54,100
	Quiché	°°°647,436
	Sacapulteco	36,823
	Simpacapense	6,000
	Spanish	4,673,00
	Tacaneco	20,000
	Tectiteco	2,600
	Tzutujil	°°°81,900
	Uspanteco	2,000
	Xinca	extinct
Honduras		
	Bay Islands English	11,000
	Garífuna	75,000
	Lenca	nearly extinct
	Mískito	10,000
	Pech	°°°300
	Pipil	nearly extinct
	Spanish	5,800,000
	Sumo	500
	Tol	°°°°°300
Nicaragua		
	Garífuna	1,500
	Matagalpa	extinct
	Mískito	154,400
	Monimbo	extinct
	Rama	24
	Spanish	4,347,000
	Subtiaba	extinct
	Sumo	6,700
	Nicaraguan Creole	30,000
Panama		
	Buglere	2,500
	Chinese	6,000
	Catío	40

Country	Language	Number of Speakers
	Emberá	8,000
	Guaymí	128,000
	Kuna	°°°70,700
	Spanish	2,100,000
	Teribe	3,000
	Waumeo	3,000
	Panamenian Creole English	299,600

°Number of speakers out of an ethnic group of 35 to 300.
°°Number of speakers, all older people, out of an ethnic group of 196,576.
°°°Corresponds to the number of speakers of different dialects of the same language.
°°°°Number of speakers out of an ethnic group of 600 to 800.
°°°°°Number of speakers out of an ethnic group of 593.

Source: Grimes, Barbara F., ed. *Ethnologue: Languages of the World.* Hp. 1996. Online. (Dallas, Texas: Summer Institute of Linguistics, Inc.) http:/www.sil.org/ethnologue/ethnologue.html (2/20/97).

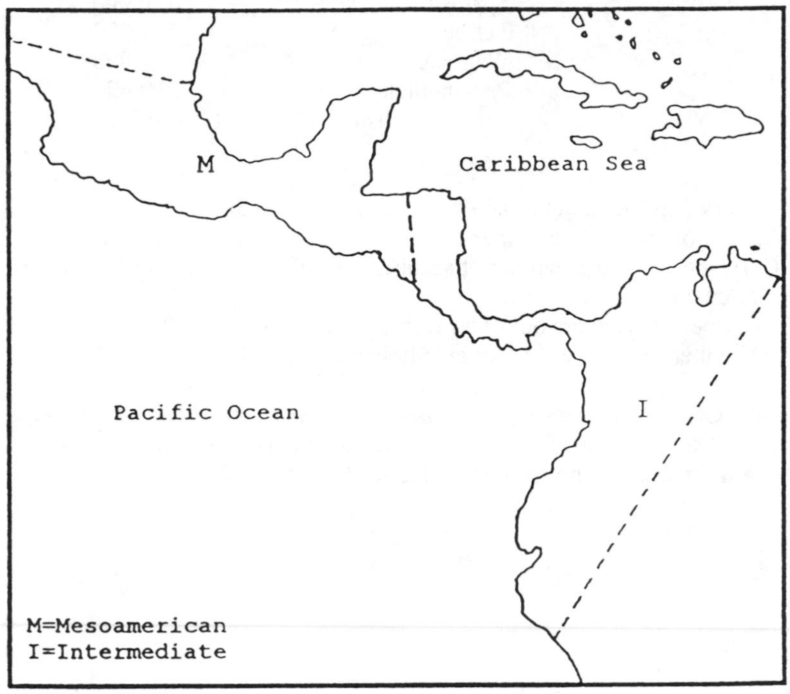

Figure 1

Intermediate and Mesoamerican Cultural and Linguistic Areas

After: Adolfo Constenla Umaña. *Las lenguas del Area Intermedia: Introducción a su estilo areal*, 1991:4.

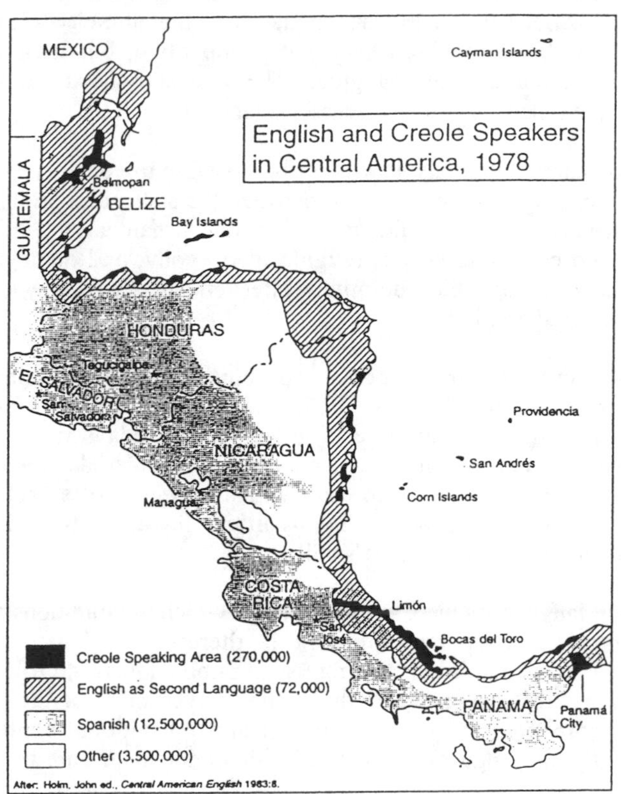

Figure 2

English and Creole Speakers in Central America, 1978

Notes

I greatly appreciate the critical comments by Kathleen Shea, Professor Margarita Bolaños, and Dr. Elizabeth Kuznesof on an earlier version of this paper.

1. That is to say, if we were to consider the case of the Maya in Guatemala for instance, it is not only the Mayan languages or the ethnicity of the people (i.e., objective markers) that will keep the group alive, but their own sense of belonging together as a cultural group. That is exactly what is happening to the Maya people today, as will be discussed later.

2. Due to space limitations, it will not be possible to consider in detail the full range of complex relations that exist between the status of a group's language in Central America and such factors as literacy, urbanization, industrialization, political and economic power, religion, geography, and demography, among many others, all of which definitely intervene in a two-way causal relation between language and identity.

3. Until recently Central America was considered to be composed of the Spanish-speaking countries only; Belize was matched to the Caribbean Islands, with which it shares ethnicity and language. Nowadays it is part of Central America. Additionally, Panama was not always considered a member country of Central America; scholars who dealt with the region often referred to it as "Central America and Panama." In this article, the linguistic situation of Belize will not be included, but Panama's will.

4. National language is the language through which the traditions and the glories of a country's past are transmitted and is, therefore, designated by the federal government as the one acceptable for use in public domains. Official language is the one formally designated by the central government of the country as the language employed in all governmental and educational contexts and it is, consequently, the language in which all official documents are written.

5. Actually this linguistic and archeological "Intermediate Area" also stretches down to the north of South America, including some areas of Colombia, Venezuela, and Ecuador.

6. It is beyond the scope of this article to take up the individual indigenous and Afro-Central American linguistic groups in detail. A thorough treatment of the former is presented in *The Mesoamerican Indian Languages* by Jorge A. Suárez, and *Las lenguas del Area Intermedia: introdución a su estudio areal* by Adolfo Constenla Umaña. The latter are dealt with in *Pidgins and Creoles: An Introduction* by Jacques Arends et al., as well as in *Central American English*, edited by John Holm.

7. Needless to say, "European" and "African" are oversimplistic generalizations that comprise groups of peoples of diverse origins. Also, the process here explained has taken place all over the world and does not apply exclusively to Africans and Europeans.

8. There are several explanations of the origin of creole languages. Basically they fall into two separate views: the monogenetic and the polygenetic theories (Herzfeld 1978:72).

9. The pidgin is a kind of "foreign" language, of limited vocabulary and restricted syntactic alternatives. The children born in the New World to African pidgin-speaking parents, for instance, found the pidgin (however variable) more useful than their parents' native languages (Holm 1988:6–7). Thus, when a pidgin develops into the native language of an entire speech community it becomes a creole. Basically the process of creolization or nativization, which is the opposite of pidginization, entails the expansion rather than reduction of the language, the elaboration of the vocabulary, and a complex reorganization of the grammar.

10. Edwards' more complex definition (1985:10) suggests that:

> Ethnic identity is allegiance to a group—large or small, socially dominant or subordinate—with which one has ancestral links. There is no necessity for a continuation, over generations, of the same socialisation [sic] or cultural patterns, but some sense of a group boundary must persist. This can be sustained by shared objective characteristics (language, religion, etc.), or by more subjective contributions to a sense of "groupness," or by some combination of both. Symbolic or subjective attachments must relate, at however distant a remove, to an observably real past.

Definitions of "ethnicity," of course, abound as do the criteria considered adequate for defining a collectivity as an "ethnic group," and as distinctive from a "racial group." Here, I will adopt the view that an ethnic unit is formed by those individuals who say they belong to ethnic group A rather than B, and are willing to be treated and allow their behavior to be interpreted and judged as A's and not B's.

11. Fishman (1977:16) states that "paternity" is a central experience around which all others can be clustered, and that

> it deals with the recognition of putative biological origins and, therefore with the hereditary or descent-related "blood," "bones," "essence," "mentality," "genius," "sensitivity," "proclivity" derived from the original putative ancestors of a collectivity and passed on from generation to generation in a biokinship sense.

In other words, heritage determines one's ethnicity. From the point of view of a person's experience, this "paternity" is probably seen as the key to that individual's ethnicity, no matter whether it is played down, or even denied to escape it.

12. Johann Gottfried Herder (1744–1803), the author of *Über den Ursprung der Sprache*, argued in favor of the human innately endowed capacity of reason and speech, which ultimately links individuals, through their mother tongue, to the expression of the nationality's soul and spirit.

13. An example of (1) is the case of Catalan in Catalonia, Spain; of (2) is Spanish in Latin America; (3) are all the indigenous languages of Latin America; (4) is the case of the West Indian speakers in Central America; and (5) is the linguistic situation of urban Paraguay, which is certainly unique. There, Spanish (from the descendants of the colonizers) and Guaraní (from the Tupí-Guaraní Indians) seem to coexist side by side, illustrating what Fishman (1972:91–106) calls "a stable bilingual society." This is the case of two groups forming a single society in which there is both bilingualism and diglossia.

14. *Diglossia* is a linguistic phenomenon defined nowadays as the existence of separate languages with socially allocated functions for each one.

15. When two populations begin to occupy the same habitat but do not share a single order, the way in which political and economic conditions are changed will determine whether conflict or a quasi harmonious assimilation will occur (Lieberson 1981:86). Initially at least, the indigenous subordinate group will try to carry on with its established set of institutions, keeping at some spatial distance from the superordinate group. If it does not succeed in its endeavors, conflicts will arise. In Latin America, these led to the decimation of the subordinate groups' sources of sustenance and disrupted linguistic, religious, and tribal forms of organization. Although at a slow rate in some cases, the language and identity of those who survived have been or are being shifted. This is the linguistic process that has taken and is taking place in most Latin American countries of subordinate indigenous populations.

16. These figures were taken from *Mayas y ladinos en cifras: el caso de Guatemala*, by Leopoldo Tzian, 1994.

17. By "rapid," I mean a substantial change in the course of only a few generations.

18. José Arévalo and Jacobo Arbenz were democratically elected when the dictator Jorge Ubico was forced to resign in 1944.

19. It is obvious that Rigoberta Menchú, the Quiché Maya Nobel Peace Prize winner, has certainly become a strong uniting voice among her people as well

as a leader in the Pan-Indian movement that is sweeping through Latin America at present.

20. Both the Universidad Rafael Landívar (sponsored by UNICEF) and the Universidad Mariano Gálvez (with the support of the Summer Institute of Linguistics) are turning out graduates in linguistics who are writing textbooks in at least 10 Mayan languages. At present, they are being used to teach reading and writing to native speakers, youngsters and adults, in the areas of high indigenous density. It is also worthwhile mentioning that the government has financed an *Academia Nacional de las Lenguas Mayas* where scholars meet to discuss problems related to the standardization of the Mayan languages.

21. To my knowledge no in-depth linguistic studies have been conducted in Livingston and Puerto Barrios, so it is not clear whether people there speak a creole or a dialect of English.

22. Only a few studies are available on the linguistic situation of the Caribbean coast of Honduras. At this point, there is not sufficient evidence to claim that the language spoken on the Bay Islands of Honduras is actually a creole. Future research should clarify whether it should be considered a non-standard dialect of English which originated in a creole or whether it is a full-fledged creole in its own right.

23. Limonese Creole is called /mekaytelyuw/ or /mekatelyuw/ by its speakers. It comes from Jamaican Creole in which "Make I tell you [something]" is equivalent to Standard English "Let me tell you [something]" (Herzfeld 1978:116).

24. The ethnic composition of the population of these Central American countries has changed considerably in the last 30 years. While some fifty years ago, approximately 46% of the Atlantic coast population of Costa Rica for example, was of African origin, the latest figures for that region are as follows:

Table 2
Atlantic Region: Population by Ethnic Groups (1984)

Ethnic group	1984
Hispanic–Latins	117,792
Blacks	58,517
Amerindians	6,000
Chinese	5,000
Total	197,316

Source: Carvajal and Driori (1987:43)

25. Although Afro-Antillean immigrants to the Central American continent originated from a variety of islands in the Caribbean, in the case of Costa Rica most of them came from Jamaica.

26. In order to export coffee to Europe, the government of Costa Rica contracted the services of a young American engineer, Minor Keith, to build a railroad between the Atlantic coast and the capital, San José. It was he who hired West Indians to work on the railroad. Later this successful entrepreneur established banana plantations and port facilities, which developed into the all-powerful United Fruit Company's operations in the region. As a result the West Indians turned into plantation laborers and stevedores in Port Limon and never returned to Jamaica.

27. Originally Afro-Antillean plantation and railroad workers spoke mostly Jamaican Creole. With the passage of time, and once these people established themselves for good away from the island, their creole developed into a linguistic code sufficiently different from Jamaican Creole, which I have designated Limonese Creole, called /mekaytelyuw/ (Jamaican Creole "Let me tell you [something]") by its speakers.

28. It is no wonder that the Afro-Caribbeans have failed to successfully adapt to a competitive society. Society has not provided them with the means to achieve satisfaction from an entirely new set of values—i.e., from the mental attitude of ex-slaves for whom work is an imposition and a burden to one in which it means the honest procurement of food, shelter, and clothing. As to the indigenous populations, their own upbringing is also at odds with the mores of the superordinate culture. While communal work and barter, responding to needs rather than profit, are emphasized among them, the macro society in which they now have to operate is highly competitive and based on a profit-making economy.

29. Although not everyone agrees that this bilingual bicultural education is going to support the indigenous cultures and thus consolidate their ethnic identity, many do feel that this educational experience is getting positive results. For instance, at present there is a much more thorough knowledge of the linguistic needs of the country, and there are many more Maya languages being studied. All this is bound to contribute to the establishment of more comprehensive linguistic policies than in the past.

30. Although there are some communal domains where Limonese Creole is still spoken, these are increasingly diminished as older generations die away and the younger ones take over.

References

Appel, R. and P. Muysken. 1987. Language contact and bilingualism. London: Arnold Edward.

Arends, Jacques, Pieter Muysken, and Norval Smith, eds. 1995. Pidgins and creoles: An introduction. Amsterdam: John Benjamins.

Augelli, John P. 1962. The rimland-mainland concept of culture areas in Middle America. Annals of the Association of American Geographers 52. 119–29.

Bickerton, Derek. 1975. Dynamics of a creole system. Cambridge, UK: Cambridge University Press.

Bryce Laporte, Roy S. 1962. Social relations and cultural persistence (or change) among Jamaicans in a rural area of Costa Rica. Unpublished Ph.D. dissertation. Institute of Caribbean Studies, University of Puerto Rico.

Carvajal, Guillermo, and Israel Driori. 1987. La diversidad étnico-cultural en la región atlántica y los problemas de integración socio-espacial al contexto regional costarricense. Revista Geográfica 107. 19–43.

Constenla Umaña, Adolfo. 1991. Las lenguas del área intermedia: Introducción a su estudio areal. San José, Costa Rica: Editorial de la Universidad de Costa Rica.

DeCamp, David. 1961. Social and geographical factors in Jamaican dialects. In Creole Language Studies II, ed. by Robert B. Le Page. New York: St. Martin's Press.

Dirección General de Estadísticas y Censos. 1984. Censo de Población de Costa Rica. San José, Costa Rica: Ministerio de Economía y Hacienda.

Dow, James R., ed. 1991. Language and ethnicity. Amsterdam: John Benjamins.

Edwards, J. 1977. Ethnic identity and bilingual education. Language and Ethnicity and Intergroup Relations, ed. by H. Giles, 253–82. London:

Academic Press.

———. 1985. Language, society and identity. Oxford: Basil Blackwell.

Fallas, Carlos Luis. 1941. Mamita Yunai. San José, Costa Rica: Editorial Soley y Valverde.

Fishman, Joshua A. 1989. Language and ethnicity in minority sociolinguistic perspective. Clevedon, PA: Multilingual Matters Ltd.

———. 1986. The rise and fall of the ethnic revival. Berlin: Mouton de Gruyter.

———. 1977. Language, ethnicity, and racism. Georgetown University round table on languages and linguistics 1977, ed. by Muriel Saville-Troike. Washington DC: Georgetown University Press.

———. 1972. Language in sociocultural change. Essays selected and introduced by Anwar S. Dil. Stanford: Stanford University Press.

Giles, Howard , ed. 1977. Language, ethnicity and intergroup relations. London: Academic Press, Inc.

———. and Bernard Saint Jacques, eds. 1979. Language and ethnic relations. Oxford: Pergamon Press.

———, and Nikolas Coupland, eds. 1991. Language: Contexts and consequences. Buckingham, UK: Open University Press.

Gudykunst, William B., ed. 1988. Language and ethnic identity. Clevedon, PA: Multilingual Matters Ltd.

Gumperz, J. J., ed. 1982. Language and social identity. Cambridge: Cambridge University Press.

Haarmann, Harald. 1986. Language in ethnicity: a view of basic ecological relations. Berlin: Mouton de Gruyter.

Hadley, C. V. D. 1973. Personality patterns, social class, and aggression in the

British West Indies. Consequences of class and color: West Indian perspectives, ed. by David Lowenthal and Lambros Comitas. Garden City, NY: Anchor Press.

Harrison, Regina. 1989. Signs, songs and memories in the Andes. Austin: University of Texas Press.

Herzfeld, Anita. 1978. Tense and aspect in Limon Creole: A sociolinguistic view towards a creole continuum. Unpublished Ph.D. dissertation. Lawrence: The University of Kansas.

———. 1980. Bilingual instability as a result of government induced policies. ITL: Review of Applied Linguistics. 48:1–20.

Holm, John, ed. 1983. Central American English. Heidelberg: Julius Gross Verlag.

———. 1988. Pidgins and creoles, Vols. I & II. Cambridge, UK: Cambridge University Press.

Huffiness, Marion L. 1991. Pennsylvania German: "Do they love it in their hearts?" Language and Ethnicity: Focusschrift in honor of Joshua A. Fishman on the occasion of his 65th birthday; v. 2, ed. by James R. Dow. Amsterdam: John Benjamins. 9–22.

Le Page, Robert B. 1960. An historical introduction to Jamaican Creole. Creole language studies, ed. by R. B. Le Page, 3–124. London: MacMillan.

Lieberson, S. 1981. Language diversity and language contact. Essays selected and introduced by A. S. Dil. Stanford: Stanford University Press.

Meléndez, Carlos. 1974. Introducción a la cultura negra. Curso de capacitación para educadores de la provincia de Limón, Siquirres, Setiembre 23–28, 1974. San José, Costa Rica: Ministerio de Educación Pública.

Olien, Michael D. n.d. The negro in Costa Rica: An historical perspective. Mimeographed copy.

———. 1972. Ethnohistorical research on Colonial Black Populations in Costa

Rica. Paper prepared for the Latin American Panel, American Society for Ethnohistory Annual Meeting. Boston: Boston University.

———. 1977. The adaptation of West Indian Blacks to North American and Hispanic culture in Costa Rica. Old roots in new lands, ed. by Ann M. Pescatello. Westport, CT: Greenwood Press, Inc.

Pacheco, Gilda. 1989. Nicaraguan refugees in Costa Rica: Adjustment to camp life. Washington, DC: Georgetown University, CIPRA.

Peñalosa, Fernando. 1981. Introduction to the sociology of language. Cambridge, MA: Newbury House Publishers.

Rickford, John. 1987. Language Contact, Variation and Diffusion: Microlevel Community Perspectives. In Georgetown University Round Table 1987, ed. by Peter Lowenberg, 25–44.

Roberts, George. 1957. The population of Jamaica. Cambridge: Conservation Foundation at the University Press.

Rona, José P. 1971. The social and cultural status of Guaraní in Paraguay. Sociolinguistics, ed. by William Bright. Berlin: Mouton.

Rossi, Anacristina. 1992. La loca de Gandoca. San José, Costa Rica: EDUCA.

Rubin, Joan. 1985. The special relation of Guaraní and Spanish in Paraguay. In Language of inequality, ed. by Nessa Wolfson and Joan Manes. Berlin: Mouton.

Scherer, Klaus R., and Howard Giles, eds. 1979. Social markers in speech. Cambridge: Cambridge University Press.

Simms Ennis, Giselle. 1990. Un análisis sociolingüístico de las esferas de uso del inglés de Limón en hablantes que residen en San José, Costa Rica, y algunas actitudes de los hablantes y de los descendientes de hablantes del inglés de Limón, que no lo hablan, con respecto a esta lengua. Unpublished Master's Thesis. San José, Costa Rica: Universidad de Costa Rica.

Smith, Anthony Douglas. 1971. Theories of nationalism. London: Duckworth.

Stewart, Watt. 1964. Keith and Costa Rica: A biographical study of Minor Cooper Keith. Albuquerque: The University of New Mexico Press.

Suárez, Jorge A. 1983. The Mesoamerican Indian languages. Cambridge: Cambridge University Press.

Thornton, John. 1992. Africa and Africans in the making of the Atlantic world, 1400–1680. Cambridge: Cambridge University Press.

Tzian, Leopoldo. 1994. Kajlab'aliil Maya'iib' Xuq Mu'siib': Ri Ub'antajiik Iximuleew. Mayas y Ladinos en Cifras: El caso de Guatemala. Guatemala, Guatemala: Cholsamaj.

More Than Wives and Mothers: Women in Latin American History

Sarah C. Chambers

In North America, we often receive contradictory images of women in Latin America. On the one hand, we hear that they are expected to model themselves upon the Virgin Mary and passively suffer a subordinate role in society. Yet in the newspaper, we see grainy black and white photos of female guerrilla fighters in fatigues. Even images of women fulfilling their traditional role as mothers defy simple stereotypes. A poster from the Nicaraguan Revolution featured a woman cradling an infant to her breast with one arm while hoisting a rifle over the other. Other mothers defiantly march across our television screens demanding the return of sons and daughters who disappeared under military regimes.

To some degree, the entrance of large numbers of Latin American women into politics is a recent phenomenon. Nevertheless, the stereotype of the Virgin Mary does not accurately represent the experiences of real women even under a powerful Catholic Church at the height of Spanish colonialism. In order to understand the position of women in Latin America today, therefore, it is necessary to explore their history in its full complexity and diversity. Only then can we see how women have actively and creatively responded to the restrictions placed upon them, at times through individual strategies of accommodation and survival and at others through collective movements for change. Such a tour through the past will reveal that divisions between private and public spheres cannot always be easily drawn, and that the meanings of motherhood vary according to the specific contexts of time and place.

Conquest and Colonization

The numerous figures of female goddesses found by archaeologists throughout the Americas attest to the power, of both life and death, attributed to women in pre-Columbian societies. The Pueblo people of what is today the Southwestern United States, for example, traced the origin of human life to Corn Mothers, and women continued to control that sacred grain and the land upon which it was cultivated.[1] But among societies like the Aztecs, which began to build empires by conquering neighboring societies, the status of women declined. In the Aztec telling of their history, a battle in which the god Huitzilopochtli defeated his sister Malinalxoch symbolized the growing political dominance of men. The primary rcute to wealth and power, service in the military, was closed to women. At birth, baby girls were given spindles and admonished to stay in the home, while boys were presented with shields and arrows and encouraged to become courageous warriors.[2] Compared to their fate after the arrival of Europeans, nevertheless, Aztec women continued to enjoy a relatively high status.

Spanish society similarly glorified masculine prowess in war, and the heroes in their tales of the conquest of America were daring soldiers. Since women were rarely warriors on either side, their role in the conquest has been overlooked. But armies on the move need to eat and be nursed, and it was primarily women who provided such services. In a few cases, such as the famous "Malinche," women took on a more active role. When Hernán Cortés came ashore in 1519, she was among a group of twenty female slaves presented as a gift to the Spanish commander by the chiefs of Tabasco. She became a mistress of Cortés, but in addition served him as a translator and invaluable source of information on native society. Although Cortés barely acknowledges her important role in his self-promotional letters to Spain, native pictographs show her in the prominent role of speaking for the conqueror. "La Malinche" later became a symbol in Mexico of the treacherous female, but like other native allies of the Spaniards, Malinche did not consider the Aztecs "her" people.

Although relatively few Spanish women arrived during the conquest era, several took on active roles in defending early settlements. Doña Isabel de Guevara requested recompense from the Princess Juana of Spain for her assistance in defending Buenos Aires. Due to a famine, she wrote:

> The men became so weak that all the tasks fell on the poor women, washing the clothes as well as nursing the men, preparing them the little food there was, keeping them clean, standing guard, patrolling the fires, loading the crossbows when the Indians came sometimes to do battle, even firing the cannon. . . because at that time, as we women can make do with little nourishment, we had not fallen into such weakness as the men.[3]

Nevertheless, her petition was denied. Spanish women would receive the material rewards of conquest only through their relationship to men.

Colonialism meant the imposition upon the Americas of Iberian norms and laws governing gender. Under the law of *Patria Potestad*, fathers had authority over all the property and people (wife, children, and servants) within the household. Daughters, unlike sons, were legally perpetual minors as they needed first their fathers' and later their husbands' permission to undertake any financial or legal transactions. Women could not hold positions within the royal bureaucracy and were excluded from many professions. Nevertheless, they did enjoy equal inheritance rights and ultimate ownership of dowries they brought into marriage, property rights that were better than those of women in many European countries.[4] Normative expectations and applications of the law varied among women of different classes and races. Wealthy women of primarily European descent enjoyed the greatest privileges, but also faced the greatest pressure to conform to dominant norms. Elite families preserved their honor and status by arranging suitable marriages and carefully controlling women's sexuality to guarantee the purity of the lineage. Other daughters came closest to the model of the Virgin Mary by entering convents.

For a few, nonetheless, the convent provided a space for intellectual pursuits. Sor Juana Inés de la Cruz, a nun in Mexico City during the late seventeenth century, gained renown in her own time for eloquent poems and religious plays. But when she wrote a theological critique of a Jesuit sermon, her bishop rebuked her, citing Saint Paul's admonition to "let women keep silence in the Church." Sor Juana's lengthy response was a subtle yet strong defense of women's rights to both study and teach. Among other arguments, she listed numerous learned women throughout history who had the approval of the church, concluding that "Saint Paul's prohibition was directed solely to the public office of the pulpit, for if the Apostle had forbidden women to write, the Church would not have allowed it."[5] Conceding that only those of learning and prudence should pursue such sacred tasks, she pointed out that such standards should apply to "not only women, who are held to be so inept, but also men, who merely for being men believe they are wise."[6]

Although marriage is often depicted as the only respectable alternative to the convent for women, they played an active role at all levels of the economy. Elite women maintained proper appearances by running estates from their homes and calling upon male relatives to act as their public agents when necessary. Those from the small "middle class" could work as seamstresses or run shops without tarnishing their reputations. Among the poor, as many as one half of the women were employed, usually in domestic service, petty marketing, and sewing trades, work that was rarely "liberating." Finally, female slaves toiling in the fields and homes of their owners suffered from poor health and abusive treatment.[7]

Women were subordinated in colonial law and did not enjoy economic opportunities equal to men's. Yet despite their lack of formal power, some, especially those of indigenous or African descent, were credited with special access to supernatural powers. Women used their knowledge of herbs in both healing and love magic, taking advantage of their control over food preparation to administer aphrodisiacs to the men they desired. Conversely, a woman who suspected her husband of adultery might hire a witch to cast a spell on the mistress to make her unattractive. Women also exchanged advice on how to magically "tame" men in order to make them less abusive and more responsible in fulfilling their marital duties.[8] Today we might attribute to psychology a man's complaint that a woman had made him impotent, but in the colonial period most people believed in the supernatural.

In preindustrial societies such as those of colonial Latin America, the division between private and public life was not as distinct as it would later become. Taverns, the ultimate public establishments and central gathering places for communities, were frequently managed by women who had traditionally produced indigenous brewed alcohol such as *pulque* made from cactus juice and *chicha* made from ground corn. The elite looked down upon female bar owners, but they were respected figures in their neighborhoods who often mediated disputes and helped out those in need. Perhaps most surprising, such taverns served as refuges for women from violence. María Valdivia escaped from the police into a "chichería" in Peru. When the officers were unable to remove her, she challenged their manhood by taunting them "to put on her skirts and give her their pants."[9]

At the highest reaches of society as well, the public and private spheres were intertwined. The power of the monarch, and by extension of colonial officials, was modeled upon the family: the king was depicted as a father figure, who enjoyed patriarchal control over his subjects. While emphasizing the absolute and divine nature of monarchical power, colonial officials also demonstrated a softer paternalism to buttress support for the royal state. During public festivities, they threw coins to the crowds, distributed alms to the poor and pardoned minor delinquents. The poor often came to expect such favors as a right, and riots broke out when high taxes or food shortages indicated that the authorities were not showing sufficient paternal concern for the fate of their subjects. Just as it was the women who tried to make husbands and fathers responsible providers within the home, they also took the lead in public revolts against officials who seemed remiss in their paternalistic duties.

In 1692, for example, when Mexico City was suffering from bad harvests and the poor believed the viceroy was not doing enough to provide corn for sale at an affordable price. One day, as women crowded into the state-run grain market, a jittery guard struck an old woman with his staff. The other women picked up her body, either unconscious or dead, and carried it to the royal palace to request redress. When the viceroy refused to come out and meet with them, they gathered a crowd of men and encouraged them to riot.[10] Nonetheless, such women, who were ready to mobilize politically when they felt the welfare of their families was threatened, can be seen as precursors to those who would protest economic austerity and human rights abuses in more recent times.

From Independence to Suffrage

Women played a central role in localized revolts against particularly abusive officials, but they were appealing to the king for justice rather than calling for his overthrow. By the early 1800s, however, the American-born, White elite increasingly resented their second-class status within the empire and began to declare independence. As in the conquest period, men dominated such military movements, but women once again played important support roles. Because royal officials were less likely to suspect women of political involvement, some worked as spies or smuggled weapons and papers under their large skirts or in the bottom of market baskets. Such women supported independence for the same reasons as men: opposition to colonialism. They were not fighting for their own political rights as women.[11]

It is not surprising, then, that women's positions changed little in the new republics after 1820. Their contributions to independence were recognized, but they were encouraged to return to their normal roles once the crisis had passed. One of the most prominent leaders, Simón Bolívar, advised his sister "not to mix in political business nor adhere to or oppose any party. . . . A woman ought to be neutral in public business. Her family and domestic duties are her first obligations."[12] The new authorities were eager to reestablish order in the wake of the wars of independence and believed the family to be the basis for social stability. Along with slaves and poor men, women were denied the right to vote, as was also true in the United States and Europe at that time. When new legal codes were drafted in each country, they similarly left unchanged the privileges of *Patria Potestad*.

There was, nonetheless, a subtle change in public attitudes toward women. Although they had always been held responsible for the care of children, the role of mother took on a new public importance. Recognizing their influence on the young, government officials encouraged women to raise sons who would become responsible, virtuous, and patriotic citizens. This growing ideology of domesticity had mixed consequences for women. Poor women, who had to work outside the home to support their families, had a hard time living up to the idealized image of the "republican mother." Some were arrested for moral "crimes," which had been considered relatively minor during the colonial period.

The stronger barrier drawn between the public and private spheres may also have restricted some of the independence of elite women, but they enjoyed privileges for serving as model mothers. The chief benefit of this ideological shift was the growing acceptance and even encouragement of female education. In contrast to the bishop who had tried to silence Sor Juana, the leaders of the new republican governments believed that in order to raise good citizens, mothers themselves needed to be educated. As one government official in Mexico put it:

> The educated woman will be truly one for the home: she will be the companion and collaborator of man in the formation of the family. You are called upon the form souls, to sustain the soul of your husband; for this reason, we educate you . . . to constitute the perpetual creation of the nation.[13]

The goal of nineteenth-century governments was to educate middle and upper-class women to be better wives and mothers rather than intellectuals and professionals, but the long-term effects would go beyond their intentions. Most educated women accepted the ideology of republican motherhood, but used it to advocate further change. The editor of a woman's magazine in Brazil in 1890 described women in typically idealized terms as symbols of tenderness, fidelity, and pure devotion, but went on to argue that "these qualities the Supreme Creator bestowed upon them prove their superiority, not their inferiority, and show that equality of action should be put into practice by those men who proclaim the principle of equality."[14] On the basis of such special qualities, women began to extend their mothering role into the public sphere as teachers, nurses, social workers, and in a few cases even doctors. As Brazilian activist Bertha Lutz put it, "Women's domain, all feminists agree, is the home. But nowadays the home is no longer just the space encompassed within four walls."[15]

By the early twentieth century, moreover, such female professionals began to assert that they deserved greater rights in accord with their important social role. Although women in the colonial and independence periods had occasionally participated in political movements, these early feminists were the first to organize collectively in order to promote their rights as women.[16] One of their chief complaints was that civil codes still defined women as the minors of their husbands. That women did not even have legal custody rights over their children was a particularly glaring contradiction to the growing idealization of mothers. Professional and working women also wanted the right to pursue employment without having to request their husbands' permission. Such demands fit the growing respect for women's roles, and in most countries feminists successfully lobbied for changes in the legal codes.

Suffrage, however, was more controversial. To justify their entrance into the public sphere, feminists were careful to stress the moralizing influence they could have on politics. Although they did not serve in the armed forces, a common constitutional requirement of citizens, feminist Paulina Luisi of Uruguay asserted "that women provide another service more than equivalent to that of the military, sometimes at the cost of their lives and always after long months of painful waiting and brutal suffering; women bring into the world those same young lives who will one day serve their country in the army."[17] Beginning in Ecuador in 1929 and ending with Paraguay in 1961, women did win the right to vote. Often the passage of suffrage hinged upon the support of a president, such as Juan Perón of Argentina, who along with his famous wife Eva, hoped to advance his career by gaining the support of women.

The emphasis on motherhood and morality convinced some politicians that granting rights to women would not threaten male dominance directly, but such symbols also restricted the agenda of the first generation of feminists. Aside from custody rights for mothers, they called for few changes within the private sphere of the family. Even activists considered issues such as divorce, birth control, abortion, and sex education far too controversial to address. When Ofelia Domínguez Navarro repeatedly introduced resolutions at Cuban feminist congresses in the 1920s advocating equal rights for unwed mothers and their illegitimate children, for example, the majority of the women delegates accused her of trying to destroy the family.[18]

Women, Work, and Revolution

The legal and political victories achieved by these early feminist movements benefitted primarily women of the middle and upper classes; poor women had more immediate survival needs. In 1937, while feminists were fighting for suffrage, Domitila Barrios de Chungara was born in a poor community in the high Andes of Bolivia. She married a mineworker and struggled to raise her family in the cramped housing provided by the company on her husband's low wages. Rather than pursue what seemed like abstract legal rights for women, Barrios joined the Housewives Committee, a group established by women in 1961 to support efforts to improve the wages and benefits of their husbands and to advocate the release of jailed union activists.

When the miners initially resisted their wives' entry into political action, the women pointed out they too were laborers. "Because, with such a small wage, the woman has to do much more in the home," explained Barrios. "And really that's unpaid work that we're doing for the boss, isn't it?"[19] As women, they also linked workplace and community issues, calling for better housing, schools, healthcare, and support for widows, who were evicted within ninety days of their husbands' often early deaths. Although initially not taken seriously by the government, as they escalated their activism the women became targets of repression. Barrios was arrested and tortured several times, and even lost a baby born in jail. The Housewives Committee, linked historically to the corn rioters of the colonial period, was also a preview of the grassroots women's organizations that would multiply during the following decades.

By the 1960s, most Latin American economies underwent severe crises. The spread of mechanized commercial agribusiness pushed millions of small peasants off the land and into crowded urban shantytowns. The lack of industrial jobs led many to work in the precarious "informal" sector as street vendors or day laborers. Those factories that were established were increasingly controlled by transnational corporations seeking cheap nonunionized labor. Growing male unemployment pushed more and more women into these low-paid sectors as domestic servants, small scale marketers and assembly-line workers.[20]

The consequences have been mixed. Some women report pride in being able to contribute to family income, a growing sense of confidence and independence from working outside the home and, in some cases, even the ability to convince their husbands to take on more of the household duties. Nevertheless, at work they often face sexual harassment in addition to long hours at low pay and unhealthy working conditions. Some female workers have begun to form unions, but their double day of wage labor and housework limits the time they can commit to meetings.

Given the extreme poverty throughout the region, it is not surprising that many men and women alike have supported revolutionary movements. After the 1959 Revolution in Cuba, poor women gained significant benefits from the expansion of public education, free healthcare, and other social programs. The government believed that socialism alone would lead to women's liberation, but it proved difficult to incorporate women into the workforce because they were still doing almost all the housework. Programs to aid working women, such as factory cafeterias, childcare, and family-leave days, ameliorated some of the problem, but the state did not have enough resources to provide adequate services. In 1975, therefore, a new Family Code in Cuba took the unusual step of legally requiring husbands and wives to share housework and childrearing. It was an important public acknowledgment that equality should exist within the home, but it has been difficult to enforce in practice.[21]

By 1979, when the Sandinista revolution came to power in Nicaragua, women had become increasingly active in politics throughout Latin America. They made up one-third of the armed guerrillas in Nicaragua, and had established an organization to represent the specific interests of women. The new government, therefore, recognized that the problem of women's subordination had to be addressed directly rather than assuming it would disappear under socialism. For example, the Sandinistas immediately banned the exploitation of women's bodies in advertisements. In 1985, the women's organization opened a legal aid office for women, which in the first year alone helped 10,000 women, many of whom filed complaints of domestic violence. Nevertheless, as Nicaragua faced intensifying opposition from counter revolutionaries funded by the United States, the government increasingly channeled funds into military defense and put women's programs on the back burner. In the wake of the electoral defeat of the Sandinistas in 1990, many women who supported the revolution have reflected that it did not do enough to advance women's issues. Ironically, Nicaragua's first female president, Violeta de Chamorro, introduced even more conservative policies for women.[22]

Women's Opposition to Military Regimes

Cuba and Nicaragua were exceptional: from the 1960s through the 1980s the military took power throughout most of Latin America to prevent further revolutions. The ruling generals believed the traditional family was the basis of political stability and asserted that a woman's place was in the home. The majority of women, however, found themselves caught in the contradictory position between the rhetoric and practices of the dictatorships. They were told to be good housewives, but social services that improved family welfare were drastically cut. The military promoted the ideal of the nurturing mother, dominant since the previous century, yet tens of thousands of young people were detained, tortured, and killed for their opposition to military rule. Female activists were physically and sexually abused for both their political beliefs and their rejection of traditional gender roles. Babies who survived birth in prison were taken from their mothers and put up for adoption.[23]

Military regimes shut down congresses, banned political parties, and outlawed labor unions, the traditional arenas in which men had participated in the public sphere. Confident that such actions would eliminate the opposition, the dictatorships were taken by surprise when resistance began to emerge from the customary spaces into which they had pushed women: the church, the kitchen, and the nursery.[24] Unable to perform their traditional roles because of repressive policies, women brought supposedly private issues into the public sphere.

Women had always been particularly active in the Church, but traditionally religious authorities had been strong allies of the various governments in power. Beginning in the 1960s, however, many priests and even some bishops began to advocate reforms on behalf of the poor, and women often made up the majority of the new "Christian Base Communities." Liberation theology called for greater involvement of lay people in interpreting how the Bible related to their own experiences. Activist priests also encouraged parishioners to translate those ideas into social action in order to build the Kingdom of God on Earth, rather than passively waiting for an improvement in the afterlife. Empowering lay people opened positions of importance to women, who were excluded from the priesthood. Azuleiko Sampaio, for example, had led a typical life for a poor Brazilian woman: working from a young age as a domestic servant, marrying at sixteen, and continuing to work in a factory. But when she joined a Christian Base Community in 1974 she quickly rose to a leadership position. The confidence she gained encouraged her to extend her activism beyond the church into community organizations and by 1983 she had been elected president of a city-wide federation of neighborhood associations.[25]

Such local grassroots movements were the second arena in which women, by extending their household duties into the public sphere, played a major role. Their influence, moreover, grew as political parties and unions were banned. Estela, a woman from a squatter neighborhood in Lima, explained that since men went off to find work it was often the women who were most active in claiming a piece of land and building houses as best they could from cheap materials. When the police tried to evict them, she continued, "we cling on by our teeth or whatever else to the very stones themselves. Just try getting me out! Why? Because we think of the children."[26] Women who had cooperated in building their neighborhoods also made collective efforts to maintain their households, establishing communal soup kitchens to stretch tight budgets and share the labor of cooking. In addition to such self-help activities, they protested that the authoritarian governments should live up to the family values they espoused by providing adequate drinking water, electricity, healthcare services, and price controls on basic foods. In their effort to be good housewives, they transformed a private and individual role into a public and collective one.

Finally, as mothers, Latin American women have been crucial in exposing human rights abuses and helping to bring down military regimes. Women at first humbly went to jails and government offices simply to find out what happened to sons and daughters who had been picked up by the police and military. But they were met with shocking denials that such arrests had ever occurred. Your children, they were told, have simply disappeared. Not knowing what happened was even more painful than the news they had expected. "I think that their absence has left me pregnant forever," reflected Hebe de Bonafini of Argentina.[27] In their rounds in search of information, women began to notice they were not alone. In 1977, a few decided to meet every Thursday afternoon in the central Plaza de Mayo of Buenos Aires. Initially, they just sat on the benches and talked, but when the police ordered them to stop "loitering," in an attempt to disperse them, they instead began to walk around the plaza in a silent vigil for their lost family members. The "Madres" soon numbered in the hundreds and were the first group in Argentina to openly denounce the secret war of torture and executions.

The Madres of the Plaza de Mayo gained the most international attention, but similar groups formed throughout Latin America. They used powerful symbols to denounce the abuses committed against their children. Some wore white scarves, even the cloth diapers they had once used for their babies, embroidered with the names of missing sons and daughters. They carried placards with pictures to assert the existence of their loved ones. In Chile, when the police turned water cannons on women protesting the human rights abuses, they spontaneously held up their hands and cried "Our hands are clean!" The message of whose hands were bloody was clear. The sight of mothers protesting the disappearance of their children was a strong indictment of military regimes, which hypocritically claimed to be supporting family values. By bringing both national and international attention to human rights abuses, women played a key role in pressuring dictatorships to step down from power.

Undeniably, the moral authority of women as suffering mothers was the primary strength of such movements. There is debate, however, on the long-term consequences of such a strategy. Have these women transformed the meaning of motherhood from a passive and private role to one of militant activism in the public sphere? Or ultimately have they reinforced the idea that women are by nature nurturing and that motherhood is the only proper role for women in Latin America? Once the crisis has passed, will mothers be expected to give up their political activities and return to the home?

It is too early to definitively answer such questions, but there are signs that at least some women who initially organized in an effort to better fulfill their traditional roles as wives and mothers have changed as a result of their political activism. Women often found it personally liberating to get out of their homes and attend meetings, and as they learned to petition the government and organize marches their self-confidence grew. When husbands objected to their activism or male leaders of grassroots organizations did not take their demands seriously, many began to defend their rights as women. Some women in church groups came into conflict with the priests when they began to advocate their right to birth control. Mothers of the disappeared in El Salvador highlighted the connection between the sexual abuse of political prisoners and the broader social problem of rape.[28] In other countries as well, women asserted that authoritarian regimes were rooted in broader patriarchal structures, and they extended their demands to call for both "democracy in the country and in the home."

Conclusion

Women's movements today in Latin America are strong and diverse, as shown by the growing attendance at region-wide feminist meetings.[29] Certainly women do not agree on all issues. At the United Nations Women's Conference in Mexico City in 1975, Domitila Barrios de Chungara, the Bolivian miner's wife, criticized middle-class feminists for not recognizing that economic survival and political repression were the key problems and required women to work alongside men of the same class. Twenty years later, poor women continue to assert that legal equality between women and men will have little impact if problems of economic and social justice are not addressed.[30] Similarly, women of color have complained of discrimination within the feminist movement. Nevertheless, it would be an oversimplification to say that working-class and peasant women reject the notion of women's rights. "We are all feminists," they shouted at a meeting of Latin American women in 1987.[31]

The activism of women in the public sphere is not a new phenomenon in Latin America. Since the colonial period they have worked outside the home and played an active role in revolts. Few openly challenged patriarchal domination, however, working instead through informal and even magical channels to ameliorate its worst abuses. The first generation of feminists early in this century did call for greater equality between men and women, but did not necessarily advocate changing other social hierarchies. Today women are increasingly drawing connections between basic human rights to political freedom and a decent standard of living and their specific rights as women, and they are demanding that the two challenges be tackled simultaneously.

Notes

1. Ramón A. Gutiérrez, *When Jesus Came, the Corn Mothers Went Away* (Stanford: Stanford University Press, 1991), 1–36. 2. June Nash, "The Aztecs and the Ideology of Male Dominance," *Signs* 4, no. 2 (1978): 349–62. For a comparison to the Incas, see Irene Silverblatt, *Moon, Sun and Witches* (Princeton: Princeton University Press, 1987).

3. James Lockhart and Enrique Otte, eds., *Letters and People of the Spanish Indies* (Cambridge: Cambridge University Press, 1976), 15.

4. For an overview, see Asunción Lavrin, "Women in Spanish American Colonial Society," *Cambridge History of Latin America*, (Cambridge, UK: Cambridge University Press, 1984), 2, 321–56.

5. Margaret Sayers Peden, ed. and trans., *A Woman of Genius: The Intellectual Autobiography of Sor Juana Inés de la Cruz*, 2nd ed. (Salisbury, Conn.: Lime Rock Press, 1987), 82.

6. Ibid., 68.

7. On women's roles in the economy, see Silvia Marina Arrom, *The Women of Mexico City, 1790–1857* (Stanford: Stanford University Press, 1985), and Mary Karasch, "Anastácia and the Slave Women of Rio de Janeiro," in *Africans in Bondage: Studies in Slavery and the Slave Trade*, ed. Paul Lovejoy (Madison: University of Wisconsin Press, 1986), 79–105.

8. See Ruth Behar, "Sexual Witchcraft, Colonialism, and Women's Powers," in *Sexuality and Marriage in Colonial Latin America*, ed. Asunción Lavrin (Lincoln: University of Nebraska Press, 1989), 178–206.

9. Archivo Regional de Arequipa, Corte Superior: Causas Criminales (Case dated May 28, 1806), "Doña María Valdivia contra el Alcalde de Socabaya por atropellamientos."

10. For an elite, eye-witness account of the riot, see Carlos Sigüenza y Góngora, "Letter to Admiral Pez" (1692), reprinted in *Don Carlos de Sigüenza y Góngora: A Mexican Savant of the Seventeenth Century*, ed. Irving Leonard (Berkeley: University of California Press, 1929), 211–77.

11. See Evelyn Cherpak, "The Participation of Women in the Independence Movement in Gran Colombia, 1780–1830," in *Latin American Women: Historical Perspectives*, ed. Asunción Lavrin (Westport, Conn.: Greenwood Press, 1978), 219–34, and Arrom, *The Women of Mexico City*, 32–46.

12. Quoted in Francesca Miller, *Latin American Women and the Search for Social Justice* (Hanover, NH: University Press of New England, 1991), 14.

13. Quoted in Mary Kay Vaughn, *The State, Education, and Social Crisis in Mexico, 1880–1928* (DeKalb: Northern Illinois University Press, 1978), 204.

14. Quoted in June E. Hahner, *Emancipating the Female Sex: The Struggle for Women's Rights in Brazil, 1850–1940* (Durham, NC: Duke University Press, 1990), 214.

15. Quoted in Hahner, 149.

16. On the early feminist movements, see Hahner, *Emancipating the Female Sex*, K. Lynn Stoner, *From the House to the Streets: The Cuban Women's Movement for Legal Reform, 1898–1940* (Durham: Duke University Press, 1991), and Asunción Lavrin, *Women, Feminism, and Social Change in Argentina, Chile, and Uruguay, 1890–1940* (Lincoln and London: University of Nebraska Press, 1995).

17. Quoted in Sara Castro-Klarén, ed., *Women's Writing in Latin America* (Boulder: Westview Press, 1991), 251.

18. K. Lynn Stoner, "Ofelia Domínguez Navarro: The Making of a Cuban Socialist Feminist," in *The Human Tradition in Latin America* (Wilmington, Del.: Scholarly Resources Press, 1987), 2:119-40.

19. Domitila Barrios de Chungara, *Let Me Speak!* (New York: Monthly Review Press, 1978), 34.

20. See, for example, María Patricia Fernández-Kelly, *For We Are Sold, I and My People: Women and Industry in Mxico's Frontier* (Albany, NY: SUNY Press, 1983), and Ximena Bunster and Elsa M. Chaney, *Sellers and Servants: Working Women in Lima, Peru* (Granby, Mass.: Bergin and Garvey, 1989). For testimonies by working-class and poor women, see Carolina María de Jesús, *Child of the Dark* (New York: Dutton, 1962), Daphne Patai, ed., *Brazilian Women Speak* (New Brunswick, NJ: Rutgers University Press, 1988), and Rigoberta Menchú, *I Rigoberta Menchú* (London: Verso, 1984).

21. See Lois Smith, *Sex and Revolution: Women in Socialist Cuba* (New York: Oxford University Press, 1996).

22. For the Nicaraguan case, see Maxine Molyneux, "Mobilization without Emancipation? Women's Interests, the State, and Revolution in Nicaragua," *Feminist Studies* 11, no. 2 (1985): 227–54, Helen Collinson, ed., *Women and Revolution in Nicaragua* (London: Zed Books, 1990), Margaret Randall, *Sandino's Daughters* (Vancouver: New Star Books, 1981), and Randall,

Sandino's Daughters Revisited (New Brunswick, NJ: Rutgers University Press, 1994).

23. For a moving testimony written by a female political prisoner, see Alicia Partnoy, *The Little School: Tales of Disappearance and Survival in Argentina* (Pittsburgh: Cleis Press, 1986).

24. María del Carmen Feijoó identifies these as equivalents of the German "Kinder, Küche und Kirche" (children, kitchen and church) in "Women and Democracy in Argentina," *in The Women's Movement in Latin America: Participation and Democracy*, ed. Jane S. Jaquette (Boulder: Westview Press, 1994), 111. See also Sonia E. Alvarez, *Engendering Democracy in Brazil* (Princeton: Princeton University Press, 1990).

25. For Sampaio's story, see Daniel H. Levine, *Religion and Popular Protest in Latin America* (Notre Dame: Helen Kellogg Institute for International Studies, 1986), 219–20. See also Sonia E. Alvarez, "Women's Participation in the Brazilian 'People's Church,'" *Feminist Studies* 16, no. 2 (1990): 381–408.

26. Quoted in Cecilia Blondet, "Establishing an Identity: Women Settlers in a Poor Lima Neighborhood," in *Women and Social Change in Latin America*, ed. Elizabeth Jelin (London: Zed Books, 1990), 29.

27. Reprinted from her *Historias de vida in Women's Writing in Latin America*, 281. See also Jo Fisher, *Mothers of the Disappeared* (Boston: South End Press, 1989).

28. Jennifer Schirmer, "The Seeking of Truth and the Gendering of Consciousness: The CoMadres of El Salvador and the CONAVIGUA Widows of Guatemala," in *'Viva': Women and Popular Protest in Latin America*, ed. Sarah A. Radcliffe and Sallie Westwood (London: Routledge, 1993), 62.

29. See the interviews in Gaby Kuppers, ed., *Compañeras: Voices from the Latin American Women's Movement* (London: Latin American Bureau, 1994).

30. See, for example, Elvia Alvarado, *Don't Be Afraid Gringo: A Honduran Woman Speaks from the Heart*, ed. and trans. Medea Benjamin (New York: Harper and Row, 1987).

31. Nancy Saporta Sternbach et al., "Feminisms in Latin America: From Bogotá to San Bernardo," in *The Making of Social Movements in Latin America*, eds. Arturo Escobar and Sonia E. Alvarez (Boulder: Westview Press, 1992), 226.

Works Consulted

Alvarado, Elvia. *Don't Be Afraid Gringo: A Honduran Woman Speaks from the Heart*. Ed. and trans. Medea Benjamin. New York: Harper and Row, 1987.

Alvarez, Sonia E. *Engendering Democracy in Brazil*. Princeton: Princeton University Press, 1990.

———. "Women's Participation in the Brazilian 'People's Church.'" *Feminist Studies* 16, no. 2 (1990): 381–408.

Arrom, Silvia Marina. *The Women of Mexico City, 1790–1857*. Stanford: Stanford University Press, 1985.

Barrios de Chungara, Domitila. *Let Me Speak!* New York: Monthly Review Press, 1978.

Bunster, Ximena and Elsa M. Chaney. *Sellers and Servants: Working Women in Lima, Peru*. Granby, Mass.: Bergin and Garvey, 1989.

Castro-Klarén, Sara, ed. *Women's Writing in Latin America*. Boulder: Westview Press, 1991.

Collinson, Helen, ed. *Women and Revolution in Nicaragua*. London: Zed Books, 1990.

Fernández-Kelly, María Patricia. *For We Are Sold, I and My People: Women and Industry in Mexico's Frontier*. Albany, NY: SUNY Press, 1983.

Fisher, Jo. *Mothers of the Disappeared*. Boston: South End Press, 1989.

Gutiérrez, Ramón A. *When Jesus Came, the Corn Mothers Went Away*. Stanford: Stanford University Press, 1991.

Hahner, June E. *Emancipating the Female Sex: The Struggle for Women's Rights in Brazil, 1850–1940*. Durham, NC: Duke University Press, 1990.

Jaquette, Jane S., ed. *The Women's Movement in Latin America: Participation and Democracy*. Boulder: Westview Press, 1994.

Jelin, Elizabeth, ed. *Women and Social Change in Latin America*. London: Zed Books, 1990.

Jesús, Carolina María de. *Child of the Dark*. New York: Dutton, 1962.

Karasch, Mary. "Anastácia and the Slave Women of Rio de Janeiro." In *Africans in Bondage: Studies in Slavery and the Slave Trade*, ed. Paul Lovejoy, 178–206. Madison: University of Wisconsin Press, 1986.

Kuppers, Gaby, ed. *Compañeras: Voices from the Latin American Women's Movement*. London: Latin American Bureau, 1994.

Lavrin, Asunción, ed. *Latin American Women: Historical Perspectives*. Westport, CT: Greenwood Press, 1978.

———. ed. *Sexuality and Marriage in Colonial Latin America*. Lincoln: University of Nebraska Press, 1989.

———. *Women, Feminism, and Social Change in Argentina, Chile, and Uruguay, 1890–1940*. Lincoln and London: University of Nebraska Press, 1995.

———. "Women in Spanish American Colonial Society." *Cambridge History of Latin America*. Vol. 2, 321–56. Cambridge, UK: Cambridge University Press, 1984.

Levine, Daniel H. *Religion and Popular Protest in Latin America*. Notre Dame: Helen Kellogg Institute for International Studies, 1986.

Lockhart, James, and Enrique Otte, eds. *Letters and People of the Spanish Indies*. Cambridge, UK: Cambridge University Press, 1976.

Menchú, Rigoberta. *I Rigoberta Menchú*. London: Verso, 1984.

Miller, Francesca. *Latin American Women and the Search for Social Justice*. Hanover, NH: University Press of New England, 1991.

Molyneux, Maxine. "Mobilization without Emancipation? Women's Interests, the State, and Revolution in Nicaragua." *Feminist Studies* 11, no. 2 (1985): 227–54.

Nash, June. "The Aztecs and the Ideology of Male Dominance" *Signs* 4, no. 2 (1978): 349–62.

Patai, Daphne, ed. *Brazilian Women Speak*. New Brunswick, NJ: Rutgers University Press, 1988.

Partnoy, Alicia. *The Little School: Tales of Disappearance and Survival in Argentina*. Pittsburgh: Cleis Press, 1986.

Peden, Margaret Sayers, ed. and trans. *A Woman of Genius: The Intellectual Autobiography of Sor Juana Inés de la Cruz*. 2nd ed. Salisbury, Conn.: Lime Rock Press, 1987.

Radcliffe, Sarah A., and Sallie Westwood, eds. 'Viva'*: Women and Popular Protest in Latin America.* London: Routledge, 1993.

Randall, Margaret. *Sandino's Daughters*. Vancouver: New Star Books, 1981.

———. *Sandino's Daughters Revisited.* New Brunswick, NJ: Rutgers University Press, 1994.

Saporta Sternbach, Nancy, et al. "Feminisms in Latin America: From Bogotá to San Bernardo." In *The Making of Social Movements in Latin America*, eds. Arturo Escobar and Sonia E. Alvarez. Boulder: Westview Press, 1992.

Silverblatt, Irene. *Moon, Sun and Witches*. Princeton: Princeton University Press, 1987.

Smith, Lois. *Sex and Revolution: Women in Socialist Cuba.* New York: Oxford University Press, 1996.

Stoner, K. Lynn. *From the House to the Streets: The Cuban Women's Movement for Legal Reform, 1898–1940*. Durham: Duke University Press, 1991.

———. "Ofelia Domínguez Navarro: The Making of a Cuban Socialist Feminist." In *The Human Tradition in Latin America*. Vol. 2, 119–40. Wilmington, Del.: Scholarly Resources Press, 1987.

Vaughn, Mary Kay. *The State, Education, and Social Crisis in Mexico, 1880–1928*. DeKalb: Northern Illinois University Press, 1978.

Malinche, Guadalupe, and La Llorona: Patriarchy and the Formation of Mexican National Consciousness

C. Alejandra Elenes

The forging of Mexican and Chicano national consciousness has been constructed through three female figures: Malinztin/Malinche, The Virgin of Guadalupe, and La Llorona (The Weeping Woman). The symbolism of each of these figures is quite different because each of them represents patriarchal constructions of Mexican and Chicana womanhood, and may even oppose one another. Needless to say, these patriarchal constructions have been contested by Chicana and Mexican feminists (e.g., Del Castillo, 1977; Alegría, 1975; Alarcón, 1981, 1989; Candelaria, 1980; Moraga, 1983; Anzaldúa, 1987). Tracing the construction of *Guadalupe, Malinche,* and *Llorona* in historical sources (primary and secondary) helps us understand the development of Mexican nationalist consciousness. Cultural practices are social constructions that change over time. History is one of these practices. As such the interpretations of events and documents change over time. In this chapter I am deconstructing "official" interpretations of these three mythical figures, based on how they have been constructed in historical texts. Through this deconstruction I am uncovering their function in the development of Mexican nationalist consciousness and its relationship with patriarchal constructions of womanhood. The purpose of this deconstruction is to demonstrate that historical texts have multiple meanings. Thus, each text can be used as a source for different interpretations, regardless of the standpoint of the interpreter. In other words, nationalists, feminists, and religious people, for example, can all examine the same historical source and come up with different interpretations. Moreover, this analysis also demonstrates that historical texts (like all texts) are not innocent or impartial. The deconstruction of historical sources is important as well to understand that these definitions of women are not inherent in the texts, but in the multiple interpretations of these texts by different scholars. The sources examined for this process of deconstruction include the chronicles of the Spanish conquest of Mexico, oral histories, and contemporary analytical historical texts.

The "origin" of these three figures can be traced to the sixteenth century. However, we can find traces of their development in the indigenous cultures of Mexico that predate the Spanish conquest. Of the three, only Malintzin/Marina/Malinche is a "real" historical figure.[1] That is, she was a "real" in-the-flesh woman who lived and participated in the Conquest of Mexico and, thus, had to made decisions accordingly. The Virgin of Guadalupe and Llorona are metaphysical beings. The legend of La Llorona is about a woman whose actual existence cannot be substantiated. What is relevant about her story are the events that led to her death and the death of her children. Her significance as a legend is her status as a ghost, not as a living human being.

And, of course, the Virgin is not human, she is a deity whether one believes she is Tonántzin (a goddess) or the Christian mother of God. Or for the skeptical, she is a painting.

Historical Narratives and Deconstruction

Historical narratives are not innocent neutral activities. Like literary texts, historical texts are not transparent, rather they are dynamic and always in flux. Thus for Scott the study of concepts (historical and cultural) "calls attention to the conflictual processes that establish meanings, to the ways in which such concepts as gender acquire the appearance of fixity, to the challenges posed for normative social definitions, and to the ways these challenges are met—in other words, to the play of force involved in any society's construction and implementation of meanings: to politics" (Scott, 1988, p. 5). Meanings are political, and historical narratives document the conflicts and contradictions in individual societies. Which events get recorded and how (the power relations involved in such documentation) vary over time, and so do their interpretations. The historical records on the formation of the myths of *Guadalupe, Malinche,* and *Llorona* are in and of themselves part of the construction of these myths and the forging of Mexican nationalism. For it was precisely in their function toward the construction of nationhood that these figures were historically documented and interpreted. In the case of the Virgin of Guadalupe, the historical documentation is related to her function in the formation of national consciousness. For example, Sahagún documents a cult to an image, while Sánchez consolidates the cult to the Virgin of Guadalupe, thus demonstrating the different beliefs of the two writers. Sánchez consolidates the cult to Guadalupe from a Creole standpoint. Therefore, it is interesting to analyze not only the events recorded in historical narratives, but the ways in which these narratives reproduce political positions not only through what they say, but also through what they do not say. Once these positions are consolidated they become invisible under the rubric of cultural traditions, myths, and the like. Deconstruction offers an exegetical strategy to uncover these processes. Joan Scott argues that deconstruction adds an important new dimension to the historical exegetical project. Scott proposes that historians can use similar methodologies as literary critics since historical texts, like all texts, are open to multiple interpretations.

For Derrida (1981) deconstruction is a strategy of displacement that seeks to reverse the hierarchies of binary oppositional terms such as good/evil, man/woman, positive/negative. Where the superior term, the one always in front, belongs to the logos and is a higher presence, the inferior term marks a fall (Culler, 1982). According to Derrida (1977), since Plato, Western metaphysicians have worked through these dualities. Culler's understanding of deconstruction is that it requires an investigation of how various discourses (i.e., historical, literary, philosophical) have constituted binary oppositions by characterizing the inferior term by its absence. Thus, in deconstruction, "the analyst seeks to locate points at which these discourses undo themselves, revealing the interested, ideological nature of their hierarchical imposition and subverting the basis of the hierarchy they wish to establish" (Culler, 1982, p. 166).

Deconstruction cannot be called a "method"; rather it is a philosophy that deconstructs methodology (Gasché, 1986). Derrida believes that method is reductive; however, this does not mean that deconstruction is not rigorous. As Gasché explains, deconstruction is not a non-method that invites to "uncontrollable free play" (p. 123). The recognition and understanding of deconstruction as a rigorous and systematic analysis makes it possible to study the conflictual process that produces meaning (Scott, 1988). In this essay deconstruction serves to reverse and displace the binary oppositions in the construction of *Malinche, Guadalupe,* and *Llorona*. By analyzing how various historical narratives have constituted the figures, I am revealing the interests and ideological nature of the construction of the myths.

Myth, Nationalism, Sexuality, and Class

During Spanish colonial times we find the roots of the construction of Mexican nationalist consciousness. In order to construct and eventually develop a sense of nation (even before the idea of independence from Spain to form the nation-state Mexico) it was necessary to understand what "Mexican" meant in cultural and political terms. Creoles initiated this identification process. Creoles, in order to construct their own cultural and political world, were obligated to differentiate themselves from the Spanish and their contemporary indigenous and mestizo counterparts. For Creoles were not Spanish, indigenous, or mestizo, but found their identity in a past that could be projected into the future. Using the religious discourse they had available, which was part of their own way of thinking and making sense of the world, Creoles constructed a glorious indigenous past. Identifying with an indigenous past is not necessarily negative or positive. What is significant and problematic of Creoles' construction of and identification with a glorious indigenous past is that it is idealized and that the identification is always with the lost, past indigenous cultures, not with their contemporaries. This is a process of identification that has not benefited the indigenous population. It is a past constructed on a reinterpretation of the ideologies that permeated Spanish expansion. It justified the conquest and gave Creoles the role of savior of the "pagan" Indian. Thus, it should not be surprising that the Virgin of Guadalupe became the first nationalist symbol, a symbol that continues in contemporary times and transcends class. Guadalupe represents all that was good of the past. For Mexican nationalism, and eventually, Chican*o*[2] nationalism is constructed by glorifying the past. As Wallerstein (1991) theorizes, "pastness" is an important element for the construction of nationalism and nation:

> Pastness is a central element in the socialization of individuals, in the maintenance of group solidarity, in the establishment of or challenge to social legitimization. Pastness therefore is preeminently a moral phenomenon,

> therefore a political phenomenon, always a contemporary phenomenon. That is of course why it is so inconstant. Since the real world is constantly changing, what is relevant to contemporary politics is necessarily constantly changing. (p. 78)

However, since the past is constant "no one can ever admit that any particular past has ever changed or could possibly change" (Wallerstein, 1991, p. 78). That is, for the past to be able to articulate nationalist sentiments, this past and the "official" representation of the past is constant. However, as the following analysis demonstrates, interpretations of the past are not constant.

The Historical Record

Malintzin/Marina/Malinche

Malintzin/Marina/Malinche did not leave any account of her own life. What we know about her life is what has been written in the chronicles of the conquest. Therefore, the historical record is rather vague, suspect, and open to speculation. Malintzin's public biography is documented in the chronicles of the conquest, archival documents, and secondary historical sources. According to Bernal Díaz del Castillo (1632/1960) Malintzin Tenépal was born in Paynala, near Coatzacualco (or Guazacualco, the spelling used by Díaz del Castillo).[3] Chicana feminist historian Adelaida del Castillo (1977) places her birth in 1505, while Cordelia Candelaria, citing Somonte, places it in 1502. What we do know is that Malintzin's parents were from the ruling elite, Caciques. Her father died when she was young and her mother remarried another Cacique with whom she had a son. Malintzin's mother and stepfather had an affinity for this son and decided he should succeed and inherit their fortune (Díaz del Castillo, 1632/1960). They gave the child Malintzin to people from Xicalango during the night and pretended young Malintzin had died. The people from Xicalango gave her to the people of Tabasco. Thus, Malintzin was able to speak Nahuatl and Mayan. After Cortés took over Tabasco, the Tabascans gave him twenty women, including Malintzin, who was given the Spanish name of Marina after she was baptized (Díaz del Castillo, 1632/1960). With Cortés she had a son. But afterwards he married her to Juan Jaramillo, one of his captains. According to Díaz del Castillo (1632/1956) her translating functions were essential for the Spanish conquest of the territory that the Spanish called New Spain and today includes Mexico and parts of Central America.

According to Candelaria (1980) Malintzin's public history ends in 1527 when Cortés leaves New Spain. Malintzin's life after the conquest and her death are even more open to conjecture than her public life. Candelaria cites archival documents with sworn testimony from contemporaries that indicate that Malintzin died around 1527 or 1528 at approximately 25 years of age of smallpox (Candelaria, 1980).

History did not record Malintzin's own voice; what we know of her was written by the chroniclers of the conquest such as Díaz del Castillo, Cortés, Gómara, and Sagahún and some of the Mexica códices. Much of what we know about her and interpretations of her life are through popular culture and literature. During Spanish colonial times she was pretty much forgotten. Moreover, the historical sources are rather contradictory. Indeed Díaz del Castillo's chronicle consistently tries to correct Gómara's text.

The contemporary and popular construction of La Malinche as a traitor began after independence (Cypess, 1991). The first construction of Malintzin as a traitor is the anonymous novel *Jicotencal* published in Philadelphia in 1826 (Leal, 1983; Cypess, 1991). According to Leal, *Jicotencal* represents Doña Marina as "the forces of evil and is characterized as wily, perfidious, deceitful, and treacherous" (p. 228). In the twentieth century the trope of treachery is consolidated with Octavio Paz's *El laberinto de la soledad* (1950) and in José Clemente Orozco's murals (Leal, 1983).

Díaz del Castillo (1632/1960) refers to Malintzin in a very positive, kind, and deferential manner. He always referred to her by her Christian name Doña Marina, the Doña being a term of respect. Díaz del Castillo described her as a "gran cacica, beautiful, self-assured, and willing to insert herself in the unfolding events of her time" (pp. 120–121). In the *Códice Florentino, Códice Ramírez,* and *Códice Aubin,* which are native narratives of the conquest documented in *Visión de los vencidos* (1959/1992), Malinche is referred to as Malintzin, also with respect since the "tzin" reflects respect and honor. Malintzin was instrumental in the conquest of Mexico not only for her translating abilities, but also as a source of information and diplomacy, despite the fact that she was not a conquistadora. Examples of her strategic importance in the conquest abound. In a significant event that is often cited as an example of her supposed treachery, Malintzin was able to provide secret information to Cortés that avoided a catastrophe for the Spanish. When the Spanish were in Cholulaas they approached Tenochtitlán, the Cholutecas were planning a surprise attack. An old Indian woman approached Malintzin and told her what they were planning and that she should leave with her. The old lady approached Malintzin because she was beautiful and rich, and she promised to marry her to her son. Malintzin pretended to agree to leave with her and told the old woman that she needed to gather her things that were of significant value. Instead she informed Cortés of the plan. With this information, Cortés was able to avoid a costly catastrophe for the Spanish.

Her function as a translator and diplomat became very significant once the Spanish entered Tenochtitlán. When Cortés decided that he needed to place Motecuhzoma under house arrest, some Spaniards were talking very loud and rude.[4] Motecuhzoma could not understand what they were saying, but was nervous about the tone of voice. Thus, he asked Malintzin what they were saying. Instead of simply translating, she inserted her own position. According to Díaz del Castillo (1632/1960) she told him: "Lord Montezuma: what I advise you is to go with them to your quarters, without noise, because I know they will honor you as the great lord you are. Any other way and you will be dead. In your quarters the truth will be known" (p. 294).[5] After hearing this, Motecuhzoma agreed to the house arrest. Todorov (1984) makes a similar argument, adding that since she was given in slavery by her own people that we can imagine that she held certain rancor against them. Regardless of what her motivations were (which can only be speculations), Todorov's point that she clearly took sides and adapted to the Spaniards' values is one of the reasons why she is so maligned in post-independence Mexico. In other words, Malintzin interpreted not only language, but also the indigenous cultures of what is called today Mexico. An interpretation and information that gave Cortés an advantage that was more powerful than the numerical superiority of the Mexicas.

The Virgin of Guadalupe

Between December 9 and 12, 1531, the Virgin of Guadalupe appeared four times to an Indian named Juan Diego in Tepeyac. The official story explains that the dark-skinned Virgin asked Juan Diego to give a message to Fray Juan de Zumárraga, the first bishop of Mexico to build a temple dedicated to her. She provided a miraculous signal by growing flowers in Tepeyac to be taken to the bishop. The Virgin also appeared and cured Juan Diego's uncle. The final miracle was that in front of the bishop as Juan Diego gave him the flowers the Virgin had made appear, her image appeared in his *tilma* (cloak). The image of the Virgin is housed in the Básilica de Guadalupe in Mexico City where every year millions of people make pilgrimages to her. The effect of these events has been historically transmitted from generation to generation, and they are of great importance for the construction of Mexican nationalist consciousness, religion, and culture (Nebel, 1995; Poole, 1995; Taylor, 1987; Lafaye, 1974).

Historical accounts of the apparition of the Virgin of Guadalupe appear in the seventeenth century. The closest approximation to historical documentation can be found in the accounts of the four evangelists of the cult of Guadalupe. In 1648, Father Miguel Sánchez wrote the first account: *Imagen de la Virgen María, Madre de Díos de Guadalupe, Celebrada en la Historia con la profesía del Capítulo doce del Apocalipsis*. The second evangelist was Lasso de la Vega who published in 1649 the *Hue Tlamahuizaltica,* which is the *Nican Mopohua* (Here it is told) written in Nahuatl. The authorship of the *Nican Mopohua* is attributed to Antonio Valeriano, a disciple of Fray Bernardino de Sahagún in the Colegio de Santa Cruz de Tlatelolco. In 1666 Luis Bezerra Tanco wrote *Origen Milagroso*, which was posthumously published by his friend Antonio de Gama with the title of *Felicidad Mexicana*. And the fourth evangelist is Francisco de Florencia, who in 1688 published *La Estrella del Norte*, which expounded Creole theology. The development of the cult of Guadalupe and modern understanding of Guadalupe is based on the writings of these four evangelists.

According to Enrique Florescano (1994) the first account of the cult of the Virgin of Guadalupe appeared in an *Información* that Fray Alfonso de Montúfar ordered in 1556. This *Información* was based on a sermon by Fray Francisco Bustamante. In this sermon Bustamante attacked the cult to the *image* of the Virgin of Guadalupe:

> It seemed to him that the devotion that this city had taken in a hermitage and home of Our Lady that they have entitled of Guadalupe is a great harm to the natives because it leads them to believe that the image *painted by the Indian*

> *Marcos* performs miracles . . . and to tell [the Indians] that an image that was painted by an Indian performs miracles, would be great confusion and undo good that had been planted there. (Bustamante qtd. in Florescano, 1994, p. 132. My emphasis)

Miguel Sánchez's *Imagen de la Virgen María, Madre de Díos de Guadalupe* was based on the preservation by old men of oral accounts of the apparition. According to this account the Virgin Mary appeared in Tepeyac to the Indian Juan Diego in early December 1531. Juan Diego heard sweet music and his name called. He then saw a lady who ordered him to go toward her and asked him where he was going. She revealed herself to Juan Diego and asked him to give her message to the bishop. Her request was to have a temple built where she appeared so she could protect her people and they could venerate her. Juan Diego obliged and paid a visit to Fray Juan de Zumárraga, the bishop of Mexico, who indifferently told him to come another day. On his way back home, when the Virgin appears to him a second time he informs her of the bishop's behavior. Juan Diego begged the Virgin to choose a person with more credibility to give her message to the Church authorities. But the Virgin assures him that he is the one who should and will convey the message to the bishop. On the third appearance Juan Diego informed her that the bishop had asked for a sign. The Virgin promised to give the sign the next day. But the next day, Juan Diego's uncle became severely ill and he had to look for a priest to perform the last rights. Juan Diego did not want to get distracted by the Virgin and tried to avoid her to no avail.

The Virgin appeared to Juan Diego and assured him that his uncle was fine and that he should not be afraid since she would protect him. The Virgin then proceeded to ask him to climb up a mount to the place where he had seen her and cut and pick up the roses and flowers he would find there. Without questioning the "odd" demand, since it was December and the nature of the terrain (stone) was not conducive for flowers to grow, with haste he went and found the flowers, which he picked and put in his cloak. Juan Diego proceeded to show the sign to the bishop. As he was waiting to see the bishop, his assistants, who were not letting him in, noted his patience and that he had something in his cloak. Once they realized that what he had were flowers and that it was not possible to take them out of the cloak, they informed the bishop. When Juan Diego was before the bishop, he related to him everything that had happened, and the miracle occurred:

> He revealed the clean blanket to present the gift of heaven to the fortunate bishop; he anxious to receive it, saw on the blanket a holy forest, a miraculous spring, a small garden of roses, lilies, carnations, irises, broom, jasmine, and violets, and all of them, falling from the blanket, left painted on it the VIRGIN MARY, Mother of God, in her holy image that today is preserved, guarded, and venerated in the sanctuary of GUADALUPE in Mexico City. (Sánchez, 1648 qtd. in Florescano, 1994, p. 141)

So the miracle of the apparition has become part of the Mexican religious and national consciousness. I will elaborate on the construction of Guadalupe as a symbol of Mexican nationalism in the next section.

La Llorona

There is much scholarly debate on whether the origins of the legend of La Llorona are indigenous or European. Limón (1990) refers to her as a syncretic figure of European and indigenous origin. For Limón she is a distant relative of the Medea story. Other similarities with European legends include the German legend of *Die Weisse Frau* (Barakat, 1965; Kirtley, 1960; Lomax Hawes, 1968), Lillith of Jewish origin, and the Lamia of Greek folk (Candelaria, 1977). The Aztec elements of the legend include the wailing, water, knife, and general appearance (Barakat, 1965). As Limón suggests, La Llorona can be traced to the Aztec goddess Cihuacóalt. Fray Bernardino de Sahagún wrote that the goddess Cihuacóalt was dressed in white, and she had a crib on her back. She was known as the goddess of adverse things (*cosas adversas*) such as poverty. When other women got near the crib, they were able to see that inside there was a knife.

According to González Obregón (1924) in the middle of the sixteenth century, not long after the Spanish conquest, people would be awakened in the middle of the night by the weeping of a woman who without a doubt had deep moral or physical pain. She would wear a white dress and cover her face with a thick veil. She was named La Llorona because nobody knew who she was. Obregón believes that the origins of La Llorona are Aztec and, as many others, cites Sahagún to maintain this claim. Obregón also claims that La Llorona is the sixth prognostication of the doom of the indigenous inhabitants of Mexico.

Obregón also writes that it was believed that La Llorona is La Malinche crying after the death of her fallen children: the Mexicans. The two figures are often believed to be the same; I do not believe that this is the case. The difference between Llorona and Malinche is that Llorona repents for a crime she committed, while Malinche did not commit a crime, and thus she does not repent. Consolidating the two figures into one assumes that Malinche did betray "her people" and repents. This position is contrary to the interpretation offered in this essay.

The legend of La Llorona continues to be transmitted through the oral tradition. Thus, there are many variants of the legend. However, the basic premise of the legend is that a beautiful young woman (she can be mestiza, Creole, and Indian; rich or poor but for the most part of humble origin) sometimes named Luisa or Rita fell in love with a rich man. They lived together and had between one and three children and lived happily. However, the man's mother demanded that he marry within his class, which he did. When she found out about his deed, in a moment of jealousy she killed their children. Some versions say that she died a violent death, others that when she died (how is not specified) and went to heaven God told her she could not enter until she found her children. That is why she is looking for them.

Over the years, the legend of La Llorona has become a "boogie man" story to keep children from straying. Children are told that La Llorona is looking for her children and she will take any child she finds. She particularly scares men, and in many versions she has a very cold breath and that when she uncovers her face, one sees her skeleton. Once a person (especially a man) sees La Llorona either he/she dies immediately or when telling the story. More recently, people don't die but do get very scared.

One of the interesting aspects of La Llorona is that she is a derivative of Cihuacóatl, the Aztec goddess. As I have demonstrated, Guadalupe and Tonántzin are related (actually the same). Mexica philosophy was based on dualism (León Portilla, 1961); this duality often was contradictory. So it should not be surprising that Cihuacóalt and Tonántzin are the same, representing different sides of the duality. In Western thought the duality is separate, one is either good or evil. Therefore, once adopted to Western thought Guadalupe/Tonántzin and Llorona/Cihuacóatl become different figures with different symbolism. But as Guadalupe and Malinche are functions of each other, so are Guadalupe and Llorona. Once Cihuacóalt/Tonántzin is appropriated in Westernized philosophy and religion, her duality becomes two different entities: one good (Guadalupe/Tonántzin) and one bad (Llorona/Cihuacóatl).

Deconstructing Malinche, Guadalupe, and Llorona

The construction of these three figures, in their similarities and differences, are all related to the forging of Mexican nationalism from colonial times to independence; and to the formation of Chicano nationalism in the 1960s and 1970s. Although there are three figures, they work in a Manichean logic between good and bad. Guadalupe is the virginal loving mother, and Malinche and Llorona are deviants. According to Lafaye (1974) and Florescano (1994) the consolidation of Guadalupe as a nationalist symbol was the work of the Creoles. Given the rigid hierarchy of the Spanish crown, Creoles who were of "pure" Spanish stock but born in the colonies could not aspire to the upper power structures of Spain and its colonies. However, they were *different* from mestizos since Creoles were at least of European extraction. Thus, Creoles articulated their cultural identity based on the racial hierarchy developed by the Spanish crown.[6] Creoles lacked their own identity and needed to forge one and construct their own sense of nationhood and ethnicity.

Creoles found this sense of ethnicity in the religious discourses available to them at the time. Spanish Catholicism was still based on a medieval notion of the eschatological, that is, the belief that the end of the world would come soon. The Spanish, especially the religious orders, believed that it was their duty to convert the pagans to Catholicism as soon as possible; otherwise, their souls would be condemned. While in the sixteenth century the Church tried as much as possible to eliminate any traces of indigenous religion, in the seventeenth century some priests tried to find connections between the indigenous past and Catholicism. Many believed that the inhabitants of the Americas were one of the lost tribes of Israel and that Mexico represented a "promised land." Therefore, even for Creoles in the seventeeth century the relationship between Tonántzin and the Virgin Mary was not an impossibility. Rather, it justified their existence in the New World and consolidated their new ethnic identity. Therefore, the notion of mestizaje and hybridity was important for the construction of Mexican national identity that transcends race. Because Guadalupe maintains her indigenous roots, and Creoles were able to accept these roots (at an idealized mode), today the veneration of the Virgin of Guadalupe either as a religious or nationalist symbol transcends class.

La Llorona also serves as a symbol for the construction of national consciousness as can be seen in Southwestern versions of La Llorona. On a ranch in New Mexico near Clayton, a tale was created to explain a heart wrenching sound (produced by coyotes, wolves, and wind blowing between the granite walls of a canyon). The tale told of an Indian maiden, La Llorona, who mourned for the young lover who had been captured by the Spaniards. She was punishing the Spaniards by crying every evening and making them as lonely as she was. The relationship to La Llorona is by name only, since most of the other elements are not present. However, it is a clear indictment against Spanish colonization and the subsequent plight of indigenous inhabitants of North America.[7] Another version of the legend of La Llorona combines the elements of the traditional story, but the male protagonist is a Spaniard. A young woman was seduced by a Spaniard, an evil one, and she has a child. Soon the Spaniard leaves her. The child dies or is killed (not by her). The woman cries and generally pines away and dies soon after the child. The legend says that "there is a weeping sound that rolls through town in a white, furry-type ball like a big snowball, that rolls through town with the weeping sounds coming from it."[8] The weeping sound can also be heard near the windows of children, which means that the woman is trying to get the children. These stories identify the Spanish (the Conqueror) as evil, and thus serve to construct an anticolonial cultural identity.

Nationalist discourses tend to be patriarchal. These three figures are constructed in a hierarchical way that reflects patriarchal definitions of proper womanhood. Guadalupe is the protecting mother that symbolizes ideal femininity; Malinche and La Llorona symbolize the negative side of women. The idealization of femininity places a double standard on women that is impossible to fulfill. As Norma Alarcón (1989) has pointed out, Guadalupe and Malinche are functions of each other, as are Guadalupe and Llorona. Once Mexican nationalism is constructed in relation to an ideal indigenous past (a construction that became important for Chicano nationalism), then it is necessary to find scapegoats for the conquest. To justify why paradise was lost, Malinche becomes such a scapegoat.

During colonial times Doña Marina was pretty much forgotten, and when remembered she had not become the Mexican Eve. The construction of Marina/Malintzin as La Malinche is a post-independence move. Although the historical record is vague about Malintzin, Bernal Díaz del Castillo has a high opinion of Doña Marina. According to Díaz del Castillo, Doña Marina was well liked by Indians and Spaniards, and many considered her a savior (Alarcón, 1989). The indigenous códices do not make any type of assessment on Malintzin's role. When she appears, she is referred to only in her function as a translator in a straightforward manner. According to the Spanish narrative, for those who lived during the Conquest, including the indigenous population, she was not considered a traitor. Then, why does she become the scapegoat of Mexico's conquest? In order to understand how Malintzin became Malinche it is necessary to appreciate the process of construction of nationalism and its relation to patriarchy. Mexican feminist Juana Armanda Alegría believes that Doña Marina is judged by history so harshly probably because she was a woman. Clearly, Malinche's gender is crucial to the construction of her treachery. To understand how this operates it is necessary to understand the development of Mexican nationalism. If Mexican nationalism, and subsequently Chicano nationalism, was based on a desire to bring back the utopian idyllic past, then, it was necessary to find a scapegoat for the loss of this past. But there are plenty of men who allied themselves to Cortés. The cacique of Cempoala, who was under the rule of the Mexicans and allied himself to Cortés can, under the same logic, be considered a traitor. Yet his place in history is negligent. Motecuhzoma has been criticized, but mostly for incompetence. Moreover, there seems to be a historical amnesia regarding his role in the conquest. The códices document that his own people were upset with him and wanted to take a more proactive attack on the Spaniards. There is speculation that he might have been killed by one of his own people. Yet these two men are not considered traitors nor are they to be blamed for the conquest.

Malinche's gender makes her a target for her position in history as a traitor. The two sins that Mexican nationalism and patriarchy do not forgive her for are sexuality and knowledge. Malintzin had sexual relations and a child with Cortés, but she also was instrumental in the conquest for the knowledge of Nahuatl, Maya, and Spanish, and in assisting the Spaniards in understanding indigenous cultures. Bernal Díaz del Castillo wrote that without her service as a translator and diplomat the Spanish would not have been able to conquer the Mexicas. After all, she was able to convince Motecuhzoma to agree to be placed under house arrest by Cortés. Thus, her status as a traitor and scapegoat is linked to her status as a woman who deviated from the traditional norm. In addition to her sexual transgressions, Malinche's other great sin is the usage of her knowledge in the service of the "enemy" or herself, not her "community." This type of critique of Malinche is based on contemporary notions of nation and community. What community did Malinche betray? Following her history, Malinche did not have a community; her own mother gave her away in slavery, and she was passed from one group of persons to another. Why should she have had any loyalty toward the Mexicas or any other indigenous nation? Given her circumstances, acting on behalf of herself was an act of survival not of treachery. To say that she allied with the foreigner as her ultimate betrayal is an ahistorical interpretation that views all indigenous peoples as one nation, which at that historical time was not the case. Moreover, Malinche allied herself to the Spanish against the Mexicas who were hated by many indigenous nations; therefore, she was not betraying anybody. The sin that patriarchy claims she committed is one created by contemporary views. As Norma Alarcón writes,

> Because Malintzin the translator is perceived as speaking for herself and not the community, however it defines itself, she is a woman who has betrayed her primary function—maternity. The figure of the mother is bound to a double reproduction, *strictu sensu*—that of her people and her culture. In a traditional society organized along metaphysical or cosmological figurations of good and evil, cultural deviation from the norm is not easily tolerated nor valued in the name of inventiveness or "originality." In such a setting, to speak or translate in one's behalf rather than the perceived group interests and values is tantamount to betrayal. (Alarcón, 1989, p. 63)

As already documented, Creoles constructed a nationalist consciousness based on the notion of a promised land based on an idyllic past. Eventually the majority of Mexicans also made the glorification of the indigenous past an essential element for nationalist consciousness. In Mexican and Chicano patriarchal nationalist discourses, the image of the Mexica warrior is one of the most visible elements. The numerical superiority of Mexicas and their military might is never in doubt. Given this superiority, Mexicans and their allies should have easily defeated Cortés and his numerically inferior army. The advantage that Cortés had was not military but the information that Malintzin provided plus germ warfare: smallpox. Therefore, if the Mexicas lost, it is not because of a military deficiency, but because of two elements that were beyond their control: biology and knowledge provided by a woman. There was no defense against biological warfare. The indigenous people were helpless against smallpox, an epidemic that killed thousands. Equally, or if not more damaging, was the cultural knowledge that Malinche was able to give Cortés. According to patriarchal notions it was through a woman's intervention that the Mexicas lost. Therefore, Malintzin becomes La Malinche, the one who betrays "her people" through communication, knowledge, and sex with the foreigner. Thus, she is considered a traitor not only because she is a woman, but because she is a woman who uses her knowledge and sexuality to survive. Because of this she is seen as betraying her people, especially against the masculine power. There is no doubt that Malintzin was instrumental in helping Cortés in the conquest. However, she could not have single-handedly defeated the Mexicas.

La Llorona is an even more enigmatic figure. As Malinche she represents the negative side of the feminine. In the most common variation of the legend, La Llorona commits one of the most unthinkable crimes: infanticide. But in other versions she does not kill her children, they die because of poverty. La Llorona is not as maligned as Malinche. After all, she did not commit her crime against all Mexicans (unless she is considered Malinche), but to her family, and ultimately repents. Moreover, Llorona's sexual activity is more acceptable since she is still subservient to the male. She is seduced by a handsome man and gives him children out of love. While Malinche exercises sexual agency, Llorona does not. She can be seen in the traditional sense that women would do anything for the men they love.

For José Limón (1990), La Llorona represents a resolution to the contradictory position of women in Mexico and Chicano patriarchal history.

This contradictory position "articulated through the iconic signs of Madonna and whore, is addressed and resolved through the historically continuous mythic project of a 'real' woman who, . . . experiences the effects of this contradiction and resolves it through the narrative's formal structure" (p. 420). The feminist symbolism of La Llorona, according to Limón, is the destruction of the patriarchal structure in order for a new structure to emerge, "one that, in the most powerful kind of feminism, speaks not only of women but through the power of women for *all* the socially weak" (p. 427, italics in the original). Limón's analysis has been criticized by Norma Alarcón, who, I agree, finds this type of feminism quite dangerous.

Conclusion

For the indigenous people who inhabited the territory that we call today Mexico, the Southwestern United States, and Central America, the Spanish conquest drastically disrupted their world, and not for the better. A new culture and racial/ethnic category emerged, although this does not mean that the indigenous cultures were lost. This new "race," the mestizas/os, and their culture have historically been in a struggle to construct their own cultural identity.[9] One of the ways this cultural identity has been constructed is through the development of nationalist consciousness. As demonstrated in this essay, Mexican and subsequent Chicano patriarchal nationalism was constructed through very specific images of women, through the mystification of the three female figures *Guadalupe, Malinche,* and *Llorona.*

The deconstruction of the construction of these three mythical figures in historical texts permits us to see how the development of the concept of nation was realized in masculine terms. However, since texts have multiple meanings which are open to different and contradictory interpretations and re-interpretations of official or masculine versions, feminists can consult the same sources to provide different standpoints.

Mexican and Chicana feminist scholars have contested the patriarchal construction of nationalism, including the role that *Malinche, Guadalupe,* and *Llorona* have played in such constructions. These three figures are an integral part of Mexican culture, cultural productions, and representation. In this chapter, I deconstructed their representation in historical texts. However, given the richness of cultural productions that challenge the dominant views of the three figures, there is a need to continue documenting alternative feminist interpretations of these figures. Alternative feminist interpretations of these figures can transform nationalism and cultural identity in ways that will benefit women and not continue to place them in a subordinate position.

Notes

This research was funded by a ASU West SRCA grant. I would like to thank and acknowledge Juan Guevara who diligently worked as the research assistant for this project. Special thanks to Manuel de Jesús Hernández Gutiérrez for his support and insightful comments in the early stages of this research. I would like to acknowledge James Griffith, of the Southwest Folklore Center at the University of Arizona, and Monique Durham, of the Center for Southwest Research at the University of New Mexico, for their assistance in my archival research. I am grateful as well to Cynthia M. Tompkins and to the editors of this volume, Julio López-Arias and Gladys M. Varona-Lacey, for their thoughtful comments on earlier drafts of this essay.

1. There are many names for Malintzin: Doña Marina, Malinal, and of course Malinche. The name I will use for her during this essay varies according to context. However, for the most part I prefer to call her Malintzin, her given Nahuatl name. Marina is her Christian name. She was known as Malinche because this is the name that indigenous people gave to Cortés. Since she was always with him, they also called her Malinche.

2. I use the italicized "o" to point out how influential patriarchy was in the development of Chicano nationalism. The "o" is the linguistic masculine identifier in Spanish.

3. See the fifth edition of *Editorial Porrúa* by Joaquín Ramírez Cabañas, the first edition of *Historia verdadera* was published in Madrid in 1632. Del Castillo's original manuscript in draft form was finished in 1568 (forty-seven years after the conquest). The manuscript was sent to Spain the same year, which was later found in the early seventeenth century by Fray Alfonso Remón in the library of Lorenzo Ramírez Prado, the Counselor of the Indies. This is the manuscript that was used for the first edition, with editorial changes by Remón. Subsequent editions came from the manuscript and *códices* archived in Guatemala and based on Del Castillo's draft.

4. The spelling of Montezuma varies in historical documents, language, and historical time. I decided to use the spelling of *Visión de los vencidos*. The variations of the spelling in this chapter reflect the spelling used in a particular document.

5. The Spanish text reads, "Señor Montezuma: lo que yo os aconsejo es que vais luego con ellos a su aposento, sin ruido ninguno, que yo sé que os harán mucha honra, como gran señor que sois, y de otra manera aqui quedaréis muerto, y en su aposento se sabrá la verdad" (my translation).

6. Contemporary social scientists agree, for the most part, that race is not biological but a social construction. However, even though race is a construction, and consistent with the arguments provided in this essay, the "fact" that race is socially constructed does not foreclose the significance that the concept of race has in the history of the colonization of the Americas, and in contemporary societies. As Howard Winant (1994) explains, based on W. I. Thomas, if people define a situation as real, the consequences are real. This is the case with the concept of race. There might not be a biological basis for the conceptualization of race, but this social construction is very real for some people. Thus, throughout this essay I use the concept of race and racism to explain the hierarchies that were developed in the sixteenth century to distinguish between Europeans (Christians) and the inhabitants of the Americas.

7. Ernest W. Baughman Folklore Collection, Center for Southwest Research, University of New Mexico (archive, box, and file unknown). (Hereafter abbreviated as EWB Collection.)

8. EWB Collection (archive, box, and file unknown).

9. Although mestizo is not a racial category per se, it does operate as a racial rather than an ethnic category. There is no doubt that mestizo is a Mexican construction to identify as the mixture of indigenous and Spanish blood. As such it has become very important in the construction of national consciousness. Therefore, even though biologically speaking it cannot be considered a "race," practically it does operate as such.

References

Alarcón, N. (1981). Chicana's feminist literature: A re-vision through Malintzin/or Malintzin: Putting flesh back on the object. In C. Moraga & G. Anzaldúa (Eds.), This bridge called my back (pp. 182–190). New York: Kitchen Table Women of Color Press.

———. (1989. Fall). Traddutora, traditora: A paradigmatic figure of Chicana feminism. *Cultural Critique*, 13, 57–87.

Alegría, J. A. (1975). *Psicología de las mexicanas* (2a edición). Coyoacán, México: Editorial Samo.

Anzaldúa, G. (1987). *Borderlands La Frontera*. San Francisco: Aunt Lute.

Barakat, R. A. (1965). Aztec motifs in "La Llorona." *Southern Folklore Quarterly, 29*, 288–296.

Candelaria, C. (1980). La Malinche, feminists prototype, *Frontiers, 5*, 1–6.

———. (1977, July/August). Marketplace: Legend of La Llorona. *Agenda, 7*, 46–47.

Culler, J. (1982). *On deconstruction: Theory and criticism after structuralism*. Ithaca, NY: Cornell University Press.

Cypess, S. M. (1991). *La Malinche in Mexican literature: From history to myth.* Austin: University of Texas Press.

Del Castillo, A. R. (1977). Malintzin Tenépal: A preliminary look into a new perspective. In R. Sánchez and R. Martínez Cruz (Eds.), *Essays on la mujer* (pp. 124–149). Los Angeles: UCLA Chicano Studies Center Publications.

Derrida, J. (1981). *Positions* (Alan Bass, Trans.). Chicago: University of Chicago Press.

———. (1977). *Limited Inc.* (Samuel Weber, Trans.). Evanston, Ill.: Northwestern University Press.

Díaz del Castillo, B. (1632/1956). *The discovery and conquest of Mexico 1517–1521.* Genaro García, Ed. (A. P. Maudslay, Trans.). n. p.: Farrar, Straus and Cudahy.

———. (1632/1960). *Historia verdadera de la conquista de la Nueva España* (5a edición) con introducción de Joaquín Ramírez Cabañas (Vol. 1). México, D. F.: Editorial Porrúa.

Florescano, E. (1994). *Memory, myth, and time in Mexico: From the Aztecs to independence* (Albert G. Bork, Trans.). Austin: University of Texas Press.

Gasché, R. (1986). *The tain of the mirror: Derrida and the philosophy of reflection.* Cambridge, MA: Harvard University Press.

González Obregón, L. (1944). *Las calles de México.* 6a ed. México: Ediciones Botas.

Kirtely, B. (1960). 'La Llorona' and related themes. *Western Folklore*, 19 (2), 155–168.

Lafaye, J. (1974). *Quetzalcótl and Guadalupe: The formation of Mexican national consciousness 1531–1813* (Benjamin Keen, Trans.). Chicago: The University of Chicago Press.

Leal, L. (1983). Female archetypes in Mexican literature. In B. Miller (Ed.), *Women in Hispanic literature: Icons and Fallen Idols* (pp. 117–242). Berkeley and Los Angeles: University of California Press.

León Portilla, M. (1961). *Los antiguos mexicanos.* México: Fondo de Cultura Económica.

———. (1992). *Visión de los vencidos:Relaciones indígenas de la conquista* (13 edición). México: Universidad Nacional Autónoma de México.

Limón, J. (1990). La Llorona, the third legend of greater Mexico: Cultural symbols, women, and the political unconscious. In Adelaida del Castillo (Ed.) *Between Borders: Essays on Mexican/Chicana history* (pp. 299–342). Encino: Floricanto Press.

Lomax Hawes, B. (1968). La Llorona in Juvenile Hall. *Western Folklore, 27* (3), 153–170.

Moraga, C. (1983). *Loving in the war years: Lo que nunca pasó por sus labios.* Boston: South End Press.

Nebel, R. (1995). *Santa María Tonántzin Virgen de Guadalupe: Continuidad y transformación religiosa en México* (Carlos Warnholtz Bustillos, Trans. Spanish). México, D.F. : Fondo de Cultura Económica.

Paz, O. (1950). *El Laberinto de la soledad.* México: Fondo de Cultura Económica.

Poole, S. (1995). *Our Lady of Guadalupe: The origins and sources of a Mexican national symbol, 1531–1797.* Tucson: University of Arizona Press.

Sahagún, F. B. (1938). *Historia general de las cosas de la Nueva España* (Vols. 1–4) México: Editorial Robredo.

Scott, J. (1988). *Gender and the politics of history.* New York: Columbia University Press.

Taylor, W. B. (1987, February). The Virgin of Guadalupe in New Spain: An inquiry into the social history of Marian devotion. *American Ethnologist, 14*, 9–33.

Todorov, T. (1984). *The conquest of America: The question of the Other.* New York: Harper & Row.

Wallerstein, I. (1991). The construction of peoplehood: Racism, nationalism, ethnicity. In E. Balibar & I. Wallerstein (Eds.), *Race, nation, class: Ambiguos idenities* (pp. 71–85). London: Verso.

Winant, H. (1994). *Racial conditions.* Minneapolis: University of Minnesota Press.

The Catholic Church in Latin America: From Privilege to Protest

Sarah Brooks and Christian Smith

Religion has long been a dominant feature in Latin American society. In a region where nearly 80 percent of the population claim some formal religious affiliation, church leaders have been powerful forces in shaping regional politics and national culture. The Roman Catholic Church has historically been the principal religion in Latin America, and its leaders have taken prominent roles in society. The status of the Catholic Church has undergone tremendous change, however, since the first Spanish missionaries arrived in the Americas. From its traditional role in the elite power structures, the Catholic Church has dramatically redefined its mission in the twentieth century with profound and at times far-reaching political consequences. The Church, once the bastion of conservatism, found itself by the 1970s embroiled in movements for radical social reform, which at times brought harsh repression from military regimes. We will see that the role of religion in Latin America has been transformed repeatedly throughout history; each time with profound implications for political and social relations throughout the region.

The Colonial Church

As early as Columbus' second voyage, the colonization of the Americas was carried out hand-in-hand with the spiritual conquest of the indigenous population by Catholic clergy. The Catholic crown of Spain under Ferdinand and Isabella was particularly favorable to the Church and lent strong support to religious forces as a means of achieving national unity and absolute loyalty to the crown. In the Americas as well as in Spain, the crown maintained solid control over the Church through the institution of the *patronato real* (royal patronage), which entailed the absolute right of the Spanish kings to nominate all Church officials, collect tithes, and found churches and monasteries in the Americas (Keen and Wasserman 1988, 103). Catholic clergy thus assumed a function in colonial society similar to the one it held in Spain in relation to the state. Where the Church assumed a new function, however, was in relation to the indigenous population of the Americas.

The Catholic priests in the early conquest were members of the elite and highly educated ranks of society. Combining missionary zeal with their emphasis on education and literary training, Catholic priests set to the task of mass conversions of the natives, and established schools for the instruction of humanities, including Latin, logic, philosophy, and Christian doctrine. The religious orders likewise placed special emphasis on the study of native languages and history and produced important works on native grammar and civilizations (Lockhart and Schwartz 1983, 110). This knowledge of native language and culture facilitated the process of conversion. In Mexico, the Franciscan priests were said to have converted more than one million Indian people by 1531, though not all by free will (Keen and Wasserman 1988, 103).

Where persuasion failed, pressure and force were often used to obtain mass "conversions." The result of such large-scale conversion efforts was in many places a lack of understanding or true devotion by the native peoples to Catholic doctrine. In many instances, this led to a fusion of old and new religious ideas, and combined worship of the Virgin Mary alongside pagan divinities. This practice of *syncretism,* or combining of indigenous beliefs and rituals with Catholic practices and symbols, remains a prominent aspect of popular religion in countries such as Peru, Bolivia, and Brazil where the indigenous cultures are pronounced (Parker 1996, 12–15).

The early generations of colonists incorporated the rural Church parish into the *encomienda*, tracts of land and forced Indian labor, as a reward to members of the conquest by the Spanish crown. Although the Church was originally in a dependent and subordinate position, it soon acquired significant economic power by accumulating large tracts of land from wealthy donors. These became the inalienable property of the Church and bolstered its economic power in relation to the competing enterprises of private landowners. The Church in the Americas generally accepted the *encomienda* system as the economic framework for colonial society, and exploited the labor and tribute of Indians who were assigned to the land. Notable voices of protest against slave labor of the indigenous population came from members of the clergy, such as Bartolomé de las Casas (1484–1566), a former encomendero and Dominican friar (Gutiérrez 1993). Nevertheless, the exploitation of Indian labor was at the foundation of vast accumulations of land and wealth by ecclesiastical missions throughout the colonies.

In addition to the economic dominance of the Church in colonial society, the clergy held a virtual monopoly over all levels of education. Primary and secondary schools administered by the Church were generally open only to children of the white upper class and the Indian nobility. This left the majority of the native population and those of mixed blood out of the primary educational system (Dussel 1992, 127). The close alliance of the Church through the colonial government allowed it to extend its influence in cultural matters to a strict censorship on written material ranging from doctrine to fiction, and even to the regulation of private and public behavior. Tribunals of the Inquisition, which originated in Spain, were set up in Mexico and Lima in 1569 to stem the spread of "dangerous thoughts" in the colonies. These tribunals were not widespread in the colonies, but where they existed, they relied on denunciations by informers, torture, and coercion to gain confessions of blasphemy and deviant behavior. Practices such as this illustrate the close relations between the religious and political authority which governed daily life in Spanish America and Brazil during the colonial era.

The Post-Independence Church

Following the struggles for political independence in the early nineteenth century, the symbiotic relationship between the Church and the State of the colonial era was significantly shaken. The new ruling political class of "liberals" embraced a profoundly distinct philosophy from that held by the colonial governments. Liberals aimed with varying success to sever ties between the Church and State and to restrict the privileges of the Church in social life, including its control over institutions of education, marriage, and burial. This new group of leaders included among its goals the withdrawal of state subsidies of the Church, the end of the public collection of tithing, and to seizure of much of the Church landholdings. Through these efforts, the new political elites aimed at the end of the nineteenth century to make the Catholic Church just another institution of society, rather than *the* institution of society.

In response to this assault, the advent of the twentieth century found the Latin American Church in a process of retrenchment. It pulled back not only for the purpose of regrouping its political energies, but truly out of necessity. The sudden loss of material resources for rebuilding was coupled with the widespread decline in vocations, since many priests died in independence struggles and fewer men were eager to join the less powerful and less dominant Church (Dussel 1992, 106). This development was particularly devastating to the Church since it was the status-oriented elites who had traditionally filled its ranks. By the turn of the century, the Catholic Church in many countries was largely wrested from its position as part of the aristocracy and became an outsider in relation to political and social elites.

In order to defend itself in response to these campaigns of secularization, the Latin American Church turned to the Vatican, its headquarters in Rome, for support. In addition to personnel and financial resources, Latin American Church leaders adopted the ideas and organizational models developed by their European counterparts. This change marked an important departure from its previous position of relative autonomy from the Church of Rome. The "Europeanization" of the Catholic Church became an important factor shaping the subsequent political and social role for the Church in the twentieth century, and cleared the way for its dramatic reinsertion into the political arena.

Closer links between Rome and the Latin American churches led to a change in the ideological and political orientation of the Latin American Church. Fueled by more activist social doctrine from Rome, the Latin American churches began to move from their traditional affiliation with the conservative elites toward a closer alliance with the working class. Pronouncements issued by the Pope, the highest Catholic leader in Rome, called for an awareness of the workers and masses as victims of capitalism. This perspective was voiced by Pope Leo XIII in the encyclical *Rerum Novarum* (literally "New Things") (1891), in which he asserted, "The whole process of production as well as trade in every kind of good has been brought almost entirely under the power of the few, so that a very few exceedingly rich men have laid a yolk almost of slavery on the unnumbered masses of non-owning workers" (quoted in Stewart-Gambino 1992, 4).

Moved by this orientation toward the middle and lower sectors, the Latin American Church began to advocate the right of association for workers against the interests of the dominant export elites (the same who had earlier campaigned for the secularization of the state). The Pope asserted that it was not only important that workers form interest associations, but that it was the duty of the Church to found and promote Catholic unions (Stewart-Gambino 1992, 4). The adoption of this politically charged and activist orientation deepened the divide between the Church and the dominant economic elites in Latin American society.

The Era of Populism: 1930–1959

The liberal model of agricultural export capitalism declined in the wake of the 1929 world depression. This economic crisis likewise occasioned an attack on the liberals from the unionized workers as well as a new stratum of economic actors: the national industrial bourgeoisie. These producers made it their goal to end the economic dependence of Latin American countries on international trade by creating domestic consumer markets. Given that these new elites considered their prime enemy to be internationally oriented capitalist forces, they were receptive to alliances with the nationalist-oriented Catholic Church. This allegiance provided a greater opportunity for the political reinsertion of the Church by providing it with a new, financially and politically powerful ally.

The doctrine of Church action at this time was called "New Christendom." It replaced the traditional model of Christendom that had patterned Church social action during the Colonial Era. The doctrine of Christendom had aspired to build up the Church institution itself by constructing a Christian society through religious education and centers of worship. New Christendom, in contrast, called for outward activity and participation by members of the Church in the political, social, and economic worlds (Dussel 1992, 140). Its alliance with the middle classes at this time permitted the Church to follow the political strategy of support for several populist regimes in the region, such as those of Stroessner in Paraguay and Samoza in Nicaragua.

By 1945, however, the Church was increasingly distancing itself from these governments and taking stronger positions as an advocate for the rights of workers. The Church contributed material and organizational resources to help labor unions bargain for wages and benefits. This new role for the Catholic Church as advocate of the working class would bear important political consequences for its relationship with the governments of the various states in Latin America. The return of the Catholic Church to the political arena in Latin America was thus motivated on the elite level by the Church in Rome, but was brought to life in concrete and distinctly political forms through the mobilization of workers under Christian slogans.

The Period of Developmentalism: 1955–1970

The declaration of the "decade of development" from 1955 to 1965 throughout Latin America followed from the exhaustion of initial Import Substituting Industrialization (ISI) efforts of the populist governments, and their downfall at the hands of repressive military regimes. The crisis of dependent capitalism jeopardized not only the economic stability in Latin America, but also threatened the process of labor mobilization on which it rested. Government repression of the working class forced the Church to establish more clearly its allegiance with the popular sectors as opposed to the elite power structures in society. This ushered in a period of political and social upheaval that was to witness the most profound transformation in the Catholic Church.

The economic and social crises generated by the exhaustion of the early phase of ISI programs fueled the spread of "developmentalist" ideology throughout Latin America. For many governments, national development was intended not only to find economic solutions to underdevelopment and poverty, but as a policy of national security. Nationalist development was particularly intended to defend against the rising tide of communist ideology after the Cuban revolution of 1959. Regional development programs, such as U.S. President John F. Kennedy's *Alliance for Progress*, were formed in order to strengthen Latin American nations from within, and to head off communist attempts at destabilization (B. Smith 1991, 111–15).

During the 1960s, Catholic unions became increasingly secularized, and militant members began to merge with revolutionary groups struggling to promote the class interests of the peasants (Dussel 1992, 153). In the political sphere, reformist movements found expression in parties of Christian Democracy. In many countries, these parties carried a revolutionary current that combined theories of dependency with calls for liberation, rather than merely reform. Such parties were first organized in Chile in 1923, spreading to Venezuela in 1947. Not only did official Church discourse turn to revolutionary change and alliance with the poor, but the political forms in which these ideas took shape embodied radical challenges to the existing political and economic order (B. Smith 1982). In this time of global upheaval, the Catholic Church in Latin America began to profoundly to renovate its doctrine and action. These changes took shape at the Second Vatican Council, a three-year meeting of Church leaders from around the world called by Pope John XXIII.

Vatican II was the watershed of global Catholicism during the twentieth century. This meeting brought not only a normative change in Catholic teaching, but a substantive alteration of the structure and practice of the Church. The Latin American presence was strongly felt at the Council, which was attended by 601 Church leaders from Latin America, nearly a quarter of the total attendance. At the same time as the Vatican Council, the Episcopal Council of Latin America (CELAM), which serves as a Church governing body in the region, held several assemblies in Rome. They discussed and formulated progressive models of Church action in Latin America in response to the social and economic crisis in the region (Dussel 1992, 153). These leaders took the occasion of transforming Church doctrine to make important and far-reaching changes in the activities of the Church in Latin American society.

Vatican II solidified the departure of the Latin American Church from its traditionally conservative stance and moved it further toward a position of confrontation and reform (Levine 1980, 21). The changes in Church structures gave new importance to parish priests and nuns as the active members of society. In the past, the Church hierarchy had been the predominant means through which the Catholic Church made its presence felt in society, and had long allied with the dominant political and economic classes. The shift in emphasis toward community activity by the common Church members, priests, and nuns thus freed the hierarchy from its role in preserving the status quo, and permitted some members of the Church to take a more activist posture in society.

This change came about through a conscious project to build community and solidarity for a more just world (Berryman 1994, 11). Throughout Latin America, this was done through the creation of *comunidades eclesiásticas de base* (CEBs), or base ecclesial communities. In these, teams of Church workers situated themselves within the communities of poor people for the purpose of worship, as well as practical efforts to improve their conditions. Church workers prioritized the formation of leaders who could carry out Bible study and other organizing functions. In addition to group prayer, CEBs engaged in practical activities such as building houses, sharing agricultural techniques, and providing health services. The base communities thus combined religious and concrete ends in a new vision of Christianity as the struggle for liberation, or freedom from poverty and misery.

CEBs flourished throughout Latin America in the 1960s and 1970s, and in many countries developed extensive networks largely independent of the Church hierarchy. This form of organizing was championed by the Brazilian Church, where base communities in urban and rural areas trained leaders of local resistance groups and provided opportunities for communities to unite regularly to discuss religious as well as socioeconomic problems (Berryman 1994, 17). In

Brazil, the political impact of Catholic base communities was most profound, and has been widely documented as an important source of resistance to the authoritarian regimes. While most base communities avoided direct political actions, they had a distinctly political impact in the 1970s. This was particularly evident in Central America, where revolutionary struggles in countries such as Guatemala, El Salvador, and Nicaragua embroiled the Church in brutal conflicts with repressive military regimes (Berryman 1994).

Amidst the backdrop of social and political turmoil, the late 1960s witnessed important transformations in the Catholic Church in Latin America. The inability of developmentalist governments to quell the demands of the sectors suffering the effects of the exhaustion of the import substitution model, led to a series of coups and the establishment of military governments throughout South America. At the same time, regional churches confronted internal disputes that arose from the mandate of change issued by Vatican II. The call to struggle against the traditional power structures with which the Church had for so long been allied spurred internal disputes between progressive and conservative members of the institution (Dussel 1992, 154–55). The 1960s were thus a period of upheaval not only in society, but within the Church as well.

The breaking of traditional models of Church action crystallized within the Latin American Church at the second Episcopal Conference of Latin America (CELAM) held in Medellín, Colombia, in 1968. The conference participants issued a critical analysis of the structures of domination in Latin America, linking the "international imperialism of money" to the "institutionalization of violence" within the social structures of the region. The Church leaders placed responsibility for these social injustices upon those who maintained through them a disproportionate share of wealth and power, and declared its commitment to becoming a Church of the poor (B. Smith 1994, 8).

Although the Catholic leaders at Medellín supported change toward "authentic liberation" of the poor, their proclamations deplored the use of violence to redress grievances (C. Smith 1991, 19). Nevertheless, the conference participants asserted that "revolutionary insurrection can be legitimate in the case of prolonged tyranny that seriously works against the fundamental rights of man, and which damages the common good of the country" (quoted in C. Smith 1994, 7–8). To many in Latin America, the Medellín proclamations were interpreted as approval for Church members to join the existing revolutionary movements. The years following this conference thus witnessed an explosion of religious activism throughout Latin America, ranging from peaceful protest to armed conflict.

The Medellín conference marked an important turning point for the Catholic Church in Latin America. It not only embraced a more progressive discourse and alliance with the poor, but also fostered an important theological renovation with a distinctly revolutionary tone. This new theology, known as *theology of liberation*, was conceived as the Latin American Church's response to what they perceived as structural sources of injustice and oppression (C. Smith 1991). By the end of the 1960s, the Catholic Church in Latin America had changed profoundly its message and action in ways that bore important political consequences. Although they fueled an era of political activation throughout the region, this activity at times brought members of the Church into bloody conflict with military regimes in the 1970s.

Liberation Theology

As a political phenomenon, liberation theology incorporates an understanding of class conflict but does not adopt a revolutionary program of political transformation (Levine 1980, 116). As a religious doctrine, liberation theology invokes Old Testament themes of "captivity, exploitation, and oppression" to explain contemporary struggles of the poor against the "structural sin" of class domination (Levine 1980, 118). Liberation theology thus reconceptualized "sin" and "salvation" in ways which assumed a broader social meaning. Sin was understood to include the support of unjust social structures and exploitation of the poor (Gutiérrez 1973). Salvation, in turn, was understood to involve and even to require social action to liberate the oppressed poor. For many religious adherents in Latin America, liberation theology fostered a deepening of the political and religious commitment to activism (Levine 1980, 13).

The doctrine of liberation theology thus became part of the broader movement throughout Latin America in the 1970s to mobilize the poor and less powerful members of society for the purpose of liberating social change. In the wake of the Medellín conference, Latin American bishops found themselves armed with a new theology as well as a new form of ministry in the CEBs. Activism was further catalyzed at this time by an influx of foreign aid from the United States and Western Europe. These monies funded the study and implementation of grassroots organizing.

The reform-minded Church thus flourished in the 1970s not only with its new plan of action, but with the resources necessary to implement it (C. Smith 1991). The impact of liberation theology in Latin America, however, was not consistently felt. The varying political contexts throughout Latin America at this time fostered distinct political expressions of Church action. Likewise, many distinct voices existed within the national churches that opposed the progressive change and reacted strongly against liberation theology and base community action at every level of the institution.

The Church and the Military Dictatorships

The rise of the liberation theology movement in the 1970s and the strengthening of the Latin American Church at the grassroots level had the effect of politicizing a previously marginalized and subordinated sector of society: the peasantry (Harrison 1980, 7). The peasants were encouraged by the priests and nuns working in base communities to challenge the dominant social structures. In previous centuries these structures had been upheld by the Church as necessary sources of stability in society. The weight of this change in perspective was not only consequential in terms of theological development, but carried with it important political consequences as well. As a result of its activism, certain members of the Catholic Church found themselves in direct opposition to violent and repressive military governments (Berryman 1984). The priests and nuns who were killed in the midst of these political struggles number in the thousands. Consequently, international support diminished as Catholic social action came to be associated with the movements of militant revolutionary groups in Central America.

Although very few members of the clergy actually took arms and joined the struggles, the implication of this association for Church-State relations was profound (Harrison 1980, 7). One of the best known revolutionary Catholics was Father Camilo Torres. A Colombian priest and sociologist, Torres worked actively to promote social change and improvement of conditions for the poor. His activism, however, brought him into confrontation with his superiors and eventually led him to renounce his priesthood and to take up arms with the guerrilla Army of National Liberation in Colombia (C. Smith 1991, 16). Torres proclaimed that "the duty of every Catholic is to be a revolutionary, the duty of every revolutionary is to make the revolution" (Gerassi 1971, xiii). Torres was killed in 1966 in a skirmish between the guerrillas and the army in Colombia. His espousal of violence caused him to find little support from even the more progressive Catholic Church leaders. Nevertheless, Torres' revolutionary legacy lived on as an inspiration to activists who formed "Camilista groups" throughout the Andes (Levine 1980, 114).

The decades of the 1960s and 1970s thus witnessed a period of immense change in the Catholic Church. Challenged by their leaders to respond to the "signs of the times," Catholics were spurred into political activism for the cause of social justice. More than any other group at this time, the Catholic Church expressed and brought attention to the grave inequalities and repression in Latin American societies. As a consequence of this advocacy of human rights, the Church in many countries found itself at the margins of social and political power. It was in conflict with ruling political regimes that saw the subordination of human rights as a necessary element of national security, and with conservative elites which opposed the advocacy of rights for the poor (Harrison 1980, 7). By the 1970s, therefore, it was the peasants rather than the powerful elites who claimed the weight of moral righteousness in the eyes of the Catholic Church (B. Smith 1994, 10–11).

Division, Transition, and Transformation

The politicization and progressive shift in the teaching of the Catholic Church in Latin America were not embraced with unanimity throughout the institution. Many conservative leaders merely signed on to the official pronouncements of change out of deference to Rome, yet made no effort to implement them (B. Smith 1994, 11). Further, some conservative Catholic leaders not only refused to support liberation movements, but also presented no opposition to military dictatorships in the region.

The 1970s and 1980s thus witnessed strong division within the Church over the theological model of Catholicism in Latin America, brought on by a strengthening current of conservatism within the national churches. Internal divisions in the Catholic Church were often temporarily set aside, however, during the years of military crackdown upon grassroots Church members throughout the region. The earliest forms of repression were felt by Brazilian clerics at the hands of the military coup of 1964 and climaxed in the torture and death of thousands of Christian activists (Dussel 1992, 169). In fact, Brazil was the sight of the most active and politicized base communities among all of the Latin American churches; its progressive hierarchy assumed the most vocal stance in opposition to the government on behalf of the indigenous populations and of the poor (Adriance 1986).

In contrast to Brazil, the distinctly conservative Argentinean Church hierarchy waged no opposition to the military regime throughout the 1970s. In fact, the Argentine Catholic Church lent support to this regime coalition of military and landed aristocrats by publicly justifying the violent repression of guerrilla movements. Absolving these on the grounds of "the common good," the Church issued a statement after a 1981 national council delineated "legitimate" and "illegitimate" forms of repression. Catholic leaders offered no moral support to the resistance movements, which often included progressive members of the clergy (Dussel 1992, 169). This position of the Church hierarchy in Argentina thus dealt a significant blow to popular mobilization movements. As a result, they suffered harsh repression at the hands of the government throughout the 1970s.

A distinct sector of the Church, however, led a "Justice and Peace" movement. It supported secular mobilizations such as the "Mothers of the Plaza de Mayo," whose peaceful vigils on behalf of the "disappeared" led to further acts of violence against priests and nuns working at the base of society. In Chile, the 1973 coup by General Augusto Pinochet ushered in a period of violent repression. The Catholic Church remained the only institutional opposition to it in the country. In each nation throughout the region, the divisions in the Church as well as the Church-State conflicts played out quite differently, and varied with the unique structures and conflicts of each society.

The "triumph of democracy" in the 1980s has left the Catholic Church in an ambiguous position. Without its unified external enemy, internal divisions and a conservative reaction from within the institution have flourished. The conservative backlash has aimed to remove the Church from the overtly political role in which some practitioners of the theology of liberation had placed it in the 1970s. The 1979 bishops' meeting at Puebla provided a forum for the Vatican and prominent conservative bishops in Peru to express their criticisms of liberation theology and to gather momentum for the reactionary current within the Church. In 1985, prominent liberation theologian Leonardo Boff of Brazil was censored by the Church and silenced for one year. Within this conservative retrenchment in the 1980s, notions of political transformation were removed from the discourse of the Catholic Church. Accordingly, conservative Catholics aimed to establish the social mission of the Church through acts of charity and self-help projects, rather than through political or protest-oriented activity.

Furthermore, the primacy of the Catholic Church as the predominant religious voice in Latin America has been challenged in recent decades by the growth of pentacostalism and other Protestant churches. By the mid 1980s, scholars estimated the size of non-Catholic Christianity in Latin America to have grown to more than ten percent of the population, or at least forty million people (Stoll 1990, 6). In Central America, El Salvador and Guatemala have witnessed the strongest growth in Protestant religions, while in South America, Brazil and Chile report up to a quarter of their populations as Protestant (Stoll 1990, 8). This growth has been partly fueled by waves of evangelical missions from North America. Indeed, they have been credited for converting millions of "born again" since the 1960s. The success of evangelical Protestantism, characterized by its emphasis on biblical authority and salvation, has been attributed to a great variety of other factors as well. These include dissatisfaction with the Catholic emphasis upon hierarchy; the structure and rigidity of Catholic ceremonies centering around the role of the priest; and evangelical Protestantism's personal and spiritual emphasis on strict moral codes of behavior (C. Smith 1994; Stoll 1990, 4–10; Burdick 1993; Cleary and Stewart-Gambino 1997; Martin 1990). Thus, in a region that was long dominated by an elite political-religious hierarchy, the religious landscape has become increasingly pluralistic and dynamic.

Conclusion

The Roman Catholic Church in Latin America has experienced a long, 500-year history, through which it has evolved from a position of privilege to a posture of protest. More recently it has adopted an increasingly disengaged political stance.

Now facing a situation of greater religious pluralism and competition, internal organizational disagreements, and the exhaustion of previously popular religious models of socio-political engagement, the Church today faces the difficult task of deciding how best to position itself to accomplish its mission of human redemption and social influence.

References

Adriance, Madeleine. 1986. *Option for the Poor*. Kansas City: Sheed & Ward.

Berryman, Phillip. 1994. *Stubborn Hope*. Maryknoll, NY: Orbis Books.

———. 1984. *The Religious Roots of Rebellion*. Maryknoll, NY: Orbis Books.

Burdick, John. 1993. *Looking for God in Brazil*. Berkeley: University of California Press.

Cleary, Edward, and Hannah Stewart-Gambino. 1997. *Power, Politics, and Pentecostals in Latin America*. Boulder: Westview.

Dussel, Enrique ed. 1992. *The Church in Latin America: 1492–1992*. Maryknoll, NY: Orbis Books.

Gerassi, John. 1971. *Revolutionary Priest*. New York: Random House.

Gutiérrez, Gustavo. 1973. *A Theology of Liberation*. Maryknoll: Orbis Books.

———. 1993. *Las Casas*. Maryknoll, NY: Orbis Books.

Harrison, John. 1980. Preface to *Churches and Politics in Latin America*, edited by Daniel Levine. London: Sage.

Keen, Benjamin, and Mark Wasserman. 1988. *A History of Latin America*. Boston: Houghton Mifflin.

Levine, Daniel. 1980. *Churches and Politics in Latin America*. London: Sage.

Lockhart, James, and Stuart Schwartz. 1983. *Early Latin America*. Cambridge, UK: Cambridge University Press.

Martin, David. 1990. *Tongues of Fire: The Explosion of Protestantism in Latin America*. Cambridge, UK.: Blackwell.

Parker, Cristián. 1996. *Popular Religion and Modernization in Latin America*. Maryknoll, NY: Orbis Books.

Smith, Brian. 1994. Religion and Social Change. In *The Roman Catholic Church in Latin America*, edited by Jorge Domínguez. New York: Garland.

———. 1982. *The Church and Politics in Chile*. Princeton: Princeton University Press.

Smith, Christian. 1991. *The Emergence of Liberation Theology*. Chicago: University of Chicago Press.

———. 1994. "The Spirit and Democracy: Base Communities, Protestantism, and Democratization in Latin America," *Sociology of Religion*. 55 (summer): 119–43.

Stewart-Gambino, Hannah. 1992. *The Church and Politics in the Chilean Countryside*. Boulder: Westview Press.

Stoll, David. 1990. *Is Latin America Turning Protestant?* Berkeley: University of California Press.

POLITICS

AND

ECONOMICS

War in Latin America
The Peaceful Continent?

Miguel Angel Centeno

The military plays an important role in our images of Latin America. Yet, the dogs of war have rarely barked on the continent.[1] Since independence in the early nineteenth century, Latin America has been relatively free of major international conflict. In the twentieth century, the record is truly remarkable, especially in light of the experience of other regions of the world. Latin America has experienced low levels of militarization and the organization and mobilization of human and material resources for potential use in warfare. The important point is not that Latin Americans have not fought each other but that they have generally not attempted to organize their societies with such a goal in mind. This chapter presents a summary of that military conflict that has occurred in Latin America (both international and domestic) and ends with a discussion of the possible reasons for the relative peace of the continent.

International Wars

When compared with other parts of the world, Latin America appears as a historically unique case of peaceful international relations. On a per capita basis, the nations of Europe and North America, for example, have had over 86 times the number of men in their armed forces, have killed proportionally 123 times as many people, and at nearly 40 times the rate per month at war. Even Africa, which had a much shorter period of independence, has witnessed more international conflicts.

If we look at the individual wars we note that they are geographically and historically concentrated. The vast number and by far the most significant occurred in the nineteenth century. Following the Wars of Independence of 1810–1825, these wars were largely "land grabs" by more powerful neighbors seeking to increase their access to resources. None of the international wars experienced by Latin America have featured an ideological, nationalistic, or ethnic hatred so much a part of the history of other parts of the globe. The wars have also tended to be concentrated in two regions: the La Plata basin shared by Brazil, Paraguay, Uruguay, and Argentina and the mid-Pacific littoral where Bolivia, Peru, and Chile meet. Two other wars deserve mention: the U.S. war against Mexico of 1846 and the Chaco War between Paraguay and Bolivia in 1932. Other disputes have flared from time to time (the most prominent being between Peru and Ecuador), but these have not involved large numbers of men or lengthy periods of conflict (Table 1).

Table 1
Major International Wars

War	Countries	Year
Independence	All	1810
La Plata	Argentina, Brazil, Uruguay	1825
War of La Plata	Argentina, Brazil, Uruguay	1836
Chile-Bolivia War	Bolivia, Chile, Peru	1836
Guerra Grande	Argentina, Brazil, Uruguay	1838
Mexican-American War	Mexico	1846
La Plata War	Argentina, Brazil, Uruguay	1851
Franco-Mexican War	Mexico	1862
Triple Alliance	Argentina, Brazil, Paraguay, Uruguay	1864
Peruvian-Spanish War	Bolivia, Chile, Peru	1865
Ten Years War	Cuba	1868
Pacific Latin American War	Bolivia, Chile, Peru	1879
Central American	Guatemala, El Salvador	1885
Independence	Cuba	1895
Secession of Panama	Colombia	1898
Central American	Guatemala, Honduras	1906
Central American	Nicaragua.,	1907
World War I	Brazil	1914
Chaco War	Bolivia, Paraguay	1932
World War II	Brazil	1939
Border Dispute	Peru, Ecuador	1941
U.S. intervention	Dominican Republic	1965
Football	El Salvador, Honduras	1969
Angola/Ethiopia	Cuba	1975
Ecuador/Peru Border Dispute	Ecuador, Peru	1981
Falklands War	Argentina	1982
Ecuador/Peru Border Dispute	Ecuador, Peru	1995

Source: G. D. Kaye et al., Major Armed Conflict, 1985; J. D. Singer and M. Small, *A Call to Arms*, 1982; Leslie Bethell, ed., *Cambridge History of Latin America.*

The Wars of Independence

The most significant international wars in Latin American history occurred at practically the very birth of the new states.[2] The Wars of Independence originated not in internal conditions of the colonies (although tensions and resentments existed), but in events in Europe. This consideration is important since the absence of a domestic or internal logic behind the wars helps to explain the almost universal political chaos that followed them.

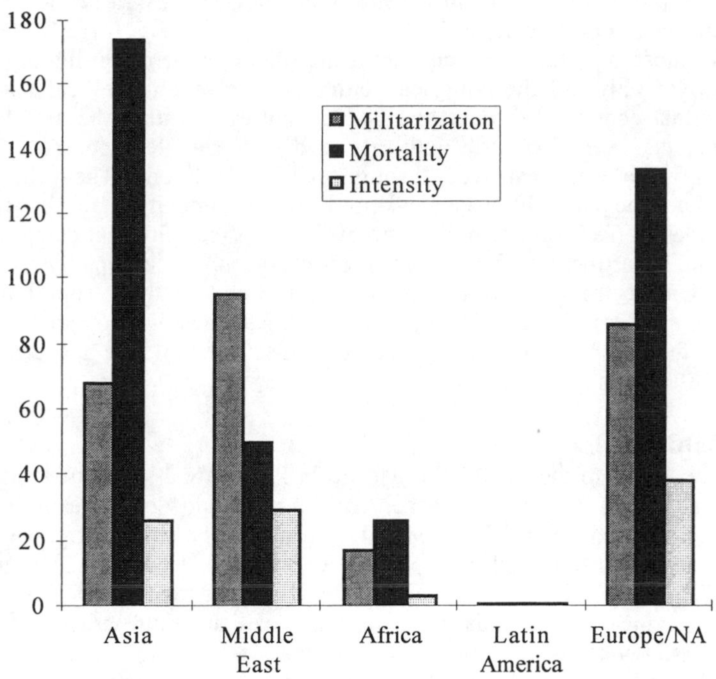

Figure 1
International Wars 1816–1980

The confusion produced by the Napoleonic invasions of Spain in 1808 provided the spark and the opportunity for Latin American independence. By 1810, colonial juntas had been declared in Caracas and Buenos Aires, and it was at that same time that Miguel Hidalgo was leading Mexican peasants against the gauchupines (Mexicans of Spanish descent). But, regional animosities, racial fears, and plain perceptions of interest served to divide the colonial population, many of whom sided with the Spanish peninsulares. By mid-decade, the loyalists had reestablished their control. Only Argentina remained autonomous, formally declaring its independence in 1816.

José de San Martín and Simón Bolívar led the rebellion's comeback. San Martín crossed the Andes from Argentina and conquered Chile in 1817–1818. Beginning in 1818, Bolívar consolidated his rule over what would become Colombia and Venezuela. The two armies cooperated in the final conquest of Peru, culminating in the defeat of the Spaniards in Ayacucho on December 9, 1824. In the north, Mexico's decade of rebellion ended with the victory of the ex-loyalist general Iturbide and his subsequent declaration of independence in

1821. Brazil avoided much of the war, but successfully declared its independence from Portugal in 1822.

The most important consequence of the wars was the fracturing of political power. Not only did the American empire dissolve into several nations (a process that continued through the 1820s), but even within the new borders, governments exercised little authority and had even less control. Civilian administration was destroyed throughout the continent. The other major institution, the Church, was weakened by its opposition to the wars of independence. The wars also did a great deal of sheer physical damage to the economic infrastructure of the Latin American economy, especially the mining sector. Unlike the case of Europe where the end of the Napoleonic wars provided a political base for 100 years of political consolidation and economic growth, the independence struggles left a legacy of violence and destruction which still haunts Latin America.

The Battle for La Plata

From the 1820s to the 1850s, the Rio de la Plata saw a series of struggles to determine which country would control the river and dominate the regional economy.[3] During much of this period, Brazil was the strongest player, either occupying the eastern bank of the old Vice-Royalty of La Plata (Uruguay) or controlling the politics of that country after its independence. War between the United Provinces of Rio de la Plata and the Brazilian empire broke out in 1825 and was only ended with British intervention and the creation of an independent Uruguay as a buffer between the two potentially hostile powers.

The struggle for the control of both banks of the Plata continued for most of the next thirty years and included wars between almost all the relevant actors and a variety of foreign interventions. At least in the case of Argentina, the war accelerated the disintegration of central authority while simultaneously beginning the long-term financial dependence on British capital. In Brazil, however, the wars arguably helped consolidate centralized rule. The end of this conflict sealed the entente between Argentina and Brazil, which is perhaps one of the most remarkable aspects of intra-regional relations in Latin America. Despite the continuing tensions between the two most obvious potential super powers, they have not fought a war against each other since 1850.

The War of the Triple Alliance

The origins of this war may be traced to a variety of sources: the colonial legacy, international competition for trade, geopolitical struggles for control over the La Plata River system, long-standing Brazilian-Argentinean intervention in Uruguayan politics, British support for the creation of a new economic system in the Southern Cone, domestic instability in both Argentina and Uruguay, and the personal dementia of the Paraguayan leader Francisco Solano López.[4]

By the 1860s, the weak Uruguayan state was helpless to prevent an almost Hobbesian chaos of civil war and caudillismo. The possible entry of Paraguay into the geopolitical mix was not welcomed by either Brazil or Argentina. The Brazilian empire had an interest in maintaining Uruguay and Paraguay pliant and weak in order to assure free passage on the Paraguay River to the increasingly important province of Mato Grosso. Argentina saw the continued existence of Paraguay (a breakaway province from the former Vice-Royalty of La Plata) as an incentive for separatist caudillos.

The singular history of Paraguay made it a worthy adversary. From 1814 to 1840, it was controlled by the dictator Dr. José Francia. He was succeeded by Carlos Antonio López, and after 1862, his son Francisco Solano López. By the 1860s Paraguay had developed an independent manufacturing capacity in small arms and ship repair. Using all the resources available to a state monopolizing the country's economy, López II raised an army of 28,000 with which he sought to finish the long-standing quarrels with his neighbors and create a new South American Empire. He believed that in conjunction with his internal allies in both Uruguay and Argentina, and with the likely Argentinean opposition to shedding blood on behalf of the slave monarchy in Brazil, the alliance between the two regional giants would not survive a single Paraguayan victory.

Unfortunately for López, he made it politically easy for both adversaries by invading the Mato Grosso in 1864 and Corrientes province in 1865. Despite the imbalance of resources, Paraguay's armed forces were arguably the best (if not the largest or best equipped) in the region. Notwithstanding the initial success of the Paraguayans, however, they could not resist the combined efforts of Brazil, Argentina, and a Colorado-led Uruguay. Lacking support from potential allies such as Bolivia and Chile, Paraguay soon faced a completely defensive struggle. López increasingly committed the entire Paraguayan society to the defense of the Republic, which allowed for the continuation of the War even after disastrous military defeats in 1866. The war did not end until López was killed in 1870 after the loss of a still disputed (but definitely large) percentage of the population of the country.

Wars of the Peruvian-Bolivian. Confederation of the Pacific

Given their very close economic and administrative links during the colonial era, the early separation of Bolivia and Peru was in many ways a political fiction.[5] In part because of their historic and economic connection and in part because of the rising strength of the Chilean state, the Bolivian president General Andres Santa Cruz sought to establish closer connections between two halves of the old Vice-Royalty of Lima. In alliance with some Peruvian caudillos, he invaded Peru in 1835, and in October 1836 he declared the Peruvian-Bolivian Confederation. This union did have some popular support, but the division of Peru into two states and the selection of Lima as the capital alienated elites in both countries. More importantly, the union threatened the geopolitical position of Chile and Argentina. Both countries viewed a strong Peru as a challenge to their predominance. The first declared war in December 1836, the latter in May 1837. Despite some early failures, the Chilean army, in alliance with Peruvian forces opposed to the union, were able to defeat Santa Cruz in the Battle of Yungay in January 1839, leading to the dissolution of the Confederation.

Chile's victory over Peru and Bolivia in the 1830s established its reputation as the regional Prussia and further solidified the political institutionalization begun under Diego Portales. For Peru and Bolivia, defeat appears to have accelerated the process of economic and political fragmentation begun with independence. (Peru did have one successful military adventure in the nineteenth century. Following the Spanish invasion of the Chincha Islands, Peru defeated the Spaniards in the war of 1864–1886.)

Beginning in 1840 various international companies began the exploration of the Bolivian coast in order to make use of the guano and nitrate deposits there. The exploitation of silver beginning in 1870 led to an economic boom. During this decade Chile and Bolivia appeared to resolve a series of quarrels by increasing the influence of the former in the disputed region. But disagreements over taxes and the nationalization of Chilean mines in the Peruvian desert in 1875 maintained the tension. Following some diplomatic efforts to resolve a new set of crises, Chile declared war in April 1879. Given a Peruvian-Bolivian alliance, this involved Chile in a war with both northern neighbors. The war quickly became a contest for plunder.

None of the countries was prepared for war, although Chile had a significant advantage in naval forces. More importantly, the Chilean state retained its institutional solidity while both Peru and Bolivia suffered from internal divisions. Chile occupied the Bolivian littoral, then Tarapaca in 1879, Tacma and Arica and most of northern coast in 1880. By this stage the Chilean army had increased significantly, with an invasion force of 12,000 men. International pressure from both the U.S. and European powers forced the two sides into negotiation, but the Chileans sought a complete victory. In 1881, with an army numbering 26,000 men, the Chileans entered Lima. They did not leave until 1884, extracting the province of Tarapaca forever and the provinces of Tacna and Arica until 1929. Chile also took the entire Bolivian coast (Atacama).

The victory helped determine the future institutionalization of both the Chilean and Peruvian militaries, as well as partially defining the development options of the three countries. Chile enjoyed an economic boom as well as unprecedented patriotic euphoria, both of which helped dissolve the gloom of the 1870s. Despite the relative shortness of the war, Peru suffered severe casualties and the destruction of much of the coastal infrastructure. The war may also be seen as the best example of the military formation of a new national identity, as the Peruvian and Bolivian memory of their defeat continues to play a large role in their respective nationalisms. The defeat of Bolivia deprived it of a great part of its wealth and left it contained within the altiplano (in which Chile had no interest). The war did help decrease the political influence of the military and helped consolidate the rule of a civilian oligarchy dominated by mining interests.

The War of the Chaco

In many ways this was the most tragic of all the international conflicts within Latin America because it involved two extremely poor and autocratic societies in which the military already played important roles, Paraguay and Bolivia.[6] The war arguably originated in earlier defeats of the two participants. For Bolivia, the Chaco promised access to the sea (lost to Chile) through the Paraguay River. For Paraguay, control of the Chaco served to ameliorate the pain of the López catastrophe. Rumors and hopes of natural wealth only served to heighten the competition.

The two countries had been in a low intensity conflict over the region since the early twentieth century. Clashes in 1928 were followed by all-out war in 1932. At first, the Bolivians appeared to lead with their early assault on Ft. López, but under the leadership of José Felix Estigarribia, Paraguay united behind the war effort, with the army growing to over twenty times its peacetime strength. Over the next three years, the armies fought in some of the most inhospitable terrain in the world. By 1935, the Bolivian army had collapsed and Paraguay was awarded the disputed territory.

Both victory and defeat led to some attempts at reform, culminating in the 1952 revolution in Bolivia and army-led regimes in Paraguay.

The Mexican-American War

In terms of geography and global historical impact, this was no doubt the most important of the wars fought by a Latin American country.[7] To a large extent, the war may have been unavoidable given the economic and ideological pressure of U.S. expansion as well as the particular political needs of the slave states. While it is undeniable that Mexico could not have been worse served than by the leadership of General Santa Ana, it is difficult to imagine any other outcome given the very different military and political capacities of the two states.

The origins of the war may be partly traced to the political instability of post-independence Mexico, particularly after 1827. This instability (and the aborted Spanish invasion of 1829) paved the way for the rise to power of General Antonio Santa Ana. His attempted imposition of greater centralized control from Mexico City led to revolt in the northern province of Texas. Despite his opening bravado and early victory in San Antonio, Santa Ana was unable to defeat the rebellion. Following his capture by the rebels, he had to recognize the independence of the new Texan Republic. The southern province of Yucatan also tried to escape increased centralized control (and also obtain more effective military support for its system of caste slavery) later in the decade, but was unable to secure its independence.

Santa Ana remained a key player in the increasingly chaotic Mexican political scene in the early 1840s, often relying on military bombast and threats to declare war on the United States should it attempt to annex the Texan Republic (whose independence Mexico had yet to recognize). Despite European efforts to mediate the dispute, the momentum of manifest destiny and Southern slavery politics led to the American annexation of the province in February 1845. Despite early efforts to avoid a war, public opinion and military pride led to Mexican refusal to accept annexation.

Three months after the beginning of hostilities in April of 1846, the U.S. army occupied most of northern Mexico. In part because of continuing instability requiring the participation of the army in civil unrest in Mexico City, the U.S. was able to land in Veracruz in March 1847. Proving that war does not necessarily unite, much of the Mexican military effort was expended on domestic struggles. When the Mexican government was able to produce an army to fight the U.S. invaders, it was largely defeated by the absence of logistical support. By September 1847 U.S. troops were overcoming the last Mexican resisters in Chapultepec Castle (the famed "Halls of Montezuma" of the U.S. Marines).

The Treaty of Guadalupe Hidalgo left Mexico without half of its territory. It may have also contributed to the rise of the new Liberal party, which under Benito Juarez would begin the construction of contemporary Mexico. For the U.S., the war brought glory and heartache. The acquisition of so many resources and the transcontinental expansion provided the basis for future U.S. power. The control over vast territories also intensified the competition between the Southern and Northern views on the union.

Civil Wars

A very different record of violence marks the domestic history of Latin America.[8] The gulf between Latin America and other regions is much less pronounced, although the level of violence (with some prominent exceptions) has tended to be lower than in other parts of the globe (Figure 2). The number of conflicts and the complexity of their historical and social origins make it impossible to give any summary description here. We may distinguish four general types of civil wars that students of Latin America need to consider.

The first type of conflict dominated the nineteenth century and was largely about defining who would govern and how they would do so. Many of the conflicts involved provinces rebelling against control by the capital. The classic example of these is Argentina, where a variety of provincial alliances sought to limit the power of Buenos Aires. Only in the 1870s can we begin speaking of Argentina as a united nation.[9] During the same period, Mexico saw unrelenting conflict between political factions, each of whom sought to control the capital. Peru and Colombia represent even more chaotic scenarios while Brazil and Chile may be seen as exceptions of stability.

A second form of civil conflict may be called "fratricidal." While these struggles often reflect underlying social and economic conditions and inequalities, they appear to take a life of their own, generating unprecedented levels of violence. Thus, competition between political parties and their adherents becomes more important than the original points of dispute. "La Violencia" of Colombia in the late 1940s and early 1950s is the prototypical example, as might also be the more recent wars in Central America.[10]

A third type may be called "race/ethnic wars." The most important of these occurred before independence, during which the vast majority of the pre-Colombian population was either killed or died from disease and overwork. In the eighteenth and nineteenth centuries, rebellions in Peru and Mexico sought to win back the region from the European population.[11] The genocide of the Indians continued as well, as frontier wars culminated with the expulsion, killing, or subjugation of native populations in Chile, Argentina, and Mexico. More recently, the civil war in Guatemala has at times taken on characteristics of a race war as the government identified Indians as automatic enemy sympathizers. The rebellion in Chiapas and the continuing insurgency in Peru indicate that this war will continue well into the next century.

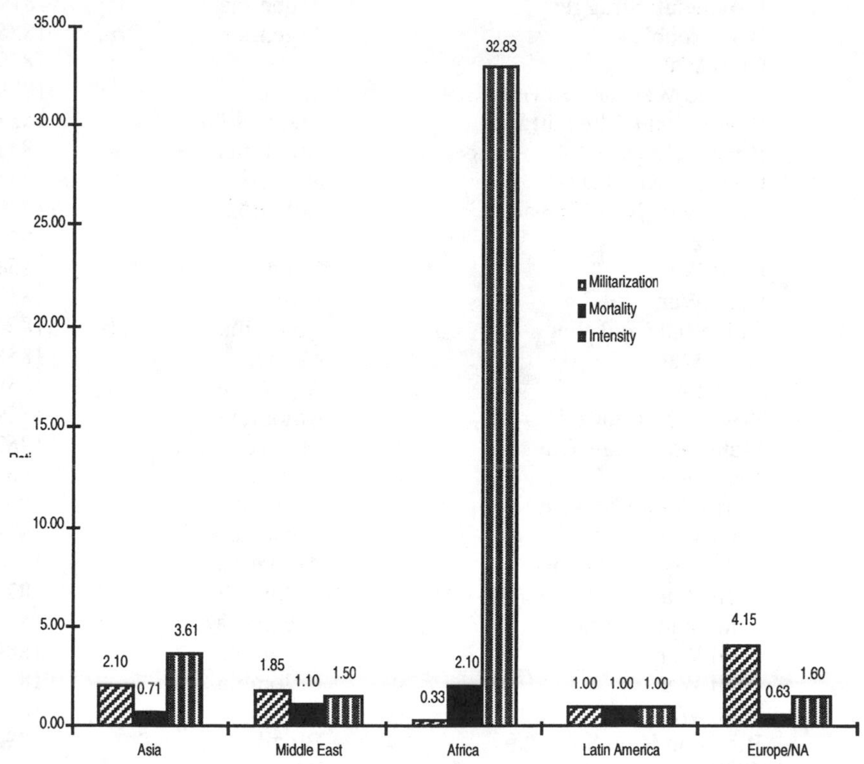

Figure 2
Civil Wars
Source: Singer and Small, *Wages of War.*

A final type of civil war is that generated by revolution. These conflicts may combine aspects of the first three with an organized effort to remake the social and economic rules of the respective countries. These wars are not so much over territory, but over the distribution of a social and economic pie. As a military struggle, the Mexican revolution deserves pride of place. In terms of cultural impact, however, the Cuban revolution of the 1950s (despite its military marginality) may be the most important case.[12]

Table 2
Major Civil Wars

War	Country	Year Started
Provincial Struggle	Argentina	1819
BA Troubles	Argentina	1828
Civil War	Chile	1829
Mexico Wars and Revolts	Mexico	1829
Revolution of the Farrapos	Brazil	1831
Buenos Aires	Argentina	1833
Conflict over Texas	Mexico	1835
Civil War (New Granada)	Colombia	1839
La Paz	Peru	1841
Civil War	Chile	1851
Civil War	Peru	1853
Colombia Civil War	Colombia	1854
Civil War	Mexico	1858
La Plata	Argentina	1859
War of the Cauca	Colombia	1859
Franco-Mexican War	Mexico	1862
Civil War	Ecuador	1863
North West Province	Argentina	1863
Civil War	Venezuela	1868
Mitre Revolt/ Pampas	Argentina	1874
Civil War	Colombia	1876
Patagonia Massacre	Argentina	1879
Civil War	Argentina	1880
Civil War	Colombia	1884
Civil War	Chile	1891
Rio Grande do Sul	Brazil	1892
Civil War	Peru	1894
Civil War/ Bahia Revolt	Brazil	1896
Colombia	Colombia	1899
Civil War	Uruguay	1904
Mexico Revolution	Mexico	1910
Civil War	Paraguay	1911
Civil War	Honduras	1924
Cristero	Mexico	1926
Civil War	Nicaragua	1928
Civil War	El Salvador	1932
Civil War	Costa Rica	1948
Civil War	Colombia	1948
Revolution	Bolivia	1952
Civil War	Guatemala	1954

War	Country	Year Started
Revolution	Cuba	1959
Argentina Dirty War	Argentina	1976
Sandinista Revolution	Nicaragua	1978
Civil War	Colombia	1978
Civil War	El Salvador	1979
Sendero Luminoso	Peru	1980

Source: G. D. Kaye et al., *Major Armed Conflict*, 1985; J. D. Singer and M. Small, *A Call to Arms*, 1982; Leslie Bethell, ed., *Cambridge History of Latin America.*

Why the Peace?

To explain peace we have to look for the reasons for war.[13] We may begin by distinguishing between short- and long-term developments or immediate versus general causes. Analyses of the former include those that emphasize diplomatic history, the process of negotiation, and different strategic scenarios. A variant of these, for example, would include theories of balance of power. These models appear to have limited value, however, in explaining the long period of peace that has prevailed on the continent. That is, unless we are prepared to accept exceptional diplomatic skill, and almost omniscient strategizing on the part of all the relevant actors, as well as an enviable structural stability in the balance of forces, none of these explanations can account for the generalized absence of war on the continent.

An important subtype of such explanations, which has enjoyed considerable popularity in Latin America and therefore cannot be ignored, is the elite or class conspiracy. According to this view, the outbreak of war can be traced to the machinations of capitalist elites in one or another of the countries involved, or in an imperial power that stands to benefit from such a struggle. As relevant as these concerns may be for exploring the outbreak of individual wars, it is difficult to imagine how such an interpretation could be applied to 100 years of relative peace. A century-long continental conspiracy of peace would require that Latin American elites exhibit a class-wide rationality for which there is little evidence.

We can therefore turn to more general or systemic explanations. Why is it that some nations appear to be more and others appear less prone to warlike behavior? Despite a great deal of research effort, there is little evidence for any consistent structural correlation between regime-type or socio-economic variables and war. One exception is the apparent link between democratic and liberal regimes and more peaceful behavior. Yet, Latin America as a whole would tend to contradict such a perspective, given that militaristic, authoritarian, and conservative countries have been so successful at avoiding conflict with each other.

Some have emphasized a cultural predisposition to war. Thus, particular societies, regions, and/or epochs might be culturally predisposed to interstate conflict. As in many of the other generalizing theories of war, this view can easily degenerate into tautology as measures of bellicosity may be products of war itself. Moreover, it is difficult to imagine a continent where cultural predispositions to violence have been more emphasized than in Latin America. While we should always be careful with culturally deterministic arguments, it is undeniable that the general political culture in Latin America is not peaceful. Certainly, following this logic it would be difficult to link the continental peace to a regional cultural predilection.

A related explanation might rely on the relatively homogeneous culture of the continent. Without the struggles between different elite cultures, there was no subsequent conflict between political claims over territory. Yet, similar cultures did not make Renaissance Italy or seventeenth-century Germany particularly peaceful. Moreover, as we have seen recently in the Balkans and in East Africa, competing political institutions can forge inimical heterogeneity out of the most apparently uniform populations.

So, how do we explain the particular pattern in Latin America? First, geography is a factor. Large-scale military operations can only be conducted under certain physical conditions. In Latin America, much of the interstate violence has been concentrated in the La Plata River system and the South-Central Pacific Coast, both of which are much more hospitable to military logistics than the Andes or the Amazon. It is also possible that international intraclass conflict did not occur because the region was large enough to allow the creation of sufficient buffer zones. That is, international conflict was precluded because competing elites never came into contact with each other. It was precisely in those areas of concentration of resources or potential for wealth (e.g., La Plata, or the Andean deserts) where we see the greatest conflict.

Second, we cannot ignore the role of external powers, which may have guaranteed borders and the status quo, thereby removing many of the immediate stimuli of conflict. The Latin American peace may be, thus, the ultimate expression of dependencia. The presence of the European powers prevented a series of military events that may have created a very different geopolitical balance. We should be careful, however, with resorting to explanations that might deny Latin American societies any control over their own fate. We might even reverse the causal order and suggest that it was the absence of war which in turn produced a weak state, and which in turn made intervention possible; since Latin America was unable to create an empire from within, it had to suffer one from without.

Third, the absence of war over time creates conditions in which countries can avoid the type of behavior (e.g., arms races) that is correlated with conflict. The long peace of the twentieth century may thus be explained by the absence of revanchist myths or long-standing cultures venerating interstate conflict. That is, Latin America does not possess the kind of cross-border hatreds and animosities that still dominate so much of international relations elsewhere.

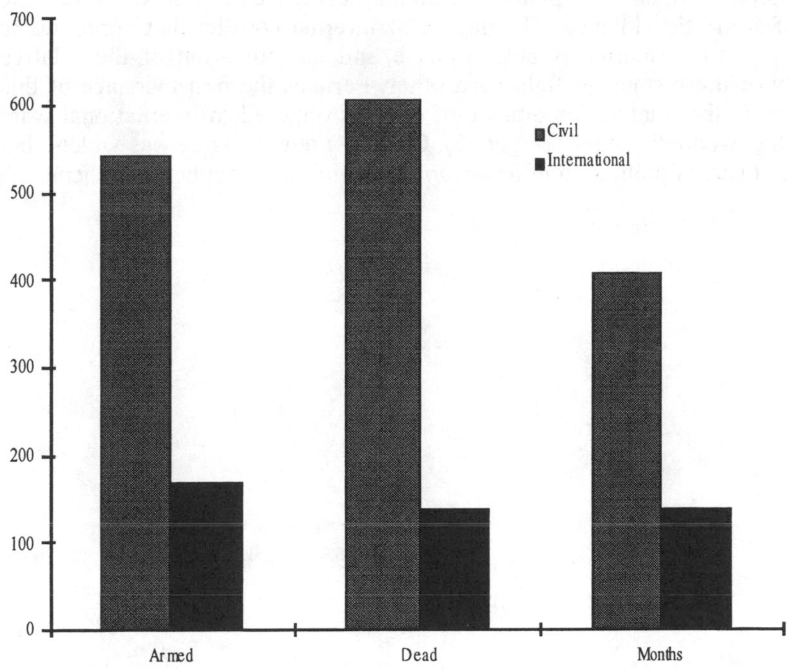

Figure 3
Latin America in the 20th Century
Source: J. D. Singer and M. Small, *Wages of War*, 1982.

Fourth, Latin America lacked a coherent elite able to impose its will and organize the capacities of the state toward war. No faction was able to establish a strong enough hegemony so as to prioritize national collective interests. In the absence of that hegemony, the monopoly over the means of violence did not coalesce around any central actor, and subordinate classes were never totally vanquished. Simply put, each nation's military remained too busy killing its own peasants to bother with someone else's. (Conversely, the absence of wars may have also retarded national integration.)

Fifth, we should question the assumption that all states are capable of war. There is a strong correlation between political and economic power, and bellicose behavior. War requires basic organizational competence and access to resources that only certain states have. From this point of view, Latin America has been peaceful because the states in the region never developed the political capacity to have prolonged wars. No states, no wars.

Finally, if we are to explain the external peace, we need only to recall the level of domestic violence. The degree of internal conflict that continues to dominate Latin America is both a cause and an indication of the relative inability of these states to fight each other. Perhaps the best evidence of this condition is the relative importance of civil as opposed to international wars during the twentieth century (Figure 3). Clearly, Latin America was violent, but the largest part of political conflict occurred within states, not between them.

Notes

1. For more details see Miguel Angel Centeno, *A Rumor of Peace: Latin America in War and Peace* (University Park: Penn State University Press, forthcoming).

2. The best single history volume is John Lynch, *The Spanish-American Revolutions*, 1808–1826, 2nd ed. (New York: Norton, 1986).

3. A good start on this topic is Tulio Halperin Donghi, *The Aftermath of Revolution in Latin America* (New York: Harper Torchbooks, 1975). For the Brazilian side see Ron Seckinger, *The Brazilian Monarchy and the South American Republics, 1822–1831* (Baton Rouge: Louisiana State University Press, 1984).

4. See John Hoyt Williams, *The Rise and Fall of the Paraguayan Republic, 1800–1870* (Austin: Institute of Latin American Studies, University of Texas, 1979).

5. See William F. Sater, *Chile and the War of the Pacific* (Lincoln: University of Nebraska Press, 1986). For a view of the internal situation in Peru see Florencia Mallon, *Peasant and Nation: The Making of Postcolonial Mexico and Peru* (Berkeley: University of California Press, 1994).

6. There are practically no sources on the Chaco War available in English. Refer to H. S. Klein, *Bolivia: The Evolution of a Multi-Ethnic Society* (New York: Oxford University Press, 1982). On Paraguay see H. G. Warren, *Paraguay: An Informal History* (Norman: Oklahoma University Press, 1949).

7. See Gene M. Brack, *Mexico Views Manifest Destiny, 1821–1846.* (Albuquerque: University of New Mexico Press, 1975); John H. Schroeder. *Mr. Polk's War: American Opposition and Dissent, 1846–1848* (Madison: University of Wisconsin Press, 1973).

8. The best background information may be found in Tulio Halperín Donghi, *The Contemporary History of Latin America*, 13th ed. (Durham: Duke University Press, 1993). See also David Bushnell and Neill Macaulay, *The Emergence of Latin America in the Nineteenth Century*, 2nd ed. (New York: Oxford University Press, 1994).

9. See David Rock, *Argentina 1516–1982* (Berkeley: University of California Press, 1985).

10. See Charles Berquist et al., eds., *Violence in Colombia* (Wilmington, Del.: Academic Press, 1992).

11. See Nelson Reed, *The Caste War of Yucatan* (Stanford: Stanford University Press, 1964).

12. For Mexico see Alan Knight, *The Mexican Revolution* (New York: Cambridge University Press, 1986). For Cuba see Hugh Thomas, *Cuba or the Pursuit of Freedom* (New York: Harper & Row, 1971).

13. See Michael Howard, *The Causes of War* (Cambridge, Mass: Harvard University Press, 1984). John Keegan, *A History of Warfare* (London: Hutchinson, 1993); Charles Tilly, *Coercion, Capital, and European States, AD 990–1992* (Cambridge, Mass.: Blackwell, 1992).

Development and Dependency in Latin America

Satya R. Pattnayak

Development became a top priority in most nations after World War II. In Latin America, however, the surge toward development based on industrialization began in the 1930s, much earlier than in other regions, such as most of Asia and Africa. It is important to distinguish between economic growth and overall social development at this stage. By economic growth, we may refer primarily to aggregate growth indices in the national economy or in any specific sector within. Overall social development can be defined in terms of progress in the areas of income distribution, life expectancy, educational attainment, health standards, and so forth; all are indicators of a general improvement in the welfare of the majority of inhabitants in a nation.

Historical Background

Ever since the discovery of Latin America, economic development in the region has been largely determined by forces located outside the region. First, it materialized in the form of the Spanish and Portuguese colonization that resulted in the exploitation of the natural resources abundantly available in the virgin lands. Subsequently, in the years following political independence in the early nineteenth century, the centers of exploitation shifted from Iberia to Western Europe and the United States. In all the recorded years of modern Latin American economic and social history, the primary natural resource sector had played a prominent role in the region's development.

Since the early sixteenth century, when the colonization of the region was begun by Spain and Portugal, until the early twentieth century, the bulk of the population was engaged in the primary sector, earning its livelihood from farming, mining, forestry, and fishing.[1] This sector, much of whose products were always destined for exports, had been the chief source of dynamism and growth in every Latin American country until the Great Depression of the 1930s. Many of the products for exports from this sector generally consisted of raw materials, such as copper, oil, gold, tin, iron ore, and agricultural products such us coffee, cocoa, and sugar. Not all of these products featured in the region's exports at the same time. In the course of the last several centuries, a variety of products had at different points in time dominated the region's trade. The changes in the location and nature of economic activity had taken place over a period of time as one product was displaced by another without affecting the position of the sector as the principal source of employment, income, and trade.[2]

The Role of Foreign Investment

In economies oriented toward external markets, foreign investment has historically played a very important role. This was true of Latin America as well. When foreign investment penetrated into Latin America from Europe in the early years of colonization, the motive was precisely to extract precious raw metals for export. The hunt for precious metals finally ended and farming became a primary occupation when they were no longer found in the region. Throughout Latin America, the search for precious metals was the principal motive for exploration and settlement. The distribution of population reflected the success of that search in different areas. The primary centers constituted virtually the only market for the output of other sectors and were mainly responsible for the diversification and development of the economy. Gradually, the exploration of precious metals turned to mining and the development of mining required food production, cattle breeding, and ranching in the surrounding areas.[3]

Now, you get the picture. A country's economy depended on the one or two major exports, which in turn depended on the international demand structure at the time. This point will be discussed later in the chapter when we turn to the theories of dependency.

The hunt for raw materials of different kinds expanded as the Industrial Revolution swept across the European continent. A worldwide search for cheap raw materials and markets resulted in the penetration of British investment into Latin America.[4] The British investment was soon followed by French, German, and Dutch investments.

With the demise of colonialism in the early 1800s, the economic power of the newly independent Latin American countries passed firmly into the hands of the primary producers, land owners, and the mine-owning class who accounted for nearly all of the region's exports.[5] The last class especially benefited from free trade by acquiring wider markets for its output of raw materials and also by being able to satisfy its consumption needs for capital goods through imports.[6] The trade of Latin America increasingly grew but remained small in volume until England developed manufacturing industries and began to specialize in producing manufactures for export.[7] As the demand for raw materials increased and technology developed, the locations shifted. The costs gradually became lower and supply increased over time with more capital investment. This actually meant a fall in prices for Latin America's raw materials. Even though the volume of trade rose quite steadily after the 1830s, the benefits to Latin America were never proportionate.[8]

To incorporate Latin America's natural resource sector into the world economy, the Europeans invested in transport and other infrastructural bases or in industries processing resources for exports.[9] Direct investment by major foreign multinational corporations (MNCs) became more prominent after the development of oil and metals, which were also meant for export. As the region became heavily integrated into the world economy in the second half of the nineteenth century, its raw material exports became increasingly subject to fluctuations in the face of industrial activity and the rise in income in more-advanced European nations.[10]

The U.S. investment followed the European path, and by the middle of the twentieth century it had replaced Europe as the main source of foreign investment in Latin America.[11] Since Latin America proved to be a greater source of raw material than Europe, and a considerable market for dumping industrial and semi-industrial goods, U.S. investors saw its enormous potential in their global strategy of profit accumulation.

Latin America as a whole, by 1960, absorbed about one-fifth of the total U.S. merchandise exports, providing thereby one of the important markets for U.S. goods of various types.[12] These included consumer durables, capital goods and equipments, semi-manufacturing goods, and the sale of arms.[13] As the sales to Latin America covered the entire range of U.S. national production, the potential of Latin American economies as a major profitable outlet and a safe market increased in the eyes of U.S. producers. Since foreign trade remained the lifeblood, this also meant that for economic health and further progress Latin American economies became dependent on the U.S. market.

However, despite the fact that Latin America became an increasingly important market for products from the U.S. and other industrialized nations, and a major source of raw material, its economic growth rate was not proportionate to its important status in these two areas. For example, according to the World Bank, the Gross National Product (GNP) per capita of the region grew 3.7 times between 1972 and 1992.[14] As a comparative frame of reference, the GNP per capita in the United States increased four times during the same twenty-year period, which signifies an increasing gap in the economic status between Latin American countries and the United States.[15]

Regional rates do not tell us much about the individual country's fate. There have been wide-ranging variations in the GNP per capita growth rates within Latin America. One of the fastest growing Latin American countries between 1972 and 1992 was Brazil, whose GNP per capita increased 4.9 times, much higher than the U.S. rate.[16] On the other hand, Venezuela, which possesses one of the largest oil reserves in Latin America, experienced an increase of only 2.2 times in the GNP per capita during the same time period.[17] Chile grew by 2.5 times, whereas Paraguay, one of the poorest countries in Latin America in terms of GNP per capita (300 U.S. dollars in 1972), experienced an increase by 4.6 times.[18] Remember that all of these countries had been historically vulnerable to fluctuations in the prices of their main export products in the international market. But since their respective national product growth rates had been wide-ranging, one thing we can safely assume is that the overall economic growth and development are complex processes. These differences within the region tell us that growth and development processes are influenced by economic, political, and social factors that are both internal and external. Unless we get a grasp of some of the dominant theories of development, we will not be able to understand why some Latin American countries did relatively well in terms of growth but others grew only modestly.

The Theoretical Underpinnings

The growth and developmental experiences of Latin American countries can be explained in terms of a variety of theories. We shall deal with four major ones in this section: liberal-pluralist, dependency/world system, developmental, and neoliberal.

The liberal-pluralist theory of development is concerned primarily with the individuals who make up society. It asserts that individual welfare is achieved when people are permitted to pursue their most appropriate economic and political interests. In this approach collective welfare is interpreted as synonymous with the "sum of individual interests."[19] Much inspired by Adam Smith's writings, liberal-pluralists believe in an invisible hand of the market-place, which in turn implies a self-regulating society. In this society, the state is subjugated to individual interest. Smith writes:

> Every individual is continually exerting himself to find out the most advantageous employment for whatever capital he can command. It is his own advantage, indeed, and not that of society, which he has in view. But the study of his own advantage naturally, or rather necessarily, leads him to prefer that employment which is most advantageous to the society.[20]

However, there is a very crucial, implicit assumption in the liberal-pluralist approach overlooked by many.[21] This assumption of a self-regulating market-place is possible only if an impartial administrative and institutional infrastructure is provided. Capitalism cannot perform well without this kind of infrastructural support. In Latin America, there are not enough private individuals or corporations to maintain the infrastructural framework needed to make capitalism work, so the role of the state becomes all the more important.

The notion of market as the supreme arbiter of economic behavior might have worked in Western Europe and the U.S., but in the context of Latin America the effective operation of markets too often requires the presence of strong and interventionist states. This scenario undoubtedly was present in the 1940s, 1950s, and 1960s, when most state-led development efforts were undertaken. Many scholars have identified this period of Latin American development as the Import Substitution Industrialization (ISI) phase.[22] The ISI in brief implies that countries undertook policy measures through a combination of incentives, subsidies, and protection to facilitate a surge of domestic industries that would essentially cater to the national market. Why such an emphasis on the national market? This ISI policy came about as a reaction to the long-standing vulnerability that the Latin American countries had experienced vis-a-vis the world market.

For a long time, they were mostly exporters of primary products, such as food stuffs, raw materials, and/or mining extracts but had little control over the prices they could command. On the other hand, the industrialized countries of North America and Europe were exporting expensive finished products to Latin America, including fine manufacturing and technology or machine-intensive products. Therefore, historically Latin American countries had faced a negative fiscal balance. In other words, they had always paid more for the products they imported than the prices they commanded for the products that were exported from their countries. The implementation of the ISI was expected to reverse that trend. An active role for the state was incorporated. The previous economic trend of laissez-faire, generally adopted throughout the nineteenth century and the early part of the twentieth century, needed an overhaul. The market as the chief arbiter of economic relations between Latin America and world economic powers did not benefit Latin America on many fronts, the most obvious of which had been the perpetuation of economic and social inequities. Obviously, then, liberal-pluralist ideas were essentially disregarded in the 1940s in favor of a controlled market-place in which states played an active role.

The second major theoretical underpinning of Latin American development came from the Dependency/World system scholars. Scholars in the dependency tradition were heavily influenced by the Marxist-Leninist intellectual vision of society.[23] In general, these scholars viewed the state as a dependent entity, an instrument of oppression serving the interest of the propertied class at the expense of the property-less class. The Latin American state was characterized as an agent of the dominant classes, who in turn served the economic and political interests of multinational corporations of industrialized countries. Wrote Frank:

> When imperialism accelerated the production and exportation of raw materials in Latin America at the end of the nineteenth century the economic and class structure of the various countries was once more transformed. The Latin American lumpenbourgeoisie became the junior partner of foreign capital and imposed new policies of lumpendevelopment which in turn increased the dependence on the imperialist metropolis.[24]

Note the terms *lumpenbourgeoisie* and *lumpendevelopment* in the preceding paragraph. *Lumpenbourgeoise* refers to a Latin American upper class that depends on the oppressive corporations of industrialized nations. Therefore, the Latin American state has very little autonomy of its own. Likewise, Latin American development is characterized by Frank as a form of *lumpen-development*, meaning that it cannot sustain itself; it depends on the dynamics of the international capitalist system.

The World System variation of this perspective adds a twist to the argument and, instead of exclusively focusing on class, gives much importance to the location of the state in the world system.[25] State capacity to facilitate growth or resolve conflict, in this view, depends on the country's structural location. In a hierarchical three-tier system, Latin American countries are likely to be located in the bottom two tiers and, therefore, the state elites do not have the capacity necessary to engage in successful societal transformation.[26]

By the 1970s and 1980s, though, these simplistic views on the state were questioned. Based on the developmental experiences of the earlier decades, many scholars began to challenge the validity of the above approaches.[27] The changing international environment which saw the United States and other leading capitalist nations becoming hardpressed in a world of more intense and uncertain economic and political competition facilitated more seemingly independent state activities worldwide.[28] Writes Skocpol:

> In today's international environment which stretches from geopolitical domination and competition to world economic competition for trade, investment, market, and finance, modern states stand at the intersection between domestic and international borders, which they must manipulate, mold, and maneuver for survival and gaining advantage over others.[29]

Many studies published in the late 1970s and early 1980s depicted the Latin American state as a forceful and a relatively independent actor in the development process.[30] Some provided reasons why and how modern state elites formulated and pursued their own goals.[31] Stepan's work on Peru and Brazil amply highlighted the factors that encouraged leading state officials to pursue necessary strategies in the face of strong opposition from more powerful domestic and foreign groups.[32] The study showed that the formation of a strong, ideologically motivated, and organizationally solid cadre could ensure relatively independent political order and promote industrial growth. Military leaders in both Peru and Brazil used state power to neutralize threats from domestically powerful social groups. Between 1964 and 1979 in Brazil, for example, partly through electoral engineering and partly through coercion, the military sought to exclude dominant social groups from attaining any direct control of the state apparatus.[33]

In Latin America, this argument is substantiated historically since the state has had a major say in the consolidation of the internal market through the adaptation of the strategy of Import Substitution Industrialization (ISI).[34] Under ISI, active state encouragement and subsidies contributed to an increasing penetration of foreign investment, especially in manufacturing. The various state incentives in the form of tariffs, foreign exchange, and imports encouraged foreign MNCs to set up subsidiaries in Latin America.[35]

In the case of foreign investment, the state provided the infrastructure and complementary economic activities to make investment productive. Of course, how well the state played its part differed from one country to another and therefore made a difference in the achieved level of industrial growth.[36]

Only recently, some dependency-oriented scholars have entertained the possibility of an alliance of foreign capital and the state elite to foster industrial growth.[37] In some cases, the alliance may incorporate domestic capital. In this line of argument, the MNCs collaborated with the state elites to stimulate the industrial sector. This helped Latin America internationalize domestic markets. Specifically, unlike classical forms of economic dependency, the new alliance facilitated diversification throughout the economy. Such industrialization, however, was possible only with the cooperation of the state elite.

The Developmental State

By the 1980s, many other regions, in particular East Asia, had overtaken Latin America in terms of the economic growth rate, relative egalitarian distribution of income, and social progress. These distinctive regional processes caused much debate in the governing circles of various Latin American countries. Therefore, an interest was shown in observing developmental trends in East Asia.

A number of East Asian states, such as South Korea, Taiwan, Singapore, and Hong Kong, had experienced dramatic success in combining fast economic growth with relatively egalitarian distribution of income. The explanations of East Asia's success have been hotly debated. For example, some studies have argued that such tremendous success in East Asia occurred primarily because of a clear emphasis on trade liberalization, private enterprise, and a restricted role of the state.[38] But the assertion that the state's role was limited has been challenged by others.[39] These latter studies have maintained that East Asian states through regulatory policy changes and selective intervention in the economy have successfully harnessed domestic and international market forces of national industrial development.[40] Notwithstanding the debate about the nature of success of the East Asian industrialization as a model for Latin America, it is fair to argue that the developmental state perspective contains a strong blend of liberal-pluralist and state-centered ideas.

The main objective of a developmental state is to lead and actively intervene in selected sectors of the economy, not in all sectors, as many Latin American states did after World War II, in order to guide and promote particular developmental goals.[41] State incentives in tax, subsidy, control over credit, and pricing are used to sway the private sector and help it become more competitive globally.

Most observers note that a successful developmental state possesses, first, a high-level bureaucratic autonomy and second, closer institutionalized cooperation with private business.[42] But as far as the non-business elements, such as labor and popular sectors, are concerned, the developmental state had been notoriously authoritarian.[43] Although the authoritarian feature seems to have been slowly changing in recent years, it still continues to play a major role in the functioning of the developmental state. Through encouragement from the U.S., many Latin American countries began to imitate at least some East Asian policy postures, in particular the sphere of institutionalized cooperation with private business. Attempts by Latin American elites to replicate the East Asian economic experiences have contributed to the rise of a "neoliberal state," to which we now turn.

The Neoliberal State

The neoliberal state is an important part of the current economic globalization process. Overall, economic globalization is characterized by: (a) greater emphasis on exports, particularly of the nonagricultural products, (b) an emphasis on manufacturing in the industrial sector, (c) an asymmetrical relationship between capital and labor in that capital is more mobile across national borders and uses the least expensive labor available, (d) substantial deregulation of state economic control and some privatization of public sector enterprises, and (e) an alliance of international financial agencies (e.g., IMF and the World Bank), foreign private capital, domestic private capital, and state elites.[44] But not all of these characteristics have manifested themselves to the same degree across Latin America. The important points for our purposes are (d) and (e). The state's role must be reduced and it must enter the economy in concert with other international and domestic agents.

In the previous section, we noted that the current neoliberal prescriptions for Latin America have largely been inspired by the economic successes of the East Asian countries. However, what is lost in the discussion is the crucial role played by the state elites, in particular the bureaucratic elite, in sustaining a high level of economic growth. For example, many scholars[45] have noted that in South Korea, Singapore, and Taiwan, the state elites implemented strategic industrial policies that guaranteed state subsidies in exchange for measurable performances. A select group of industries was chosen to be the lead industries, enjoying an enormous advantage over the rest of the industrial sector. These industries became more efficient as they gradually were exposed to foreign competition and markets. But they were effectively supervised by a competent meritocracy, selected from the best available talent in these societies.[46] An effective combination of bureaucratic autonomy and strategic implementation of an industrial policy facilitated the East Asian, export-led growth. In the case of Latin American countries, these conditions are rarely observed. Furthermore, the experiments with the neoliberal state in the past fifteen years have produced some important trends to be examined in the next section. However, prior to that, let us summarize Latin America's economic development history in light of the theories presented earlier.

Throughout the nineteenth and early twentieth centuries, Latin America generally acted as prescribed by liberal-pluralist theory. The state was not greatly interventionist in the economy. Its economic policies facilitated foreign investment, first from Europe, and subsequently from the United States. However, despite the fact that Latin America pursued such a model of economic growth, its level of development remained behind most of Europe and the U.S. The lack of much self-sustaining economic growth contributed to the rise of dependency and world system theories. These theories argued that it is the nature of the world economy that perpetuates Latin America's status, which is dependent on the U.S. and Western Europe. This status also limits how effective a role states can play in modifying market forces. Since World War II, most Latin American countries have pursued development models that required active intervention by states in the economy. States made policies relevant to all sectors in the development arena. They built infrastructure, regulated foreign investment, and guaranteed certain social safeguards to the poor and lower middle classes against economic malaise, largely caused by price fluctuations in the international market. However, the economies continued to depend on the international market for valuable foreign exchange they must earn to pay for the goods and services they must import. When prices fell, or when there was an urgent need to build and expand economic activity, states borrowed from foreign banks and international agencies, such as the World Bank and the International Monetary Fund (IMF). Borrowing is a good idea if the capacity to pay back the debt exists. But because these countries depend so much on the sale of their export products, a slight decline in the export prices caused havoc in their capacity to repay. Throughout the 1980s, one Latin American country after another faced the tremendous burden of repaying foreign debt to international banks and agencies.[47] These perpetual problems of fiscal imbalance partly contributed to a revision in the perception of the state's role in development. Comparative analyses were conducted, which generally highlighted greater developmental achievements in other regions of the world, in particular East Asia.[48] Furthermore, the nature of ideological warfare internationally underwent change. With the statist, socialist models changing in favor of the market in the former Soviet Union and its erstwhile partners in the East and Central Europe, a thorough reanalysis of development thinking was conducted, a process that eventually produced the neoliberal state. But it has been about fifteen years since most Latin American countries have begun experimenting with some form of neoliberal policy. We must analyze how they have fared in terms of major economic growth and social development indicators in order to be able to reach tentative conclusions on the current status of the Latin American economies.

Recent Trends in Growth and Development

Despite all the hoopla about the superiority of the neoliberal experiment, economic growth has not materialized on a sustained basis. The World Bank reported that except for Chile, which averaged a growth rate over 6.1% in GNP per capita between 1985 and 1995, all other Latin American countries have experienced a growth rate under 3%.[49] Some, in particular Honduras, Bolivia, Guatemala, Ecuador, Paraguay, Venezuela, Mexico, and Argentina, experienced a growth rate of under 2%. Brazil (-0.8 percent), Panama (-0.4%), and Peru (-1.6%) did even worse; they experienced negative growth rates.[50] These rates are not impressive at all.

Note that foreign trade had been a critical sector for most Latin American countries because they had to sell their best product(s) overseas so they could buy what they needed from abroad. The share of foreign trade, which includes both imports and exports, in the economy remained very high. Countries whose share of foreign trade in the economy exceeded 50% are: Honduras (80%), Ecuador (56%), the Dominican Republic (55%), El Salvador (55%), Paraguay (82%), Costa Rica (81%), Panama (79%), and Chile (54%).[51] As a comparative frame of reference, the share of foreign trade in the U.S. economy was 24% in 1995, up from 21% in 1980. In fact, since 1980 the importance of foreign trade in the economy increased for Ecuador, Bolivia, the Dominican Republic, Paraguay, Colombia, Chile, and Argentina. For the three largest economies in the region, namely, Brazil, Argentina, and Mexico, foreign trade as a percentage of total economic activity remained relatively low. Brazil's foreign trade volume was only 15% of the economy, Argentina's was 16%, and Mexico's was 48%. The unusual high percentage for Mexico can be explained on the basis of its status as the second largest trading partner of the U.S., and its recent membership in the North American Free Trade Agreement (NAFTA). But note the important distinction: Smaller countries remain quite susceptible to the fluctuations in prices in the international market, whereas larger countries, because of the much larger domestic market, are less vulnerable.

Recent indicators of income inequality and poverty have depicted a bleak picture for Latin America as well. The income distribution among the population has consistently worsened in the region. The World Bank reported that in the early 1990s, the richest 10% of the population's share of total income was 42% in Honduras, 32% in Bolivia, 47% in Guatemala, 38% in Ecuador, 40% in the Dominican Republic, 40% in Colombia, 34% in Peru, 34% in Costa Rica, 42% in Panama, 43% in Venezuela, 39% in Mexico, 51% in Brazil, and 46% in Chile.[52] As a comparative frame of reference, in the U.S. the richest 10% earned 25% of total income in the 1990s.[53] At the other end, the share of the bottom 40% of the population earned 11% of total income in Honduras, 15% in Bolivia, 8% in Guatemala, 14% in Ecuador, 11% in Colombia, 14% in Peru, 13% in Costa Rica, 8% in Panama, 11% in Venezuela, 12% in Mexico, 7% in Brazil, and 10% in Chile. Again, as a comparative frame of reference, in the U.S. the bottom 40% earned 16% of total income.[54] Regardless of how you examine it, the distribution of income among the population is highly unequal in Latin America. Since the late 1970s, these distribution figures have not improved; if anything, they have gotten worse in the majority of the countries.[55]

Table 1
Percent of Urban Households Below or on the Poverty Line, 1980–1990, Selected Countries

Country	1980	1992
Argentina[a]	5	10
Bolivia	–	47
Brazil	30	39[b]
Chile	–	26
Colombia	37	39
Costa Rica	16	25
Guatemala	41	49[b]
Mexico	29	30
Panama	31	33
Paraguay	–	37
Uruguay	9	8
Venezuela	19	31

a) Greater Buenos Aires only; b) 1990. Source: CEPAL, *Panorama Social* 1994, p. 18.

If income distribution, as an important dimension of overall development, is not favorable to most social groups, then, we may expect greater poverty as well, as the two are generally positively correlated. Since the early 1980s, when some of the current neoliberal economic policies were initiated, poverty has worsened, particularly in urban areas. Note that Latin America has become a predominantly urban region now, with an estimated 72% living in cities.[56] For example, according to Table 1, the extent of urban poverty has increased in nine out of the ten countries on which more complete data are available. Between 1980 and 1992, in Argentina the relative increase was the most severe, 10% of the urban population being characterized as poor as opposed to 5% in 1980. During the same period, in the rest of the group the increase has been wide-ranging: In Brazil the percentage of poor in urban areas increased from 30% to 39%; in Costa Rica from 16% to 25%; in Mexico from 29% to 30%; in Colombia from 37% to 39%; and in Venezuela from 19% to 31%. Only in Uruguay has it declined (by a percentage point) from 9 to 8. Although there are some indications that in Argentina, Chile, Mexico, and Venezuela the percentage of urban poor had declined slightly by 1992 from the 1990 level, it remained substantially higher than the 1980 level. If both income inequality and poverty have increased, then how can we explain the trend? Since the neoliberal experiment calls for, among other things, a reduction in the state's involvement in social development, a decline in the state's social expenditure patterns may be expected.

Table 2 compares the trends for two social expenditure indicators between 1980–81 and 1990–91: Social expenditure as a percentage of Gross Domestic Product (GDP) and per capita public social expenditure. Using two indicators instead of one reduces bias in analysis. Note that generally the two are positively correlated. The only country in which case both indicators did not behave in the same way was Colombia. In the case of Colombia, the share of social expenditure in terms of percentages of GDP declined, but the per capita social expenditure increased. Generally, social expenditures include monies spent on public education, health, social security, and housing. Note that these expenditures can be used to examine whether the country has provisions for a safety-net for the needy. Of the ten countries under observation, social expenditure as a percentage of GDP registered a decline in seven; in Costa Rica, it remained constant. In Brazil and Uruguay it increased. In the case of per capita public social expenditure, six of the ten countries under observation noted a decline from 1990 to 1991 compared to 1980 and 1981. Costa Rica registered no gain; Brazil, Colombia, and Uruguay noted increases. Note that Brazil and Uruguay also registered increases in the first indicator, so they have been consistent.

Overall decline may not mean much unless it is decomposed and the sectoral distribution of social expenditure is also examined. According to Table 3, which is based on CEPAL reports, in comparison to the 1980–1981 period, from 1990 to 1993 the level of per capita expenditure in education declined in seven of the ten countries on which complete data were available. In Uruguay it stayed constant; in Brazil and Colombia the educational expenditure per capita registered increases. In the case of public housing expenditure, eight out of ten Latin American countries registered declines between 1990 and 1993 over the level they had previously registered in the 1980 to 1981 period. The exceptions were Uruguay and Chile. Note that Chile had registered a decline in its per capita educational expenditure, but its housing expenditure per capita increased.

Health expenditure per capita decreased in only five of the ten countries on which complete data were available. The countries registering increases in 1990–1993 over their registered level of expenditure in the 1980 to 1981 period were: Uruguay, Costa Rica, Chile, Brazil, and Colombia. As far as expenditure on social security during the same period was concerned, only two out of the seven on which complete data were available registered declines; Uruguay, Costa Rica, Chile, Brazil, and Colombia registered increases.

Based on the overall and sectoral distribution, it is *not* possible to establish a strong link between the decline in public social expenditures and the increase in poverty and income inequality in the urban areas. As we saw in the earlier paragraph, although poverty and inequality increases have been more widespread, public social expenditure declines have not. Perhaps such sectoral variations can be explained in terms of specific contextual and political factors in the countries under observation.

Since much has been said about the neoliberal state, it would be prudent to examine some other trends with regard to at least one specific state characteristic: its coercive capacity. We limit our observation to this for one very important historical reason: Latin American countries had traditionally been more militarily dominated than otherwise. The recent turn toward civilian government and democracy should not detract us from observing this trend. In addition, this area has been amply justified in recent scholarship as the most important area of state domain.[57]

The same reports (Table 3) indicated that in the case of health the picture was somewhat different. Table 4 illustrates trends in military expenditure of Latin American states. Note that this does not include regular expenditures on police and other law-and-order related maintenance.

Combine the two, and one would expect a much higher figure than what has been reported in Table 4 on the security related expenditures of these countries. But given the lack of proper accounting, we must analyze the figures that come clean. Between 1980 and 1993, total military expenditure as a percentage of Central Government Expenditure (CGE) increased in four of the nine countries on which data are available. These countries are: Argentina, Brazil, Colombia, and Mexico. Notice that all of these have experienced a decline in social spending as a percentage of GDP. In the case of per capita social expenditure, all but Colombia noted declines (see Table 2). It is possible to draw two tentative conclusions from this rather cursory examination of these trends: One, the larger Latin American countries, namely, Argentina, Brazil, Mexico, and Colombia have increased their military capacity in the face of decreased social spending. And two, for other relatively smaller countries, military expenditure as a percentage of total Central Government Expenditures declined in 1993, compared to 1983. Three of these five countries, Bolivia, Chile, and Venezuela, also registered declines in their social expenditures. Costa Rica registered no change, and Uruguay indicated an increase in social expenditures.

Table 2
Trends in Social Expenditure, Selected Countries

Country	Period	Social Expenditure as % of GDP	Per Capita Public Social Expenditure
Argentina	1980–81	17.0	570
	1990–91	15.5	450
Bolivia	1980–81	6.0	75
	1990–91	4.5	50
Brazil	1980–81	9.8	160
	1990–91	11.0	175
Chile	1980–81	17.9	270
	1990–91	14.5	240
Colombia	1980–81	8.0	95
	1990–91	7.8	105
Costa Rica	1980–81	15.5	260
	1990–91	15.5	260
Mexico	1980–81	8.7	230
	1990–91	7.0	175
Peru	1980–81	4.5	37
	1990–91	2.0	20
Uruguay	1980–81	15.0	275
	1990–91	17.5	330
Venezuela	1980–81	11.0	480
	1990–91	8.5	300

Source: CEPAL, *Panorama Social,* 1994, p. 51.

Table 3
Sectoral Evolution of Social Expenditures:
1990–1993 expenditures compared to 1980–1981

	Education	**Health**
Argentina	Declined	
Bolivia	Declined	Declined
Brazil	Increased	Increased
Chile	Declined	Increased
Colombia	Increased	Increased
Costa Rica	Declined	Increased
Mexico	Declined	Declined
Peru	Declined	Declined
Uruguay	Same	Increased
Venezuela	Declined	Declined
	Social Security	**Housing**
Argentina	Declined	Declined
Bolivia		Declined
Brazil	Increased	Declined
Chile	Increased	Increased
Colombia	Increased	Declined
Costa Rica	Increased	Declined
Mexico		Declined
Peru		Declined
Uruguay	Increased	Increased
Venezuala	Declined	Declined

Source: CEPAL, *Panorama Social,* 1994, pp. 165–166.

Table 4
Military Expenditure as % of Central Government Expenditure (CGE) Selected Countries

	Military Expenditure as % of CGE	
	1983	1993
Argentina	14.9	24.8
Brazil	2.8	4.9[a]
Chile	12.7	9.2
Colombia	8.4	13.9[aa]
Costa Rica	3.0	1.4[a]
Mexico	2.0	2.8
Peru	24.7	13.3
Uruguay	12.4	7.8[a]
Venezuela	10.4	7.8

[a] = data for 1991, [aa] = data for 1992. Source: *World Military Expenditures and Arms Transfers*, Bureau of Weapons, Washington, D.C., 1993–94.

The relative increase in military expenditure in the larger countries of Latin America at the expense of social development expenditure is troubling. These countries are the leaders of the group and any recurring trend must be examined with concern. In particular, Brazil and Argentina had been home to some of the long, protracted military dictatorships in the region prior to the late 1980s. An increase in military spending is doubly troublesome when the percentage of the population without basic sanitation remains quite substantial in these countries. For example, analyst Sivard reported that by 1990, Argentina had 31% of the population living without basic sanitation facilities; for Brazil, the corresponding figure was 36%; for Mexico, 42%; and for Colombia, 30%.[58] In light of these dismal sanitation figures, a relative increase in military spending causes concern regarding elite priorities.

Conclusion

Briefly, then, we can summarize some major trends in regard to Latin America's development and dependency patterns. First, the continuing dependency on foreign trade for economic growth has not changed substantially since the early 1800s. It is particularly severe for smaller economies as they rely disproportionately on the international market. With such dependency on foreign markets comes a desire to invite foreign investment, even into areas that were previously considered vital to national pride and security, such as public utilities and communications.[59] The four countries that registered increases in military expenditure are also the ones that attracted most net foreign investment in the early 1990s, a substantial amount of which originated in the U.S. For example, in Argentina, the net annual foreign investment registered a nine-fold increase in 1993, compared to ten years earlier. In Colombia this increase was five-fold during the same time span; in Mexico and Brazil the increase was about two-fold each.[60] These trends could make the extent of capital and trade dependency worse in the region, unless of course properly guarded by the respective states.

However, as far as the state in Latin America is concerned, we notice a number of hybrid features. First, the state remains in many important sectors interventionist and, in many instances, it dictates policy changes that facilitate economic growth. Second, the state seems to be more embedded with domestic private monopoly capital as well as foreign capital without the required bureaucratic autonomy to make policies (and implement them) that make sense for most social groups.[61] And finally, there is some disturbing evidence that the new Latin American state, particularly in the larger countries of the region, as we noted in the earlier discussion, has bolstered its military capacity at the expense of incurring declines in many social expenditure patterns.

Notes

1. See Joseph Grunwald and Philip Musgrove, *Natural Resources in Latin American Development* (Baltimore: The Johns Hopkins University Press, 1970), 4–6.

2. Celso Furtado, *Economic Development in Latin America* (New York: Cambridge University Press, 1970).

3. United Nations, Economic Commission for Latin America, Department of Economic and Social Affairs, *Reports on External Financing in Latin America* (New York: 1965), 15–18.

4. See J. Fred Rippy, *British Investments in Latin America* (Minneapolis: University of Minnesota Press, 1959), 22–25.

5. See Rodolfo Stavenhagen, ed., *Agrarian Problems and Peasant Movements in Latin America* (New York: Doubleday, 1970); also see Celso Furtado, *Economic Development of Latin America* (New York: Cambridge University Press, 1970); and Solon Barraclough, *Agrarian Structure in Latin America* (Lexington: Lexington Books, 1973).

6. Stanley J. Stein and Barbara H. Stein, *The Colonial Heritage of Latin America: Essays on Economic Dependence in Perspective* (New York: Oxford University Press, 1970).

7. G. M. Oxley, A Private Enterprise in Latin America, *Stanford Research Institute International* 9 (1968): 13–17.

8. Fernando H. Cardoso and Enzo Faletto, *Dependencia y desarrollo en América Latina* (Mexico: Siglo Veintinuo, 1977).

9. See Grunwald and Musgrove, *Natural Resources in Latin American Development*.

10. United Nations, *Report on Foreign Capital in Latin America* (New York: Department of Economic and Social Affairs, 1955).

11. Cleona Lewis, *America's Stake in International Investments* (Washington D.C.: The Brookings Institution, 1938).

12. See *Historical Statistics of the United States: Colonial Times to 1970* (Washington D.C.: U.S. Department of Commerce, Bureau of the Census, Bicentennial edition, parts I and II), 905–6.

13. *Historical Statistics of the United States from Colonial Times to 1970* (Washington D.C.: U.S. Department of Commerce, Bureau of the Census, Bicentennial Edition, parts I and II).

14. The World Bank, *World Tables 1994* (Baltimore: The Johns Hopkins University Press, 1994), 4–5.

15. Ibid.

16. Ibid.

17. Ibid.

18. Ibid.

19. See Alan Bullock and Maurice Shock, eds., *The Liberal Tradition: From Fox to Keynes* (Oxford: Oxford University Press, 1977); also see Theodore J. Lowi, *The End of Liberalism: Ideology, Policy and the Crisis of Public Authority* (New York: Norton, 1969); and Sheldon Wolin, *Politics and Vision* (Boston: Little & Brown, 1960).

20. Adam Smith, *An Inquiry into the Nature and Causes of the Wealth of Nations* (Nashville, Tenn.: Parthenon, 1937), 398.

21. Alfred Stepan, *The State and Society: Peru in Comparative Perspective* (Princeton: Princeton University Press, 1978), 9.

22. Albert Hirschman, *The Strategy of Economic Development* (New Haven: Yale University Press, 1964). Also see Warner Baer, *Industrialization and Economic Development in Brazil* (Homewood, III.: Irwin, 1965); and Helio Jaguaribe, *Economic and Political Development: A Theoretical Approach and a Brazilian Case Study* (Cambridge, Mass.: Harvard University Press, 1968).

23. Andre G. Frank, *Capitalism and Underdevelopment in Latin America* (Harmondsworth, UK: Penguin, 1971), and Terrence Hopkins and Immanuel Wallerstein, *World-System Analysis* (Beverly Hills: Sage, 1982); also see Christopher Chase-Dunn, *Global Formation* (London: Blackwell, 1991).

24. Andre G. Frank, *Lumpenbourgeoisie: Lumpendevelopment* (New York: Monthly Review Press, 1972), 15.

25. Volker Bornschier and Christopher Chase-Dunn, *Transnational Corporations and Underdevelopment* (New York: Praeger, 1985).

26. Terry Boswell and William Dixon, "Dependency and Rebellion: A Cross-National Analysis;" *American Sociological Review* 50 (1990): 540–59.

27. See Alfred Stepan, *The State and Society: Peru in Comparative Perspective* (Princeton: Princeton University Press, 1978). In particular, see a number of articles in this regard in Peter Evans, Dietrich Rueschemeyer, and Theda Skocpol, eds., *Bringing the State Back In* (New York: Cambridge University Press, 1985).

28. Theda Skocpol, "Bringing the State Back," in Peter Evans, Dietrich Rueschemeyer, and Theda Skocpol, eds., *Bringing the State Back In* (New York: Cambridge University Press, 1985), 3–43.

29. Skocpol, 7.

30. See Stepan, *The State and Society:* Also see Stepan's *Rethinking Military Politics: Brazil and the Southern Cone* (New Haven: Yale University Press, 1988). See as well Peter Flynn, *Brazil: A Political Analysis* (Boulder, Colo.: Westview, 1978).

31. Stepan, *The State and Society.*

32. Stepan, *The State and Society.*

33. David Fleischer, "Constitutional and electoral engineering in Brazil," *Inter-American Economic Affairs* 37 (1984): 3–36.

34. Peter Evans, *Dependent Development* (Princeton: Princeton University Press, 1979).

35. Gary Gereffi and Donald Wyman, eds., *Manufacturing Miracles* (Princeton: Princeton University Press, 1990); Stephen Haggard, *Pathways from Periphery* (Ithaca: Cornell University Press, 1990).

36. See Peter Evans, "State, Capital, and the Transformation of Dependence," *World Development* 14 (1986): 791–808. Also see Satya R. Pattnayak, "Direct Foreign Investment, State, and Levels of Manufacturing Growth in Asia and Latin America," *Journal of Military and Political Sociology* 20 (1992): 83–106.

37. See in particular, Peter Evans, *Dependent Development.*

38. William Galenson, ed., *Foreign Trade and Investment: Development in the Newly Industrializing Asian Economies* (Madison: University of Wisconsin Press, 1985); J. Woronoff, *Asia's Miracle Economies* (New York: Sharpe, 1986).

39. Alice Amsden, *Asia's Next Giant* (New York: Oxford University Press, 1989); Frederick Deyo, ed., *The Political Economy of the New Asian Industrialism* (Ithaca: Cornell University Press, 1987); and Stephen Haggard and C. Moon, "The South Korean State in the International Economy," in *The Antinomies of Interdependence*, ed J. Ruggie. (New York: Columbia University Press, 1983).

40. In addition to the above, also see Gary Gereffi and Donald Wyman, eds., *Manufacturing Miracles* (Princeton: Princeton University Press, 1990), and G. White, ed., *Developmental States in East Asia* (London: MacMillan, 1988).

41. See also Bela Balassa, "The Lessons from East Asian Development: An Overview," *Economic Development and Cultural Change* 36 (1988): 273–90.

42. Peter Evans, *Embedded Autonomy: States & Industrial Transformation* (Princeton: Princeton University Press, 1995).

43. Amiya Bagchi, "The Terror and the Squalor of East Asian Capitalism," *Economic and Political Weekly*, 7 January 1984, 21–22.

44. See Frances Rothstein and Michael Blim, ed., *Anthropology and the Global Factory* (New York: Bergin & Harvey, 1992) for a number of essays in this area.

45. In particular, see the essays in Frederick Deyo, ed., *The Political Economy of the New Asian Industrialism*.

46. See Peter Evans, *Embedded Autonomy.*

47. Satya R. Pattnayak, "External Debt, State Extractive Capacity, State Coercive Capacity, and Industrial Growth in the Third World," *Journal of Developing Societies* 10 (1994): 148–60.

48. Stephen Haggard, *Pathways from the Periphery* (Ithaca: Cornell University Press, 1990); Gary Gereffi, " Rethinking Development Theory: Insights from East Asia and Latin America," *Sociological Forum* 4 (1989): 505–33.

49. The World Bank, *World Development Report* (New York: Oxford University Press, 1995), 214–15.

50. Ibid.

51. The World Bank, *World Development Report 1997* (New York: Oxford University Press, 1997), 218–19.

52. The World Bank, *World Development Report 1997*, 222–23.

53. Ibid.

54. Ibid.

55. See CEPAL, *Panorama Social de America Latina 1994* (Santiago, Chile: Comision economica para America Latina y el Caribe, 1994).

56. Alejandro Portes and Richard Schauffler, "Competing Perspectives on the Latin American Informal Sector," in *Globalization, Urbanization, and the State.* ed. Satya R. Pattnayak. (Lanham, Md.: University Press of America, 1996): 145–77.

57. See for a review of literature, Satya R. Pattnayak, "Modernization, Dependency, and the State in Asia, Africa, and Latin America," *International Journal of Comparative Sociology* 37 (1996): 274–86.

58. See Ruth L. Sivard, *World Military and Social Expenditures 1993* (Washington, D.C.: World Priorities, 1993), Table III.

59. *El Mercurio de Valparaiso*, Various Issues, 1997. Also see *La Jornada* (Mexico City), Various issues, 1997.

60. All net foreign capital figures are from the World Bank's *World Development Report 1997* (Washington, D.C.: Oxford University Press, 1997), 218–19.

61. The argument has been inspired by the writing of Peter Evans, in particular his *Embedded Autonomy: States & Industrial Transformation* (Princeton: Princeton University Press, 1995).

Mixed Blessings of Foreign Capital Flows: Latin America's Record of Development Performance

Susan Randolph

This chapter reviews Latin America's record of development performance from 1960 to 1995. The concept of economic development is contentious. Orthodox definitions of the term narrowly focus on economic growth and the evolution of the structure of the economy toward that characterizing European and North American economies, with industrialization as the primary goal. If one considers the whole 35-year period from this perspective, Latin America's development progress has been modest at best, but this long view masks periods of rapid progress and pronounced regress. Broader definitions of economic development emphasize broad-based gains in health, knowledge, standards of living, and other aspects of human well-being. Latin America's development record is mixed from this perspective. Without exception, Latin American countries witnessed remarkable, broad-based gains in health and knowledge throughout the 35-year period, although income inequality in the region remained high, and the standard of living for the poorest 40% of the population in all countries remained low throughout the period.

Healthier, Longer Lives Empowered by Knowledge

Latin Americans' health and life expectancy increased dramatically over the 1960 to 1995 period. The typical Latin American infant boy born in 1960 could expect to live just over 52 years, while infant girls could expect to live just over 56 years, as can be seen from Table 1. Life expectancy at birth differed by over 25 years across Latin American countries. Infant boys and girls in Bolivia faced a life expectancy of 40 and 42 years, respectively, while in Uruguay the comparable figures were 65 and 71 years, a life expectancy similar to that in the high income, industrial economies at the time. By 1993, the average life expectancy at birth had been extended by roughly 15 years. Infant boys could expect to live almost 67 years and infant girls almost 72. While there remains considerable variation across countries, the variation has been reduced by about 10 years. Costa Rica currently boasts the highest life expectancy, 74 for males and 79 for females, while Bolivian children continue to face the lowest life expectancy, 58 and 61 years for males and females, respectively. The gains in life expectancy were most marked during the decade of the 1960s, and decelerated through the 1980s, but during the 1990s the pace of improvement has quickened.

The improvement in life expectancy was led by rapid declines in the infant mortality rate, the number of infant deaths per 1,000 live births. The average infant mortality rate in the region stood at 108 in 1960, but declined by about 20 per decade to 35 by 1994 (World Bank, 1991, 1994, 1996).[1] The cross-country range in life expectancy diminished substantially over the period as well. In 1960, infant mortality rates exceeded 160 in Bolivia and Peru, whereas in Uruguay the rate was only 51 (World Bank, 1991).

Table 1
Male and Female Life Expectancy: 1960–1993

	1960		1970		1980		1993	
	M	F	M	F	M	F	M	F
Argentina	62	68	64	71	66	73	69	76
Belize	–	–	–	–	–	–	–	–
Bolivia	40	42	45	49	49	53	58	61
Brazil	53	57	58	62	61	66	64	69
Chile	54	59	61	67	67	73	71	78
Colombia	49	57	58	63	61	66	67	72
Costa Rica	60	63	66	70	71	76	74	79
Ecuador	49	52	57	61	62	66	67	72
El Salvador	49	52	57	61	63	67	65	69
Guatemala	46	48	53	56	57	61	63	68
Guyana	–	–	62	66	66	71	63	68
Honduras	45	48	52	56	58	62	66	70
Mexico	55	59	60	64	64	68	68	74
Nicaragua	46	48	54	56	59	61	65	69
Panama	61	63	65	68	69	73	71	75
Paraguay	54	58	61	65	63	68	68	72
Peru	47	49	54	57	57	61	64	68
Uruguay	65	71	66	72	67	74	69	76
Venezuela	55	60	64	69	66	72	69	75
Average	**52**	**56**	**59**	**63**	**63**	**67**	**67**	**72**

Sources: World Bank (1984). *World Development Report*. New York: Oxford University Press; World Bank (1991). *Human Development Report*, 1996 New York: Oxford University Press.

By 1994, only three countries –Bolivia, Brazil, and Nicaragua– had infant mortality rates in excess of 50 (71, 56, and 51, respectively), and five countries – Chile, Colombia, Costa Rica, Panama, and Uruguay– had rates of 20 or less (12, 20, 13, 20, and 19, respectively) (World Bank, 1996b).The improvements in life expectancy and infant mortality rates over the last 35 years are indicative of improvements in general health. Morbidity and mortality are closely linked; decreases in infant mortality rates and increases in life expectancy go hand-in-hand with reductions in the incidence and severity of disease.

Improvements in the quality of life of Latin Americans also resulted from the rapid expansion of the educational system over the 1960 to 1995 period. A rapid expansion of the educational system during the 1950s led to reasonably high primary school enrollment rates by 1960. On average, 85% of primary school aged children were enrolled in primary school in 1960 (World Bank, 1984). Enrollment rates exceeded 95% in eight countries; Argentina, Brazil, Chile, Costa Rica, Panama, Paraguay, Uruguay, and Venezuela; only Guatemala's enrollment rate fell below 50% (World Bank, 1984). The region's gross primary school enrollment rate increased to 95% in 1970, and exceeded 100% by 1980 (World Bank, 1991).[2] By 1990, the regional average climbed to 104%, and only two countries, Bolivia and Guatemala, had fewer than 95% of primary school aged children enrolled in primary school (World Bank, 1993b,1995b).

As primary education expanded, the illiteracy rate of the population fell. In 1960, the regional average illiteracy rate stood at nearly 35% (World Bank, 1991). By 1995, this figure was cut by two-thirds (World Bank, 1996c). The decadal fall in the illiteracy rate was most pronounced during the 1970s, after which the rate of decline was substantially reduced (World Bank, 1990, 1991, 1995a, 1996b). The cross country variation in illiteracy rates also decreased. In 1960, the illiteracy rate exceeded 60% in Bolivia and Guatemala and was below 20% in Argentina and Chile (World Bank, 1991). By 1995, no country had an illiteracy rate above 45%, and the illiteracy rate exceeded 30% in only two countries, Guatemala and Nicaragua (World Bank, 1996c). The illiteracy rate is currently below 10% in 12 of the 19 Latin American countries (World Bank, 1996c).

The 1960s and 1970s witnessed the most rapid expansion of the secondary school system. As can be seen from Table 2, the secondary school enrollment rate increased by over 50% between 1960 and 1970 and again between 1970 and 1980. While some additional gains occurred between 1980 and 1985, secondary school enrollment rates were essentially unchanged between 1985 and 1990. The growth in the secondary school system meant that while fewer than 20% of the secondary school aged population had access to a secondary education in 1960, by 1990, nearly 50% did. The pace of expansion was uneven across the region. Therefore, there are stark differences in secondary school enrollment rates by country. The rate remains below 30% in El Salvador, Guatemala, and Honduras, while it equals or exceeds 70% in Argentina, Chile, Peru, and Uruguay.

Table 2
Gross Secondary School Enrollment Rate: 1960–1990

	1960	1970	1980	1990
Argentina	23	44	56	71
Belize	–	–	–	–
Bolivia	12	24	36	34
Brazil	11	26	34	39
Chile	24	39	53	74
Colombia	12	25	44	55
Costa Rica	21	28	48	42
Ecuador	12	22	51	53
El Salvador	13	22	24	25
Guatemala	7	8	18	28
Guyana	–	55	60	–
Honduras	8	14	30	19
Mexico	11	22	46	55
Nicaragua	7	18	43	40
Panama	29	38	61	60
Paraguay	11	17	26	30
Peru	15	31	59	70
Uruguay	37	59	60	81
Venezuela	21	33	41	34
Average	**19**	**28**	**43**	**48**

Note: Average excludes Belize and Guyana. Data on Argentina are for 1979 and 1988. Data for Colombia and Ecuador are for 1989, not 1990. Data for El Salvador, Guatemala, and Honduras are for 1991, not 1990.

Sources: World Bank. (1984, 1993b). *Worl development report.* New York: Oxford University Press; World Bank. (1990). *Social indicators of development 1990 Data Disk.* Washington, DC: The World Bank; World Bank (1995). *World tables.* Baltimore: Johns Hopkins University Press.

The broad-based educational gains witnessed over the last three and a half decades empowered Latin Americans by increasing their access to information and enhancing their ability to effectively participate in political life. A democratic transition swept the region in the 1980s and was no doubt in part a response to the greater capacity and desire for self-governance conferred by knowledge. In the late 1970s, only Colombia, Costa Rica, and Venezuela had democratic governments. By the end of the 1980s, two-thirds of the Latin American countries were under democratic rule. The broad-based gains in health and education also enhanced Latin America's productive capacity. Human capital, the level of knowledge and health among the labor force, is simultaneously a productive force. The gains in human capital contributed to rapid output growth in the 1960s and 1970s. As will be seen, however, they were not sufficient to prevent a decline in per capita output during the 1980s.

Modest and Uneven Improvement in the Standard of Living

The general standard of living rose between 1960 and 1995 in all Latin American countries, with the exception of Nicaragua and Venezuela. Table 3 shows the average per capita Gross Domestic Product (GDP), a measure of average income by decade in constant 1985 international dollars (ICP$). Converting currencies to international dollars enables one to compare living standards across countries relative to the living standard in the United States. Ordinary exchange rate conversions are generally biased given distortions to trade, such as tariffs, and the common practice of fixing exchange rates. Exchange rate conversions also fail to take into account differences in relative prices between countries, and, accordingly, tend to underestimate purchasing power in low income countries. As Table 3 shows, real per capita income in the region rose from an average of ICP$ 2,265 to ICP$ 3,559. This increase amounts to an average annual rate of increase of 1.3% for a total gain of nearly 60% over the 35-year period. In comparison, in 1992, the per capita income in sub-Saharan Africa, East Asia excluding China, and the western industrial countries stood at ICP$ 1,346, ICP$ 8,009 and ICP$ 15,291, respectively (UNDP, 1995). The industrial market economies saw their standard of living rise at a rate exceeding 2.5% per year between 1960 and 1995, and East Asia and the Pacific saw their standard of living rise at a rate exceeding 5% per year over the same period (World Bank, 1983, 1995a).

There were substantial differences in both the standard of living and the rate of growth in the standard of living between Latin American countries. Venezuela's per capita income is the highest in the region and exceeded the poorest country's per capita income by a factor of 6.1 in 1960 and 5.4 in 1994. Whereas the gain in per capita income over the 35-year period exceeded 100% in Colombia, Mexico, and Panama, it was less than 40% in Ecuador, Honduras, Uruguay, and Peru, and negative in Nicaragua and Venezuela.

In contrast to the record of continuous improvement in health and education, the long-run improvement in the standard of living was far from continuous. Between 1960 and 1970, all countries in the region experienced significant growth in per capita income averaging 2.5% per annum.

Table 3
Per Capita Gross Domestic Product: 1960–1994
Constant (1985) ICP $

	1960	1970	1980	1990	1994
Argentina	4462	5637	6506	4706	6031
Belize	–	–	3943	3464	–
Bolivia	1148	1661	1989	1658	1753
Brazil	1784	2434	4303	4042	4123
Chile	2885	3605	3892	4338	5477
Colombia	1684	2140	2946	3300	3628
Costa Rica	2096	2904	3717	3499	4015
Ecuador	1461	1789	3238	2755	2901
El Salvador	1427	1810	2014	1824	2142
Guatemala	1660	2028	2574	2127	2231
Guyana	1596	1816	1927	1094	–
Honduras	1039	1237	1519	1377	1422
Mexico	2836	3987	6054	5827	5944
Nicaragua	1606	2359	1853	1294	1165
Panama	1575	2584	3392	2888	3524
Paraguay	1177	1394	2534	2128	2137
Peru	2019	2736	2875	2188	2396
Uruguay	3968	4121	5091	4602	5342
Venezuela	6338	7753	7401	6055	6276
Average	**2265**	**2889**	**3545**	**3095**	**3559**

Note: 1994 GDP per capita figures are estimates based on the growth of per capita GDP. Averages for 1960 through 1994 exclude Belize. Average for 1994 also excludes Guyana.
Sources: The Penn World Table (Mark 5.6), see R. Summers and A. Heston (1991). The Penn World Table (Mark 5): an expanded set of international comparisons 1950–1988". *Quarterly Journal of Economics, 106*, 327–68; World Bank. (1996). *World development report*. New York: Oxford University Press.

The cross-country average per capita income stood nearly 30% higher in 1970 than in 1960. With the exception of Nicaragua, all countries in the region saw their per capita income rise during the decade of the 1970s as well. The average gain in per capita income during the 1970s was just under 25%, or 2.1% per annum.

Growth screeched to a halt in the 1980s and per capita incomes plummeted. Only Chile and Colombia escaped a steep decline in the standard of living during the 1980s. The decline of the 1980s was so pronounced that by 1990, per capita income in Argentina, Bolivia, Guyana, Nicaragua, Peru, and Venezuela was below its 1970 value; it was only slightly above the 1970 value in Guatemala and El Salvador. For Guyana and Nicaragua, per capita income in 1990 stood well below its 1960 level; it was only slightly above the 1960 level in Argentina and Peru. The 1990s has witnessed a return to growth and with it a rise in per capita income averaging 2.2% per annum. Between 1990 and 1994, per capita income rose in all countries except Nicaragua, albeit the rate of gain was uneven across countries. In Brazil, Honduras, Mexico, Paraguay, and Venezuela the average annual rate of growth in per capita income was below 1%, while in Argentina, Chile, El Salvador, and Panama, it was above 4%.

Income inequality in Latin America has historically been high, and the rapid growth of the 1960s and 1970s did not succeed in eliminating poverty. While evidence of poverty and inequality in Latin America is incomplete and tenuous, available evidence indicates that in 1970, the poorest 20% of the population received between 2% and 5% of the total income, while the poorest 40% of the population received between 5% and 14% of the income (Table 4). Of the 12 countries for which data exist, the per capita income of the poorest 20% was below ICP$ 400 in six, while that of the poorest 40% was below ICP$ 600 in seven. In general, the crisis of the 1980s did not fully erode the gains of the poor during the 1970s. On average, the income of the poorest quintile rose by roughly 30% between 1970 and 1990, but poverty intensified in Guatemala and Nicaragua. Although growth in income was generally the rule for the poorest quintile, by 1990, the group's per capita income was below ICP$ 400 in 5 of the 17 countries for which there are data.

Between 1970 and 1990, the average income of the poorest 40% of the population increased as well, but by an average of less than 20%. The average income of this group fell in Argentina, Guatemala, Nicaragua, and Venezuela between 1970 and 1990. By 1990, the per capita income of the poorest 40% was below ICP$ 600 in only 5 of the 17 countries. Although the data here show some tendency for the income share of the poorest two population quintiles to increase, softening the blow of the crisis of the 1980s on the poor, income inequality in the region tended to rise; the middle class bore the brunt of the free fall in living standards given a rise in the income share of the wealthiest quintile.

What accounts for the dramatic growth of the 1960s and 1970s, and the devastating fall in incomes during the 1980s, followed by recovery in the 1990s? Domestic policies, official and private international financial institutions, and external shocks all played a role.

Table 4
Income Share and Average Income of Poorest 20% and 40% of the Population: 1970 and 1990

	1970				1990			
	Income Share Poorest		Average Income Poorest (ICP$)		Income Share Poorest		Average Income Poorest (ICP$)	
	20%	40%	20%	40%	20%	40%	20%	40%
Argentina	4	14	1127	1973	5	14	1177	1647
Belize	–	–	–	–	–	–	–	–
Bolivia	4	13	332	540	6	15	497	622
Brazil	3	9	365	548	2	7	404	707
Chile	–	–	–	–	4	10	868	1085
Colombia	4	11	428	589	4	11	660	908
Costa Rica	3	12	436	871	4	13	770	1137
Ecuador	2	5	179	224	5	14	689	964
El Salvador	–	–	–	–	–	–	–	–
Guatemala	5	13	507	659	2	8	213	425
Guyana	–	–	–	–	6	17	328	465
Honduras	–	–	–	–	4	11	275	377
Mexico	3	10	598	997	4	12	1165	1748
Nicaragua	3	9	354	531	4	12	259	388
Panama	2	7	258	452	2	8	289	578
Paraguay	–	–	–	–	6	16	638	851
Peru	2	7	274	479	5	14	547	766
Uruguay	–	–	–	–	6	15	1381	1726
Venezuela	3	10	1163	1938	4	11	1211	1665

Sources: Income share: World Bank. (1996a). *Social indicators of development.* Baltimore: Johns Hopkins University Press. Average income; author's calculations based on income share data and per capita income figures in Table 3.

Domestic Policies and Foreign Capital Flows during the 1960s and the 1970s

Domestic policies in Latin America differed by country and overtime, but important commonalties among countries shaped the regional trends. During the 1960s and 1970s, Latin America continued to follow an inward oriented development strategy that was adopted decades earlier, which emphasized industrialization through import substitution. The import substitution strategy of industrialization imposes taxes (tariffs) or quantity restrictions (quotas) on selective imports in order to create industrial investment opportunities. The theoretical appeal of this strategy is that the restriction of imports simultaneously creates gaps in the economy, making it obvious where demand patterns support the establishment of new industries, encourages domestic entrepreneurs to invest in these new industries by increasing the profitability of the ventures, and protects domestic infant industries from foreign competition until they can mature and become internationally competitive. In theory at least, the strategy also reduces dependency on the global economy.

The practical appeal of the strategy is two-fold. First, it is administratively a straightforward matter to curtail imports in order to induce structural change, specifically industrialization. Second, one means of overcoming a balance of payments crisis (an acute shortage of foreign exchange) is to tax or otherwise curtail imports. While most Latin American countries consciously promoted an import substitution industrialization strategy during the 1960s, in many if not most cases the strategy had come about by default. Countries slipped into it in response to recurrent balance of payments crises; certainly balance of payments crises played a role in deciding which imports were restricted and by how much, and, accordingly, which domestic industries were stimulated.

During the 1960s, tariffs and quotas predominantly affected consumer goods imports. Several factors favored concentration on domestic production of finished consumer goods. First, the cost disadvantage between domestically produced and imported intermediate goods (e.g., cloth to produce clothing) or capital goods (e.g., sewing machines to produce clothing) was greater than for consumer goods. Second, demand for domestically produced consumer goods follows directly from curtailing imports, whereas demand for particular intermediate and capital goods presupposes the existence of sufficient domestic consumer goods industries to absorb the full output of the intermediate or capital goods producing firms. Finally, many consumer goods (especially luxury goods and consumer durables) are inessential to development; increases in the costs of these goods do not impede development, whereas increases in the costs of capital or intermediate goods would. This factor also made finished luxury consumer goods the obvious target of import restrictions imposed in response to balance of payments crises.

As a further impetus to industrialization, Latin American countries maintained overvalued local currencies. That is, they administratively fixed their exchange rate (number of units of domestic currency required to purchase a unit of foreign currency such as the dollar) below the market clearing level.

Overvalued currencies further increased domestic profit margins in the new consumers goods industries by reducing the cost of imported intermediate and capital goods. Elaborate import licensing schemes were used to ration scarce foreign exchange to the new industries and other priority activities. State involvement in the industrialization process extended beyond the provision of incentives for industrialization; most states were directly involved in production activities.

The import substitution industrialization strategy was a major force behind the economic expansion of the 1960s. The 5.2% average annual rate of investment growth fueled continued industrial expansion (World Bank, 1984). In most countries, the industrial sector's growth rate exceeded that of other sectors so that by 1970, industry's share in output rose modestly from a regional average of 29% to just under 31% (World Bank, 1991). Gains exceeding three percentage points were realized by El Salvador, Mexico, Nicaragua, and Panama, although Colombia, Ecuador, Peru, Uruguay, and Venezuela failed to realize the desired structural transformation during the 1960s (World Bank, 1991). Government expenditures remained within reason, despite the extensive government involvement in production and the rapid expansion of education and health infrastructure. At the beginning of the 1970s, government expenditures were less than 20% of output in all but four countries, Chile, Panama, Uruguay, and Venezuela (World Bank, 1984). Government deficits for the most part remained within bounds (only Chile and Panama ran deficits in excess of 5% of output), and as a consequence, inflation rates averaged less than 12% per annum over the decade of the 1960s in all but four countries (Argentina, Brazil, Chile, and Uruguay) (World Bank, 1984, 1992a).

The import substitution process bogged down in most of the Latin American countries in the 1970s. Several forces closed in. Once expansion of finished goods industries saturated the domestic market, further industrialization came to depend on the establishment of intermediate or capital goods industries or the export of consumer goods. Since the cost disadvantage of domestically producing capital and intermediate goods is greater, shifting more heavily into these industries raised the cost of growth as well as investment requirements. The domestic industries that were spawned tended to use overly capital intensive production techniques as a consequence of overvaluing domestic currencies (capital imports were cheap for those granted import licenses), further increasing the investment requirement for expansion.

The option of exporting industrial goods required the attainment of international competitiveness. Few of the new domestic industries could compete in the international market. The lack of competitiveness in part reflects the time required for infant industries to mature; however; the chaotic structure of tariffs and incentives that emerged over time, the use of overvalued exchange rates, and insulation of government-owned industries from competitive forces are perhaps more to blame. The chaotic structure of protection implied that industries did not emerge along the lines of their potential comparative advantage, that prices failed to gauge efficient resource use, and that profitability depended less on increasing the efficiency of production than on lobbying the government for import licenses, greater tariff protection, and other benefits. Overvalued domestic currencies implicitly taxed export activities by reducing the domestic currency yield on a given quantity of exports. Exporters were typically required to surrender their foreign exchange earnings to the government, so they could not legally offset this disadvantage by selling their foreign exchange receipts in parallel markets. Since government enterprises could realistically expect subsidies to offset any operating losses, neither profitability nor efficiency were a driving force.

Reform became a priority. Several countries, notably Chile and Argentina, experimented with alternative development strategies (Griffin, 1989). Most Latin American countries, however, stayed the course of import substitution but took steps to rationalize incentives and otherwise increase its momentum, albeit, generally at the behest of the International Monetary Fund (IMF), in return for balance of payments support. Tariff structures were rationalized by reducing the average tariff level and moving toward a more uniform tariff structure. Currency devaluations became more common. Many governments increased the scope of their activities, including direct investment in productive activities.

What ultimately proved to be of greater consequence, however, was the growing reliance on foreign capital markets, specifically foreign commercial banks, to boost the investment rate so that the momentum of growth could be maintained, and the more costly and difficult phase of import substitution, domestic production of intermediate and capital goods, could be established. Prior to 1973, official transfers from bilateral and multilateral agencies (such as the United States Agency for International Development and the World Bank), along with direct foreign investment (the establishment of business enterprises by multinational corporations or foreign nationals) accounted for the preponderance of foreign capital inflows to Latin America.

The success of OPEC, the Organization of Petroleum Exporting Countries, in raising the price of oil in 1973 provided both the impetus to tap private foreign capital markets and the potential to dramatically increase foreign borrowing. The huge increase in oil prices induced unexpected and abrupt balance of payments crises. The Latin American economies had grown increasingly vulnerable to interruptions in the flow of imports; success in the first phase of import substitution shifted the composition of imports from non-essential consumer goods to essential capital and intermediate goods. The non-oil-exporting Latin American countries needed to rapidly mobilize funds to support their balance of payments, given steep declines in the terms of trade (the quantity of imports that could be purchased for a given quantity of exports decreased). Dramatically cutting imports was not an option if growth was to be maintained. Commercial banks in Europe and the United States, awash with a rapid influx of funds from OPEC countries, sought new lending opportunities. They actively peddled loans to Latin American governments and private investors. The terms offered were too good to pass up. Prior to 1974, the real rate of interest was negative 0.8%; over the 1974 to 1978 period, the real rate of interest was barely positive, 0.5% (Cline, 1983). Further, the commercial bank loans could be mobilized more quickly than official transfers, were not tied in any way, as foreign aid typically was, and were offered without any political strings attached.

A rapid buildup of debt ensued. Even oil-exporting countries increased their commercial borrowing, in large part to build capacity in their oil industries. Between 1970 and 1982, Latin America's total long-term disbursed and outstanding debt increased nearly ten-fold from US$ 25.2 billion to US$ 233.3 billion (World Bank, 1985, 1993a). Long-term public and publicly guaranteed debt increased twelve-fold from US$ 15.2 billion to US$ 184.7 billion (World Bank, 1985, 1993a). The rate of public and publicly guaranteed debt build-up was far more rapid in Brazil, Costa Rica, Ecuador, Mexico, Nicaragua, and Venezuela, where outstanding debt expanded by a factor of 16 or more.

For the most part, the inflow of foreign capital enabled Latin American countries to maintain imports of essential goods, increase their investment rates, industrialize further, and achieve a healthy rate of growth. The growth rate of investment during the 1970s exceeded that of the 1960s, so that gross domestic investment as a percentage of output increased in all Latin American countries. It averaged in excess of 20% between 1970 and 1979 in all but six countries (Chile, Colombia, El Salvador, Guatemala, Nicaragua, and Uruguay) (World Bank, 1992b). Industrialization proceeded at a slightly higher average pace during the 1970s than the 1960s, but the average hides substantial variation in outcomes. The share of industry in output increased by 4 percentage points or more in Belize, Brazil, Costa Rica, Ecuador, and Paraguay, while it fell in Argentina, Bolivia, Chile, Panama, and Venezuela (World Bank, 1991). Growth and industrialization were accompanied by a rise in the size of the government sector. By 1981, the number of countries with government expenditures in excess of 20% of output more than doubled to nearly two-thirds of the countries (World Bank, 1984).

Debt, External Shocks, and the Crisis of the 1980s

Toward the end of the 1970s, problems began to emerge that were exacerbated by the second oil price shock in 1979 and other changes in the external environment. Inflation accelerated, fueled by the increase in oil prices over the decade and deficit financing. Whereas only two countries, Chile and Panama, had budget deficits in excess of 5% of output in 1972, seven countries did by 1981 (World Bank, 1984, 1992a). The regional inflation rate averaged 33.8% per annum over the 1970 to 1982 period (World Bank, 1984). The annual average rate of inflation exceeded 100% in Chile and Argentina (World Bank, 1984).

The oil price shocks induced inflation in the industrial countries as well. In 1978, the United States and Britain contracted their money supplies in an effort to combat inflation. This sharply increased real interest rates in the international markets. By 1981, the real interest rate rose to 11% (Cline, 1983). Because most of the commercial bank loans to Latin America carried a variable interest rate, debt service obligations ballooned. The effect of the high interest rates was magnified due to the commercial bank practice of "front loading" loans, that is, repayment burdens were heaviest during the initial years of the loan as opposed to being flat over the life of the loan.

Table 5
Ratio of Long-Term Public and Publicly Guaranteed Debt (DOD) to GNP and Ratio Resultant Debt Service Obligations to Export Earnings (TDSDOD/XGS): 1970–1982

	DOD/GNP %		TDSDOD/XGS %	
	1970	1982	1970	1982
Argentina	21.6	23.1	8.6	30.5
Belize	–	–	7.7	38.9
Bolivia	11.3	31.5	48.2	93.8
Brazil	12.5	43.3	8.2	19.7
Chile	19.2	19.8	25.8	23.3
Colombia	11.6	17.3	18.5	15.6
Costa Rica	10.0	11.7	13.8	109.3
Ecuador	8.6	42.0	11.8	35.1
El Salvador	3.6	7.4	8.6	28.8
Guatemala	7.4	7.8	5.7	13.3
Guyana	3.8	17.9	33.5	158.3
Honduras	2.8	18.9	12.9	53.4
Mexico	23.6	34.1	8.7	31.5
Nicaragua	10.5	35.8	19.5	109.5
Panama	7.7	6.6	19.5	73.6
Paraguay	11.8	10.2	19.2	16.8
Peru	11.6	36.3	12.0	28.1
Uruguay	21.7	13.4	11.3	18.8
Venezuela	2.9	16.2	6.6	18.6
Average	**11.2**	**21.9**	**15.8**	**48.3**

Source: World Bank. (1989). *World debt tables 1988–1989*. Washington, D.C.: World Bank.

Tight monetary policy in the United States also induced an appreciation of the dollar against other currencies. Because most of the commercial bank loans to Latin America were denominated in dollars, there was a sharp increase in the amount they had to pay back in terms of their own currencies and the currencies of their other developed country export partners. Global recession in the early 1980s further eroded the ability of Latin American countries to service their debts. The global recession reduced demand for Latin American exports so that both the quantity of exports and the price received per unit fell.

By the beginning of the 1980s, Latin America's debt burden grew to unsustainable levels as a consequence of the rapid accumulation of debt, the increase in interest rates, and the fall in Latin America's capacity to earn foreign exchange. Table 5 shows the change in the ratio of long-term public and publicly guaranteed debt (DOD) to Gross National Product (GNP), a measure of total output, and the ratio of debt service obligations (principal and interest payments due) on that debt to export earnings between 1970 and 1982. The average debt to GNP ratio was 11.2% in 1970; it rose to 21.9% by 1982. Debt exceeded 30% of GNP, a historically unprecedented level, in Bolivia, Brazil, Ecuador, Mexico, Nicaragua, and Peru. Debt service obligations averaged just under 16% of export earnings in 1970; they averaged close to 50% of export earnings in 1982. In Costa Rica, Guyana, and Nicaragua debt service obligations exceeded export earnings.

The death knell sounded on Latin America's growth in 1982 with Mexico's announcement that it could not meet its debt service obligations. Mexico was not the first Latin American country to experience difficulties in servicing its debt. In 1980, fully half of the Latin American countries were drawing on credits with the IMF to shore up their balance of payments (World Bank, 1988). But Mexico's announcement that it was near default carried with it the risk of insolvency for major U.S. banks. It alerted all creditor banks to the possibility of systematic Latin American default. The specter of systematic default not only posed a threat to individual banks, but a threat to the viability of the international financial system. Creditor banks for their part reacted by sharply curtailing new lending to all Latin American countries whether they were at imminent risk of default or not. The commercial banks' competition to shore up their individual lending portfolios turned a serious problem into an immediate crisis of huge proportions. The abrupt curtailment of credit threatened to transform what was essentially a problem of illiquidity (short run cash flow) into one of widespread insolvency.

A highly decentralized consortium emerged that served as a lender of last resort in an effort to avert collapse of the international financial system (Devlin, 1992). The consortium was comprised of international financial institutions, including the International Monetary Fund, the World Bank, and the Bank of International Settlements, as well as North American and Western European central banks, treasuries, export credit agencies, and the creditor banks themselves. The "rescue" package typically consisted of bridging loans from OECD country central banks or treasuries until negotiations could be concluded with the IMF for a "stabilization" loan to tide the countries over the crisis period and with creditor banks to reschedule debt service payments and guarantee minimal continuation of capital flows. Stabilization loans were eventually followed by longer-term 'structural adjustment' loans from the World Bank.

Stabilization and structural adjustment loans imposed policy reforms that ended Latin American governments' dogmatic reliance on the import substitution strategy of development and pushed them toward a more outward oriented, market-based development strategy. IMF stabilization loans were designed to last typically three to five years and imposed conditions intended to restore balance of payments equilibrium and macroeconomic balance in general. The prototypical conditions imposed included significant currency devaluation, credit restriction to both the public and private sectors, scaling back the size of the government sector, removing price controls and subsidies, and restraining wage growth. World Bank structural adjustment loans were longer in duration (typically in excess of 20 years), and focused on microeconomic reforms to increase the market orientation and efficiency of the economy. Trade liberalization, entailing abandonment of import substitution, financial sector reform, privatization, and price deregulation were the *quid pro quo* for structural adjustment loans.

The rescue package succeeded in ensuring an orderly repayment of commercial bank debt and averted destabilizing defaults. Creditor banks were spared financial ruin. In fact, as noted by Devlin, "throughout the crisis years of 1982–1986 the international earnings of United States banks remained buoyant, and indeed their overall growth of net income accelerated" (1992, p. 210). The banks have increased their primary capital and successfully diversified their loan portfolios. The international financial system is essentially secure; today even complete default by major debtors could be absorbed by the system (Blitzer, 1986).

The Latin American countries for the most part lived up to their commitment to meet their debt service obligations. The creditor banks on their part placed higher priority during the 1980s on strengthening their balance sheets than living up to their commitments to help meet the debt or countries' financial needs for restructuring. The result was a hemorrhage of funds from the Latin American countries to the West. Between 1983 and 1984, the net transfer (total capital inflows minus total capital outflows) to Latin American countries turned negative, and the outward transfer of funds exceeded US$ 9.4 billion (World Bank, 1988). Between 1985 and 1989, the net outward transfer of funds was just under US$ 98 billion, an amount that exceeded the total positive net transfer over the 1970 through 1982 period by a hefty margin (World Bank, 1978, 1980, 1981, 1988, 1993a, 1996b).

While the policy reforms undertaken in Latin America during the 1980s do not merit unreserved applause, they do merit applause. Many of the recommended policy reforms were implemented, and it is this fact that enabled Latin American countries to continue servicing their debts. The resultant outward transfer of funds was essentially policy-induced. Fiscal reforms typically included reining in government expenditures via privatizing government enterprises, repressing public sector wages or laying off public sector employees, and scaling back service provision and infrastructure investments. Despite the fall in output, most Latin American countries reduced government expenditures; in 1990 government expenditures averaged 20.2% of GNP, whereas in 1981 the average was 22.2% (World Bank, 1984, 1992a). The average tends to hide the extent of progress in scaling back the size of the government sector; in all but six Latin American countries, government expenditures were below 20% of GNP in 1990 (World Bank, 1984, 1992). Tax systems were also overhauled to increase tax revenues and reduce distortions. Budget deficits were reduced as a result of the expenditure and tax reforms. By 1990, only three countries, Brazil, Panama, and Peru, had budgetary deficits of 5% of GNP or more. Financial reforms extended beyond credit restraint and raising interest rates to liberalization of financial markets in many cases. The financial reforms (along with tax reforms) did stimulate savings to some extent; between 1982 and 1987, the savings rate averaged 7% higher than the 1980 value (Devlin, 1992). Tariffs and quotas were reduced further and rationalized to some degree. Significant currency devaluation took place, and many Latin American countries moved from a fixed exchange rate regime toward a more market-oriented flexible exchange rate regime. The reforms made it possible for the region as a whole to convert its persistent trade deficit into a massive trade surplus that averaged US $26 billion per annum between 1982 and 1988, despite the fall in the terms of trade (Devlin, 1992).

The policy reforms enabling the outward transfer of funds had as their counterpart a fall in the investment rate, accelerating inflation, and deindustrialization as well as the devastating fall in living standards. Whereas gross domestic investment averaged 22.3% of GDP between 1970 and 1979, it averaged 20% of GDP between 1980 and 1984, and only 17.4% of GDP between 1985 and 1989 (World Bank, 1992b). Between 1980 and 1990, the inflation rate averaged 106% per annum; the annual rate of inflation exceeded 200% in Argentina, Bolivia, Brazil, Mexico, and Peru (World Bank, 1992a). The share of industry in output fell an average of two percentage points between 1980 and 1989. It fell in all but six countries; only Colombia, Ecuador, and El Salvador succeeded in raising the share of industry in output by more than a negligible amount between 1980 and 1989 (World Bank, 1991).

Recovery and Prospects for the Future

The 1990s have witnessed a remarkable return to growth in all the Latin American economies. The growth rate of GDP was positive over the 1990–1994 period without exception and averaged 4.3% per annum; per capita growth was positive as well in all countries except Nicaragua. Gross domestic investment as a share of GDP was up by 2 percentage points over the previous five years and averaged 19.3% over the 1990 to 1994 period. What accounts for the turnaround (World Bank, 1996c)?

The wrenching and far-reaching reforms of the 1980s helped set the stage for the recovery of the 1990s. Price distortions were reduced so that prices served as a far better gauge of efficient resource use than before. Production was depoliticized; profitability came to be more strongly linked with productivity growth. Central authorities came to view the attainment of international competitiveness as a priority goal and began allocating preferences based on performance. Many inefficient state-owned enterprises had been privatized or otherwise subjected to the discipline of the market by 1990. The continuous improvement in human capital since 1960 undoubtedly served to boost the productivity of labor now that efficiency concerns guided its deployment.

The external environment also posed fewer hurdles during the first half of the 1990s. Although commodity prices for Latin American exports have not fully recovered, oil prices have fallen. The global economy is no longer beset with recession. While real interest rates have not returned to the level of the mid-seventies, they remain well below the peak value of the early eighties. All of these factors played a role in Latin America's recovery during the first half of the 1990s. They are likely to continue to exert a positive influence on Latin America's economic development for the next several years.

As important as these factors were, the dramatic return of foreign capital was likely of greater consequence to the turnaround of the 1990s. Between 1990 and 1994, the net transfer to Latin American countries exceeded US$ 63.5 billion, an inflow equal to 60% of the value of the outflow over the previous five years (World Bank, 1996b). One of the more significant trends in international capital flows, including flows to Latin America, is the growing share of portfolio investment (the purchase of domestic stocks and bonds by foreigners). Net Portfolio Investment Flows to developing countries increased from practically zero in 1983 to US$ 13 billion in 1992 (Grakel, 1996). Between 1989 and 1993 alone, they increased by 277% (Grakel, 1996). Portfolio investment flows are more volatile than other forms of capital inflows. Their volatility results from their high degree of liquidity in the context of financial openness. Investors' perceptions regarding the attractiveness of opportunities available in particular markets are fleeting and can change rapidly in response to news or speculation regarding political stability, currency devaluation, changes in interest rates abroad, the emergence of new markets with potentially higher returns, or any number of other factors.

As welcome as the return of foreign capital flows is, it poses a mixed blessing. Latin American countries remain highly debt ridden, and accordingly vulnerable to any sudden reduction in foreign capital inflows. As Table 6 shows, total debt as a percentage of GNP has fallen since 1982, but remains high. It exceeded 30% in 1994 in Brazil, Honduras, Mexico, and Nicaragua. In 1994, total debt service obligations as a percentage of export earnings not only remained dangerously high, but exceeded their 1982 value in over half of the Latin American countries. The Mexican crisis of 1994 was triggered by a rapid outflow of portfolio investment in response to the Chiapas' revolt and an increase in interest rates in the United States. It serves as a warning that any unexpected change in the internal or external environment holds the potential to cut short Latin America's recovery.

Table 6
Ratio of Total Debt (EDT) to GNP and Resultant Ratio Debt Service to Export Earnings (TDSEDT/XGS): 1982–1994

	EDT/GNP%			TDSEDT/XGS		
	1982	1990	1994	1982	1990	1994
Argentina	50.0	41.1	31.8	83.8	46.0	27.8
Belize	6.5	7.5	7.0	42.4	39.1	33.2
Bolivia	59.2	33.0	28.6	114.7	85.9	89.4
Brazil	81.3	22.4	31.8	34.8	26.0	27.9
Chile	71.3	26.4	19.2	76.7	67.4	45.5
Colombia	29.5	38.4	29.8	27.0	45.4	30.9
Costa Rica	21.4	24.2	14.6	167.5	68.1	47.8
Ecuador	78.4	33.1	21.8	66.9	122.7	94.6
El Salvador	13.7	16.7	14.5	43.2	45.6	26.9
Guatemala	11.3	12.3	10.9	17.9	38.1	23.4
Guyana	20.7	117.3	22.9	227.8	707.7	445.0
Honduras	31.1	36.9	34.9	67.9	135.8	151.6
Mexico	56.8	25.9	33.9	53.4	43.8	35.2
Nicaragua	44.2	3.9	38.2	111.6	1081.1	800.6
Panama	6.8	4.1	4.6	99.8	140.4	106.3
Paraguay	17.9	16.5	9.7	23.7	39.1	25.1
Peru	48.7	11.5	20.2	45.0	68.2	45.8
Uruguay	30.5	40.8	14.8	29.6	55.0	33.2
Venezuela	29.5	23.2	19.9	42.1	70.3	64.0
Average	**37.3**	**23.2**	**21.5**	**72.4**	**154.0**	**113.4**

Note: Belize EDT/GNP% data shown as 1994 are for 1993. Venezuela TDSEDT/XGS data shown as 1982 are for 1980.
Source: World Bank. (1993a, 1996b). *World Debt Tables.* Washington, D.C.: The World Bank.

Latin America's recovery will remain fragile until several related problems are resolved. First, Latin America's savings ratios remain among the lowest in the world. Between 1983 and 1992, they averaged 15.3% of GDP (Edwards, 1996). In contrast, the high performing East Asian countries had aggregate savings rates ranging between 30% and 40% of GDP, and government savings represented about one-third of aggregate savings (Edwards, 1996). Unless Latin America can substantially increase its rate of savings, growth will remain dependent on fickle foreign capital inflows. Second, income inequality is not only high, but is increasing. This not only has reduced the improvement in human well-being derived from the recent economic boom, but promises to increase political instability. Political instability reduces domestic savings and investment, two factors crucial to Latin America's sustained recovery. Of more immediate concern, the recent capital inflows will be reversed at the first sign of trouble.

Notes

1. The Latin American countries considered in this chapter include all 19 countries in Central and South America (Argentina, Belize, Bolivia, Brazil, Chile, Colombia, Costa Rica, Ecuador, El Salvador, Guatemala, Guyana, Honduras, Mexico, Nicaragua, Panama, Paraguay, Peru, Uruguay, and Venezuela). All averages and regional totals are computed for these 19 countries.

2. The primary school enrollment rates reported here are gross primary school enrollment rates. These are calculated as the number of children enrolled in primary school as a percentage of the number of children of primary school age. Gross primary school enrollment rates frequently exceed 100 as universal primary school enrollment is reached because some pupils are younger or older (due to grade repetition) than the country's standard primary school age.

References

Blitzer, C. (1986). Financing the World Bank. In R. E. Reinberg (Ed.), *Between Two Worlds: The World Bank's next decade* (pp. 135–160). Washington, D.C.: Overseas Development Council/Transaction Books.

Cline, W. (1983). *International debt and the stability of the world economy.* Washington, D.C.: Institute for International Economics.

Devlin, R. (1992). Options for tackling the external debt problem. In C. Wilber and K. Jameson (Eds.), *The political economy of development and underdevelopment* (pp. 210–233). New York: McGraw-Hill.

Edwards, S. (1996). Why are Latin America's savings rates so low? An international comparative analysis. *Journal of Development Economics, 51,* 5–44.

Grakel, I. (1996). Marketing the Third World: The contradictions of portfolio investments in the global economy. *World Development, 24,* 1761–1776.

Griffin, K., (1989). *Alternative strategies for economic development.* London: MacMillan Academic and Professional.

Summers, R., and Heston, A. (1991). The Penn World Table (Mark 5): An expanded set of international comparisons 1950–1988. *Quarterly Journal of Economics*, 106, 327–368.

United Nations Development Program. (1995). *Human development report 1995*. New York: Oxford University Press.

United Nations Development Program. (1996). *Human development report 1996*. New York: Oxford University Press.

World Bank. (1978). *World debt tables*. Washington, DC: World Bank.

World Bank. (1980). *World debt tables*. Washington, DC: World Bank.

World Bank. (1981). *World debt tables*. Washington, DC: World Bank.

World Bank. (1983). *World tables*. Baltimore: Johns Hopkins University Press.

World Bank. (1984). *World development report 1984*. New York: Oxford University Press.

World Bank. (1985). *World debt tables*. Washington, DC: World Bank.

World Bank. (1988). *World debt tables*. Washington, DC: World Bank.

World Bank. (1989). *World debt tables*. Washington, DC: World Bank.

World Bank. (1990). *Social indicators of development 1990: Data Disk*. Washington, DC: The World Bank.

World Bank. (1991). *World development report 1991: Supplementary data disk*. Washington, DC: World Bank.

World Bank. (1992a). *World development report 1992*. New York: Oxford University Press.

World Bank. (1992b). *World tables*. Baltimore: Johns Hopkins University Press.

World Bank. (1993a). *World debt tables*. Washington, DC: World Bank.

World Bank. (1993b). *World development report 1993*. New York: Oxford University Press.

World Bank. (1994). *World development report 1994*. New York: Oxford University Press.

World Bank. (1995a). *World development report 1995*. New York: Oxford University Press.

World Bank. (1995b). *World tables*. Baltimore: Johns Hopkins University Press.

World Bank. (1996a). *Social indicators of development*. Baltimore: Johns Hopkins University Press.

World Bank. (1996b). *World debt tables*. Washington, D.C.: World Bank.

World Bank. (1996c). *World development report 1996*. New York: Oxford University Press.

ARTISTIC

MANIFESTATIONS

Five Hundred Years of Latin American Literature

Gustavo A. Alfaro

Introduction

Five hundred years ago Spanish explorers emerging from the Middle Ages and eight centuries of struggle to reconquer Spain from the Moors "discovered" the New World. This world across the Atlantic Ocean had been inhabited for thousands of years by peoples of Asian origin who had developed advanced civilizations in Mesoamerica and Peru. In México, Aztec culture, the last of a number of splendid cultures, was on the ascendancy at the time of Cortés' arrival. The Incas in Peru had forged a vast empire stretching from what is now Ecuador to northern Chile. Unfortunately, the Spanish war of conquest and the iconoclastic fury of the Christians left little standing of these civilizations. In the first century after Columbus' arrival the Spaniards explored a vast territory stretching from northern California to Patagonia. A Latin American culture gradually emerged in these lands, a synthesis of the Indian, the Iberian, and the African cultures, and writing in Spanish began as soon as Columbus set foot in the New World.

The Literature of the Conquest and the Colonial Era

It is not surprising that the first literary manifestations in Spanish should be concerned with the events of the discovery and conquest. Columbus' letters and diary communicate his excitement, and though uncertain of what exactly he had discovered, he immediately began describing it. He saw the Caribbean islands as a kind of paradise inhabited by a beautiful people living in their natural state. He also praised the natural beauty of the islands and in his desire to reassure the Spanish monarchs about their investment in his enterprise, Columbus held out the dual prospect of gold and docile subjects. The Indians, according to Columbus, were peaceful, generous, and without guile and saw the Spanish as heaven sent. One senses, however, that it is gold that pushes Columbus forward from island to island in the Caribbean.

The letters of the conqueror of the Aztec empire, Hernán Cortés inform the Spanish emperor of his military feats and of the riches he has found in México, hoping to obtain Charles V's pardon for his unauthorized expedition. Cortés describes the Aztec capital, Tenochtitlan, as an imposing city with large squares, temples, and palaces, superior to any in Spain. In the total war of conquest, however, all this greatness was reduced to rubble. Years later, Bernal Diaz del Castillo, a foot-soldier in Cortés' army, wrote a chronicle in order to set the record straight and to obtain royal recognition for his contributions. *La verdadera historia de la conquista de la Nueva España* (written in the mid-sixteenth century but published in 1632), a detailed account of the conquest by this untutored soldier with a prodigious memory and great narrative skills, offers the immediacy and drama that only an eyewitness and participant can provide. He admires the achievements of the Aztecs but is revolted by some of their practices, in particular, human sacrifice and ritual cannibalism. In his account we come to know the personalities of the Machiavellian Cortés and the introspective Moctezuma, who seemed confused by the arrival of the strangers with their superior weapons and horses. Bernal Diaz candidly states that he and his companions had come to México to spread the faith but also to get rich.

Most of the Spanish writings in the first century are not, properly speaking, literature. The Spaniards first wrote histories, ethnographic studies, and tracts describing the continent, the inhabitants, and their customs. Most tend to justify the conquest of the Indians, but occasionally there is someone who takes up their cause. The best-known defense of the Indians is Bartolomé de Las Casas' *Brevísima relación de la destrucción de las Indias* (1552), an impassioned attack against the evils of the Spanish conquest. This work by a Franciscan friar, who had originally arrived in the New World as an ordinary settler, contributed to the creation of the Black Legend of Spain. Las Casas believed that the Indians must be converted, not enslaved, and that conversion should be accomplished by peaceful means. Other important works written by Spaniards who came in the sixteenth century are still valuable for an understanding of the conquered peoples, including Bernardino de Sahagún's *Historia general de las cosas de Nueva España* (1570–82), Toribio de Benavente's *Historia de los indios de Nueva España* (written in 1541, published in 1848), and José de Acosta's *Historia general y moral de las Indias* (1590). These histories, written by members of religious orders, are syntheses of the knowledge the scholarly evangelizers had gathered in the first century of the conquest.

As a result of Spain's strict control of education and cultural life, particularly of the printed word, relatively few works of literature were published during the three centuries of conquest and colonization. The paucity of literature in the beginning was also due to the fact that the vast majority of the conquerors were poorly educated, and that they had more pressing tasks, such as exploration, warfare, and survival. Moreover, Spain prohibited the importation of works of fiction or their publication in America. Education of the native population was not encouraged. When the authorities saw that a school in México City, founded soon after the conquest for the education of the Aztecs, was extraordinarily successful in teaching them Latin, music, and the arts, they promptly closed it. They no doubt saw in the education of the Indians a threat to their authority.

During the first century, the great majority of writers were Spanish born and their most important literary accomplishments were epic poems. *La Araucana* (in three parts, 1569, 1578, 1589) by Alonso de Ercilla, is considered the outstanding work of this genre. Ercilla was a nobleman, product of the Spanish Renaissance, and familiar with the European epic tradition. His epic poem, however, deals with an American theme, the Spanish war against the Araucanian Indians of Chile, a war in which the author himself took part, and

Ercilla is a hero of his own narrative. His work inspired several other epic poems in the New World but none that artistically surpassed it.

By the seventeenth century a few authors born in the New World appear on the scene. Some of them were of pure Spanish descent and others of mixed Spanish and Indian blood. Inca Garcilaso de la Vega, a contemporary of Cervantes, was the son of a Spanish nobleman and an Inca princess. As a young man he left Peru and settled in Spain, where he wrote *Comentarios reales* (1609) and translated Leon Hebreo's *Dialoghi d'Amore*, both considered models of Spanish prose of the Golden Age. His *Comentarios reales* deal with the origins of Inca civilization and its history and traditions until the arrival of the Spaniards. Inca Garcilaso embraces the Spanish culture of his father without rejecting the Inca culture of his mother. The other outstanding Latin American author of the seventeenth century is the Mexican nun, Juana Inés de la Cruz. The daughter of a *criolla* and a Spaniard, Sor Juana was possessed of a remarkable intellect, combining a talent and passion for poetry and a curiosity for science. She became a victim of the age and culture in which she was born. As a woman she was not expected to develop her intellect to the fullest, and she was prevented from pursuing her scientific interests. Eventually she was completely silenced by the Church, but not before she had written a body of poetry that gained for her a high place among the Baroque poets of her time. Her poetry is strongly influenced by Góngora, the highest exponent of the Baroque in Spain. Other important Latin American works of poetry are the Mexican Bernardo de Balbuena's *La grandeza mexicana* (1604), a description of the beauty of Mexican nature and of the refinement of life in the viceroyal capital; the Peruvian Diego de Hojeda's *La Christiada*, a long religious poem; and the Chilean Pedro de Ona's *El Arauco domado* (1596), an epic poem about the Araucanian Indians.

Independence: The Age of Civil Wars (1810–1910)

With the exception of Cuba and Puerto Rico, the Spanish colonies in the New World gained their independence between 1810 and 1825. French revolutionary ideas of freedom and equality, and the example of the U.S. revolution, inspired Latin Americans to proclaim their independence. In the new republics the main political and social change was the transfer of power from Spanish officials to the *criollo* elites. However, because of Spain's long cultural hegemony, Latin Americans found it difficult to break away from their old traditions. Gradually a more autochthonous literature began to emerge, even though conditions were not ideal for culture to flourish. Civil wars raged for nearly a hundred years following independence. The stability of the republics was constantly threatened by tyrants, but the principal antagonists were the liberals and the conservatives. The liberals stood for progressive social reforms, including separation of church and state, lay education, and a more democratic form of government such as existed in the United States. The conservatives, on the other hand, stood for tradition, particularly Spanish tradition, strong ties to the Catholic Church, and political power based on the *latifundio*, the great landed estates.

The first important literary work of this period is the novel *El Periquillo Sarniento* (1816) by the Mexican José Joaquín Fernández de Lizardi. Following the form of the Spanish picaresque novel, it is critical of Mexican society at the time of the War of Independence. Lizardi proposed a more liberal, progressive, and rational society, in which the virtues of study and hard work were cultivated. By the middle of the century, Romanticism had made its way to Latin America, particularly Argentina, where the struggle against the tyrant Manuel Rosas inspired two works of fiction: Esteban Echeverría's *El matadero* (1838), a novella in which the hero, a representative of the educated, Europeanized class, is set upon by a mob at the Buenos Aires slaughterhouse because he is perceived as an enemy of their idolized ruler, the dictator Rosas. The young man dies from the indignation he feels when the mob is holding him down. José Marmol's novel *Amalia* (1851) is also an attack against Rosas: two young lovers persecuted by the dictator manage to escape and get married, only to be finally captured and killed. The most influential work from this period, however, is *Facundo. Civilización y Barbarie* (1845) by Domingo Faustino Sarmiento who later became president of Argentina. The book is mainly a biography of Facundo Quiroga, a barbarous regional caudillo, and Rosas' strongest rival. The book also examines Argentina's political and social problems, which Sarmiento attributes to the semi-savage way of life in the pampas and the negative effects of both the Spanish and Indian heritages. The solution he proposes is to kill the Indian, tame the gaucho, and populate the pampas with "civilized" people. In the second half of the century, the Colombian Jorge Isaacs wrote *María* (1867), widely regarded as the best romantic novel in Latin America. It portrays an unhappy love story set in an idyllic yet recognizable Colombian landscape.

Poets made a more conscious effort to proclaim Latin America's cultural independence from Spain. The Ecuadorian José Joaquín de Olmedo's poem to Bolivar, "La victoria de Junin" (1825) is a neo-classical poem praising the great Liberator and the Latin American heroes of the final battle of the War of Independence. The Venezuelan poet, lawyer, and educator Andrés Bello wrote two neo-classical poems, *Alocución a la poesía* (1823) and *Silva a la agricultura en la zona tórrida* (1826), in which he adapts the classical tradition to the New World. A more authentically American expression is a series of narrative poems about the gauchos in the Argentine pampas. José Hernández' *Martín Fierro* (Part I, 1872; Part II, 1879) is a sympathetic portrayal of a gaucho's difficult existence at a time when his way of life is threatened by advancing "civilization." The first poetic movement to originate in Latin America and to have an influence on Spanish poetry in America and Spain is Modernismo. Toward the end of the nineteenth century the Nicaraguan poet Rubén Darío, inspired by the French Parnassian and Symbolist schools, revolutionized poetry in Spanish. In a musical, sensual, and poetic language, not inspired by his Latin American experience, Darío writes an escapist poetry dealing with distant, elegant, and decadent worlds. Although most of his poetry ignores his Latin American origins, in his later years Darío returns to the American scene in poems like "A Roosevelt," in which he compares the U.S. president to the Assyrian conqueror Nemrod, invader of an innocent, Spanish speaking and Indian America. Modernism proved very seductive, and many Latin American poets imitated Darío, among them the Colombian José Asunción Silva, the Cuban Julián del Casal, the Mexican Manuel Gutiérrez Nájera, and the Argentinian Leopoldo Lugones.

Independence: The Age of Revolutions (1910-Present)

Cuba's war of independence from Spain was the prelude to the present century of revolution in Latin America. It was a time when Latin Americans began to address some of the questions arising from the final retreat of Europe from the New World and the filling of the vacuum by the United States. The entry of the U.S. into Cuba's war of independence in 1898 signaled the beginning of a new political reality for Latin America. José Martí, the hero of Cuban independence, who died in the first battle for the liberation of his country, left an important body of poetry and essays. He was a precursor of Modernismo in his poetry and a visionary in politics, calling for Latin American unity and warning of the dangers from the giant to the north. A more influential essay of that time was the Uruguayan José Enrique Rodó's *Ariel* (1900), in which he contrasted the materialism of the United States and the spirituality of Latin America, which, according to him, was the true descendant of the classical culture of Greece and Rome.

The Mexican Revolution

The Mexican Revolution of 1910 was the first real social and political revolution of the twentieth century, and its repercussions were felt throughout Latin America. México's revolution gave hope that change was possible in the condition of the traditionally downtrodden, particularly the Indians. The cultural revolution that followed the armed struggle was equally significant. Literature and the arts were inspired by the culture of the masses and their struggle. Mariano Azuela's *Los de abajo* (1915) was the best novel to emerge from the Revolution. Written by a small town doctor who joined the Revolution in its early stages, it stays close to the battlefield and observes human behavior under revolutionary conditions. Azuela's disillusionment with the war includes both the peasants, whose ignorance condemns them to brutality, and the leaders, whose selfishness makes them cruel and cynical. Another masterpiece dealing with the Mexican Revolution, Martín Luis Guzmán's *El águila y la serpiente* (1928), is valuable for its portrayal of the leaders of the Revolution. The author, an intellectual who became Pancho Villa's secretary, describes in detail the character of the bandit turned general, showing Villa's courage and charisma as well as his brutality.

The Mexican Revolution gave rise to many other works of fiction. Martín Luis Guzmán's *La sombra del caudillo* (1927) is a *roman à clef* about the deadly politics of post-revolutionary México in the 1920s, when presidents began to be appointed by the outgoing ruler in the same manner in which it is still done today. Agustín Yánez' *Al filo del agua* (1947) deals with the origins of the revolution, describing life in a typical small town dominated by the Church and stifled by conservative traditions. The stagnant and suffocating life in México is communicated by the slow pace of the action. An undercurrent of restlessness suggests that the revolutionary storm, in the form of a rebel army on horseback, will be most welcome. In 1955 Juan Rulfo published *Pedro Páramo*, a phantasmagorical depiction of Mexican village life before and after the Revolution, in which life and death, myth and reality are deftly interwoven. The local caudillo, Pedro Páramo, survives the war through his clever manipulation of the peasants he has always dominated, only to die at the hands of one of his illegitimate sons. Although Pedro Páramo has always taken what he wanted, including many women, at the end he realizes that his only true love was unattainable. Carlos Fuentes has dealt with the Mexican Revolution in two major works: *La muerte de Artemio Cruz* (1962) and *El gringo viejo* (1986). In the first, the best-known of the Mexican Revolution cycle of novels, Fuentes presents a comprehensive history of the upheaval, beginning with its origins at the end of the nineteenth century and ending in the 1950s when the Revolution seems to have reached its nadir under president Miguel Alemán. This long history is seen through the trajectory of the hero, Artemio Cruz, the illegitimate son of a landed oligarch, who joins the Revolution and rises to great political and economic power, being corrupted in the process. Fuentes returns to the subject in *El gringo viejo*, this time with a different interest, to confront and contrast the two cultures he knows best: the Mexican and the North American. He invents a final chapter in the life of the American journalist Ambrose Bierce, old and disillusioned with his life in America, who goes south to die in the revolutionary struggle. Nothing is known of the real life of Bierce in México, but Fuentes fulfills his dream of dying in the Revolution.

Revolution in Prose

Three major writers born at the turn of the century may be considered the precursors of the literary Boom of the sixties and seventies: Jorge Luis Borges, Miguel Angel Asturias, and Alejo Carpentier. Their long and prolific lives allowed them to be both precursors and contemporaries of the Boom generation. Experimenting with language and structure, they wrote works of metaphysical, mythical, and historical interest. Asturias' *El Señor Presidente* (1946) is the first of the dictator novels, a sub-genre of the Latin American novel modelled on Ramón del Valle Inclan's *Tirano Banderas* (1926). Asturias depicts an unnamed Central American country reminiscent of the author's native Guatemala, existing in a state of terror under a tyrant not unlike Manuel Estrada Cabrera, who ruled the country when Asturias was a young man. The author describes a perverse world in which goodness is punished and evil rewarded. This work is also the first surrealist novel of Latin America. In his other major novel, *Hombres de maíz*, Asturias portrays the mythical world of the exploited and persecuted Guatemalan Indians. Their world seems so dehumanized and impenetrable that its fictional representation would later be called "magic realism."

The Argentine writer Jorge Luis Borges was the most famous and influential Latin American writer of his time. A poet, essayist, and short story writer, his fame is mainly due to two small collections of short stories, *Ficciones* (1944) and *El Aleph* (1949). The labyrinth is his favorite image for communicating the human condition, and he has a preference for intellectual games in which the world, real or imaginary, makes us reconsider our assumptions about time, history, and human destiny. In one of his stories Borges compares the universe to an enormous library; in another, he sees the whole world in an object that fits into the palm of his hand; in another, he makes it possible for a writer to will the suspension of time in order to complete the work that will redeem him; and in yet another, he shows that the desert can be a greater labyrinth than any constructed by man. For Borges, human beings will never be intelligent enough to comprehend the universe or God.

The Cuban novelist, Alejo Carpentier, heir to the cultures of France and of his native Cuba, studied architecture, music, history, and literature, and his novels reflect his cosmopolitanism and erudition. His fiction centers on the culture of the Caribbean, its history, its politics, and its racial complexity. He notes that Latin American reality often seems unreal and proposes the concept of the "marvelous real," to describe it. Latin American writers, by merely describing their reality, could achieve what Europeans could only imagine. In his early novel, *El reino de este mundo* (1949), he portrays Haiti's struggle for independence from France and life under its first black ruler, Emperor Henri Christoph. Tyranny is perpetuated by the new emperor who wants to replicate the splendor of Versailles in Haiti, a nation of former slaves still given to superstition and voodoo. One of Carpentier's latest and most ambitious novels, *La consagración de la primavera* (1978), traces the relationship of a young Cuban and a Russian ballerina, an emigree from the 1917 Revolution, who meet in Paris and whose lives are affected by the Spanish Civil War, the Second World War, and the Cuban Revolution. These novels, together with *El siglo de las luces* (1962), *El recurso del método* (1974), and *Los pasos perdidos* (1953), fictionalize the cultural and political history of the Caribbean peoples and their search for freedom and identity. In *Los pasos perdidos*, Carpentier contrasts Latin American, North American, and European cultures. The narrator, a Latin American musicologist living in New York, undertakes a journey in search of artifacts to prove his theory of the origins of music. The journey is a return to his homeland, a typical Latin American republic undergoing a violent change of government, followed by a journey to the heart of South America, deep in the Amazonian jungle, where he finds an earthly paradise and true love. But it is a tale of paradise lost: the hero leaves, intending to return, and can never find his way back.

Revolution in Poetry

Pablo Neruda is the first great revolutionary poet of Latin America. His early, and still popular, *Veinte poemas de amor y una canción desesperada* (1924) is strongly influenced by Modernismo. But he soon abandoned his modernist style for a poetry of desolation expressed often in surrealist images. *Residencia en la tierra* (1933–1935) reflects his experience in the Far East where he was posted as Chilean consul, and where he felt alienated and fatalistic. Neruda's next critical experience was the Spanish Civil War; it changed his politics and his poetry. It would no longer be self-centered but would be in the service of the proletariat. He wrote *España en el corazón* (1937), protesting, in a direct and often colloquial language, the horrors of Franco's war. Returning to Chile, he entered politics and was elected to Congress as a communist candidate only to see his party outlawed and himself become a fugitive. In these years he completed his monumental poem *Canto general* (1950), an epic history of Latin America from pre-Columbian times to his own time in Chile under the dictator who persecutes him. Another major political poet, César Vallejo, left his native Peru as a young man, settled in Paris, and also found himself on the side of the Republic during the Spanish Civil War. At age 26 he had already published an important book of poetry, *Los heraldos negros* (1918), followed a few years later by *Trilce* (1922). The experience of poverty and alienation made Vallejo alert to the absurdity and inhumanity of the world. These feelings he expressed in a hermetic poetry made up of startling language and images. He spent the last sixteen years of his life in Paris in difficult circumstances and like Neruda joined the communist party. His support of the Spanish Republic is expressed in *España, aparta de mi este cáliz* (1938), and *Poemas humanos* (1939).

Born almost a generation later, the Mexican Nobel laureate, Octavio Paz, also was involved in the Spanish Civil War on the side of the Republic, and like Neruda, spent time in the East in the diplomatic service. In 1950 he published one of the most influential essays on Mexican culture, *El laberinto de la soledad.* Although he wrote many other cultural and political essays, his fame rests mainly on his book of poetry, *Libertad bajo palabra* (1935–1960), in which he suggests that man can overcome isolation and attain love through poetry.

The Cuban Revolution

The Cuban Revolution of 1959 is the other political upheaval that has had a major impact on the course of Latin American history. It inspired revolutionary movements throughout South America, as well as writing in Cuba and outside of Cuba that was politically committed and revolutionary in structure and style. Writers put down the pen and took up the gun. Poets and priests headed for the jungle to fight alongside the guerrillas and some of them died in battle. Still others became exiles from their countries, and the 1960s saw García Márquez, Vargas Llosa, and José Donoso ironically finding shelter in Franco's Spain. Latin American writers and artists have traditionally been critics of dictatorial regimes and often radical in politics. Borges and the early Julio Cortázar were among the exceptions, but in his later years Cortázar was drawn into the battle and wrote works in favor of Latin American revolutionary movements. García Márquez' dictator novel, *El otoño del patriarca*, can be read as an anti-imperialist attack against all the powers that have dominated Latin America beginning with Spain and ending with the United States. However, as the Cuban Revolution evolved toward a more extreme form of communism, some writers began to drift away. Guillermo Cabrera Infante worked for the Revolution in the beginning but became disenchanted and fled to England. While in Cuba he had written *Tres tristes tigres* (1965), a novel inspired by Joyce's *Ulysses*, in which a group of friends spend a night in Havana visiting the entertainment spots while talking endlessly in a language rich in wordplay. *La Habana para un infante difunto* (1979), closer to Marcel Proust in inspiration, is an autobiographical account of his childhood and youth in Havana, with the emphasis on his erotic life. Edmundo Desnoes remained in Cuba until the eighties when he emigrated to the U.S. but never declared himself for or against the Revolution. His novel *Memorias del subdesarrollo* was made into a film that was acclaimed inside and outside of Cuba. It describes the experience of an intellectual, not unlike the author, who decides to remain on the island even when his wife, parents, and friends have left. He stays, not because he is in favor of the Revolution, but because he is curious to see if Cuba will cease to be a society devoted to trivial pursuits. What he observes, however, is that Cuba has exchanged one set of problems for another.

Many of the major novels of the sixties and seventies took the form of dictator novels. Following Asturias' example, three major Latin American writers published novels in which the main character is the dictator who has ruled Latin American republics so often. Carpentier's contribution, *El recurso del método* (1974) is about a Francophile Caribbean tyrant who spends all the time not committed to putting down rebellions in his country, enjoying the refinements of Parisian life. The Paraguayan Augusto Roa Bastos' *Yo el Supremo* (1974) portrays the tyranny of the eccentric Dr. Francia, ruler of Paraguay for a few decades after independence. And Gabriel García Márquez' *Otoño del patriarca* (1975) describes the absolute power and solitude of a typical Caribbean tyrant.

The Literary "Boom"

Among the novelists of the "Boom" of the sixties and seventies, four have enjoyed the greatest popularity and have had the most influence: Julio Cortázar, Carlos Fuentes, Mario Vargas Llosa, and Gabriel García Márquez. The Argentine Cortázar inherited from Borges the love of intellectual games, but he made them less obviously philosophical and more psychologically playful. Living in Paris for most of his adult life, Cortázar created in his work a bridge between Paris and Buenos Aires. In *Rayuela* (1963), structured so that it can be read in several ways by following different chapter sequences, Cortázar contrasts the rational French mind and the more instinctive Argentinian spirit. This exercise underlines the element of chance or accident in life.

Carlos Fuentes is the most prolific of the Latin American writers of the Boom. Author of many novels, he has also written short stories, plays, literary criticism, and journalistic articles and is a frequent lecturer in universities and on television. His novels deal almost exclusively with México's historical and social reality. Besides *La muerte de Artemio Cruz*, his novella *Aura* is considered a masterpiece. It is a gothic tale of perverted love in which the divine and the satanic are subtly combined to suggest ideas about generations and reincarnations. His most ambitious novels are *Terra Nostra* (1975) and *Cristobal Nonato* (1988). The first, an attempt at writing the total novel, is a brilliant, imaginative critique of imperial Spain, encompassing the sixteenth and seventeenth centuries but briefly jumping back to the time of Christ and forward to the end of the millennium. The second novel is equally ambitious, but here Fuentes undermines his achievement by attempting to imitate Cabrera Infante's prodigious wordplay, which is not Fuentes' forte.

The Peruvian novelist Mario Vargas Llosa is a playwright, academic, essayist, and politician (he ran for President of his country). His novels have managed to outrage the authorities of Peru, resulting in a public burning of one of his books. Of his shorter works, L*os cachorros* (1967) tells the story of a boarding school student who is castrated by a dog while taking a shower. His condition deeply affects his relationship with his parents and even more with his classmates. His condition is especially aggravated as they become adults and follow ordinary lives of courtship and marriage. Written as one paragraph with sudden shifts in point of view, time, and place, this story is one of the most successful stylistic achievements in Latin American narrative. Vargas Llosa is the author of a series of masterpieces: *La ciudad y los perros* (1963), a novel which explores the cruel and corrupt world of a military academy not unlike the one the author attended; *La casa verde* (1966), a technically complex narrative dealing with equally complex social situations, and set in both the jungle and desert regions of Peru; *Conversación en la catedral* (1969), a dark vision of politics in Peru in the 1950s; *La guerra del fin del mundo* (1981), a creative retelling of the episode of Brazilian history dealt with by Euclides da Cunha in *Os sertões* at the beginning of the century: the rebellion of the Canudos, religious fanatics who wanted to live independently but were crushed by the army. Other novels are written in a lighter, satirical vein: *Pantaleón y las visitadoras* (1971), a story of soldiers and prostitutes in an Amazonian jungle outpost and *La tía Julia y el escribidor* (1978), a semi-autobiographical work in which Vargas Llosa, the character in the novel, tells of his marriage to his aunt when he was a young aspiring writer.

Among the writers of the Boom, Gabriel García Márquez must be singled out as the most influential in Hispanic and world literature. If Latin America is in the middle of a literary Golden Age, García Márquez is its Cervantes and *Cien años de soledad* its *Don Quixote*. García Márquez' novel, like Cervantes', gained instant popular and critical acclaim and was translated into many languages. García Márquez has changed not only the world's perception of Latin America, but also the way many authors write today. *Cien años de soledad* chronicles Latin America's first hundred years of independence by tracing several generations of a family in a remote Caribbean town. On a larger scale it refers to Latin American history since the arrival of Columbus, and with its biblical overtones, it suggests the story of mankind, from the Creation to the Apocalypse. And yet this novel, like the book about the Spanish knight-errant, flows effortlessly and humorously, so that all can enjoy it. García Márquez has written several other recognized masterpieces, including *El coronel no tiene quien le escriba* (1961), *Crónica de una muerte anunciada* (1981), *El amor en los tiempos del cólera* (1985), and *El general en su laberinto* (1989). He is also a short-story writer, a writer of filmscripts, and a journalist. As a politically committed writer, García Márquez has occasionally played a role in mediating international crises. His speech before the Swedish Academy on the occasion of receiving the Nobel Prize is a memorable statement about the destiny of Latin America, a continent whose dream of solidarity has yet to become reality.

Conclusion

It took Latin America approximately 500 years to go from the epic writings of the conquerors to the fiction of García Márquez. It is a time-span comparable to the time between Spain's medieval epic, *Poema de Mio Cid* (1140) and Cervantes' *Don Quixote* (1605, 1615), the masterpiece of the Spanish Golden Age. The Boom, however, is a literary phenomenon that also required the confluence of unprecedented creativity and a vastly expanded readership in Spanish and in those languages into which Latin American literature has been translated. Besides the writers discussed above, a more complete list would have to include Manuel Puig, Reinaldo Arenas, Alfredo Bryce Echenique, Isabel Allende, Nicanor Parra, Salvador Elizondo, Fernando del Paso, Rosario Castellanos, Antonio Skármeta, Luisa Valenzuela, Rosario Ferré, Cintio Vitier, Severo Sarduy, Elena Poniatowska, David Viñas, Ernesto Cardenal, Gustavo Sainz, Luis Rafael Sánchez, and Roberto Fernández Retamar, to name only those that come to mind. These writers have made significant contributions to the literary flowering and no doubt will inspire new generations of writers that will insure a high place for Latin America in the literature of the twenty-first century.

Works Cited

Asturias, Miguel Angel (Guatemala). *El Señor Presidente*. 1946. San José, Costa Rica: EDUCA, 1973.

———. *Hombres de maíz*. Buenos Aires: Losada, 1949.

Azuela, Mariano (México). *Los de abajo*. 1915. México: Fondo de Cultura Económica, 1958.

Bello, Andrés (Venezuela). "Alocución a la poesía." 1823. *Antología poética*. Buenos Aires: Angel Estrada y Cía, 1952.

______. Silva a la agricultura en la zona tórrida. 1826. In *Antología poética*. Buenos Aires: Angel Estrada y Cía, 1952.

Borges, Jorge Luis (Argentina). *El Aleph*. 1949. Buenos Aires: Emece Editores, 1957.

———. *Ficciones*. 1944. Buenos Aires: Emece Editores, 1956.

Cabrera Infante, Guillermo (Cuba). *Tres tristes tigres*. 1965. Barcelona: Seix Barral, 1969.

Carpentier, Alejo (Cuba). *La consagración de la primavera*. Madrid: Siglo XXI, 1978.

______. *Los pasos perdidos*. 1953. México: Compañía General de Ediciones, S.A., 1959.

———. *El recurso del método*. México: Siglo XXI, 1974.

———. *El reino de este mundo*. 1949. Barcelona: Editorial Seix Barral, S.A., 1993.

———. *El siglo de las luces*. Barcelona: Editorial Seix Barral, S.A., 1993.

Colón, Cristóbal. *Diario de Colón; Libro de la primera navegación y descubrimiento de las Indias*. Carlos Sanza, Ed. Madrid, 1962.

Cortázar, Julio (Argentina). *Rayuela*. 1963. Buenos Aires: Editorial Sudamericana, 1970.

Cortés, Hernán (Spain). *Cartas de relación*. México: Porrúa, 1960.

de la Cruz, Sor Juana Inés (México). *Antología*. Ed. Elias L. Rivers, Biblioteca Anaya, Salamanca, 1965.

Darío, Rubén (Nicaragua). *Poesías completas*. Madrid: Aguilar, 1960.

Desnoes, Edmundo (Cuba). *Memorias del subdesarrollo*. México: Joaquín Mortíz, 1983.

Donoso, José (Chile). *El lugar sin límites*. México: Joaquín Mortíz, 1966.

Echeverría, Esteban (Argentina). *La cautiva y El matadero*. 1938. Buenos Aires: Sopena, 1962.

Ercilla, Alonso de (Spain). *La Araucana*. 1569. Santiago: Editorial del Pacífico, 1956.

Fernández de Lizardi, José Joaquín (México). *El Periquillo Sarniento*. 1816. México: Porrúa, 1962.

Fuentes, Carlos (México). *Aura*. Ediciones. México: Era, S.A., 1962.

———. *Cristóbal Nonato*. México: Fondo de Cultura Económica, 1988.

———. *Gringo viejo*. México: Fondo de Cultura Económica, 1986.

———. *La muerte de Artemio Cruz*. 1962. México: Fondo de Cultura Económica, 1970.

———. *Terra Nostra*. México: Fondo de Cultura Económica, 1970.

García Márquez, Gabriel (Colombia). *Crónica de una muerte anunciada*. Bogotá: Editorial La Oveja Negra, 1981.

———. *El amor en los tiempos del cólera*. Bogotá: Editorial La Oveja Negra, 1985.

———. *Cien años de soledad*. Buenos Aires: Editorial Sudamericana, 1969.

———. *El coronel no tiene quien le escriba*. Buenos Aires: Editorial Sudamericana, 1970.

———. *El otoño del patriarca*. Buenos Aires: Editorial Sudamericana, 1975.

———. *El general en su laberinto*. Madrid: Mondadori, S. A., 1989.

Garcilaso de la Vega, El Inca (Peru). *Comentarios Reales.* 1609. Madrid: Espasa–Calpe, 1961.

Guzmán, Marín Luis (México). *El águila y la serpiente.* 1928. México: Porrua, 1984.

———. *La sombra del caudillo.* México: Compañía General de Ediciones, S. A., 1962.

Hernández, José (Argentina). *Martín Fierro.* Garden City, NY: Doubleday & Company, Inc., 1962.

Isaacs, Jorge (Colombia). *María.* 1867. México: Porrúa, 1967.

Las Casas, Fray Bartolomé de (Spain). *Tratados.* México: Fondo de Cultura Económica, 1966.

Mármol, José (Argentina). *Amalia.* 1851. Buenos Aires: Estrada, 1944.

Motolinia, Fr. Toribio de Benavente (Spain). *Historia de los indios de Nueva España.* Barcelona, 1914.

Paz, Octavio (México). *El Laberinto de la soledad.* México: Fondo de Cultura Económica, 1970.

———. *Libertad bajo palabra.* México: Fondo de Cultura Económica, 1968.

Roa Bastos, Augusto (Paraguay). *Yo el Supremo.* Buenos Aires: Siglo XXI, 1975.

Rodó, Enrique (Uruguay). *Ariel.* Montevideo: Dornaleche y Reyes, 1900.

Rulfo, Juan (México). *El llano en llamas.* México: Fondo de Cultura Económica, 1970.

———. *Pedro Páramo.* 1955. México: Fondo de Cultura Económica, 1969.

Sahagún, Bernardino de (Spain). *Historia general de las cosas de Nueva España.* 1570. México: Porrúa, 1956.

Sarmiento, Domingo Faustino (Argentina). *Facundo. Civilización y barbarie.* 1845. Garden City, NY: Doubleday & Company Inc., 1961.

Vargas Llosa, Mario (Peru). *Conversación en la catedral.* Barcelona: Seix Barral, 1969.

———. *La casa verde*. Barcelona: Seix Barral, 1966.

———. *Los jefes. Los cachorros*. 1967. Madrid: Alianza Editorial, 1987.

———. *La guerra del fin del mundo*. Barcelona: Seix Barral, 1981.

———. *Pantaleón y las visitadoras*. Barcelona: Seix Barral, 1973.

———. *La tía Julia y el escribidor*. Barcelona: Seix Barral, 1982.

Yánez, Augustín (México). *Al filo del agua*. 1947. México: Porrúa, 1967.

The Indigenous and Neo-Indigenous Literature of Peru

Blas Puente-Baldoceda

Introduction

Peruvian literary production which deals with the Indians as a subject matter during the nineteeth and twentieth centuries has two phases: indigenous and neo-indigenous literature. The first, indigenous literature, or the so-called classic or orthodox phase, has in its turn two branches: the first tends to idealize, and the second focuses on the economic conditions of the Indian. Ideologically, both branches represent the reformism or the antioligarchical radicalism of a middle class that sought to modernize the supposedly archaic structure of Indian society by integrating and acculturating it into national society. On the other hand, these two branches can be explained in terms of a heterogeneous literary production: one socio-cultural sector produced and consumed the text, whereas another one, the Indian, served as a referent of that text. The writers of indigenous literature still have an external and dualistic vision of the "Indian problem." It doesn't matter whether it is the idealized view of Ventura García Calderón, the naturalism of Enríquez López Albújar, or the economicism and acculturation of the fiction of Ciro Alegría. In the second phase, neo-indigenous literature, a greater national integration of Peruvian society took place because of an intensive process of transculturation and ethnical hybridization. In this context, neo-indigenous literature rediscovered and revalued the intrinsic features of the autochthonous and crystallized an internal vision of Indians but was at the same time enriched by the modern contribution of mestizo culture.

Literature about Indigenous Peoples

Writers of the indigenous literature of the nineteenth century emphasized exoticism and commiseration in dealing with the Andean population, but they fell short in understanding their real social and economic conditions. Most of their plays, poetry, short stories, and novels were filled with romanticism, although an exceptional case seems to be *El padre Horán* (1848) by Narciso Aréstegui. This novel is the first in the Peruvian context to show an authentic concern for the vindication of the Andean peasants. In the nineteenth century, there was no definite political plan to rehabilitate this ethnic group, only isolated efforts to question the taxation imposed on them. In 1860, a project for promoting exportation was proposed to develop the economy and eventually incorporate peasants into the working class. This proposal was based on the idea that the misery of the peasants was the result of exploitation by the landlords of the Andes. This liberal project was rejected by the conservatives, who wrote in their journal *El progreso católico* that exportation was a sacrilege, and the solution should be to assimilate the Indians to the Spanish culture through the reconquest of Perú by the Spaniards. At the end of the nineteenth century, a schism disrupted the political scene: one sector of the Civil Party argued in favor of accumulating national capital to avoid foreign domination, whereas a second one –including Manuel González Prada– was opposed to the land exploitation of the oligarchy and supported the industrialization of the country.[1] González Prada argued that the nation was constituted not only by the descendants of the Spanish but also by the Andean population, whose exploitation was the source of wealth for the upper class. He also argued that the problem was not local nor transitory; on the contrary, it had a national magnitude and was characterized by the following social typology: Indians are ignorant servants; the white exploiters are free but also ignorant; and the intellectuals, educated and free, do not assume their responsibility of liberating the oppressed group by suppressing the ignorance of the white exploiters. Based on this typology, Clorinta Matto de Turner (1852–1909) pioneered realism with an indigenous theme. In her novels, the educated whites fail in their attempt to suppress the ignorance and corruption of the wealthy whites, and the integration of the peasants to the economy of the national society is only feasible through Western education. Although her novels do not deal specifically with the exploitation of the peasants by the landlords, they reveal the ideology of the liberal middle class, which rejected the semifeudal system of the Andean landlords.

In the second decade of the twentieth century, an ideological movement concerning the Andean populations evolved in Perú, Bolivia, Ecuador, and with less resonance in Mexico and Guatemala. This movement sought not only the social and economic rehabilitation of the peasants but also an understanding and appreciation of their cultural and artistic values. The literary expression of this movement was the indigenous literature written by mestizo writers. In this respect, Mariátegui has pointed out:

> A rigorous and credible account of the Andean spirit can not be provided by the mestizo writers. They have to idealize and to stylize the Indians. For this reason it is called indigenous and not Indian. An authentic Indian literature will eventually arrive when the Indians are in condition of publishing it. (qtd. in Rama, *Transculturación* 140)

However, the production of indigenous literature cannot only be explained from the ethnic perspective. A sociological approach reveals that a middle class with access to education and social mobility assumed the vindication of the oppressed since the Indians were not capable of reclaiming their rights themselves. Using literature as a critical instrument, this middle class promoted a process of acculturation and incorporation of the natives to the national society in order to facilitate modernization according to a capitalistic mode of production and an economy of dependency:

> An emergent middle class in social mobility usurps the reclamations of other oppressed social groups in order to reinforce themselves with massive popular support. Solidarity with the oppressed peasant who suffers social injustice is a mere disguise. In spite of having created an original culture in the past, the Indian population remains silent because a middle class which has at its

disposition the written system or the plastic expression speaks for them. (quoted in Rama, *Transculturación* 142–43)

To be more precise, these middle-class writers came from the provinces, and they accomplished their literary work in the cities. That is to say, the indigenous literature took place in an urban and modern context, although the first artistic experiences of the writers belonged to the provincial context, especially in the rural area (Cornejo Polar, *Literatura* 16).[2] Written by and for an emergent middle class, this indigenous literature, inserted in an urban-capital space, did not let the natives speak for themselves. On the contrary, this literature speaks for them to an audience that is exclusively white or mestizo but not Indian. However, the fragmentation of Peruvian reality in the twentieth century could not be restricted entirely to issues of ethnicity (white, mestizo, and Indians), to region (coast and highland), and social factor (middle class and peasants). The fragmentation of the country involved other areas such as linguistics, culture, and economics. José Carlos Mariátegui says:

> The problem of unity in Peru is very complex. It is not a matter of putting together a plurality of local or regional traditions but of understanding the diversity of race, language and feelings as a historical outcome of the conquest of Perú by a foreign race which was not able either to eliminate, to merge nor to assimilate the vanquished Peruvians. (quoted in Cornejo Polar, *Literatura* 11)

In this context of social and cultural opposition between oppressor and oppressed arose a heterogeneous literature in which the production of the text and its reception is located in one sociocultural sector of the Peruvian society, whereas the subject matter of this literature is located in another. The essence of indigenous literature is this conflictive heterogeneity in the literary process; that is, the asymmetric relation between the modern and Western sector that produces and consumes the text and the indigenous sector that makes up the subject matter of the text. This internal contradiction reflects obviously the fundamental contradiction of Andean reality (Cornejo Polar, "Sobre el 'Neo-indiginismo'" 550). The use of standard Spanish instead of Quechua or Aymara as channels of communication shows obviously the Western orientation of the writers of indigenous literature. Also, the use of the novel as genre is reflected in the different schools adopted by these writers: romanticism, naturalism, realism, and magic realism. On the other hand, the literary text reproduces clearly the tension and ideological interference between the Western world view of the producer/receptor and the world view of the Indian.

However, it is not sufficient only to look at the cultural mixture, ethnic conflict, and regional opposition of the twentieth century in Perú as causes of the heterogeneity of the indigenous literature; it is also necessary to do a careful analysis of the economic conditions of that disintegrated society. In the undeveloped urban sector within a capitalistic economic system, a confrontation took place between the modern and pro-imperialist bourgeoisie and the radical middle and lower social classes, whereas in the agrarian sector of the Andes the peasants confronted the landlords who oppressed them within a feudalistic regime. In fact, this complex economic situation served as the infrastructure of the heterogeneity of the indigenous literature.

For Mariátegui any political, juridical, ecclesiastical, ethnic, or cultural solution to the problem of the Indian population was prone to fail because it disguised or distorted the real cause of their oppression: their miserable economic condition.

> According to Mariátegui, the problem of the Indians is the possession of land. The solution would be to liquidate the feudal system of the Andean landlords. The perpetuation of the latifundium and the servitude is an agrarian problem with national implications. (Escobar 27)

Textual Production of Indigenous Writers

Inca culture was idealized when new archaeological and bibliographic material was discovered (Paracas, Macchu Picchu, Guamán Poma de Ayala), and this tendency to nostalgia was intensified to the extent that a utopian restoration of this historical period was proposed by the indigenous movement. This revalorization generated a vision of the Indian as a historical entity. The most representative works of this phase of indigenous literature in Peru are *La venganza del condor* (1924) by Ventura García Calderón and the collection of short stories *Los hijos del sol* (1921) by Abraham Valdelomar. With a florid prose in the modernist style, García Calderón fantasizes his Indian characters as being an essential component of Andean nature without hiding a historical perspective that glorifies the Spanish conquest:

> Obviously Ventura García Calderón represents the ideology of the Peruvian oligarchy which legitimates the cruel and violent conquest by presenting it as legendary and historical. In spite of being barbaric, it is glorious and fascinating and this is enough to justify any abuse committed against the defeated and exploited Indian population. According to Mariátegui this perspective corresponded to the spirit of cast of the Spanish conqueror and the colonist who was granted Indian laborers by royal decree. (Cornejo Polar, *Literatura* 46–47)

This historical nostalgia is manifested in some of the short stories of Valdelomar, whose work in general does not belong to the indigenous trend. However, he portrays the rural space with its Indian inhabitants in a concise style, and in this sense he surpasses the verbose prose of some modernists.

Another branch of the first period of indigenous literature is grounded in the belligerent rehabilitation of the Indians proposed by Mariátegui. The most representative work in the Peruvian context are short stories, *Cuentos andinos* (1920) and *Nuevos cuentos andinos* (1937) by Enrique López Albújar (1872–1966), whose naturalistic realism is a continuation of the trend initiated by Aréstegui and Matto de Turner. Nevertheless, López Albújar is the first writer to describe the psychology of the Indians. In spite of having created complex characters without false embellishments or idealizations, he was not able to penetrate to the core of the Indian interiority since his approach is restricted to individual cases of delinquency. For this reason, his characters are depicted as being violent, cruel, and dominated by primitive passions, so that the view is partial, deformed, and negative. This external and objective vision is derived from the positivistic psychology practiced by the writer in his experience as a judge. In any case, the Indian in López Albújar's fiction is not the flat character of nineteenth-century indigenous literature; on the contrary, he seems to have a life of his own for the first time.

The well-known novel *El mundo es ancho y ajeno* (1941) by Ciro Alegría (1909–1967) deals specifically with the Indian community from its origin until its extinction, prompted by the avarice of the landlords. This novel exemplifies the heterogeneity of indigenous literature in the realistic mode and, in general, is concerned with the soul of the Andean man, agrarian production, the history of oppression, the spirit of solidarity, the failure of the judicial system, the privileges of the country represented by the central government, and the misery of the real country represented by the peasants and shepherds of the highland (Castro Arenas 227). The most relevant feature of this work is its economic perspective. It emphasizes the ownership of the land and the exploitation of the peasant, the dual conception of coast and highland, and the idea of modernization as a vehicle to acculturate and integrate the Indian population as a productive force within the national society. Integration is to be achieved through an intensive campaign of literacy, modern technology, and a gradual change of the collective habits of the Andean people. In Rumi, the Indian community, there is a harmony between man and nature that allows for the socialization of its inhabitants. When this magic and mythical world is disrupted by the rapacity of the landlords, some of its members migrate to the cities of the coast where they fail to adapt themselves to an alien environment. This inability to change depicts the value system of the native culture –the so-called barbaric or primitive– is superior to that of the urban, civilized area where the writers of indigenous literature originate. Moreover, the return of Benito Castro from military service in the capital signals the emergence of a historical consciousness that allows the natives to conceive of events within a causal and objective order without recurring any longer to supernatural explanations.

> There is a mixture of a magic consciousness with a historical one and eventually the latter prevails. At the beginning the historical consciousness is the privilege of the narrator, but afterwards it spreads among the characters when the rejected western social order has destroyed the ideal enclosure of the elders in the community. Benito Castro has learned the social rules in the territory of the enemy and when he returns to the highland he confronts the members who still believe in the magic power of a lake in the social dynamic. This novel shows undoubtedly the contradictory aspects of the indigenous literature. (Cornejo Polar, 1987, xxiv)

On the other hand, Alegria's novel also presents some of the new features that characterize neo-indigenous literature. Narrative techniques such as the use of folklore affect the structure of the Western novel and generate an original narration with roots in popular culture. Also, the use of the voices of the oral tradition as minor narrative units are fitted in the setting and the plot of the novel. This Western genre is adapted to represent the idiosyncrasies of the native referent and undergoes a transformation in its structure and style; therefore, a peculiar conception and praxis of the novel arises whose instability and multiplicity reflects the heterogeneity of indigenous literature.

Neo-Indigenous Literature

For Tomás G. Escajadillo, the neo-indigenous literature is not a cancelation but a transformation of traditional indigenous literature, and this new phase starts with *Los ríos profundos* (1958) and "La agonía de Rasu „iti" (1960) by José María Arguedas and the short stories by Eleodoro Vargas Vicuña (1924). The characteristics of neo-indigenous literature are the following: a) use of magic realism to incorporate Andean mythology; b) intense lyricism as part of the narration; c) experimentation with narrative technique; and d) increase of the fictional representation by including other spaces according to the transformation of the national society (Cornejo Polar, "Sobre el 'Neo-indiginismo'" 550). Gutiérrez rejects the term neo-indigenous and prefers "rural Andean" for this indigenous narrative form that arose during the fifties. He argues that it is different from the rural pertaining to the coast and also from the urban narrative. The adjective rural alludes to the subject matter rather than to the space where the literary production takes place, since the neo-indigenous phase as well as the indigenous are urban phenomena that are influenced by Andean culture and urban modernism.

Furthermore, the neo-indigenous phase differs from the indigenous phase not only in terms of narrative technique but also in terms of the relation that exists between narrator and fictional representation. In the indigenous literature, the confrontation between the Indian community and the landlord who was in alliance with the state apparatus was the main factor in the plot, but in neo-indigenous literature the narrator, besides taking sides with the peasants in their struggle, promotes the forms of life and the value system of the natives. Social struggle become secondary and the human condition of the Indians turns into the most relevant factor in the neo-indigenous narrative (Gutiérrez 1988, 103). Adopting an internal perspective, the neo-indigenous writers aspire to revalue, to legitimize, and to preserve the intrinsic features of native culture, and for this reason the movement is called "culturista." This promotion of native culture involved not only a generation of intellectuals in the literary field but also comtributors from other disciplines such as sociology, anthropology, ethnology, linguistics, and folklore. Without neglecting the social, economic, and political reclamation of Indian populations, these writers were able to penetrate very deeply into the cultural identity and the value system of the Indian world, and for them both are the main sources of national culture. This cultural movement was intensified with the massive migration of the Andean population to the industrialized cities of the coast, which generated an accelerated process of transculturation along with an accelerated process of hybridization.[3] Arguedas argues that a cultural –not necessarily racial-hybridization– has emerged as a result of the coexistence and reciprocal influence of European and Indian culture for several centuries:

> For many centuries European and Indian cultures have coexisted in the same territory and between them there was an uninterrupted interaction. Through diverse, powerful and numerous channels the former has influenced the latter, which has been able to keep its internal structure and to remain in its native setting; the result of this unceasing and reciprocal influence is the emergence of a human product who is showing an overwhelming activity: the mestizo. We are arguing in terms of culture; we do not consider the concept of race at any moment. Anyone can see in Peru Indians who are white by the color of their skin, and also dark colored individuals whose behavior corresponds to a western culture. (quoted in Escobar 52–53)

The mestizo is the key element in the foundation of the national culture because of his skill, energy, and ability for preserving the Indian heritage within an intensive process of transculturation. He revived the artistic traditions of the Indian and moved them from a provincial space to a national space. The resulting cultural identity used the value system of the native culture as the foundation for absorbing the Spanish heritage (religion, clothes, instruments, farming, celebrations) and assimilating them to its own tradition (Rama, *Transculturación* 183–86). For instance, in *Yawar Fiesta,* Arguedas shows that there is no way to know whose *modus pensandis* prevails: the white's, the mestizo's, or the Indian's. The world represented in the novel is a large community where different ethnic groups coexist by forming a complex net of mutual influences.

On the other hand, this intense process of hybridization has narrowed considerably the distance between coast and highland, capitalism and feudalism, urbanism and ruralism, western and native; consequently, a process of integration has taken place in Peruvian society. However, this does not imply an egalitarian society; on the contrary, there is still a dichotomy between a hegemonic economic sector and the subordinate and dependent sectors. In this context of relative socio-cultural integration in which the distance of the traditional dichotomies has decreased, the writers of neo-indigenous literature faced, as did those of the previous phase: "how to reveal the indigenous world [although the indigenous now appears strongly mixed] from the perspective of another socio-cultural sector" (Cornejo Polar, "Sobre el 'Neoindiginismo'" 550). From my point of view, the question raised by this critic is undoubtedly valid for the indigenous literature, but not for the neo-indigenous literature since the knowledge and appreciation of the writers of the second phase toward indigenous culture is intrinsic insofar as they inherit it from their predecessors; therefore, they are capable of assuming an ideology and esthetic that are both autochthonous. Their revelation and appraisal of the intrinsic features of Indian culture is enriched by the contributions of modernization in order to form an Andean discourse. This immersion of the original sources of the native culture within the instruments of modernity crystallizes in the creation of formal innovations in the narrative and linguistic structure of the story. These innovations constitute characteristics of the neo-indigenous narratives, equivalent to the neo-cultural features of the transculturation created by writers who originated from the Andean socio-cultural sector and lived in the coastal cities.

The transition from the indigenous to the neo–indigenous literature is illustrated by linguistic transformations of the literary discourse. Under the influence of regionalist writers such as Gallegos, Rivera, and Azuela, the writers of the former imitate the speech of popular characters in order to obtain a more realistic representation. This stylization of the regional dialects is made by a phonetic deformation of words and by syntactic interferences. On the other hand, the narrator –urban, educated, and familiar with the idiomatic norms of Standard Spanish– uses strictly a literary language that is suitable for artistic creation. This linguistic unbalance between the narrator and the characters can be explained in terms of the class and culture division of the first phase of the indigenous literature. In *Agua, Yawar Fiesta,* and *Diamantes y pedernales,* which represent the first period of Arguedas' writing, the author accommodates the Spanish vocabulary into the Quechua syntax; in other words, he creates a mixed language in order to represent the speech of Andean characters with a higher degree of authenticity, whereas the fluid, rigid, strongly standardized speech of the narrator functions as a directing norm in the text. In the first period of Arguedas's fiction, the dialogues are written using a dialectalized speech that serves as an artificial sign to indicate that the character is Indian or mestizo (Rama, *Transculturación* 239). In his later work, Arguedas replaced this conventional language with a literary discourse that is linguistically more integrated; for that reason, the text has artistic unity.[4] In sum, in the literary discourse of the neo-indigenous writers there is a considerable reduction of regional vocabulary, phonetic alterations of the words, and syntactic inferences from Quechua. Instead, all these elements are contextualized in the text to obtain a linguistic unification of the text:

> [The] original contribution of the writers who participate in the transculturation [or neo-indigenous writers] is the linguistic unification of the literary text according to the principles of artistic unification by using their own language instead of the learned language. In sum, they return to their own linguistic community to be able to speak from inside and using openly their own idiomatic strategies. [This community] is rural and strongly indigenous, and its linguistic system is re-elaborated artistically by the neo-indigenous writers from inside instead of imitating a regional dialect from an external position. (Rama, *Transculturación* 212–213)

Textual Production of the Neo-Indigenous Writers

The neo-indigenous writers are divided into two groups: Carlos Eduardo Zavaleta (pioneer of neo-indigenous literature since 1954), and Manuel Scorza, Marcos Yauri Montero, and Edgardo Rivera Martínez form part of the first group. A younger generation of writers form part of the second group: Félix Huamán Cabrera, Hildebrando Pérez Huaranca, Víctor Zavala Cataño, and

Oscar Colchado Lucio. With the exception of Huamán Cabrera, all of them write exclusively short stories, while Scorza and Yauri Montero are novelists (Escajadillo 85–86). Subsequently, I will analyze the narrative structure and the literary language in Manuel Scorza's novel and Oscar Colchado's short stories in order to exemplify the narrative innovations and the literary language of the neo-indigenous trend.

In his fiction, Scorza recreates the atrocious massacre perpetrated by the repressive Peruvian government in order to defeat the Indians in their struggle for liberation during the 1950s and 1960s. The author considers his saga of five novels *La guerra silenciosa,* as a chronicle of the peasant war or the "Andean Vietnam." In the *Redoble por Rancas* (1971), the narrative structure is organized in the following way: first, a third-person narrative voice, omniscient and omnipresent, registers different spaces and times through zero perspective or external perspective.[5] This voice provides the interpretation, generalizations, and evaluations concerning events related to ethnography, history, and the oneiric world of the characters. The explicit, concise, objective, and linear narration of events can be characterized as the high style of the written register. Second, a third-person narrative voice with an internal perspective describes the interiority of the characters. The style of this voice tends toward the oral register. Third, a first-person narrative voice corresponding to one of the characters is situated in a second narrative level. This voice belongs definitively to the oral register. Fourth, a narrative voice of one of the characters participates directly in narrated events as an invisible witness whose style is a mixture of written and oral registers. Furthermore, this manifold or polyphony of voices is manifested in the text by means of different discursive strategies such as narratized speech, direct speech, indirect speech, free indirect speech, and free direct speech.[6]

On the other hand, among third-person narrative voices there is an authorial voice that makes a parody of the style of Cervantes in the title of each chapter. The ideology of this narrative voice is congruent with that of the implied author and also with that of the biographical author.[7] The latter, Scorza, assumes in his creative work an ideological and political compromise with the peasant struggle. For this reason, the ideological norms of the implied author impugn four parts of the ideological apparatuses of the state: the religious, the judicial, the cultural, and the educational[8]; at the same time the army and the police –the repressive apparatus of the state– are denounced. These ideological and repressive apparatuses are in alliance to defend the economic interests of the American company Cerro de Pasco Corporation, which has appropriated the land of the Indian communities. The fact that the enemy is not only the Andean landlord but also an American company shows an increase of the fictional representation in the neo-indigenous narrative. In any event, Alfonso Rivera, as representative of the community, suggests the use of the legal system as a strategy for liberating the peasants, but Fortunato, aware of the real cause of injustice, persuades Rivera to use the same strategy as the oppressor: violence, because for him to believe in the judicial system of the oppressor is part of false consciousness. The demystifying purpose of the authorial ideology is manifested in another character: the lucid and courageous Hector Chacón who, aware of the farce of the judicial system, challenges the repressive apparatus of the state when he adopts violence as the only way for liberation.

The rejection of religious dogma –another ideological apparatus of the state by the implied author is seen through the behavior of Teodoro Santiago– a religious fanatic, who uses the biblical apocalypse to spread supernatural explanations for the apparition of the wired fence built by the Cerro de Pasco Corporation to protect its property. After a massacre perpetrated by the police, in a magic realist scene, the soul of Santiago talks to Fortunato's in the cemetery, and the latter persuades the former of the real cause of the oppression of the indigenous community:

> —You are right, little toad. It is no Christ who punish us, but the Americans.
> — Are you convince now, Santiago?
> — You convince me, Fortunato! (Scorza 284)

As far as the cultural ideological apparatus is concerned, the social, linguistic, and ideological stratification of Peruvian society is reflected in the plurality of narrative voices; this heteroglossia determines the polyphonic structure of the novel.[9] The narrator's intention orchestrates skillful stylizations of diverse discourses such as those of the historiographer, ethnographer, and the oneiric world of the characters. In particular, the parody of high style speech demonstrates the author's intention of mocking the literary canon. In other words, the florid, ornamental, and wordy style of the so-called high or canonical literature is ridiculed by means of parodic stylization;[10] on the contrary, the oral tradition forms the sediment of a new literary language proposed by this neo-indigenous writer. Finally, as for the educational ideological apparatus, the authorial intention rejects the sacred canon of the official history; using humor, irony, and parody, the official history is shown to be nothing but a masquerade, a farce, a fable of lies that the hegemonic group uses to justify their economic, political, and cultural oppression of the Indian community. Instead, the authentic history is given by the oral tradition based on songs, legends, myths, and folktales.[11]

In the short story "Cordillera negra" by Oscar Colchado Lucio, linguistic integration provides artistic unity to the narrative text. In his literary discourse there is some morpho-syntactic interference from an indigenous language, Quechua, but the author is able to accommodate this interference through a process of stylization; consequently, the enunciation of the narrator and the enunciation of the characters are linguistically uniform.

The following are some of the linguistic features of this literary language: final position of the verb in the sentence as a result of the Quechua order subject-object-verb; inversion of verbal periphrasis; the use of gerund to translate the Quechua suffixes of syntactic subordination; some lexical and phonetics features such as elision of articles and rephonologization of Spanish words according to the Quechua sound system; the use of a verb "*decir*" (to say) in its forms "*diciendo*" (saying) or "*dizque*" (say that); the adjective "*seguro*" (sure) to translate the Quechua suffixes for discursive validation -shi and -chi; the borrowing of Quechua words; onomatopoeias; archaisms; translations of the

Spanish suffix -ción to translate the Quechua suffix -na; the adverb "*nomás*" (only) to translate the Quechua suffix -na; and the diminutive -ito to translate the derivative suffix: -lla and -chay. All these features of Andean Spanish are not merely glossed in the text, but they have acquired stylistic relevance and function as rhetorical strategies of a new literary language. On the rhetorical level of the discourse –metaphor, simile, and hyperbole– are used very often in the descriptions, and their semantic content alludes to the Andean flora, fauna, and climate of which the author shows a deep knowledge.

Conversely, the events are narrated from an internal perspective by using the indirect free speech of a narrator who acts as protagonist and witness. His narration has an epic tonality when it deals with collective actions; for instance, the battles between the Indians and the whites, and a lyric tonality when he deals with his individual actions (evocation of his childhood, his idyllic relations, or his doubts about his Christian beliefs). In any case, the narration starts in *media res* and the subplots –the collective ones as well as the individual ones– are organized in a relatively chronological sequence of scenes with flashbacks and anticipations. Although these scenes, which have a certain degree of autonomy, appear to be merely juxtaposed, there is a relation of causality between some of them. In addition, the narrative distance between the narrator and the events narrated is minimal due to his role as protagonist as well as witness. Nevertheless, at the end of the short story, the verbal tense, preterit and imperfect, changes suddenly to present tense in which the narrator-protagonist turns out to be the voice of a rock that heals the sickness of the hearts according to the pattern of Andean mythology. At any rate, the ideological inference from the text is that in this supernatural remembrance of a rock there is the purpose of rewriting the official history from the indigenous perspective.

Atusparia, the mestizo leader, conceives the rebellion as a protest against tributes and the exploitation of workers. On the contrary, the Indian Uchcu Pedro considers it as a violent and radical revolution against the dominance of the Spanish descendants, and his ultimate goal is the restoration of the Inca empire. For this reason, Uchcu Pedro denounces the defensive position of Astuparia as treason and as a sign of defeat. When the latter changes his mind about setting the towns on fire, the oppressor allows him to return to his farm. For his part, Uchcu rejects the peace treaty that is proposed by the priest. In exchange for his surrender, the oppressor promises the Indian leader and his followers a pardon and the possibility of returning to their land, but Uchcu Pedro decides to continue his struggle until he is executed. Furthermore, he mocks the firing squad by pulling down his pants and showing his buttocks. During the battles, Uchcu Pedro reinforces the courage of his few faithful followers by mentioning examples from Andean mythology. For instance, he tries to convince them that Wiracocha is asking for revenge, testing their endurance, and also predicting the future each time the Andean deity shows them the bloody strings of Huascarán mountain, a flying condor, or an aggressive puma hiding in the sanctuary that served as refuge to Uchcu Pedro when he was persecuted by government troops. Another mentioned Andean deity is Mama Quilla (mother moon), who cries blood instead of tears for the defeat of her sons, the Indians.

Similarly, during the Inca Empire the deserters were turned into rocks and were later considered deities by Uchcu Pedro and his followers, who hope to resuscitate them by praying. At any rate, the failure of the Indian insurrection is not only attributed to the defeat of the leader Atusparia and Justo Solís, but also to the relinquishment of small farmers, an absence of followers from Conchuco, the failed participation of the riders of Trujillo and Huánuco, and to the impossibility of recruiting new contingents among the youngsters who are hiding because the defeat of the Indian uprising is imminent. Besides, the troops of the government were reinforced by ethnic minorities –blacks and Chinese– who brutally raped Indian women. As a last resort, Toman Nolasco, the narrator-protagonist, organizes a procession for Taita Mayo (the statue of Christ), who made a miracle of healing him when he was a child, so they can get help from Him, but Uchcu Pedro attempts to attack the stretcher with a knife because he thinks that Christ is the God of the whites. Before plundering and setting towns on fire, Tomás Nolasco admits reluctantly his ungratefulness to Christ, but he justifies his participation in the popular war since it constitutes a defense of his race. As one can see, the revolution comprises not only socio-economic factors but also the ideological apparatus of religion as in the case of *Redoble por Rancas.* In any case, a combination of epic and lyric narration is shown in an idyllic scene where Tomás Nolasco falls in love with Marcelina. Also, there is a humorous scene: the soldiers of the government die as a result of an ambush after being lured by the song and the beauty of the lover of one of the leaders of the insurrection. Humor in the form of irony and parody are rhetorical strategies used quite often by the neo-indigenous writers.

In sum, Scorza and Colchado Lucio, within the sphere of influence of Arguedas, created a neo-indigenous narrative as participants in an intensive process of transculturation that has been taking place in Peru since the 1950s. Based on an autochthonous esthetic and ideology and a profound knowledge of the language and culture of the Andean region, they were able to crystallize a new literary language. Their artistic restructuring or transfiguration of the oral and popular traditions is incomparable. Undoubtedly, this contrasts with the prejudice of the dominant Peruvian culture and its canonical literature, which pretends to deny or to ignore the literature created by the subordinate social classes or by the oppressed ethnic groups.

Notes

Thank you to John Alberti from the Department of Literature and Language at Northern Kent University for collaborating generously in the editing of this article.

1. Manuel González Prada was the ideological and political leader of the post-romantic generation; he was not only a great orator and polemicist but also an esthete and a poet. He is the author of *Páginas libres* (1894), *Horas de lucha* (1908), and other political books about Peruvian society.

2. A more careful sociological approach would also note the relations between the lower middle class along with the first manifestations of the working class and the peasant movement in Peru. Evidence of such popular movements in the tuentieth century are the foundation of the Central Organization of Workers in 1929, the appearance of the journal *Amauta* in 1926 with Mariátegui as a director, the situation of *Resurgimiento* in Cuzco in 1927, the foundation of the political party APRA in 1928, and the insertion of the communist party in the political scene in 1930. The indigenous movement took place in this social and political world full of conflict and tension, "in which there are two essential aspects: a) the consolidation and the modernization of the capitalistic structure of the country and its inclusion in the orbit of American imperialism; and b) the increasing radicalization of the low and the middle classes" (Cornejo Polar, *Literatura* 17).

3. Rama used the definition of transculturation proposed by Fernando Ortíz: "Transculturation subsumes the different phases of the transitional process from one culture to another. However, this concept is different from acculturation, which consists basically in acquiring another culture. Transculturation implies the loss or detachment of the preceding culture, that is to say, a partial deculturation, but at the same time implies the creation of new cultural phenomena, which could be called neoculturation." (Rama, *La Novela* 209). Rama emphasizes the importance of the element of the original culture that survives and develops "in such a way that 'deculturation' is not valuable without a parallel 'reculturation,' that is to say, the relevance of internal characteristics that identify a particular culture. The importance of these two variables allows to measure the effort of the 'neoculturation' for absorbing external elements from a modern culture" (Rama, *La novela* 211).

4. "In sum, what is relevant in the narrative syntax of Arguedas is a double linguistic valence in the same surface structure. This double valence does not correspond to two regional or social dialects, or two registers, but corresponds to two different languages. More exactly: the fiction solves the dilemma in this way: the Quechua speaker expresses himself fluently as if he/she were using

his/her native language, and the reader reads it as if he/she were able to understand it. This mechanism presupposes two questions: a) the reader knows that he does not know how to speak Quechua; and b) knows that the Indian does not have enough competence in Spanish and appears as if he would speak Quechua. In this way, the translinguistic relation between languages in contact actualizes the Quechua message, making visible what is underlying; in fact, there is a correlation between two terms of the equation: the Spanish is what is present and the Quechua is co-present, as a result of linguistic structure of the literary language of Arguedas" (Escobar 72).

5. Narration is mediated through three points of view (called also focalization or perspective): a) zero: when the narrator knows more than the character; b) internal: the narrator says what the character knows and sees things through his individual consciousness of the latter; c) external: the narrator knows less than the character and sees things from outside without being able to penetrate the thoughts and feelings of the characters (Genette, *Narrative Discourse* 189–90).

6. The three main techniques of representation are the following: 1. Narratized speech, an analysis of the character's interiority assumed by the narrator. It is divided into two subcategories: a) diegetic summary, which mentions the verbal act without specifying its content (Marcel spoke to his mother for an hour); b) summary, less purely diegetic, which specifies the content: (Marcel informed his mother of his decision to marry Albertina). 2. Transposed speech, which is divided into three subcategories: a) indirect content-paraphrase (governed indirect speech): (Marcel declared to his mother that he wanted to marry Albertine); b) governed indirect discourse, mimetic to some degree, faithful to certain stylistic aspects of the discourse being reproduced: (Marcel declared to his mother that he wanted to marry that little bitch, Albertine; c) free indirect speech: (Marcel went and confided: he absolutely had to marry Albertine). 3. Reported speech: also divided into two subcategories: a) direct discourse: (Marcel said to his mother: "I must marry Albertine;" b) free direct discourse, without any demarcating sign; this is the autonomous state of immediate speech: (Marcel goes to see his mother. "I must marry Albertine. It is important for me.") (Genette, *Narrative Discouse* 56).

7. "[The] implied author must be seen as a construct inferred and assembled by the reader from all the components of the text. Indeed, speaking of the implied author as construct based on the text seems to me far safer than imagining it as personified 'consciousness' or 'second self'" (Rimmon-Kenan 87).

8. The ideological apparatus of the state is manifested in the form of institutions specialized in education, religion, the family, the juridical, the political, the unions, communication, and the cultural; on the other hand, the repressive apparatuses of the state are formed by the government, the public administration, the army, the police, and the prisons (Althusser 80–87).

9. This concept can be understood "as the internal stratification of any single national language into social dialects, characteristic group behavior, professional jargons, generic languages, languages of generations and age groups, tendentious languages, languages of the authorities, of various circles and of passing fashions, languages that serve the specific sociopolitical purposes of the day, even of the hour (each day has its own slogan, its own vocabulary, its own emphasis) –this internal stratification present in every language at any moment of its historical existence is the indispensable prerequisite for the novel as genre" (Bakhtin, *Dialogic Imagination* 263).

10. Parodic stylization consists of using a discourse of someone else but imprinting a different semantic intention from the original one, so that there is a conflict between discursive voices. The narrator not only parodies the surface structure or style, but also the underlying structure or the cosmovision. Both are interdependent (Bakhtin, *Problems* 193).

11. Scorza's *Redoble por Rancas* was treated extensively in "Narrativa, lenguaje e ideología en la literatura neoindigenista y la literatura de la negritud del Perú" (Puente-Baldoceda 45–178).

Works Cited

Althusser, Louis. *Lenin and Philosophy, and Other Essays*. Trans. Ben Brewester. London: NLB, 1971.

Bakhtin, Mikhail. *The Dialogic Imagination*. Trans. Caryl Emerson and Michael Holquist. Austin: University Press, 1981.

———. *Problems of Dostoevsky's Poetics*. Trans. Caryl Emerson. Ed. Wayne Booth. Minneapolis: Minnesota University Press, 1984.

Castro Arenas, Mario. *La novela hispanoamericana del Siglo XX: Una vista panorámica*. Lima: J. Godard, 1966.

Colchado Lucio, Oscar. "Cordillera negra." *Nueva crónica: Cuento social peruano, 1950–1990*. Ed. Roberto Reyes Tarazona. Lima: Editorial Colmillo Blanco, 1990.

Cornejo Polar, Antonio. *Literatura y sociedad en el Perú: La novela indigenista*. Lima: Lasontay, 1980.

———. "Prólogo" to Ciro Alegría, *El mundo es ancho y ajeno*. Caracas: Biblioteca de Ayacucho, 1987.

———. "Sobre el 'Neoindigenismo' y las novelas de Manuel Scorza." *Revista Iberoamericana* 127 (1984): 549–50.

Escobar, Alberto. *Arguedas o la utopia de la lengua*. Lima: IEP, 1984.

Genette, Gérard. *Narrative Discourse*. Trans. Jonathan Culler. Ithaca: Cornell University Press, 1980.

———. *Nouveau Discours du Récit*. Paris: Seuil, 1983.

Gutiérrez, Miguel. *La Generación del 20: Un mundo dividido*. Lima: Labrusa, 1988.

Puente-Baldoceda, Blas. "Narrativa, lenguaje e ideología en la literatura neoindigenista y la literatura de la negritud en el Perú." Dissertation. Texas University Press, 1989.

Rama, Angel. *Transculturación narrativa en América Latina*. México: Siglo XXI, 1982.

———. *La novela en América Latina. Panoramas 1920–1980.* Bogotá: Procultura, 1982.

Rimmon-Kenan, Shlomith. *Narrative Fiction: Contemporary Poetics.* London: Methuen, 1983.

Scorza, Manuel. *Redoble por Rancas*. Caracas: Monte Avila Editores, 1977.

Mexican Colonial Art and Architecture from the Conquest to Independence

Carol Callaway

The Sixteenth Century

The 1519 appearance of Spanish ships off the shores of Mexico was the first of a dramatic series of events that irreversibly transformed every aspect of indigenous life in that part of the New World. At the time, Mesoamerica, composed of what is now Mexico, Guatemala, Belize, parts of Honduras, and El Salvador, was dominated by the Aztec empire. The Spanish captain Hernando Cortés and his men marched inland and were met on the outskirts of the Aztec capital by the ruler Montezuma. Cortés was amazed by the size and magnificence of the capital. He described the wealth of the city and the religious practices he observed there to the Spanish king.[1] He knew that human sacrifice would be so abominable to the deeply religious sovereign that the king would consider the conversion of the population to Christianity as justification for a Spanish conquest of the Aztecs.

What the Spanish did not understand was the importance of their religion to New World people. The Aztecs and other Mesoamericans believed that the very survival of their universe depended upon continuous offerings of human blood. They let their own blood and practiced human sacrifice to make sure that the sun would rise every day and time would continue.[2] Elaborate ceremonies in honor of the gods took tremendous time and energy. After the Spanish captured Montezuma, devastated the city, and conquered the empire, they tried to destroy all vestiges of native religion.

On the recommendation of Cortés, the Spanish king assigned the task of evangelism to friars, rather than to parish priests. The Franciscans, Dominicans, and Augustinians who arrived in Mexico in the early years of colonial rule were part of a reform movement in Europe of highly idealistic humanists dedicated to service. Pedro de Gante, a close relative of the king, was among the three Franciscans who came in 1523. The following year a group of twelve Franciscans arrived. Allied with the crown they protected native people against exploitation as cheap labor by the colonists. The friars established schools such as *San José de los Naturales* in Mexico City, which was under the direction of Fray Pedro de Gante. Here the friars encouraged the continuation of native crafts and taught mural painting using European prints for inspiration.[3]

The friars often built large and impressive monasteries in order to attract the populace. One of the finest examples of monastic architecture is the sixteenth-century Augustinian convent located at Acolman in the valley of Mexico (Figure 1). Typical of such churches, the nave is long and narrow and has no transept. The crenelations that surround the exposed vaults resemble a medieval fortress.[4]

Figure 1. Augustinian Church at Acolman showing façade and open chapel. After de la Maza, et al., pp. 32–33, plate 5.

The architectural treasure of the church is the sophisticated Plateresque façade. Deriving from the art of silver working, the word Plateresque defines a very late Renaissance decorative style originating in sixteenth-century Europe. Pairs of Plateresque columns, called candelabra, flank the arched opening. As their name implies, these look like elaborately ornamented candlesticks. Each pair frames a gothic niche containing sculptures of St. Peter and St. Paul, respectively. Paul is identifiable by his sword and book, and Peter holds the keys of heaven. Together these calm, contained figures represent the founders of the Christian church. Above, there is a scene of the annunciation, feisty sawhorses, classical urns, shields, and lion heads. The window above illuminates the choir located in the second story balcony at the back of the church. The façade is so purely Spanish in style that it has been accredited to a European sculptor, even though most façades from this period were crafted by local artists.[5]

Figure 2. Angel from the baptismal font of the Church of San Juan Evangelista. After Weismann, *Mexico in Sculpture*, p. 66.

Between the church and the monastery there is a second-story open chapel where the friars conducted religious ceremonies before great crowds of people gathered below. Since the people of New Spain were accustomed to participating in spectacular religious ceremonies in the plazas of their temples, this outdoor space was a logical forum for all types of religious events, such as schools, processions, Christian plays, marriage ceremonies, and mass baptisms.[6]

Since baptism was essential for salvation, the baptismal font was an important piece of church equipment. The ceremony brought people into the Christian community and purged them of the stain of original sin. It was extremely popular among adults who wanted the process repeated over and over again. Since the natives believed that sacred water cured disease, they took it home in containers for their personal use.[7] Baptismal fonts were large and elaborate since they were a focus of this ritual and had to accommodate many people. An example is the baptismal font belonging to the Franciscan mission of San Juan Evangelista located in the town of Acatzingo in the state of Puebla. Two angels flank a chalice and paten, symbolic of the sacrifice of Christ. On its base is the pre-Columbian date "4 rabbit." The large hands and mask-like faces are characteristic of the art of local people working under Spanish domination[8] (Fig. 2).

Most sixteenth-century monastic churches had a large stone cross located in the center of the atrium that was the focal point of all religious activity performed there. Like baptismal fonts, these were carved by native craftsmen and deviate in subtle ways from their European counterparts. The cross belonging to the monastery of Acolman is similar in many ways to most of these Mexican crosses since it is adorned with the symbols of Christ's passion and has a large face of Christ located in the center. The head of Christ and the foliated terminations of the crossarm transform the atrium cross into an animate being.[9] The crossarm is adorned with foliate, floral, and swirling forms, making it a symbol of a living tree or Eucharistic tree of life. It also is reminiscent of pre-Columbian trees that end in trefoil terminations. Since Mesoamericans associated flowers with life and renewal, the arms and shaft of the cross represent life, death, and life-after-death, or rejuvenation in Christian and Mesoamerican religion.[10]

Church interiors were elaborately adorned at an early date with murals that were inspired by European sources. In most cases the transfer was very direct, and there is no obvious interpretation or manipulation of themes by the artist. An exception is the murals in the church of St. Michael at Ixmiquilpan in the state of Hidalgo. Warriors dressed in tiger skins wield obsidian-bladed weapons and defeat dragon-like creatures and other warriors, metaphorically representing the victory of Christian good over evil.[11]

The Paradise Garden murals on the cloister walls of the Augustinian monastery at Malinalco in the State of Mexico contain motifs deriving from European sources as well as New World symbols known only to the group of artists who painted manuscripts before the conquest.[12]

Perhaps the greatest symbol of religious syncretism in Mexico is the Virgin of Guadalupe. According to the legend, she appeared to a native named Juan Diego in 1531 at a place called Tepeyacac that was the sacred site of a shrine dedicated to the Aztec mother goddess Tonantzin. This painting, according to popular belief, was miraculously present on the cloak of Juan Diego when he opened it to show the bishop of New Spain the roses he gathered at the time of one of the Virgin's apparitions. The Virgin gave the roses to Juan Diego during the winter, when roses did not bloom in Mexico, as proof of her desire to have a church built in her honor at the site.

Early in the sixteenth century, the painting was enshrined in a church built on the site of her appearance where devotees from all backgrounds began to pay her homage despite the objections of the Franciscans. The Spanish, who were deeply devoted to the Spanish Virgin of Guadalupe, may have added Guadalupe to her name in remembrance of the peninsular Virgin. Her cult, which probably combined elements of the two folk cultures, grew in popularity until the eighteenth century, when she became the patron saint of Mexico.[13]

While the friars were building monasteries and working as evangelists, civil authorities were establishing the colonial government of the territory known as New Spain. By 1522 the decision was made to transform the city of Tenochtitlan into the new capital. An important consideration was the military presence provided by the concentration of conquistadores in the city. The island metropolis, which had withstood the attack from the Spanish and their allies, would be easy for Europeans to defend. The new Europeanized capital would build on the reputation of the area as a governmental center without being a monument to Aztec glory.[14]

The construction of the Cathedral of Mexico was part of the project to transform the city. The church had three aisles, a flat, wooden ceiling, and octagonal pillars that defined the central nave. It was located near the main Aztec temple and within the sacred precinct. In the second half of the century, a new cathedral was begun north of the original church. This structure was designed to have vaults lit by clerestory windows.

Following Spanish tradition, the choir was placed in the center of the nave blocking the view of the main altar as one entered the cathedral. In this system, the sixteen side chapels are more important to the general public than the inaccessible main altar.[15] Since construction lagged on for several centuries, and the plan was constantly revised, the interior lacks the unity and cohesiveness of a European cathedral begun during the same period.

The Mexican Baroque

By the late sixteenth century, most church construction and renovation occurred in urban areas where priests and bishops were establishing parishes and building cathedrals. As cities grew in size, and the ritual population decreased due to disease, the priesthood grew in power. The secular, urban church was supported by private citizens who paid the commissions of Europeans hired to construct churches and build altarpieces adorned with paintings and sculpture. Such artists, who often arrived with viceroys and bishops, were Spanish, Flemish, and Italian and were trained in the late Renaissance European Mannerist style. They owned European prints and architectural treatises that they used for inspiration.[16] These artists and architects continued to use these models long after Mannerism had gone out of style in Europe.

Colonial Mexican churches contained didactic screens called retablos that were placed behind the altar, sometimes entirely covering the east end of the apse. The earliest example was made for Cortés and his men soon after they took up residence in the Aztec capital.[17] The most beautiful extant example from the sixteenth century is the Franciscan monastic church of Huejotzingo in the State of Puebla (Fig. 3). It is composed of three horizontal levels of equal size, each composed of seven vertical divisions consisting of a central panel flanked by alternating sculptures and paintings. The style is considered Renaissance/ Plateresque since the columns are either classic, and therefore Renaissance, or Plateresque candelabra like the columns that adorn the façade of the Augustinian church at Acolman. The Mannerist paintings of episodes from the life of Christ alternate with wooden sculpture representing the history of the church.[18] These figures have extremely realistic, lacquer-like flesh as well as richly patterned drapery. Typical of Mexican colonial art from this period, both the paintings and the sculpture are inspirational, calm, and easy to understand (Fig. 4).

By the second half of the seventeenth century the Baroque style began to influence Mexican retablo design. Classic and Plateresque columns were replaced with Salomonic columns, which were twisted or spiral in form. Later in the century, pediments began to break, cornices became curvilinear, and ornamentation became more profuse. Some surfaces were covered entirely with organic forms such as grapevines.[19]

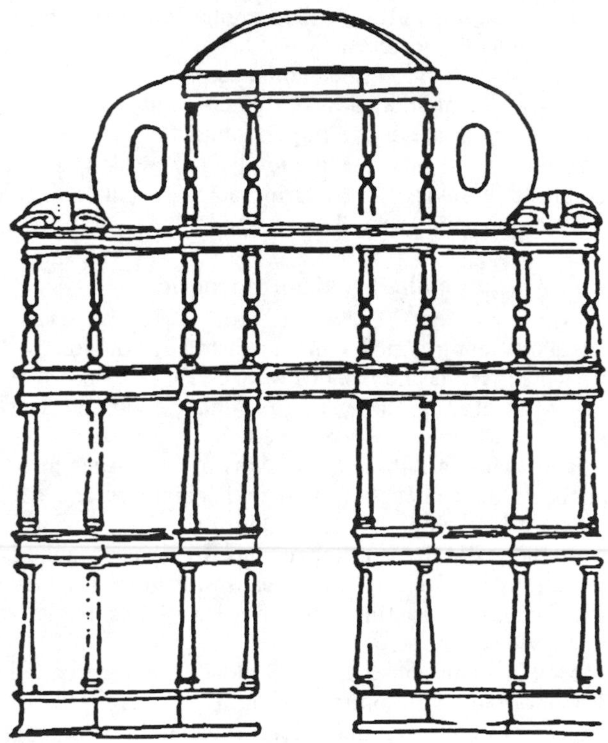

Figure 3. Framework of the retablo at Huejotzingo. After de la Maza. "Simbolismo del Retablo de Huejotzingo," p. 27.

During the seventeenth century, Mexico City was one of the richest and most spectacular cities in the world. Outdoor events and performances took place in the three main plazas in the city, as well as in the tree-lined Alamadapark. People arrived in their elaborate, horse-drawn carriages dressed in fine fabrics adorned with jewels, and accompanied by their flamboyantly dressed black slaves. Citizens supported the church with gifts of land, church furnishings, and endowments for prayers after their death. Church inventories include elaborate liturgical vestments embroidered with gold and silver, along with many silver and gold articles sometimes set with jewels.[20]

During the seventeenth century, people born in the New World began to develop a national consciousness. Such citizens resented the fact that they were denied privileges reserved for peninsular Spaniards. New World Spaniards called creoles were considered socially inferior to people born in Spain. Indigenous people, blacks, and those of mixed blood were classified into a caste system based on their ancestry. Mestizos were people of mixed Spanish and indigenous heritage.[21]

Figure 4. Bishop from the Retablo at Huejotzingo. After Weismann, *Mexico in Sculpture*, p. 76.

Perhaps the first event to attract national pride was the 1627 beatification of the Mexican martyr Fray Felipe de Jesús. Of even greater importance was the publication in 1648 of the first book on the Mexican Virgin of Guadalupe. In1737, this New World saint became patroness of Mexico. Equal excitement was expressed by Mexicans of all ethnic origins when the famous Aztec calendar stone and colossal figure of the fertility goddess Coatlicue were discovered. Such local pride in indigenous culture of Mexico paralleled the work of seventeenth-century creole scholar Don Carlos de Siguenza y Gongora. In 1680 he designed a triumphal arch adorned with pre-Columbian gods.[22]

A major project of the seventeenth century was the building of the façade of the cathedral of Mexico (Fig. 5). The three portals are set between two towers and divided by pier buttresses. The central portal is composed of many classical elements, such as the arched opening. The crowded quality of all the forms and the degree of surface ornament are typical of Mexican Mannerism. The "eared" frame that surrounds the relief sculpture of the Assumption of the Virgin also is Mannerist. The "ears" are the extra geometric forms located in the corners. The movement and degree of expression found in the sculptures of Saints Peter and Paul make them appear quite different from the same saints on the façade at Acolman. These new characteristics are typical of the Mexican Baroque style that was developing at this time.

These two tiers of the central portal were designed by the main architect or *Maestro mayor* at the time, and the general foreman. Their successors included Salomonic columns on the second tier of the side portals, which they built between 1684 and 1689. This is the first appearance of such columns on the outside of a Mexico City church.[23]

During the seventeenth century, many parochial churches were built in Mexico City and other Mexican cities. A good example of a Mexican parochial church is San Miguel, built in Mexico City between 1690 and 1714. The Mannerist façade is composed of an arched portal surrounded by pairs of columns with a relief in an "eared" frame. Above, in the third tier, is an oval, Baroque window. Typical of Mexican churches throughout the Viceregal period, European Baroque influence is restricted to details and does not affect special planning, which is dynamic in Europe but conservative and static in Mexico.[24]

One of the greatest pilgrimage churches of Mexico is Nuestra Señora de la Soledad, built at the end of the seventeenth century in Oaxaca to enshrine the southern Mexican equivalent of the Virgin of Guadalupe. The retablo façade extends out, literally like a huge folding screen completely masking the church behind it. It is constructed of a full framework or architectural elements derived from a multitude of European styles. The most important image of the façade is a relief of the Virgin kneeling at the foot of a shroud-draped cross. Her position, costume, and gesture of grief establish that she derives from an image of Mary Magdalene.

Figure 5. National Cathedral of Mexico showing main facade and facade of the Sagrario. After Baird. *The Churches of Mexico*, p. 94.

As a combination of the two Marys, the figure in relief becomes a pluralistic concept. Such ambiguity, allowing for multiple and diverse interpretations, sets this image apart from European antecedents of the Virgin. Through her roles in the birth and death of Christ and her participation in the atonement of sins through her sorrow, the Virgin of Solitude is intimately involved in the complete cycle of life. As a conflated image, the figure assumes that personality of the Magdalene considered the ultimate sinner because of her sexual transgressions as well as the penitent who was saved by Christ. Such associations with sexuality, penance, and purification suggest that the antecedents for such a mixture evolved from the pre-Columbian past, rather than the Christian tradition.[25]

The mid-seventeenth century was a virtual golden age for painters who established elaborate workshops to meet the demands of the church. In Mexico City the major painters were associated with one family, their students, and occasional new arrivals from Spain. This group established a Mexican school of painting basically Mannerist in style that grew more emotional and elaborate as the century wore on.[26]

The most representative Mexican painters of the eighteenth century were Juan Correa the Elder and Cristóbal de Villalpando. Both of these artists were influenced by the dynasty of painters who came before them. Although their subjects were European, their distorted anatomy, use of certain formulas, and other painterly freedoms distinguished their work from contemporary Spanish painting.[27]

Similar changes occurred in sculpture. Figures showed greater and greater amounts of movement. Realism was increased by incorporating actual eyelashes, human hair, and natural teeth. New materials were used, such as marble and wax, and there was increased emotion in faces.

In 1718, a Spaniard, Jerónimo Balbas, was commissioned to build a new retablo to fill the main apse of the Cathedral in Mexico City. His Altar of the Kings includes four colossal forms called *estipites*, composed of a base, an inverted obelisk, various blocks, moldings, and a capital. This retablo is no longer compartmentalized like those of the sixteenth and seventeenth centuries nor is sculpture contained in niches. The decoration includes two huge paintings, many geometric and multifaceted forms, and a profusion of fruits and flowers[28] (Fig. 6).

Before the Altar de los Reyes was completed a new *sagrario* or parish church of the National Cathedral was begun. The city was growing rapidly, and the two chapels within the cathedral could no longer accommodate the crowds. After the epidemic of 1737, there was not sufficient space to bury the dead. As an expression of piety and civic pride, the congregation entirely supported the project without the aid of the crown.[29]

The architect of the project was a Spaniard named Lorenzo Rodríguez His plan, based on the designs of the Italian Mannerist architect Sebastiano Serlio, is an ideal Renaissance central plan with five domes. The two magnificent facades on the south and west fronts of the church are made of dark red volcanic stone called *tezontle* and gray-white limestone or *chiluca*. Broken pediments, stepped moldings, and vertical estipites give them a soaring movement.[29]

Figure 6. Detail of the stucco decoration from the interior of the church of Santa María Tonanzintla. After González Galvan, *Barroco y su desarrollo formal en México.*

Elements of these revolutionary façades were widely copied throughout Viceregal Mexico. Although *estipites* were especially popular for façades built in the silver mining area northwest of Mexico City, they were used in all parts of the country and were made of a plaster substance called *argamasa* as well as stone. The beautiful façade of the pilgrimage church dedicated to the Virgin of Ocotlan outside the city of Tlaxcala is a wonderful example. The stark white façade made of plaster, consisting of *estipites*, three-dimensional archangels, and the Virgin is contrasted against the solid lower half of the towers sheathed in red tile.

Equally unique is the Church of Santa María Tonanzintla, located in the State of Puebla not far from the pyramid of Quetzacoatl at the pre-Columbian site of Cholula. The interior is a magical world of exuberance and luxury created by the riot of stucco decoration that covers the vaults, arches, dome, apse, and pilasters. It is made of a combination of Renaissance, Plateresque, and Baroque styles.

Although the Coronation of the Virgin is represented, the feeling of luxurious growth and abundance connotes pre-Columbian sensibilities of the sacred. The word *Tonantzintla* means "place of our little mother" in Nahuatl. The name is linked to the cult of Aztec fertility goddesses associated with the earth, water, agricultural abundance, health, and human fecundity.[31]

The end of such exuberant decoration came with the establishment of the neoclassical style. Architectural forms based on the clean, clear, structural lines of classical antiquity came into vogue. Churches were remodeled and the old-fashioned retablos and elaborate altars were replaced with cold, often stark structures based on Roman temples painted white with gold detail. The nontraditional, international style was part of the independence movement in Mexico. Such an idea received the support of the Bourbon monarchy anxious to modernize New Spain, reform the administration, and centralize cultural institutions.[32]

The remodeling of the *Zocalo*, or central plaza, was one of the large projects supported by the Spanish government. The equestrian statue of Charles IV for the plaza was based on a famous Roman sculpture. It therefore associated Mexico City with Rome. This was popular with the creole and mestizo population, who believed that Mexico could be a great New World capital independent from Spain. Indeed, the revolution that followed made this creole dream a reality.[33]

Conclusion

Like Mexico, other parts of Latin America that fell under Spanish domination developed colonial art that drew from two deeply religious traditions: one European and the other indigenous. Yet the New World colonial art that developed outside of New Spain evolved under different circumstances and, therefore, is stylistically different. The Inca empire, for instance, was conquered by the Spanish much later than the Aztecs. Political turmoil, economic chaos, corruption, abuse, and geography retarded the process.[34] The Viceregal capital did not overlay a pre-Columbian city but was designed as a new Spanish metropolis on the coast. This allowed the Inca capital city of Cuzco to develop an indigenous colonial art style based on the rich culture retained there.[35]

Mexico, however, developed a major national art style in the colonial period with specific characteristics that crossed regional boundaries. It is rooted in the sixteenth century when a small number of mendicants and native craftsmen built huge churches adorned with paintings and sculpture. Consistent with later Mexican churches, such structures are simple geometric forms with a concentration of ornamentation around entranceways. Consistent with other art from the period, they sometimes contain subtle references to the indigenous past. Later, Baroque structures lacked the complex spatial relationships characteristic of contemporary European churches. Instead they were elaborate because of the profusion of decoration around entrances, on retablos, inside domes, on arches, around windows, and in other places. Manerism, introduced in the mid-sixteenth century, remained the dominant European style found in Mexico. Other styles from a wide range of sources were added in a variety of ways. Such unorthodox and highly imaginative use of forms resulted in Mexican art developed primarily to serve the church and associated ritual. Such elaborate constructions came to an end with the introduction of Neo-classicism, a style that lasted to the end of the colonial era.

Notes

At Dumbarton Oaks, I wish to thank Bridget Gazzo, Pre-Columbian Studies librarian, for help in bibliographic matters. Thank you also to Jeffrey Quilter, Director of pre-Columbian studies, for editorial advice. Janice Williams, Assistant to the Director of Pre-Columbian Studies, was of invaluable service for final production of the manuscript.

I want to thank Jean Caswell for suggesting that the relief of the Virgin at the foot of the cross came from a sixteenth-century image of Mary Magdalene.

1. See Hernán Cortés, *Hernán Cortés: Letters from Mexico,* ed. and trans. by Anthony Pagden (New Haven: Yale University Press, 1986), 83–107.

2. See Cecelia F. Klein, "Post-Classic Mexican Death Imagery as a Sign of Cyclic Completion," in *Death and the Afterlife in Pre-Columbian America*, ed. Elizabeth P. Benson (Washington, D.C.: Dumbarton Oaks, 1975), 69–85.

3. See George Kubler, *Mexican Architecture of the Sixteenth Century*, 2 vols. (Westport, Conn.: Greenwood Press, 1972), 1: 1–15, 2: 366–67.

4. See John McAndrew, *The Open-Air Churches of Sixteenth-Century Mexico*, (Cambridge: Harvard University Press, 1965), 272.

5. Ibid., 174.

6. See Louise Burkhart, *The Slippery Earth* (Tucson: University of Arizona Press, 1989), 20; McAndres, 295.

7. Burkhart, 172.

8. See Elizabeth Wilder Weismann, *Mexico in Sculpture: 1521–1821* (Cambridge: Harvard University Press, 1950), 67.

9. See Alfred Neumeyer, "The Indian Contribution to Architectural Decoration in Spanish Colonial America," *Art Bulletin* 30 (1948): 107.

10. See Carol Callaway, "Pre-Columbian and Colonial Mexican Images of the Cross: Christ's Sacrifice and the Fertile Earth," *Journal of Latin American Lore* 16, 2 (1990): 199–231.

11. See Albelardo Carrillo y Gariel, *Ixmiquilpan* (Mexico: Instituto Nacional de Antropología, 1961).

12. See Jeanette Favrot Peterson, *The Paradise Garden Murals of Malinanco* (Austin: University of Texas Press, 1993), 16, 25.

13. See Peggy K. Liss, *Mexico Under Spain: 1521–1556* (Chicago: University of Chicago Press, 1975), 153–54.

14. Kubler, 1, 69.

15. Baird, 94–96.

16. See Jorge Alberto Manrique, "The Progress of Art in New Spain," in *Mexico: Splendors of Thirty Centuries* (New York: The Metropolitan Museum of Art, 1990), 240–41.

17. See Francisco de la Maza, "Mexican Colonial Retablos," *Gazette de Beaux Arts*, March 1944, 176.

18. See Francisco de la Maza. "Simbolismo del Retablo de Huejotzingo," *Artes de México* XV segunda época, 106 (1968): 26–28.

19. See Ma. del Consuelo Maquívar M., "Retablos del Siglo XVII," in *El Arte Mexicano, Arte Colonial IV* (Mexico: Salvat Mexicana de Ediciones, 1986), 1121–25.

20. See Thomas Gage, *Thomas Gage's Travels in the New World*, ed. and introduction by J. Eric S. Thompson (Norman: University of Oklahoma Press, 1958), 70–71.

21. See Irving A. Leonard, *Baroque Times in Old Mexico: Seventeenth-Century Persons, Places, and Practices* (Ann Arbor: The University of Michigan Press, 1959), 40–52.

22. Leonard, 225–26.

23. See Marta Fernández, "Algunas reflexiones en torno a las portadas de la Catedral de México," in *Anales del Instituto de Investigaciones Estéticas*, vol. XIV (1983) 53: 81–94.

24. See Elizabeth Fuentes Rojas, "Las parroquias," in *El Arte Mexicano, Arte Colonial IV* (Mexico: Salvat Mexicana de Ediciones, 1986), 1207–13.

25. See Carol Callaway, "The Church of Nuestra Señora de la Soledad in Oaxaca, México" (Ph.D. diss., University of Maryland, 1989).

26. See Manuel Toussaint, *Colonial Art in Mexico*, trans. and ed. by Elizabeth W. Weismann (Austin: University of Texas Press, 1967), 225–31.

27. See Marcus Burke, "A Mexican Artistic Consciousness," in *Mexico: Splendors of Thirty Centuries* (New York: The Metropolitan Museum of Art, 1990), 321–23.

28. See Clara Bargellini, "Escultura y retablos del siglo XVIII" in *El Arte Mexicano, Arte Colonial IV* (Mexico: Salvat Mexicana de Ediciones, 1986), 1142.

29. See Margaret Collier, "New Documents on Lorenzo Rodríguez and His Style," *Latin American Art, in the Baroque Period in Europe*, International Congress of the History of Art, 20 (Princeton: Princeton University Press, 1963), 203–18.

30. Ibid., 209.

31. See Manuel González Galván, "Tonantzin Coronada en el Tlalocan," *Anales del Instituto de Investigaciones Estéticas*, vol. 12 (1978) 48: 47–61.

32. See Marcus Burke, "The Academy: New-Classicism and Independence," in *Mexico: Splendors of Thirty Centuries* (New York: Metropolitan Museum of Art, 1990), 487–88.

33. Ibid.

34. See Kenneth J. Andrien, "Spaniards, Andeans, and the Early Colonial State in Peru," in *Transatlantic Encounters: Europeans and Andeans in the Sixteenth Century*, eds. Kenneth J. Andrien and Rolena Adorno (Berkeley: University of California Press, 1991), 121–48.

35. See Tom Cummins, "A Tale of Two Cities: Cuzco, Lima, and the Construction of Colonial Representation," in *Converging Cultures: Art & Identity in Spanish America*, ed. Diana Fane (New York: The Brooklyn Museum in Association with Harry N. Abrams, 1996), 157–70.

The Music of Latin America

Walter Aaron Clark

Latin America exhibits manifold forms of musical expression. The three principal sources of this diversity are Native America, Spain, and Portugal, and Africa. The commingling of the musical traditions of these various cultures has produced many styles of music that are entirely unique to Latin America. The numerous regional and national styles are largely the result of the relative balance of these influences. In Argentina, for instance, where the indigenous population is very small, the music exhibits much more of a European character. In Peru, however, Indian influence on the music is very strong. In Brazil and Cuba, regions that imported large numbers of slaves, the music has a markedly West African flavor. The blending and layering of traditional types of music that went on during the colonial period provided a rich source of inspiration for composers in the nineteenth and twentieth centuries seeking to infuse their classical compositions with the melodies and rhythms of folk and popular music. Classical music of the colonial period was very European in style, but during the post-colonial era there gradually developed, in response to nascent nationalism, a very intimate connection between classical and vernacular traditions in Latin American music. After World War II, however, these paths diverged: classical composers abandoned nationalism for the international avant-garde, while folk and popular music achieved global impact and in turn absorbed elements of jazz and rock.

Pre-Columbian Period

Before the arrival of Columbus in 1492, however, there was already a vast array of cultures and peoples living in what is now Latin America. There was also a splendid richness of musical traditions among them. However, none of the indigenous peoples developed a system of musical notation, and what we know of their music comes largely from three other kinds of sources.[1] The first is archeological remains. Instruments excavated at burial sites, for example, reveal the various pitches and sound colors used by ancient American musicians. Sculptural relief depicting actual performance can show us how the instruments were played and in what context. But such artifacts cannot tell us what the music itself actually sounded like.

The second source of information is more helpful to us in this regard and consists of accounts by European explorers, particularly the Spanish. Some of the conquistadors and missionaries who invaded and colonized Indian areas had musical training, and their narratives often include detailed information about the types of instruments the Indians used, about the organization of the music itself, and about the ritual or ceremonial context in which it was performed. A final, and less reliable, source of information about pre-Columbian music comes in the form of "survivals," musical practices that persist today in Indian communities and that historians believe predated contact with Europeans. But we must be cautious here, for without precise knowledge of ancient American music, we are not able to declare that a particular melody has survived for over five hundred years without any "contamination." Yet we are positive that some melodies sung today, particularly in Mexico and Peru, are of pre-contact origin. Certainly many of the instruments and the ceremonies in which they are used can be traced with confidence back to those times. The two music cultures about which we know the most, and whose music has survived in any record, correspond to the two great civilizations of the ancient Americas that were not flourishing when the Spaniards arrived, the Aztec and the Inca.

The Aztecs moved into the valley of Mexico in the early fourteenth century. Their language was Náhuatl, which is still spoken by a large number of people in Mexico today. We know quite a lot about Aztec music because the Spaniards toppled this civilization at the height of its development. As with most ancient American peoples, music had for them no separate existence but was always performed in a ceremonial context and combined instrumental music with singing and/or dancing. In fact, Náhuatl has no word for music or musician, but rather for singing and various instrumentalist functions. There was a professional caste of musicians who controlled all public performances, similar to the Levites of ancient Israel. There were schools for dancing and music, and the training was extremely strict; performances had to be flawless, as errors were punishable by execution. Because of their importance, musicians enjoyed considerable social prestige, but names of individual musicians have not come down to us. Each piece was composed for a certain time, place, and occasion, and musicians needed a wide repertoire for the 260-day religious calendar. Their memories had to be very good, for we recall that they had no method of writing the music down. As a result, any reconstruction of their music now is highly conjectural.

The two main Aztec instruments were the *huehuetl* and the *teponaztli*.[2] The *huehuetl* was an upright drum consisting of a hollowed-out log, about three feet long, with the skin of a jaguar or deer covering one end. It was tuned by heating the interior with live coals to dry and tighten this head. The *teponaztli* was a horizontal slit drum, about the same length as the *huehuetl*. It had an H-shaped opening in its side, forming two tongues that were struck with mallets. The sound carried a great distance, even when, during certain rituals, it was filled with blood. Both of these instruments were used for ceremonies involving song and dance, and they were played on a grass mat at the center of the dancing area. Often hundreds of beautifully costumed dancers would move in concentric circles around the musicians, with the nobility closest in. Movements, rhythm, and melody were all tightly coordinated.

In general, the Aztecs preferred strident, loud, shrill sounds, even in their laments. Their vocal quality was, by European standards, thin. They associated it with gold (the metal of the sun god) and with the roar of the jaguar. There were four basic kinds of Aztec songs and dances: (1) lascivious songs, (2) laments, (3) communal dances, and (4) penitential dances. Some of these survive among Native peoples in Mexico today, though the penitential dances have been Christianized.

The Inca empire flourished from the fourteenth to the sixteenth centuryes and extended over a vast area from northern Ecuador to halfway through Chile. The Inca language persists in various forms today, including Quechua and Aymara. Like the Aztecs, the Incas prized high, strident sounds. Their music frequently employed a five-note scale in which there were no half steps (called a pentatonic scale). They had a wide variety of instruments, including flutes, trumpets, and drums. They also had an advanced system of music education similar to that of the Aztecs. As with most Native American music, the texture typically consisted of a single melody, without chordal accompaniment (homophony) or other melodies going on at the same time (polyphony). Although there was a wide variety of percussion and wind instruments, string instruments were unknown in the western hemisphere until the arrival of Europeans, who introduced the guitar, harp, and bowed-string instruments like the violin.

Colonial Period

The Aztecs were conquered by Cortés in 1521, while the Inca empire fell to the conquistador Pizarro in 1532. Spanish missionaries tried very hard to extinguish the religious ceremonies and associated musical practices of the Indians. In this they were not entirely successful, and the Indians often simply incorporated the former rituals into their new, Christian system of belief. Even while struggling to maintain their own music, the talented Indians readily adopted European methods of notation, printing, instrument building, and performance. In fact, because of the Indians' enthusiasm for music, the Spaniards soon realized that it could be an effective tool for religious conversion. The Spaniards reported that many of the Indian choirs were as good as any in Europe. This gives us pause to reflect on the fact that long before the Pilgrims landed at Plymouth, Massachusetts, in 1620, European music of the highest caliber was flourishing in the valleys of Mexico and the highlands of Peru. Musical culture in what is now the United States would not come close to rivaling that of Latin America until well into the nineteenth century.

Most of the composers working in Latin America during the colonial period came from Spain and Portugal. Some later ones were indigenous, and a few were *mestizos* (of mixed Spanish and Indian background). Chief among these was the Mexican Manuel de Sumaya (1678–1756), the foremost composer in eighteenth-century Latin America.[3] But the heyday of *mestizo* music would come much later, after independence was gained in the early nineteenth century. Almost all the music that has come down to us from the colonial period was composed for Catholic worship, i.e., the Mass and the Divine Office (folk music was not deemed worthy of being written down, and folk musicians usually could not read notation anyway). Some of the finest sacred music was composed by Hernando Franco (1532–1585), the preeminent composer in Nueva España (Mexico in the sixteenth century. Franco was born in Spain and received his musical education at the famous cathedral in Segovia. He emigrated to Guatemala City in 1554 and was later appointed *maestro de capilla* (chapel master, or the music director) at Mexico City Cathedral during the last decade of his life. All of his sacred music exhibits the Renaissance polyphonic style of contemporary European masters such as Tomás Luis de Victoria and Giovanni Pierluigi da Palestrina.

There was another important genre of music brought by the Spaniards that had a loose connection to the liturgy, and this we know as the *villancico*. The *villancico* originated as a form of secular entertainment during the late Middle Ages in Spain (the word comes from the Spanish *villano*, or "rustic"), but by the late sixteenth century it was increasingly associated with sacred occasions, especially Christmas. *Villancicos* were written in Spanish for various combinations of voices and instruments and were performed during and after worship. They retained from their early history a popular and lively musical flavor and were useful in attracting people to services, which were often followed by gatherings featuring food and music. Thus, though written by composers of "serious" music, *villancicos* sometimes employed Native dialects and allusions to folk music to make them more attractive to the local population. A *tocotín* is a *villancico* blending Náhuatl and Spanish. *Negros* (or *negritos*) are *villancicos* integrating Spanish and West African dialects and musical characteristics (slaves were brought to Mexico from Guinea). An important composer of such *villancicos* was Gaspar Fernández, who was born in Portugal in 1550 and died in Nueva España in 1629 (from 1580 to 1640 Portugal was part of Spain). Like Franco, Fernández started his career in the New World in Guatemala City, but he eventually became *maestro de capilla* at the cathedral in Puebla, another important musical center during the centuries of colonial rule.

One of the most eminent composers of sacred music in seventeenth-century Latin America was Juan de Padilla (1590–1664), who was born in Málaga, Spain, and worked at Puebla Cathedral. He wrote very elaborate, sumptuous music in the Venetian style that was quite popular in Europe at that time. The Venetians developed a type of sacred polyphony involving two or more choirs performing simultaneously and in alternation. It was especially effective in the resonant environs of St. Mark's Cathedral in Venice. It was also impressive in the spacious cathedrals of the New World, such as the one in Puebla.

Of course, the principal music of the Catholic service remained Gregorian chant, a strictly monophonic kind of singing with roots in the early Middle Ages. The Indians adapted very well to the Catholic liturgy in general and chant in particular because their own liturgy and mythology exhibited similar complexity, and their musicians were already capable of committing hundreds of monophonic songs to memory. But clearly the composition, performance, and publication of sacred polyphony were important new activities. In fact, some of the most valuable collections of Renaissance and Baroque music in the world are located in such cities as Puebla, Guatemala City, and Bogotá. There were other important centers located in the Andean region of the former Inca empire. Bolivia, for instance, was part of Peru during the colonial period, and its current capital was then called La Plata (changed to Sucre in the nineteenth century), reflecting the importance of silver mining in that region. La Plata Cathedral was a major musical center, and its archives today are rich in holdings of manuscripts and printed music from the Americas and Europe. The most famous composer associated with La Plata was Juan de Araujo (1646-1712). He was born in Spain but studied in Lima and later served as *maestro de capilla* at La Plata Cathedral from 1680 to 1712.

Lima was also musically prominent, and in 1701 it witnessed the production of the first opera composed in the New World, *La púrpura de la rosa* ("The Purple of the Rose") by Tomás Torrejón y Velasco. Torrejón y Velasco was born in Spain in 1644 and eventually entered the service of the future viceroy of Peru. He was appointed *maestro de capilla* at Lima Cathedral, where he remained until his death in 1728. He was not a prolific composer, and his reputation today rests on this opera, created to celebrate the birthday of Philip V. The libretto ("little book," the text of an opera) had been written decades earlier by the celebrated playwright Pedro Calderón de la Barca for an opera by the Spanish composer Juan Hidalgo. That opera was produced in 1659 for another political event, the marriage of King Louis XIV of France to the Spanish Infanta María Teresa (it was common at this time for more than one composer to set a libretto, as there were no copyright restrictions).

The musical style of Torrejón y Velasco's opera is very conservative by standards of the early eighteenth century because he had been in Peru for thirty years and was not up-to-date with operatic developments in Europe. Whereas the typical Italian opera of the day lasted two or three hours, *La púrpura de la rosa* is short, lasting only about ninety minutes. Torrejón y Velasco does make colorful use of instruments: the *trombones* are used for serious moments, and flutes and oboes are used for pastoral scenes. The novel employment of the guitar (and popular music like *seguidillas* and *jácara*) gives a Spanish flavor to some numbers. The opera commences with a lengthy prologue praising "ever invincible Spain" for offering the crown to Philip V. The story itself is taken from Greek mythology. Venus is married to Mars but falls in love with the beautiful youth Adonis. Mars is jealous of their love affair and sends a boar to kill Adonis. Venus is heartbroken, but Adonis is transformed into a purple rose, and Venus and the rose ascend to heaven and live happily ever after. Of course, there are nymphs and shepherds, who serve as comic foils to the principals. The happy ending was dictated by the circumstances of the opera's performance.[4]

Post-Colonial Period

The colonial period came to a rather abrupt end in the early nineteenth century, three hundred years after it began. Spain and Portugal were busy fighting Napoleon, and in their weakened and distracted state could not prevent the colonies from following the example of the United States in seeking their independence. The nineteenth century, however, was a period of turbulence, as the old power structure was gone but new ones had difficulty establishing control. During this time of transition, the old system of church patronage was thrown into disarray, and the music took on a new, secular character. Composers in nineteenth-century Latin America generally wrote small-scale compositions, such as piano pieces and songs, that were suitable for performance in the salons and parlors of the bourgeoisie. Musical theater was also popular, but there was not a strong tradition of symphonic writing, and concert organizations devoted to serious music developed only gradually. As elsewhere in Europe and the United States, composers looked to Paris for their inspiration, and the music of Chopin in particular exerted a great influence on piano composers in Latin America. Another important occupation of composers was to write national anthems for the countries newly liberated from colonial rule. Thus, the classical music of Latin America in the nineteenth century does not have much of a regional flavor. It was only toward the end of the century that economic and political stability was achieved throughout most of Latin America, allowing for a sense of nationhood to take root. In response to increasing nationalism, composers began to use elements from folk and popular music to give their compositions a distinctive national quality. This helped to reinforce a sense of national identity and pride and reached out to a wider public than ever before. Of course, the development of folk and popular traditions had continued unabated, but it is hard for us to trace the evolution of what was essentially an oral tradition. The publication of folk song collections and the advent of recording technology in the twentieth century, however, have made that job easier. We will now examine the folk, popular, and classical music of Latin America from the last two centuries by large geographical region: Mexico, Central America, and Panama; the Andean region; Argentina, Paraguay, and Uruguay; Brazil, Venezuela, and Colombia; and Cuba and the Caribbean.

Mexico, Central America, and Panama

Mexico is a land of many distinct regions, each with its own unique style of music. The generic term for the peasant or rural music of the *mestizo* culture of Mexico is *son*, literally "sound." Some of the most prominent regional *sones* include *mariachi*, *chilena*, *haupango*, *música norteña*, and *son de marimba.* Other important folk styles that are not associated with any particular region include the *jarabe*, *corrido,* and *canción ranchera.*

Some scholars believe *mariachi* to mean "little Maria," a combination of the name María and the Náhuatl diminutive suffix "chi." (María is an all-purpose reference to women in Mexican popular song, somewhat like "baby" in rock.) It represents the tradition of *son* indigenous to the region south of Guadalajara in the state of Jalisco, although it has undergone much transformation during the decades since its birth early in the twentieth century and has spread throughout Mexico. The characteristic instruments employed in *mariachi son* are violins, *vihuela* (small five-course guitar), *guitarrón* (large bass guitar with four strings), and trumpets (added in the 1930s). *Mariachi* sometimes employs a female vocalist dressed as a *soldadera* (female soldier), a feature added during the same period as the trumpets. *Chilena* is short for *cueca chilena*, songs introduced to Mexico by Chilean sailors during the California gold rush. (Before the transcontinental railroad, the fastest route for gold seekers from the eastern U.S. was to sail to the isthmus, now Panama, cross on land, then sail up the west coast of Central America and Mexico to California.) *Chilena* is indigenous to the Pacific coast south of Acapulco to Oaxaca. The instruments used to accompany it include violin, guitar, and *requinto* (a small guitar tuned higher than a normal guitar). When *chilena* is danced, various wind and brass instruments may be added. *Huapango* is a term derived from the Náhuatl word for the raised wooden platform on which the dance is performed. It refers both to a type of *son* and the *rasgueado*, or guitar strumming, that accompanies it. *Huapango* comes from the Huastec region, which extends from the Gulf coast south of Tampico to the central highlands. Instruments used to accompany it include the violin and *huapanguera* (a large five-course guitar with eight to ten strings that is played in *rasgueado* fashion).

Música norteña is, as its name implies, native to the northern region of Mexico along the U.S. border. It includes European dance forms such as the mazurka, waltz, and polka, which became popular in that area in the nineteenth century. They continue to be performed and feature the characteristic sound of the accordion, as well as the guitar. The *son de marimba* is the generic name for *sones* of southern Mexico using the marimba. The marimba is a type of xylophone, with wooden keys of varying lengths struck by mallets. Tubes placed below the keys at right angles increase its resonance (gourds instead of tubes were often used in the past). It is very popular in the southern Mexican states of Oaxaca and Chiapas, but it was brought over by African slaves and is neither Native American nor Spanish. The *jarabe* is a song and dance that originated during the Mexican struggle for independence in the early nineteenth century. The most famous piece in this style is the *jarabe tapatío*, commonly known as the "Mexican Hat Dance" because the men toss their hats on the ground so they and their partners can dance around them. The *corrido* is a narrative ballad accompanied by guitars. It came into being during the Mexican Revolution in the early twentieth century, and the texts often deal with that period of conflict. One of the most famous *corridos* is *La cucaracha*. Like the *corrido*, the *canción ranchera* was born during the early twentieth century in association with the Mexican Revolution. These songs "have working class and romanticized-rural associations [and] are the Mexican equivalent of North American country and western."[5]

Also popular throughout Mexico and Central America are the so-called conquest dances. These are dramatic reenactments in dance of the reconquest of Spain from the Moors (hence their other name, *Moros y Cristianos*). They are characterized by the use of *sonajas* (rattles) and the *chirimía*, a double-reed instrument resembling the oboe. Holy Week processions also employ the *chirimía*. It is played from a church tower and accompanied by a drum during the dramatization of scenes from the crucifixion of Christ.

After the revolution, the new Mexican government promoted music and art with nationalist, patriotic themes. Composers looked to folk music and the pre-Columbian past for inspiration. The general idea was to bring culture to the masses through "high art" music that reflected their heritage. The greatest of these composers were Ponce, Chávez, and Revueltas. Manuel Ponce (1882–1948) was an avid student and collector of Mexican folk music, and he taught musical folklore at the university. He is justly famous for his guitar music, which was championed by the Spanish guitarist Andrés Segovia. His *Sonata mexicana* for guitar strongly suggests Mexican folk music in an otherwise classical genre. In 1912 Ponce composed the song *Estrellita* ("Little Star"), which became the most popular art song in Latin America. Ponce's foremost student was Carlos Chávez (1899–1978), who gained renown as a composer, critic, and conductor. Chávez also took an active interest in folk and popular music, but his own style was more modern than Ponce's and reflected the influence of Igor Stravinsky in particular. Chávez's most celebrated work is the *Sinfonía india*, in which he employs actual Indian melodies and traditional instruments. Silvestre Revueltas (1899–1940) was a conductor, composer, and teacher whose promising career was cut short by alcoholism. His best-known work is *Sensemayá* for orchestra, inspired by a poem of the Cuban revolutionary poet Nicolás Guillén about the ritual killing of a tropical snake. The brutal magic of this ceremony is expressed through jarring dissonance and irregular rhythms that reveal the influence of Stravinsky's *Rite of Spring*, which deals in a similar manner with the subject of sacrifice.

The music of Central America has much in common with that of Mexico. For example, the national dance of Guatemala is the *son guatemalteco*. The customary instruments for this dance are the marimba (the national instrument of Guatemala), the maracas (a kind of rattle), and the guitar. In this partner dance the couples move without touching. Ladinos (those with European ancestry) also enjoy the *corridos* and *canciones rancheras* of Mexico. The strong African presence in this region is reflected in the use of the musical bow, a single-string instrument of African descent found throughout Central America. The Black Caribs of Honduras retain musical traditions similar to those of their West African ancestors.

African influence is very pronounced in Panama. Though a small country, it is rich in folk music and dance that reflect the blending of Spanish and African traditions. The national dance of Panama is the *tamborito*. The melody of the dance is sung by women in the call-and-response (soloist alternating with a group) fashion typical of much West African singing. It is accompanied by the *tambora*, *pujador*, and *repicador* (large, medium, and small drums of African origin). A man and a woman dance together in the middle of a circle, and they are followed by other individual couples in turn. Guitars are popular in Panamanian music, especially a five-string variety called the *mejoranera*. The violin and accordion are further European contributions. All these instruments are used in two other dances, the *mejorana* and the *cumbia*. When the *mejorana* is danced, it involves two rows, male and female, which advance and retreat from one another. At some point they cross through each other and reverse sides. Like most of the dances of Mexico and Central America, it exhibits both *paseo* (walking or gliding) and *zapateo* (stomping) steps. The *cumbia* is a courtship dance of mulatto-creole origin. Both vocal and instrumental versions are danced to the accompaniment of lively drumming. The dance involves several mixed pairs circling the musicians, and each woman carries a lighted bundle of candles. The music of the *cumbia* has spread throughout Central

America and Mexico. It figures prominently in *tejano*, a popular music of Mexican-Americans.

During the post-colonial period, and particularly in our century, Central America has suffered enormously from civil war and general economic and political instability. This has affected its musical culture as well. Thus, despite a rich tradition of folk music, it has not produced composers of the caliber of Chávez and Ponce, though there are some very good ones. We should mention the nationalist composer María de Baratta (b. 1894) of El Salvador, who wrote the ballet *Nahualismo* in 1936 and who also collected the folklore of her country. She was one of the few women composers in Latin America to achieve any stature. The Guatemalan composer Salvador Ley (b. 1907) studied in Germany before returning to Guatemala to direct the conservatory there. His style is very international but has an ethnic flavor in its rhythms and scales. Prominent among Panamanian composers is Roque Cordero (b. 1917), whose large output includes ballets as well as nationalist works for orchestra, such as the *Obertura panameña no. 2*.

The Andean Region

The Andes mountains include the highest peaks in the western hemisphere and form the principal geographical feature of the South American continent. They also play a central role in its culture. The countries along the west coast of South America were all Spanish colonies, but the acculturation of the native peoples in many areas was less thorough than in Mexico, and as a result the music of the Andean highlands (or *altiplano*) is much more Indian in character than the *mestizo* folk music of Mexico. Many of the rituals, instruments, and musical practices of these people can be traced to pre-Columbian times. In Bolivia and Peru especially the Indians play the *zampoñas*, or panpipes, whose haunting sound has become a hallmark of Latin American music. They consist of a series of pipes of varying lengths fastened together and played by blowing across them. They are usually made of cane. The playing of panpipes is a tradition that stretches from Panama to Chile and goes back at least 1,500 years. Although they are used in a wide variety of musical styles, *k'antu* is the ceremonial panpipe music from the *altiplano* of Bolivia and serves as an excellent example of this phenomenon.[6] It is the music of the Kallawaya people, who inhabit the eastern slope of the Andes, near the Peruvian border, and speak both Quechua and Aymara. Their *k'antu* ensembles consist of twenty to thirty dancers who move in a circle playing these instruments (which they call *phukunas*). However, they play the panpipes only during the dry season, from June to September. During the rest of the year they play vertical and transverse flutes, whose clear sound they believe attracts rain.

In northern Ecuador there are Indians living at high altitude in little clusters of houses (*comunas*) on the slopes of tall mountains. They play the harp, an instrument introduced by Spanish missionaries hundreds of years ago. These people also speak a dialect of Quechua, Quichua.[7] Their particular type of music, *sanjuan*, was once associated with the festival of St. John (June 24). Now, however, it is played for private masses, weddings, and wakes, to accompany singing or dancing on these occasions. Their harps are not like the modern orchestral variety in that they have fewer strings and lack the complex pedal mechanism that permits a performer to adjust the pitch of a string while playing. Their sound boxes are also wider and deeper than those on the harps one normally sees in Europe and the U.S. Just as with the guitar, Latin American musicians have taken the basic European prototype and invented many new varieties of harp that are found nowhere else in the world.

In Peru, the national song and dance is the *huayno*, and it comes in several varieties. The *huayno* is a social dance that dates back to Inca times when it was performed by Quechua Indians for funerals. It employs the pentatonic scale and is very lively. The *quena* is a vertical flute still used to accompany the *huayno* and, like the panpipes, was played by the Incas. Other instruments include the harp, guitar, *bombo* (bass drum), and *charango*, a small ten-string guitar whose body is often made from an armadillo hide.

Not all the music of the Andes, however, is Indian in character; there are also Black genres. In Peru, Blacks sing and dance the *festejo*, to the accompaniment of a box-like drum called the *cajón*. In Ecuador they sing the *bomba*.[8] Creoles (those of European ancestry) have certain types of dance and music they enjoy. In Peru the local variety of the waltz is called the *vals criollo*, while in Ecuador it is called the *pasillo*. The instruments used to perform the *pasillo* include harp, mandolin, guitar, and the *cuatro*, a guitar with four strings. The population of Chile is primarily European and *mestizo*, with only a small percentage of Blacks and Indians. One of the most important musical trends to emerge in Latin America in the last thirty years began in Chile and is known as *Nueva Canción*, or "New Song." *Nueva Canción* was a musical response to political repression in the 1950s and 1960s. Its purpose was to extol indigenous traditions and to protest economic and cultural imperialism, especially from the U.S. One of the most important composers of this type of song was Víctor Jara, whose *El lazo* ("The Noose") must be counted among the most poignant and beautiful songs of Latin America in our time.[9] In it, the composer employs the rhythms of the *cueca*, a Chilean folk dance. Jara was murdered in 1973 by the military dictatorship of Augusto Pinochet (which was supported by the U.S.).

Argentina, Paraguay, and Uruguay

As we cross the Andes we come to an area of broad plains and expansive river systems flowing from the mountains. Argentina, a land of much natural wealth, has been among the most prosperous countries in Latin America. Like Chile, it is very European in character, especially its cosmopolitan capital, Buenos Aires. This city is home to one of the world's great opera houses, the Teatro Colón. Argentina also possesses a wealth of traditional and classical music that has had a strong impact throughout the world. The many types of folk music include the *vidala*, a carnival song; *zamba*, a rural Argentine dance (not to be confused with the Brazilian *samba*); and the *cueca*, which is popular in the western provinces and is related to the *zamba*, though it is more lively and varied in rhythm. The best-known dance from Argentina, of course, is the *tango*. The origins of the word are uncertain. It may come from the Spanish *tañer*, meaning "to play," or it may come from an African word meaning either a dance or instruments used to accompany dance. The main progenitor of the *tango* was the Cuban *habanera*, a dance that was popular throughout Latin America in the late nineteenth century. These elements blended with the following Argentinean genres to produce the *tango*: first, the *milonga*, a *gaucho* (Argentinean cowboy) dance possibly of African origin that contributed certain rhythms to the *tango*; second, the *payada*, a *gaucho* song of social and political protest; and third, the *candombe*, a dance with African roots associated with Carnival.

The *tango* grew up in the suburban slums of Buenos Aires in the late nineteenth century among disaffected European immigrants and out-of-work urban *gauchos*. It became the music of the brothel, and its choreography, postures, and gestures reflect the mannerisms of pimps, known as *compadritos*. The stiff upper body was typical of this character, as was the impassive face, outwardly unaffected but inwardly passionate. The smooth patterns of steps were derived from the choreography of the *duelo criollo*, a creole knife fight that was done, like fencing, with a definite set of moves. The theme of the dance for couples is the domination of male over female, expressed through suggestive movements. (The man's need to dominate the woman emanated from the fact that the lower-class men often lost their women to wealthier men.) The *tango* was looked down upon in middle- and upper-class Buenos Aires until it became popular in Paris in the early twentieth century. There it spawned a whole *tango* culture, including novels and poetry. Finally, it gained general acceptance in Argentina in the 1920s. The typical *tango* orchestra features strings and a squeeze box called the *bandoneón*. Some *tangos* are sung, and the lyrics to these are often pessimistic and bitter in nature. Carlos Gardel (1887–1935) was the greatest of tango singers.Other *tangos* are strictly instrumental. The *tango* may have its roots in folk music, but it evolved into a composed urban genre; among the most celebrated of *tango* composers was Astor Piazzolla (1921–1992). Perhaps the best-known *tango* melody is *La cumparsita* ("The Masquerade"), by the Uruguayan composer Gerardo Matos Rodríguez (1900–1948).

Throughout its history, Argentina has attracted composers from Spain and Italy with its wealth. In the twentieth century, composers born in Argentina have taken the lead not only at home but on the international scene. The greatest of Argentinean composers was Alberto Ginastera (1916–1983). Early in his career he wrote pieces using a modern musical idiom but was inspired by the music and lifeways of his own country. His nationalist phase in the 1930s and 1940s paralleled that of Chávez and Revueltas in Mexico. Among the most important of his early works is the ballet *Estancia* (1941), which premiered as an orchestral suite at the Teatro Colón in 1943 (it was finally done as a ballet in 1952). The one-act drama in five scenes is about a young man from the city who goes to live with the *gauchos* on an *estancia* (ranch) in the *pampas* (grasslands). The young man falls in love with a local girl, who considers him a weakling in comparison to the *gauchos*. In the "Final Dance" he beats the *gauchos* at their own game by dancing the *malambo*, a fast, vigorous dance that tests one's endurance.

The creole music of Paraguay includes the *polca*; its name is misleading because it more closely resembles the Argentinean *zamba* than the Polish polka. When sung, the texts deal with military, political, or patriotic subjects. One of the most colorful figures in Latin American music was the Paraguayan guitarist and composer Augustín Barrios (1885–1944). He was among the greatest classical guitarists of this century and performed in concerts throughout South America and Europe. He was also the first guitarist to make a gramophone recording. When attendance at his concerts began to slacken, he started to dress up as an Indian chief (he actually had some Indian ancestry himself) and adopted the stage name Big Chief Mangoré; the ploy was successful. One of his finest works for guitar is entitled *La catedral*, and it expresses the composer's emotions after hearing an organist perform some music of Johann Sebastian Bach in church. In fact, this piece sounds a lot like a Bach toccata.

Uruguay has little indigenous music left because the Indians were deliberately exterminated in the nineteenth century. Its creole tradition has much in common with that of neighboring countries Brazil and Argentina. Classical music flourished later there than elsewhere in South America because the capital of Montevideo was not established until the eighteenth century; there was not much missionary activity in the area before then. In this century several composers have distinguished themselves in the classical vein, writing music in a nationalist style. Luis Cluzeau-Mortet's (1889–1957) delightfully evocative *Tamboriles* for piano is inspired by the *tamborils* (African drums) played during their summer from December through the end of Carnival.

Brazil, Venezuela, and Colombia

Brazil was settled by the Portuguese and gained its independence bloodlessly in 1822. The principal influences on Brazilian music are Iberian and African. The main Iberian contribution is in melody and harmony and the use of the guitar. African contributions include the musical bow, called a *berimbau*, the *reco-reco* (a scraper), and many different types of drums. Lively and complex rhythm is paramount, exemplified by the chief Afro-Brazilian genre, the *samba*. *Samba* is a song and dance of which there are several varieties, both rural and urban. The word *samba* originally designated the choreography of certain African circle dances involving the touching of navels. The urban *samba* is associated with Rio de Janeiro, especially the *samba de morro* from the hillside slums of Rio, which is performed during the city's annual Carnival celebrations. The accompaniment consists largely of percussion instruments. The urban *samba* evolved into a ballroom dance played by an orchestra, and this gradually became popular among whites in Brazil in the 1920s and 1930s. It was this style of *samba* that was introduced to U.S. audiences during the 1940s in films featuring the sensational Brazilian entertainer Carmen Miranda.

Out of the *samba* grew another Brazilian musical craze, the *bossa nova.* It originated in the late 1950s and was popularized in the U.S. in the early 1960s by jazz greats Charlie Byrd and Stan Getz. *Nova* means "new," while the word *bossa* is Rio de Janeiro slang for "special ability." The most famous *bossa nova* song is *The Girl from Ipanema* by Antonio Carlos Jobim (1927–1994). Jobim, together with the singer and guitarist João Gilberto (b. 1931), defined the genre. *Bossa nova* is more relaxed and mellow than the *samba*. The singer avoids an extroverted, emotional delivery and finds a middle ground between speech and song. Rhythm, harmony, and melody are equal in importance, and percussion is less prominent than in the *samba*. Instead, the guitar is emphasized as the accompanying instrument. As in the *samba*, the rhythm is syncopated, a hallmark of Brazilian music. Its characteristic rhythm can be rendered by clapping at a speed of four times a second in equal lengths but emphasizing the beats in the following way: I i i I i i I i i i I i i I i i. The lyrics of the *bossa nova* express a kind of bittersweet melancholy.

Because the country was sparsely settled, there is not much Brazilian art music from before the eighteenth century, and all of what survives from before 1800 is liturgical music. In the nineteenth century European salon music and opera predominated, and it was not until the twentieth century that nationalism became a strong current in Brazilian music, just as it did elsewhere in the Americas. The greatest of Brazilian composers was Heitor Villa-Lobos (1887–1959). Villa-Lobos (the double "l" in Villa is pronounced like an "l," not like a "y," as in Spanish) received some musical instruction from his father but was otherwise largely self-taught in composition. He studied the cello seriously, played the guitar well, and composed an astonishing amount of music, over 1,000 works, many of them for the guitar (Segovia also championed the music of Villa-Lobos).

Villa-Lobos led a bohemian life as a youth in Rio, playing in groups of popular musicians known as *chorões* (the word *choro* came to signify their music as well). They were serenaders who strummed guitars of various kinds and played sentimental music, often inspired by European dances but permeated with Brazilian melodic and rhythmic flavor. During early adulthood he traveled throughout Brazil collecting folk tunes and observing various peoples and their customs. His fiery temperament made study at the conservatory in Rio difficult. He spent several years in Paris, however, familiarizing himself with the latest developments there. He in turn was considered exotic, and his music gained tremendous popularity among the Parisians. He then returned to Brazil, where he finally gained acceptance as a composer. The government asked him to organize music education throughout the country, and he was responsible for the establishment of a system of conservatories in the provinces. During this period (1930s and 1940s) he wrote a series of suites known as the *Bachianas Brasileiras*. These suites are permeated with the melodies and rhythms of Brazil, but they also reflect the composer's love of the music of Johann Sebastian Bach. In fact, he considered Bach's music "a universal 'folk' source and language, accessible to all humankind."[10] Villa-Lobos felt that there was a great similarity between the rhythmic quality of Brazil's music and that of Bach. Of these suites, No. 5, for solo soprano and eight cellos, is the most famous. The aria from this suite was inspired by the *modinha*, a sentimental song from the nineteenth century. Though it has an improvised and spontaneous quality, this movement is very logically laid out in the form of an eighteenth-century aria (ABA).

Venezuela was not colonized as rapidly as other South American territories because the area was considered poor. Its heritage of colonial music is, therefore, not outstanding. Venezuelan folk music exhibits mostly the influence of Spain and Africa. The national song and dance of Venezuela is the *joropo*, a lively number that uses the *cuatro*, maracas, and harp. The most famous *joropo* is *Pajarillo* ("Little Bird").[11] Nationalism took root in the twentieth century. Antonio Lauro (1917–1986) is perhaps the most celebrated Venezuelan composer. Though a violinist, most of his works were written for the guitar; his *Suite venezolana* for that instrument subtly evokes the folk music of his native land. The *joropo is also popular in* Colombia, whose capital of Bogotá, was an important musical center during colonial times. The country's popular Andean dance is the lively *bambuco*, in which the woman and the man alternately pursue one another.

Cuba and the Caribbean

Cuba was the last Spanish possession in the Western hemisphere to gain its independence. During colonization, as elsewhere in the Caribbean, most of the indigenous peoples (Arawaks and Caribs) died from diseases brought by Europeans. African slaves provided the necessary labor to work the plantations, and the impact of West African music, culture, and religion on this region was enormous (the local syncretist form of religion is called *Santería*). The characteristic African drum of Cuban music is the conga (or *tumbadora*). It stands about three feet high and is played with the hands. Another Cuban percussion instrument is the bongos, two small, squat, upright drums also played with the hands. The güiro (a hollow gourd with groves cut across it that are then scraped with a stick), claves (two cylindrical sticks that are struck together), and maracas are all typical percussion instruments of the Cuban *conjunto* ("musical group"). A popular form of guitar is the *tres*, which has three sets of double strings. There are many styles of folk and popular music in Cuba, several of which have achieved popularity around the world.

The *danzón*, instrumental music for ballroom dancing, was very popular in the 1930s and 1940s. The *rumba* is a very lively song and dance with a distinctive beat, and it remains popular in the ballroom today. The *conga* dance is possibly of African origin, as its name suggests. The music exhibits a syncopation (accented upbeat) that is expressed with a kick or sidewise movement of the dancer's leg. The *guajira* is a rural song and dance accompanied by the *tres*. The most famous *guajira* is *Guantanamera.* The *guaracha* originated as a theater dance and is a lively, cheerful song. The word *chachachá* is an onomatopoeic reference to the stamping of the feet; it is an internationally famous ballroom dance. The *bolero* is a popular song and dance that originated in the nineteenth century (it bears no relation to the Spanish *bolero*). The *comparsa* is a genre associated with masquerade carnivals. One of Cuba's finest composers, Ernesto Lecuona (1896–1963), drew inspiration from these songs and dances and composed memorable versions of his own, including *La comparsa* and *Panama.* Another composer whose early works captured the rhythms and melodies of Cuban music is the guitar virtuoso Leo Brouwer (b. 1939), who composes chiefly for that instrument.

Haiti, colonized by the French, is located on the island of Hispañola and is famous for the *Vodou* (Voodoo) cult practiced there. Music plays a central role in this form of worship, which is brought to a fever pitch through the use of drums, bells, and gongs. The tree that provides the material for the drums is blessed before cutting and during construction. Finally, the drums are clothed like human beings, given names, and feted with an elaborate ceremony. The *juba* drum lies on its side as one drummer sits astride it, pressing his heel against the drumhead to change the pitch, while another strikes it from behind with sticks. Another important instrument is the *ogan*, a bell.

The Dominican Republic forms the eastern part of the island of Hispañola. As with the other islands in the Caribbean, little of the indigenous culture remains, and there is a mixture of African and Spanish ancestry. The *merengue* is the national song and dance of the Dominican Republic. It is a fast dance with lyrics that often comment on society and politics.

Puerto Rico was colonized in 1508 and taken from the Spaniards by the U.S. in 1898. The principal genre of folk music is the *seis*, which exhibits strong Spanish influence. Its lyrics employ the *décima*, a ten-line stanza with eight or nine syllables per line. There are various varieties of *seis*, many of them named after a particular region or musician.

Jamaica was colonized by Spain but later captured by England. African influence on the music is strong, and drums play an important role in social life and communication. Sacred drums are baptized in the name of a deity and provide a direct connection to the spirit world. Rastafarianism is a religion practiced on the island, and its followers claim allegiance to Africa and maintain that their music is African. Reggae music expresses many Rastafarian beliefs, and its distinctive beat and relaxed good spirits have spread far beyond the shores of Jamaica.

Trinidad is an island just off the coast of Venezuela and is best known for *calypso*. This is an eclectic mix of African and European elements that grew up during the nineteenth century in association with Carnival celebrations in Port of Spain. Its lyrics tend toward satire and social commentary, and it uses call-and-response singing. The most prominent feature of the music is the use of steel drums of various sizes, which became popular in the 1940s when they were made from oil drums.

After World War II

Following World War II, composers in Latin America began to turn away from nationalism and to look outward toward the latest trends in Europe and the United States for inspiration. They came increasingly under the influence of the post-war avant-garde and began writing music without any tonal center (or key), and even without a discernible beat. This music is generally very complex and dissonant. Chávez, Cordero, Ginastera, and Brouwer have all experimented in this style. Mario Davidovsky (b. 1934) and Mauricio Kagel (b. 1931) are two contemporary Argentinean composers who have spent most of their careers outside their homeland (in the U.S. and Germany, respectively) and who have become leaders of the avant-garde. The long-term impact of this music remains to be seen, but listeners would find nothing about it to remind them of Latin America, and like most of the avantgarde music of the last forty years, it has gained little favor with concert audiences.

By contrast, the folk and popular music of Latin America has had a tremendous impact around the world and continues to flourish, especially in the U.S., where there is an increasingly large Hispanic population. *Tejano*, *mariachi*, *mambo*, *salsa*, *bossa nova*, *tango*, *merengue*, Andean panpipe music, and many other styles of Latin American song and dance have gained great currency in the U.S. and elsewhere. Artists such as Gloria Estefan, Tito Puente, Selena, Antonio Carlos Jobim, Sergio Mendes, and Inti-Illimani have brought the musical bounty of Latin America to the world. However, much of this music reflects the influence of jazz and rock, and the process of hybridization so characteristic of Latin American music shows no sign of abating in a world where the global dissemination of music and ideas is instantaneous.

Notes

1. See Robert M. Stevenson, *Music in Aztec and Inca Territory* (Berkeley: University of California Press, 1968), 17–18.

2. The Aztecs had many musical instruments in addition to these. For a detailed description of their construction and use, see Stevenson, *Aztec and Inca*, 30–85 (the instruments are treated in alphabetical order).

3. Most of the information for this chapter comes from the twenty-volume *New Grove Dictionary of Music and Musicians* (1980), edited by Stanley Sadie, which is the world's largest and most authoritative reference work on music. Those wishing more information on particular musicians, countries, or types of music should consult this work (a new edition is in preparation). In addition, the *New Grove Dictionary of Musical Instruments* (1984), also edited by Stanley Sadie is an excellent additional source of information on organology.

4. Up-to-date information on Torrejón y Velasco and his opera is available in the *New Grove Dictionary of Opera* (1992), edited by Stanley Sadie. Entries in this three-volume dictionary include not only composers but terms and titles of specific works.

5. Thomas Turino, "Music in Latin America," in Bruno Nettl, Charles Capwell, Isabel K. F. Wong, and Thomas Turino, *Excursions in World Music*, 2d ed. (Upper Saddle River, N.J.: Prentice Hall, 1997), 237.

6. For more discussion of *k'antu* and an example of the music, see the text and accompanying recordings for Jeffrey Todd Titon, ed., *Worlds of Music*, 3d ed. (New York: Schirmer, 1996), 437–42. The excellent chapter on Latin America/Ecuador was written by John Schechter.

7. Consult Titon, *Worlds of Music*, 443–86, for a thorough presentation of Ecuadorian folk music.

8. Ibid., 485–86. Includes a recorded example of the *bomba.*

9. Ibid., 430–37. Includes a recording of Jara's song.

10. Gerard Béhague, *Heitor Villa-Lobos: The Search for Brazil's Musical Soul* (Austin: Institute of Latin American Studies, University of Texas, 1994), 105.

11. See Titon, *Worlds of Music*, 429–30. Includes a recording of *Pajarillo.*

Select Bibliography

Appleby, David P. *The Music of Brazil*. Austin: University of Texas Press, 1983.

Austerlitz, Paul. *Merengue. Dominican Music and Dominican Identity.* Philadelphia: Temple University Press,1997.

Béhague, Gerard. *Heitor Villa-Lobos: The Search for Brazil's Musical Soul.* Austin: Institute of Latin American Studies, University of Texas, 1994.

———. *Music in Latin America: An Introduction.* Englewood Cliffs, N.J.: Prentice Hall, 1979.

Chase, Gilbert. *A Guide to the Music of Latin America.* 2d ed., revised and enlarged. Washington: Pan American Union, 1962 (reprinted New York: AMS Press, 1972).

———. *Bibliography of Latin American Folk Music.* New York: AMS Press, 1972.

Ficher, Miguel, Martha Furman Schleifer, and John M. Furman, eds. *Latin American Classical Composers: A Biographical Dictionary.* London: Scarecrow Press, 1996.

Manuel, Peter, Kenneth Bilby, and Michael Largey. *Caribbean Currents: Caribbean Music from Rumba to Reggae.* Philadelphia: Temple University Press, 1995.

McGowan, Chris and Ricardo Pessanha. *The Brazilian Sound, Samba, Bossa Nova and the Popular Music of Brazil.* New ed. Philadelphia: Temple University Press,1998.

Nettl, Bruno. *Folk and Traditional Music of the Western Continents.* With chapters on Latin America by Gerard Béhague. 2d ed. Englewood Cliffs, N.J.: Prentice Hall, 1973.

Olsen, Dale A. "Folk Music of South America –A Musical Mosaic." In Elizabeth May, ed. *Musics of Many Cultures: An Introduction.* Berkeley: University of California Press, 1980.

Sadie, Stanley, ed. *New Grove Dictionary of Jazz.* New York: Macmillan, 1988.

———. *New Grove Dictionary of Music and Musicians.* New York: Macmillan, 1980.

———. *New Grove Dictionary of Musical Instruments*. New York: Macmillan, 1984.

———. *New Grove Dictionary of Opera*. New York: Macmillan, 1992.

Schechter, John. "Latin America/Ecuador." in Jeffrey Todd Titon, ed. *Worlds of Music*, 3d ed., edited by Jeffrey Todd Titon. New York: Schirmer, 1996.

Schreiner, Claus. *Música Brasileira. A History of Popular Music and the People of Brazil.* Translated by Mark Weinstein. New York: Marion Boyars, 1993.

Slonimsky, Nicolas. *Music of Latin America*. New York: Thomas Y. Crowell, 1945.

Stevenson, Robert. *Music in Aztec and Inca Territory*. Berkeley: University of California Press, 1968.

———. *Music in Mexico: A Historical Survey*. New York: Thomas Y. Crowell, 1952.

———. *The Music of Peru*. Washington, D.C.: Pan American Union, 1959.

Titon, Jeffrey Todd, ed. *Worlds of Music*. 3rd ed. New York: Schirmer, 1996.

Turino, Thomas. "Music in Latin America. " In Bruno Nettl, Charles Capwell, Isabel K. F. Wong, and Thomas Turino. *Excursions in World Music*, 2d ed. Upper Saddle River, N.J.: Prentice Hall, 1997.

Latin American New Song

Colleen Kattau

Latin American *Nueva canción* or "New Song" is a fascinating cultural movement whose unfinished history develops somewhere around the late 1950s and continues into the present. This movement has different names depending on the country: in Chile it is *Nueva canción* and later becomes *Nuevo canto*; in Argentina it begins as *Nuevo cancionero*; in Cuba it is identified as *Nueva trova*; in Nicaragua it is lovingly referred to as "Volcanto; in other countries it has been referred to as *canción protesta. Nueva canción* is a particular way of approaching musical expression, yet is not easy to define, for its roots, traditions, and forms vary from country to country, and it has come to include many different genres of music. From Argentine Ramón Ayala's *galopa* and *gualambao* compositions to the salsa rhythms of Panamanian Ruben Blades, *Nueva canción's diversity* cannot be overemphasized. Keeping in mind that, though useful, a concise definition cannot account for all the variations of music to which that term applies, we can trace the history of the movement and examine its status today while underscoring the diverse nature of its cultural manifestations.

New Song began as an international phenomenon utilizing traditional instrumentation of Spain and the Americas in combination with lyrics whose aim was to reflect the cultural, economic, and political realities of oppressed peoples. Realizing the communicative power of song, and reacting to the cultural effects of colonialism and imperialism, the artists of *Nueva canción* specifically sought a genuine musical expression reflective of their own reality. Therefore, the language of both music and poetry are blended in this tradition to reach people in a way to which they can relate. The songs often suggest new ways of thinking and draw on authentic experiences of daily life. As one of the foremost performers and theorists of *Nueva canción,* Patricio Manns, has stated,[1] this musical genre is a special kind of text in which melody and rhythm combine with carefully chosen lyrics to produce an art form full of meaning. For Manns, a key element of *Nueva canción* is that the artist must *know: "Para cantar es primordial saber."*[2] The singer/songwriter must be completely cognizant of the words selected to express a certain content in order to create a successful composition. This is one of the most specifically identifiable characteristics of New Song material—its *content* or lyrics play a major role for both artist and listener. Manns argues that this is the power of *Nueva canción* when he states that "a song is written for many people and (since there is no defense against a good song) its mobilizing power is such that it was, is, and will be a multidirectional tool of enormous constructive potential."[3]

Nueva canción has its roots in cultural traditions particular to each country of Latin America. Thus its rhythms, melodies, and words may include Spanish, Portuguese, African, and indigenous derivations, blended and transformed by the new cultural context of Latin American reality. In Chile, Equador, and Peru, for example, *Nueva canción*, in addition to Spanish influence, is much indebted to Quechuan and Aymaran music, while in Brazil and in Caribbean nations, such as Cuba and Puerto Rico, in addition to Spanish and Portuguese rhythms, African rhythms are apparent. While Spanish and Portuguese are the languages employed in these compositions, it is not unusual for indigenous words and expressions to be present, as well as vocabularies and dialects typical of the particular country in which the song is produced. Thus referentiality is a key component of New Song. As a popular art form, *Nueva canción* follows in many ways the tradition of the thirteenth-century Spanish *mester de juglaría*, or travelling minstrel, who would relate events and news through performance in song.[4] A type of Old World journalist, the minstrels would go from town to town singing romances for the townspeople in a way that both instructed and amused. That practice parallels the attempt in the twentieth century to inform and entertain via folk music, or as Chilean musician Osvaldo Rodríguez suggests, to become a chronicler of one's time.[5] The *cantautor* or singer/songwriter of New Song revives and celebrates the cultural contributions of ordinary people, the vast majority of whom are *campesinos*—poor peasants living in the countryside where a strong oral tradition is present to this day. When Víctor Jara sings the "*Lamento Borincano*" (Borinquen Lament) about the *jíbaro* or Puerto Rican peasant of Spanish descent whose way of life is being challenged by the new exigencies of urban life, he is articulating not just one particular case, but rather the plight of rural people in general. In this way, the spirit of this genre is to remind citizens of the rich cultural legacy that abounds within the borders of their own nation. Similarly, in countries such as Chile, Argentina, and Uruguay, *Nueva canción* was explicitly engendered as a response to the bankruptcy of commercial or "mass" culture, and was shaped by specific historical and social events. The movement was created indigenously at the grassroots level through a process linking past to present that sought social and cultural transformation. To understand the phenomenon called *Nueva canción* then, one must place it in the context in which it was and continues to be produced, while also considering its historical circumstances.

Chilean New Song

Chile was one of the most important countries for the development of the New Song Movement in Latin America. While Atahualpa Yupanqui of Argentina is thought of as the father figure of *Nueva canción*, Violeta Parra of Chile is considered its matriarch. In the late 1950s and early 1960s, Parra nearly single-handedly transformed the Chilean music scene by doing what few if any had done before in her work to reclaim popular folk traditions. Parra traveled throughout the Chilean countryside, particularly the Southern regions where an authentic Chilean expression was to be found, painstakingly interviewing, annotating, and recording peasants who shared their versions and memories of songs with her. Molded by an oral tradition where music is passed on among families, neighborhoods, and particular geographical regions, these folksongs often contain multiple variations in rhythm, lyrics, and instrumentation, thus adding to the richness of their expression. Parra's work and that of others such as Margot Loyola, Hector Pávez, and Gabriella Pizarro, was particularly significant since it was being done at a time when most music playing on the radio consisted of commercialized and idealized recordings aimed at a homogeneous audience. This ingenuous music did not address any of the pressing social concerns of ordinary Chileans and tended to portray a smoothed-over vision of rural experience. Rather than celebrating what made Chilean society different from the rest of the Americas, mainstream forms tended to rehash stereotypical portraits of everyday life. In contrast to the music heard over the airwaves that came from "without" rather than from "within," Parra's aim was to change all that by speaking to and learning from the Chile of the countryside and of the poor. She was the first to use an indigenous name for her folkloric group *Cuncumén* (meaning "the murmur of water" in Mapuche).[6] Parra's initiative began what later would become a crucial social-artistic phenomenon unprecedented yet directly related to older musical forms. Her work was an indispensable contribution to other artists in their quest to rediscover as well as to create an authentic Chilean aesthetic, and was pivotal to a movement that came to encompass the full spectrum of artistic expression, including dance, theatre, and the visual arts. Parra herself was not only a musician and musicologist, but also was successful as a visual artist who produced ceramic sculpture and *arpilleras* (Chilean tapestries that typically relate a story or an event on embroidered cloth).[7]

Chilean poet and literary critic Marjorie Agosín and her colleague Maria Dölz-Blackburn have compared the songs compiled and performed by Violeta Parra to established oral traditions. Their work shows how Parra drew on centuries-old music that has lived on into the present as shown in the hundreds of folksongs she collected and reinterpreted as well as in her own compositions. Though her work drew on popular culture, Parra's art was really, as one critic suggests, "countercultural" –a term popular in the 1960s– but appropriate for Parra's music given its innovative alternative to then acceptable and marketable music and to the complexity of her lyrics.[8] The songs compiled and written by Parra were as varied as the instruments used to play them, such as the guitar (the central instrument for much of New Song), *quena* (flute), *charango* (mandolin-like four-stringed instrument), *zampoña* (panpipes), and *bombo* (drum). Tragically, Parra's most famous work, *"Gracias a la vida"* (Thanks to Life) was written shortly before her suicide in 1967. In this song Parra evokes the incredible multiplicity that is life and praises it for allowing the coexistence of the most simple to the most profound things:

> Thanks to life which has given me so much
> It has given me laughter and has given me sorrow
> Thus I distinguish happiness from despair;
> The two elements of my song –and of your song,
> which is my own and the same song.[9]

Sung throughout Latin America, *"Gracias a la vida"* is included in many musical and literary anthologies and was given even greater distribution in the United States when folksinger Joan Baez, a Hispanic, recorded it. That song is only one among many by Parra in which lyrics and melody interweave to create a work of art able to touch people deeply, and is indicative of the appeal to eternal human truths that characterizes her artistic production. The outspoken lyrics of *"¿Qué dirá el Santo Padre?"* (What Will the Holy Father Say?) are testimony to Parra's often candid style embedded in a folk heritage that by no means minces words when issues of injustice are at stake:

> Look how they speak to us of freedom
> When in reality they deprive us of it.
> Look at how they beseech us to be calm,
> While the authorities torment us.[10]

In this song Parra openly points to the societal contradictions befalling her country while questioning the hypocrisy of a state that speaks of freedom yet restricts liberty at every turn. In a manner characteristic of the New Song approach, Parra engages the listener by asking the same question repeatedly (What will the Holy Father say?) and by utilizing a conversational tone that invites participation and dialogue. In another composition *"La carta"* (The Letter) she explains how her brother was arrested for being an alleged "communist" and concludes:

> Fortunately I have a guitar to sing my sorrow.
> I also have nine brothers besides the one behind bars.
> All nine are Communists in God's favor, indeed![11]

As these samples suggest, her criticism is usually not posited in a theoretical way but rather by simply relating observed and lived experience, reformulated in a creative context.

Parra's repertoire extends beyond the political sphere to include many other universal themes. *"Volver a los diecisiete"* (Return to Age Seventeen) is one of her best loved songs for its ability to poetically name the deepest of universal emotions of one experiencing a profound and poignant period akin to adolescence.

Violeta Parra's own family offers us a microcosm of the evolution of New Song. While she brought the authentic folk music of Chile to a larger audience, expanding and modernizing the content of those songs, her children Angel and Isabel Parra, both performers in their own right, take that process a step further by incorporating instruments, rhythms, and lyrics from other countries of Latin America as well. Isabel became well known for her work on the *cuatro*, a four-stringed Venezuelan instrument similar to the mandolin, and has recorded songs by Silvio Rodríguez of Cuba and other artists outside of Chile. Her efforts are one example of the Pan-American nature that has come to define the movement in which New Song artists may share material, interpret each other's compositions, and incorporate instruments indigenous to their specific country while also utilizing an array of techniques from other nations.

Another central figure of Chilean New Song was not originally a singer per se, but rather the actor and director named Víctor Jara Ironically, Violeta Parra was influential in Jara's formation as a musician since she saw that with his rich tenor voice and charismatic stage presence he had a rare potential to reach people. Like millions of other poor peasants, circumstances brought Jara from the countryside to the urban center of Santiago when he was very young, and it is there in the *población* Nogales –one of the many shanty towns surrounding the city, that Jara began to play and learn in earnest. In the sixties, he along with many other musicians would play in the *peñas* or coffeehouses, the most famous of these being the *Peña de los Parra*, where in an often crowded setting people would come to eat, connect, and listen intently. From these humble beginnings, Jara would become the best-known individual artist of *Nueva canción* as the political climate in which he lived transformed him into one of Chile's most outstanding *cantautores comprometidos* (politically committed singer/song writers).

To understand the unique nature of Chilean New Song we must take a brief detour into the political context in which it was produced. In the sixties Chilean society became increasingly polarized, with many different factions vying for power. Among them was a broad coalition called *Unidad Popular* (Popular Unity) that joined distinct groups on the Left. Communists, socialists, labor unions, and *campesinos* united to support socialist Salvador Allende's election in 1970. Amidst a tense political atmosphere and with the vote divided among three candidates, Allende was surprisingly elected by a very slim margin. Before, during, and after the campaign, Allende expressly sought out artists to help develop and shape his agenda with the aim of connecting with the disenfranchised people of the nation through education and through the arts. Indeed, the cultural consciousness of Chilean workers at that time was reflected in their increased devotion to the arts and literature.[12] Ironically, two of the most emblematic songs of the electoral campaign were actually translated adaptations of two popular folksongs from the U.S.: *"El martillito"* (If I Had a Hammer) by Pete Seeger, and *"Las casitas del barrio alto"* (Little Boxes) by Malvina Reynolds.[13] While Reynolds' song critiqued the suburban sameness of prefabricated houses and consumer society in the U.S., *"Las casitas del barrio alto"* directed its criticism toward the wealthy Chileans who were generally out of touch with the way that the vast majority of poor Chileans lived. These songs and others written during the brief but intense Allende years (songs such as *"A desalambrar, La batea, Angelita Huenum,"* and countless others) underscored the marked social divisions of Chilean society. In Jara's case, Allende's campaign and subsequent election coincided with his definitive break from theatre in order to concentrate more fully on political and cultural work through music. Like many other musicians such as Patricio Manns, Osvaldo Rodríguez, and Eduardo Carrasco, Jara participated actively in Allende's campaign, addressing union groups, schools, universities, and wherever working people congregated. Jara found himself constantly playing at union meetings, rallies, cultural benefits, and essentially providing an artistic link to what many perceived as the road toward creating a new society. Groups such as Inti-Illimani and Quilapayún, whose artistic expression was closely linked to indigenous music of the Andes, served as "cultural ambassadors" of the Chilean experiment, travelling abroad and performing popular New Song selections.[14] As one observer noted, however, the *cantautores* of this tradition perhaps would not bring about a societal revolution, but would create an incredibly effective genre of music the likes of which had not been realized before on such a grand scale.[15]

Allende's presidency was short-lived. In 1973 his government was overthrown during a coup d'état supported by the CIA and the Chilean military in which Allende was killed in the National Palace. Subsequent to Allende's overthrow, many thousands of Chileans disappeared, were tortured, or forced into exile. Immediately following the coup, Jara became one of the earliest casualties when he and approximately 5,000 others were rounded up inside the Santiago Stadium where for one week they were deprived of food and water and were tortured. Víctor Jara, then a celebrity in his country, was singled out, brutally tortured and killed. This legendary figure has been immortalized in song by artists like Holly Near, Judy Collins, and Pete Seeger, in festivals held in his name, and in albums dedicated to his memory.

Most if not all of Jara's lyrics reflect the realities of the poor and working class in some way and attest to his unyielding idealism and commitment to justice for all of Latin America. One of Jara's most famous compositions, *"Plegaria a un labrador"* (Prayer to a Laborer), recorded later in the States by Judy Collins, invokes the farmers of the earth to rise up and join hands to unite for a better tomorrow:

> Rise up and look at your hands
> Extend them to your brother that you may grow
> Together we will go united by our blood
> Today is the day that can become tomorrow.[16]

In the tradition of Liberation Theology, which takes literally the idea that the meek shall inherit the earth—this earth, Jara employs a Christian discourse to entreat workers to struggle for release from oppression. This song was the winner at the first festival of Chilean Song in 1969, which took place in the midst of the campaign for Popular Unity. That festival marked the culmination of a growing Chilean song movement and a thriving of the arts in general.[17]

Jara's lyrics often intertwine the personal and the political, as in his acclaimed composition *"Te recuerdo Amanda"* (I Remember You, Amanda), which joins the tenderness of a love story with the politicization of a worker who must go to the mountains to fight:

> I remember you Amanda in the wet streets,
> Running to the factory where Manuel worked
> The rain in your hair, your broad smile,
> Nothing else mattered, you were going to meet him.[18]

Jara's repertoire also includes musical adaptations of the words of poets such as Nobel Prize winner Pablo Neruda, as in *"Yo no quiero la patria dividida"* (I Don't Want My Country Divided). Indeed, it is not unusual that Neruda's poems were set to music by several New Song artists since his innovative and revolutionizing poetry was momentous for a whole generation of Latin American young people throughout the 1960s.

Like the Mexican *corrido* (ballad) or the age-old *trova*, the lyrics of New Song frequently derive their inspiration and material from actual events. The cultural and economic tensions in Chile at the time and the power of songs to incite emotions on the right and left had become the context and content of the songs being written. *"Cantata Santa María de Iquique,"* for instance, is a lyric drama by composer Luis Advis for Inti-Illimani inspired by and dedicated to the thousands of peasants massacred in that village at the turn of the century. *"Preguntas para Puerto Montt"* (Questions for Puerto Montt) by Víctor Jara recounts an incident that occurred in the mid-sixties when unarmed peasant squatters were attacked and killed by the military, producing an intensification of the country's political situation. That song further identified Jara as a "subversive," such that even prior to the coup, as Chilean society grew increasingly polarized between the Right and the Left, Jara himself became a symbol for a progressive movement that the extreme Right wanted to eradicate, and was thus the target of threats and acts of violence.

While Jara was perhaps the most important individual artist, he was by no means the only one performing and composing in Chile, nor the only one affected by the coup. Ironically, both Quilapayún and Inti-Illimani were marooned in Europe while on tour during the overthrow, and were only able to return more than a decade later when a period of reconciliation took hold. Their situation was indicative of the great exile of artists and intellectuals from Chile during the Pinochet dictatorship that followed Allende's government. For *Nueva canción* musicians this meant that the movement once so conspicuous and celebrated within their country was now censored, went underground, or became a movement in exile. Exile proved to be a double-edged experience. On the one hand, it afforded access to an international audience. From Toronto to Rome and in Britain, Germany, Scandinavia, and other parts of Europe, musicians forced into exile found an international community in solidarity with their music and their politics. People could now hear of and relate to political events in other countries made more real by representative artists who could educate and provide information not readily accessible otherwise. Record labels such as Columbia, Polygram, and Monitor recorded these artists, thus affording their work an even wider distribution. For these Chilean groups, traveling in the international arena necessarily influenced the shape and sound of their subsequent artistic production as they heard new rhythms and experienced the folk culture of other nations. Inti-Illimani's exile in Italy for nearly 15 years, coupled with their continuous touring, gave their music a different sound. As Inti-Illimani member Jorge Coulón states:

> When the take-over came, we experienced a very intense solidarity around the world... We are no longer in contact with the human experience of the people who live under the dictatorship, but we now have in our songs all this new experience... it has changed the complexity of our songs.[19]

Changes such as these meant that while New Song originally began as a way of reclaiming the cultural roots of individual countries, it soon became, in addition, a music genre of even greater experimentation, with increased opportunities for international collaboration and education. One example of this international (and intertextual) focus characteristic of New Song lyrics is Quilapayún's signature song *"La muralla"* (The Wall), a work based on the poem by Cuban poet Nicolás Guillén that promotes inclusion of all that is just and good, and exclusion of all hatred and harmful things.

In Chile then, as was the case for many countries of Latin America throughout the 1970s and 1980s, the status of *Nueva canción* changed with the political landscape. With the rise of the dictatorship, Chilean artists came to produce what one critic termed a differentiation in the forms that the artistic struggle took.[20] Under the military regime, New Song became known as *Canto nuevo* where within a strict limitation of possibilities of expression there emerged less overt forms of communicating through song. Metaphoric language became even more important, and one word or intonation uttered in song took on an overload of meaning for its listeners. When, for instance, Argentine singer Mercedes Sosa performs Violeta Parra's haunting composition *"Volver a los diecisiete"* a song about love, the audience breaks into a powerful applause as she reaches the words "it sets the prisoners free," even while that song as a whole is not distinctly political in content.[21] Thus with *Nuevo canto*, the listener had to read between the lyrics rather than rely on more directly stated words, while the challenge for *Nuevo canto* itself was to be able to convey a message without being censored.

Cuba's Nueva Trova

While Chilean *Nueva canción* was integral to a resistance movement, and was then incorporated however briefly as part of a socialist experiment celebrated in song, the shape and direction of a similar movement in Cuba was different given the special cultural context in which it was produced. The creators of the New Song phenomenon in Cuba, known collectively as the *Nueva trova,* deliberately chose its name to underscore its link to the tradition of the *troveros* of the 1930s and 1940s who utilized folk styles such as *bolero, guaracha, canción, guajira, bambuco,* and *son,* with minimal use of instruments (usually the Spanish guitar, maracas, and single conga) to create a necessarily unplugged sound. The *nueva trova,* whose principal figures include Silvio Rodríguez, Pablo Milanés, and Sara González, savored the roots of their sound in the *trovero* tradition while creating a musical expression immersed in the realities of a revolutionary society. The *trova* was institutionally recognized and supported by the Cuban government and found its home eventually in ICAIC, the Cuban Film Institute in Havana. There these artists continue to work in an official capacity and are seen by international audiences as live emissaries of the Revolution. Their songs are heard as documents of the history, struggles, problems, and dreams of that social process.[22]

While the overriding premise of New Song was to rescue forgotten popular cultural forms not part of the mass culture of radio and television and thus to return to traditional Spanish, African, and indigenous roots of music, Cuba's movement was also shaped by the folk and rock rhythms coming out of the U.S. and Britain in the sixties.[23] The urban youth of Havana heard the urban sounds of recording artists such as the Beatles and Bob Dylan, to name only a few, and began to cultivate their own authentic new sounds, thus ridding themselves of the "obsolete cultural baggage of the 1950s."[24] Illustrative of this shift is Cuba's perhaps best known representative of the *Nueva trova*, Silvio Rodríguez. When his song *"La era está pariendo un corazón"* (Time Is Giving Birth to a Heart) was released in the mid-sixties it became a sensational hit throughout Latin America, for it expressed the restlessness and longing for change that characterized the international youth culture of the 1960s in general:

> Time is giving birth to a heart
> It cannot take any more and is dying of pain
> And one must come running for the future is falling–
> For whatever being, in every street, in every home.[25]

The little 45s on which *"La era"* was recorded were smuggled in and out of countries, and, though censored in nations like Argentina, it nevertheless was learned and sung by thousands of young people on the continent. (In fact the song was so different from anything else to come out of Cuba that Silvio's particular falsetto style confused listeners as to the gender of its author: Was it Silvia Rodríguez?— while the innovative use of a synthesizer and the poetic lyrics announcing the birth of a new age gave "*La era*" an alternative sound.)[26]

Sloganeering is entirely absent in the songs of the *Nueva trova*. Instead, they illustrate the personal and political in the broadest sense intertwined with highly metaphoric language that suggests more often than it instructs, as in the fascinating song by Silvio Rodríguez *"Yo digo que las estrellas"* (I Say that the Stars):

> I say that the stars thank the night
> Because atop any other carriage, they couldn't shine as bright.
> And I say it is the night's fault, the universe's
> That verses of poetry are culpable
> for the fact that there are nights and stars.[27]

In other selections from this prolific artist we hear of the solidarity with the people of Nicaragua, the heroism of those who defended themselves at Playa Girón during the Bay of Pigs invasion, the homage to the bravery of *"El mayor"* (The Elder), which poetically chronicles a leader of the Cuban revolution for independence at the end of the nineteenth century, and, more recently, of the double-edged promise that tourism holds for contemporary Cuba. Rodríguez's songs are interpreted by many artists throughout the Americas including Isabel Parra of Chile, Mercedes Sosa of Argentina, and Holly Near of the United States to name only a few.

The intricacies of Pablo Milanés' melodies and his beautiful tenor voice also make him an international favorite. One of his most important pieces, *"La vida no vale nada"* (Life is Worthless), merges folk and jazz elements with an intricate instrumentation and a powerful message:

Life is worth nothing if I remain seated
After seeing and dreaming that they beckon me from everywhere
When others are being killed and I go on singing
As if nothing were happening.[28]

In the spirit of *Nueva canción,* these troubadors affirm that song should inspire the listener, provoke critical thinking, and critique as well as celebrate. Through personal reflection, its authors seek to convey universal aspirations and sentiments while ever striving toward high artistic standards of excellence. Their songs are international favorites in Spain and other parts of Europe. Despite the current U.S. blockade against Cuba, their music is still marginally available to these audiences, especially in urban areas. Artists like David Byrne, in collaboration with Cuban musicians have helped make Rodríguez's *oeuvre* available in the United States, though Rodríguez's position as Cuba's top recording artist of New Song prohibits him from touring in the U.S.

Nueva canción throughout the Americas

Chile and Cuba are by no means the only Latin American countries with a New Song tradition. In fact, it could be argued that Argentina was one of the first nations to identify *Nueva canción* as an intentional direction for its authentic folk music. As in other countries, Argentina's new song utilizes a variety of rhythms, among them being the *zamba* and *chacarera.* In the early sixties, Argentina's most famous representative of New Song, Mercedes Sosa, along with other artists, drafted a manifesto outlining the basic premises of what they termed *Nuevo cancionero.* Establishing their complete identification with the people of the countryside instead of the idealized landscape that mass culture chose to portray, their express aim was to reveal the realities that the great majority of Argentines were experiencing daily –from poverty and lack of education to the solidarity felt toward the rest of Latin America. Nationally acclaimed *cantautor* and visual artist Ramón Ayala's *son "El mensú"* (The Monthly Worker) was one of the earliest compositions to document the plight of contract workers who were forced to labor under horrendous conditions for little compensation. This piece parallels Horacio Quiroga's short story *"Los mensú"* published decades earlier in 1914, once again underscoring the tendency of New Song to mirror themes and contents found in other artistic genres, and to build on the established cultural heritage.

In Argentina, roots of *Nuevo cancionero* can be seen stretching back to its most famous tango composer, Carlos Gardel. In 1917 Gardel composed a tango in remembrance of World War I in which he relates the story of a French woman with five sons, all of whom died in the war. This earlier piece resonates with yet another antiwar composition written by Argentine León Gieco in the 1970s entitled *"Solo le pido a dios"*–a song that beseeches God to never let one become jaded or indifferent to the injustices of war, greed, exile, or violence. Made even better known by groups such as Inti-Illimani and artists such as

Mercedes Sosa of Argentina and Ana Belén of Spain, Gieco's composition is internationally recognized as one of New Song's most powerful anthems.

In between military governments in Argentina, *Nueva canción* music moved from having a semi-clandestine status to achieving national distinction only to be suppressed again when the military resumed power.

In the Dominican Republic the New Song movement existed in a climate in which competition between foreign and commercial genres and popular authentic music was pronounced.[29] The post-Trujillo era brought a re-evaluation of cultural forms either suppressed or forgotten during Trujillo's dictatorship, which lasted from 1930 until 1961. As Deborah Pacini Hernández has noted, the Dominican New Song group *Convite* was one among several musical collectives central to reviving the country's autochthonous roots. This group of musicians, anthropologists, and musicologists was particularly interested in reexamining the African and indigenous musical influences that they saw as persistently overlooked by folklorists and the ruling elite who tended to emphasize only Hispanic origins, which, while central to Dominican music, was not the only source shaping it.[30]

Like Jara of Chile and others before them, members of *Convite* experienced censorship of expression due to their activism in outwardly opposing the Balaguer government that followed Trujillo's. In fact, they were arrested for singing a *salve*, a traditional Dominican style of song which in this case related the story of Mamá Tingo, a peasant killed while defending her land. As part of their goals to revisit Dominican musical traditions and educate audiences, *Convite* participated in conferences and festivals in which questions specific to the roots of Dominican sound were discussed.[31] While *merengue* is indeed the Dominican Republic's best known music genre, in the 1970s the lesser known guitar based music of *bachata* became even more popular than *merengue* among rural Dominicans. *Bachata* is significant as a music style in that it represents the authentic popular expression of Dominican culture and of the poor despite having little of the economic and commercial support enjoyed by other forms that depended on influences outside of the country for their musical approach.[32] While most recorded *bachatas* do not have identifiably political contents, a few that do illustrate the unequivocal and direct language of the very poor (a characteristic not uncommon in New Song compositions), as in this text by Ramón Torres:

> The rich keep moving ahead
> While the poor move backwards
> There are singers who sing to love and beauty
> And they forget their people who are sunken in poverty
> But I tell the people to struggle and not let up
> To keep protesting though they cut out our tongues.[33]

Turning to Central America, we find that the 1970s and the 1980s constituted, with the exception of Costa Rica, an extremely violent period of history for these nations. The political and social turmoil experienced by these countries was chronicled in song by many groups. While a successful socialist revolution was realized in Nicaragua (1979–1990), in El Salvador, and in Guatemala, all-out civil war was claiming the lives of thousands, and human rights abuses were notorious. During the 1980s in Nicaragua, the Sandinista government made an effort to foment a genuine cultural renaissance.[34] The Ministry of Culture, led by acclaimed poet Ernesto Cardenal and later Rosario Murillo, was established to promote the arts for all sectors of the populace. That initiative took place on many fronts; from the highly successful literacy campaign modeled on Brazilian Paolo Freire's *Pedagogy of the Oppressed* to the establishment of the *talleres de poesía* or poetry workshops that allowed people of humble origins the opportunity to create their own writings, to the revival of public mural paintings. The emphasis on and support for the arts fostered the creation of New Song too as groups and soloists such as *Guitarra armada,* Salvador Bustos, Carlos Mejía Godoy, Luis Enríque, and others gave expression to the new cultural milieu in which they found themselves. Mejía Godoy and Luis Enríque were instrumental in their creative initiatives on behalf of Nicaraguan New Song's radical political messages and opened the door for other musicians in the genre. One such group, called *Guardabarranco* (named for the official bird of Nicaragua), is a brother-sister duo who combine the melodic and poetic genius of Salvador Cardenal with the superior voice of Katia Cardenal. The lyricism and notable melodic structures of this group reflect the fact that Nicaragua is truly the "land of poets." One of their most recent efforts, *Casa abierta* (Open House) (1995), is deeply indebted to Liberation Theology concepts and it critiques the futility of war, racism, and discrimination by appealing to the heart and offering a more positive vision of life. The recording's title cut, for instance, emphasizes inclusion of all regardless of color or creed:

> Here is my open house.
> There's a place for you at our table,
> A shade tree for your head,
> My door is an open book for your life.
> Open house
> Friendship does not question your creed.
> The Earth likes it when we love each other
> Without distinction of belief or flag.[35]

The interchange among various artistic genres that we have seen elsewhere follows a similar pattern in Puerto Rican New Song. Contributors to that movement include *Borinqueños* such as "El Topo," Roy Brown, and Zoraida Santiago. Brown's work is complemented by his inclusive approach to songwriting, which at times uses the poetry of Julia de Burgos, Luis Palés Matos, and Juan Antonio Corretjer to create songs of far-reaching influence. *"Casi alba"* (Almost Dawn) and *"Ay, ay, ay de la grifa negra"* (Alas, the Lament of the Black Woman), both poems by Julia de Burgos, are linked up with jazz and folk instrumentation. Through the marriage of music and poetry, Brown seeks to broaden the listener's cultural awareness and celebrate the cultural legacy of Puerto Rico, in direct contrast to and rejection of the increasing influence of U.S. imported commercial music.

Ironically, the term New Song may have little meaning for many young people living in the U.S. since many of them are only recently hearing songs that were composed and produced decades earlier. Yet, immigration from the Caribbean nations and Central America, coupled with an increased Latino population in general, has necessarily advanced the popularity of Latino sound. Commercial artists Ruben Blades of Panamá and Juan Luis Guerra (D.R.) are two well known musicians who often incorporate very progressive lyrics into the salsa and merengue songs they compose, and thus are additionally identified as New Song artists.

The reaches of *Nueva canción* have not gone wholly unnoticed by U.S. artists, both Anglo and Latino. Individual artists such as David Byrne, Sting, Holly Near, Pete Seeger, and Bernardo Palombo, and groups such as Sabiá, Altazor, New Song Quintet, and Flor de caña have brought the diverse sounds of New Song to U.S. audiences with much success. Some solidarity groups such as Witness for Peace have done the same. Many of these artists continue to travel to Central and South America and the Caribbean in a spirit of cultural interchange and collaboration –a phenomenon that finds a clear articulation in the music they produce. The all-women band Sabiá exemplifies the attempt by U.S. based artists to experiment with instruments and rhythms from Latin America in combination with a politicized text. In their first recording they use an eclectic mix of guitar, *jarana*, electric bass, conga, chekere (a large gourd percussive instrument), and bombo. Sabiá has performed for the benefit of many international human rights and assistance organizations including Oxfam International and Amnesty International. Their songs offer a wide variety of themes that explore human relationships, promote non-sexist values, and affirm solidarity with people of all nationalities. *"La andina"* (Andean Woman), written by Libby Harding, one of the group's founders, is one song that seeks a connection between women of the U.S. and of the Andean region:

> Daughter of the Andes, sister of the sun
> Woman of culture and of sadness
> They have destroyed your silver castle
> How will your children grow?[36]

Their artistic creation largely comes out of solidarity efforts taking place during the 1970s and 1980s when organizations like Sanctuary, Witness for Peace, and Sister City Projects, to name only a few, were working toward offsetting U.S. government policies that promoted a large military build-up in nations to the south of its borders.

This brief overview of Latin American *Nueva canción* has focused on several representative instances in specific countries, yet in concluding, it is crucial to recognize that New Song is an important part of the cultural landscape in all countries of the Americas (including Canada, where for many years groups such as *Los compañeros* and Lillian Allen have performed), particularly given the non-commercial value of that production. While this essay has been limited to a discussion of New Song throughout the Americas, and to Latin America in particular, it is important to note the movement's importance in Spain where artists such as Ana Belén, Juan Manuel Serrat, Víctor Manuel, Luis Llach, and many others have contributed to the genre. There are many other New Song artists that deserve mention as well for their outstanding contributions to the genre: Daniel Viglietti (Uruguay), Chico Buarque (Brazil), Soledad Bravo (Venezuela), and Amparo Ochoa (Mexico). The common thread uniting all of these artists is an obligation to a critical artistic content and consciousness that envisions music as part of a larger struggle for basic human rights that is played out locally, nationally, and internationally. As Víctor Jara suggests:

> Artists, if they are authentic creators, are as dangerous as guerrilla fighters because their power to communicate is mighty.[37]

The ideology of the left, which largely defines the music of New Song,[38] thus makes it "instrumental" in the broadest sense of the word.

Notes

1. Patricio Manns, "Problemas del texto en la Nueva Canción," *Literatura chilena: Creación y crítica*, 9 (1985): 22–24.

2. Manns, "Problemas," 24.

3. Manns, "Problemas," 24.

4. Marjorie Agosín and Elizabeth Dölz-Blackburn, *Violeta Parra o la expresión inefable* (Santiago: Planeta, 1992).

5. Osvaldo Rodríguez, "Acercamiento a la canción popular latinoamericana," *Literatura chilena: Creación y crítica*, 9 (1985): 61–65.

6. Joan Jara, *Víctor: Una vida truncada* (Barcelona: Editorial Vergara, 1980), 53.

7. During the Fascist regime of Augusto Pinochet, the *arpilleras* took on a political significance, and many were produced to convey a specific event having to do with repression under his rule.

8. Naomi Lindstrom, "Construcción folklórica y desconstrucción individual en un texto de Violeta Parra," *Literatura chilena: Creación y crítica*, no. 9 (1985): 57.

9. Patricio Manns, *Violeta Parra* (Madrid: Ediciones Jucar 1977), 127–28. All translations of songs are this author's, unless noted otherwise.

10. Manns, 151–52.

11. Manns, 1977, 130.

12. Leonardo Vargas, conversation with the author, 16 July 1996.

13. Jara, 107.

14. The names these groups chose illustrate their allegiance to indigenous forms: "Quilapayún" means "three bearded men" in Quechua, while Inti-Illimani refers to the Incan concept of sun worship.

15. Leonardo Vargas, interview.

16. Víctor Jara, *"Plegaria a un labrador"* Galvarino Plaza, (Madrid: Ediciones Júcar 1976), 130.

17. Jara, 211.

18. Galvarino, 131.

19. Juan Pablo González, "Inti-Illimani and the Artistic Treatment of Folklore," *Latin American Music Review*, 2 (1988–1989): 273.

20. Gustavo Becerra Schmidt, "La música culta y la nueva canción chilena," *Literatura chilena: Creación y crítica* 9 (1985): 14–21.

21. Violeta Parra, *Gracias a la vida: Testimonio* (Santiago, Chile: Editora Granizo, 1982).

22. See Rina Benmayor, "La Nueva trova: New Cuban Song,"*Latin American Music Review* 2, no.1 (1981): 11–30.

23. Interestingly, a song consisting of the traditional Cuban *son* and lyrics by Cuba's foremost statesman and intellectual José Martí became a hit on U.S. charts when Pete Seeger interpreted *"Guantanamera"* (Woman of Guantanamo).

24. Rina Benmayor, 14.

25. Silvio Rodríguez, *"La era está pariendo un corazón," Canción protesta: Protest Song of Latin America* (Brooklyn: Paredon Records, 1970).

26. Bernardo Palombo, conversation with the author, 2 June 1996.

27. Silvio Rodríguez on *Días y flores* (La Habana: EGREM records).

28. Pablo Milanés, *Pablo Milanés, Album de canciones*, vol. 1, 28–30.

29. Deborah Pacini Hernández, "*La lucha sonora:* Dominican Popular Music in the post-Trujillo Era," *Latin American Music Review,* 12, no. 2 (1991): 105–20.

30. Hernández, 113.

31. One of these forums entitled "Encounter with Merengue" sparked an important debate about the African influences in the Dominican Republic's musical patrimony, as well as accentuated the key role that music and its interpretation plays in the construction of Dominican national identity. Hernández, 119.

32. A festival held in 1974 in Santo Domingo entitled *Siete días con el pueblo* (Seven Days with the People), where artists such as El Topo and Danny Rivera of Puerto Rico, and Silvio Rodríguez, Mercedes Sosa, and Víctor Manuel of Spain performed, was indicative of the international focus of New Song during the period of the 1970s and 1980s.

33. *Hay que seguir protestando* cited by Pacini Hernández,118.

34. For a discussion of the arts in Nicaragua during the revolutionary period see David Craven, *The New Art of Nicaragua: Art and Cultural Policies Since the Revolution 1979–1989"* (New York: Edwin Mellen, 1992).

35. Salvador Cardenal on *Casa abierta* (Oakland: Redwood Records, 1995).

36. Sabiá, "Sharing a New Song," *Sing Out,* April-June 1985, 13.

37. Jara, 64.

38. Jan Fairly, "La nueva canción latinoamericana," *Bulletin of Latin American Research,* 107–15.

“New” Latin American Cinema, 1954-1974

John Hess

Introduction

When Latin American cinema began to interest me in the early 1970s, my friends and I could see very few films. Some Cuban documentaries circulated and then, slowly, the classic films of the period began to appear. In 1972, a film distribution company called American Documentary Film organized an ambitious Cuban film festival in New York City, but the Treasury Department shut them down and confiscated all the prints, thus bankrupting the distributor.[1] All this, of course, was BV (Before Video); now you can go to your neighborhood video store or your local library and bring home many Latin American films to watch. Various mail order video houses carry others.

This greatly enhanced opportunity accompanies a growing interest in Latin American and Latin cultures in the United States. The sounds of Salsa, Merengue, and Tango; the writings of Isabel Allende, Carlos Fuentes, Gabriel Garcia Márquez, and Luisa Valenzuela; and the images of Pedro Meyer and Sebastião Salgado have all become quite popular in the United States. Most towns and cities offer lessons in Latin dance, touring Tango shows introduce new audiences to this sensual music and dance; books on Latin music abound in bookstores.[2] Many radio stations now boast *Ritmos Latinos* shows. Since the 1960s Latin American literature has gained an increased presence in our schools and universities. Books of photography, museum shows, and even websites demonstrate a growing interest in and familiarity with Latin American photography –especially the work of the Mexican Pedro Meyer, who has pioneered in the digital manipulation of photographs, and the powerful images of the Brazilian Sebastião Salgado.[3] All this does not mean that Latin Americans had not done interesting and important work in these and the other arts before the 1960s, but certainly their work has never before gained such popularity and appreciation in the United States.[4] Moreover, this burgeoning of art and literature in Latin America has encouraged, influenced, reinforced, and also learned from *Latin* artists in the United States (e.g., artists with Mexican, Puerto Rican, Dominican, Cuban, and other Latin American heritages).

A number of recent films coming from Latin America have probably become the most widely known Latin artistic expression today. For example, many people have seen Alfonso Arau’s *Like Water for Chocolate* (Mexico, 1991), as well as Tomás Gutiérrez Alea,s *Strawberry and Chocolate* (Cuba, 1993). We know Maria Luisa Bemberg’s Argentine films: *Camila* (1984) and *Miss Mary* (1986), María Navaro’s *Danzón* (Mexico, 1991), Luis Puenzo’s *The Official Story* (Argentina, 1985) and *Old Gringo* (U.S./Mexico, 1989), Suzana Amaral's *Hour of the Star* (Brazil, 1986), Hector Babenco’s *Kiss of the Spider*

Woman (Argentina/U.S., 1985), and Victor Gaviria's *Rodrigo D: No Futuro* (Colombia, 1989). In the same breath we can easily include Latino films made in the United States, such as Luis Valdes's *Zoot Suit* (1982) and *La Bamba* (1987), Robert Young's *The Ballad of Gregorio Cortes* (1984), Gregory Nava and Anna Thomas's *El Norte* (1984), and Richard Cheech Marin's *Born in East L.A.* (1987). These explosions of creativity came on the heels of a reemerging democracy in many Latin American countries (Argentina, Brazil, Chile), a long struggle on the part of many Mexican filmmakers to break away from stifling and conventional economic structures and aesthetic methods, and an energetic Latino civil rights movement in the U.S. But as quickly as doors open, they can shut. Both severe economic hardship in most of Latin America, intensified, if not actually caused, by the economic restructuring demanded by the international financial organizations, U.S. banks, and the U.S. government and powerful anti-immigrant (especially those from Mexico) sentiment here threaten the continuation of this vibrant work in both hemispheres.

I put the quotes around the New of "New" Latin American Cinema in the title in order to indicate both this very recent, quite popular work coming from Latin America and also the film movement, beginning in the mid-1950s the filmmakers themselves called New Latin American cinema and which forms an important base for this recent work. I want to demonstrate here that in order to understand this contemporary work we need to know about the important film movement that preceded it. One quickly notices, for example, that these high budget (for Latin America) contemporary feature films, unlike most Hollywood films, deal quite specifically with social and political issues from a critical point of view. Many of them pointedly critique or even vigorously attack various seats of power-authoritarian governments, the wealthy as a class, the church, the military, and patriarchal gender relations. We might conclude from this that Latin Americans are more politically involved or perhaps more courageous or even less commercially minded than our filmmakers. To some extent all are true. Films and filmmakers in Latin America have played an important role in creating and sustaining what public sphere has existed there. That is, they have played an important part in the national dialogues of their respective countries. Since the 1950s filmmakers have been seen as and have performed as public intellectuals, a role filmmakers do not usually consciously play in the United States.[5]

Since we know of Latin America's legendary *machismo*, we might be surprised to see how many women have directed these recent films (many more than we find commonly in Hollywood). We also notice that most of these films use a pronounced melodramatic form, that is, they often deal with the family, human relationships, and intergenerational and sexual conflicts.[6] Without knowing some of the background of these films, how they have emerged as part of new democratic movements in many Latin American countries, and their ties to a previous movement called "New" Latin American Cinema, a contemporary viewer may find them hard to grasp. I want to set out this essential background here.

An Opening Image

First, though, I want to describe an image, as emblematic of the earlier "New" Latin American Cinema as it is unlikely in the newer Latin American cinema. The film it comes from appeared in 1981, indicating that we are not dealing with two distinctly separate time periods in Latin American filmmaking, but much more complex issues that I want to explain in the rest of this essay. We see the following on the screen. A peasant woman stands expectantly in a jungle clearing. The camera pans right to reveal a filmmaker dressed as a guerrilla soldier emerge from the jungle, a rifle slung over his shoulder and a 16 mm Arriflex camera in his hands. He places the camera in her basket of clothing and she gives him a pistol. She covers the camera and he helps her hoist the basket on to her head. They leave the clearing in opposite directions.

The scene suggests the imperfect, even dangerous, conditions of filmmaking in the midst of highly politicized and revolutionary situations. It reminds us of the necessary cooperation between the filmmakers and the peasants and workers of Latin America, without which many of the films I will discuss here would not exist. This particular scene comes at the very end (even after the credits) of *El Salvador: El Pueblo vencerá* (El Salvador: The People Will Win, 1981). Diego de la Texera from Puerto Rico and Têtê Vasconcelos from Brazil made this film together with a crew of Salvadoran filmmakers, university students, and, of course, Salvadoran peasants and guerrillas early in the insurgency that dominated the 1980s in El Salvador, causing the death of tens of thousands of people and the devastation of the country.[7]

Latin America's New Wave

"New" Latin American Cinema, a continental New Wave in film, began simultaneously in Argentina, Brazil, and Cuba in the mid-1950s, then spread to most of the rest of the continent, and was all but extinguished by both severe repression and extensive social, political, and economic changes by the mid-1970s. Yet its oppositional and independent spirit lives on in many areas of Latin American film and video. And its notion of *cine imperfecto* affected filmmakers around the world.[8]

This period, focused primarily on the 1960s, saw great turmoil and achievement in Latin America. Encouraged by President Roosevelt's Good Neighbor Policy in the 1930s, extensive U.S. economic aid and trade during the Second World War, and a number of strong populist, nationalist leaders, such as Getulio Vargas in Brazil and Juan Domingo Perón in Argentina, Latin America experienced strong economic growth and rising expectations during and just after the war. This situation greatly strengthened nationalist sentiments as well as a continental sensibility, and encouraged calls for greater democratic participation in governments across the region. After the war, however, the United States shifted its attention away from Latin America to Europe and its cold war with the Soviet Union.

From then on Latin American countries only warranted U.S. attention when they presented the threat of communism –real or imagined. For example, the

United States instigated the overthrow of the democratically elected government of Jacobo Arbenz in Guatemala in 1954, organized the disastrous Bay of Pigs invasion of Cuba in 1961, occupied the Dominican Republic in 1965, supervised the murderous military coup against democratically elected Chilean President Salvador Allende in 1973, invaded Grenada in 1983, and conducted a bloody and costly proxy war against Nicaragua's Sandinista government throughout the 1980s. "New" Latin American Cinema emerged, flourished, and died in this context of rising expectations and quickly dashed hopes, of revolutionary struggles for national liberation, and powerful U.S. resistance and intervention. This filmmaking, however, often created the necessary pools of talent and physical infrastructure for subsequent filmmaking, and it also left a strong radical legacy for new generations of filmmakers. Moreover, it established the filmmaker as an important public intellectual –both a privilege and a dangerous responsibility.

This Cinema, moreover, represents only the cinematic aspect of an explosion of artistic creativity during these years. We best know *el boom* in literature, led by novelists like Gabriel García Márquez (Colombia), Carlos Fuentes (Mexico), Mario Vargas Llosa (Peru), José Donoso (Chile), and Julio Cortázar (Argentina). Similarly, there emerged the folk music-based New Song movement, with its earliest roots in Argentina and Chile and figures like Mercedes Sosa, Violeta Parra, and Víctor Jara. Similar developments occurred in theater, photography, painting, and other art forms.

All these arts movements, as is usually the case, combine important influences from abroad with internal developments. In the new literature, for example, modernist influences of Faulkner and Joyce jostle against magical realist modes of narrative indigenous to Latin American story telling. Equally, the new cinema depends upon and yet radically alters modernist ideas about film coming from Europe, especially those of Italian Neorealism.

Italian Neorealism

Briefly, Italian Neorealism was a movement in Italian cinema that began at the end of World War II in 1945 and lasted into the early 1950s; it had a major influence not just on subsequent Italian cinema, but on much world cinema as well, especially on the emerging cinemas in much of Africa, Asia, and especially Latin America. In films such as Roberto Rossellini's *Rome, Open City* (1945), and *Paisan* (1946), Luchino Visconti's *La Terra Trema* (1947), and Vittorio De Sica's *The Bicycle Thief* (1948) and *Miracle in Milan* (1950), the Italians developed a radically new, austere cinematic realism.[9] With low budgets and small crews they shot their films on location in natural light with a mix of nonprofessional and little-known professional actors. Their grainy black and white visual style more closely resembled documentary than traditional fiction films. They consciously set themselves against the Hollywood style cinema, a studio-produced style that had also dominated fascist filmmaking in Italy in the 1930s. Their films concentrated on the everyday lives of ordinary people who struggled with the physical, economic, and psychic devastation of the immediate post-war years.

Robert Kolker has written that Italian Neorealism is not just a certain number of films made from 1945 to the mid-1950s, but also "a concept, an aesthetics, a politics, a radical reorientation of cinema that changed the perspective on what had gone before and made possible a great deal of what came after."[10] These Italian directors worked to oppose the conventions of the Hollywood-style film that placed the spectator in the passive position of simply consuming conventionalized emotions and experiences. In contrast they sought to make films that would draw the spectator into an active intellectual and emotional relationship with a film and its director. They wanted their films to be, like other modernist art forms, a critical dialogue with the spectator about the contemporary world, its problems, and its possibilities.

These Italian films had a tremendous impact on young filmmakers in Latin America, a few of whom were able to study filmmaking at Rome's famous film school, the *Centro Sperimentali*. These young men certainly did not have the means to make a Hollywood style film. Nor did they simply want to produce entertainment. They experienced a social and political development that created a strong desire to document the peoples and problems of their own countries rather than imitate the fantasies of filmmakers in the United States or Europe. They grew to maturity in the context of a burgeoning film club movement and an expanding use of film for social documentation. They saw in the Italian films a mode of production (low budget, small crew), an aesthetic (documentary realism), and a cultural politics (critical dialogue with the audience) that fit their passionate interest in discovering and studying their own countries. They wanted to use film to participate in the vigorous national dialogues then taking place.[11]

Origins: Messengers from Europe and Early Work

New Latin American Cinema begins nearly simultaneously in Brazil, Cuba, and Argentina. Here, I want to first highlight these initial moments and then indicate briefly how things developed from there. In 1949 the Brazilian-born filmmaker Alberto Calvalcanti returned home after a successful filmmaking career in Europe and became head of the Vera Cruz film studio in São Paulo where he participated in an effort to create a truly national cinema, one that would achieve the same high level as the well-known European cinemas. Calvalcanti brought in accomplished European filmmakers and technicians and made some interesting films in a variety of genres. *O Cangaceiro* (Lima Barreto, 1953), a Brazilian Western set in the dry, impoverished Northeast, won fame internationally and a prize at the Cannes film festival. This barren landscape became a major setting for the younger filmmakers who followed. However, since the Vera Cruz studio never established a firm economic base and since they placed distribution of the films in the hands of Columbia Pictures, which had no interest in encouraging a strong, national cinema in Brazil, the project collapsed in 1954. Out of the ashes arose Cinema Novo.[12]

A few years prior to the collapse of the Vera Cruz studio, Tomás Gutiérrez Alea and Julio García Espinosa returned to Cuba from studying film in Rome. With several friends they made a short documentary-style fictional film on impoverished charcoal workers, called *El Mégano*, in 1954.[13] Cuban dictator Batista quickly confiscated the film. This group of filmmakers and their friends in several Havana film clubs went on to participate actively in the Cuban Revolution and formed the core of the Cuban Film Institute, established in the spring of 1959, only a few months after the triumph of the Revolution.[14]

Two years after the Cubans made *El Mégano*, Fernando Birri returned to his native Argentina and began teaching sociological photography and then documentary film at the provincial University of Santa Fé. He, too, had studied in Rome and returned to his homeland wanting, as he said, "to discover the face of an invisible Argentina –invisible not because it couldn't be seen, but because no one *wanted* to see it."[15] Birri made Latin America's most famous documentary film in 1958 –*Tire dié* (Throw us a Dime)– and a neorealist comedy *Los inundados* (The Flood Victims, 1962) before he was forced to flee Argentina. He then traveled through Latin America with his films, inspiring young filmmakers and intellectuals as he went. Let's see how these initial efforts developed.

Troubled Argentina

Latin Americans often refer to Fernando Birri as the Father of "New" Latin American Cinema. He earned this honor not just because the few films he made in Argentina embodied so many of the dreams and desires of a young generation of filmmakers, but because after going into permanent exile he taught and influenced so many of them directly. While teaching at what became known as the Documentary Film School, Birri worked together with a large number of students to make photo essays about the city and its marginal barrios. This early sociological field work led to the group's production of *Tire dié*. The film begins with an aerial shot of the city; a voice-over narration gives statistics about it. This could be a tourist film or a conventional documentary about a city. But as the statistics become increasingly silly numbers of hair salons, loaves of bread, street lamps, ink and erasers used in government offices –we understand that Birri has something else in mind. Suddenly, we are at ground level interviewing residents of a poor barrio on the banks of the Salado river. As the interviews proceed, informing us about their precarious living conditions, we see children gathering near a long, low railroad bridge over a swampy area. We see and feel their excited energy, but don't yet understand what is going on.

Shortly, however, the sighting of an arriving train draws our attention back to the bridge. There follows a surprising and remarkable documentary sequence. Dozens of children run along side the train as it crosses the bridge, begging for the few coins that some of the passengers throw out to them. We see the dangers, the incredible agility and skill of the children, the sense of superiority in the faces of the bored passengers, the dire need on the faces of the children. We understand from what we have already seen and heard in the film that no matter how great the danger and how much the parents fear for their children, the small change they pick up each day makes a considerable difference in the economy of each family. Clips from this amazing sequence have turned up in numerous Latin American films since then.[16]

Los Inundados (The Flood Victims), a picaresque comedy, recounts the story of the kind of people we met in *Tire dié* –Dolorcito Gaitán, his wife Optima, and their several children– after a seasonal flood forces them and all their friends and neighbors from their lowland shacks in the barrio of Centenario on the Salado river. They camp out in an open lot by the railroad tracks, courtesy of a briefly sympathetic city administration during a humorously rendered political campaign. The Gaitán and a few other families make new homes in some idle cattle cars on the tracks. One night, the family's cattle car is attached to a freight train and they begin an involuntary trip to the North. At first, the railroad officials try to get rid of them, but since, bureaucratically speaking, the car does not exist, they can't send it back to Santa Fé. Finally, they come to rest in a larger village, where the locals welcome them and Dolorcito becomes an honored guest because of his skill at bocci ball.

Inevitably, however, bureaucratic incompetence cannot help the poor for long. One fine day, the officious station master triumphantly emerges from his office and announces their immediate departure; they throw their belongings helter-skelter into their cattle car, and Dolorcito, called from a championship game, just barely catches up with the train and has his considerable bulk hauled aboard by his desperate family. At the end, we see them rebuilding their shack in the lowlands and reconnecting with their friends and neighbors –and waiting for the inevitable next flood.

In Santa Fé, Birri developed a new approach to cinema in the midst of an Argentine cinema in cultural and industrial disintegration. So, very much like the neorealists in Italy after the war, Birri stands amidst the ruins of a studio mode of production whose image of Argentina was one of unreality, a foreign and alienating image, one that avoided looking at the real, actual Argentina of the 1950s. Fernando Birri brought the message and method of Italian Neorealism to Argentina and to Latin America and began the process of adapting it to local conditions. He made the first truly sociological film about the poor and disenfranchised majority and showed subsequent filmmakers what was possible with even very limited resources.

The subsequent development of cinema in Argentina is a difficult one to tell in any coherent way because of the escalating violence of military interventions and dictatorships. In 1966, the military overthrew a temporary civilian government and initiated the New Argentine Revolution; it included extensive censorship along with harassment of artists, intellectuals, and students. Many left the country under threat of death. Others became more politically active. One group of filmmakers (Grupo Cine Liberación, including Fernando Solanas, Octavio Getino, and later Gerardo Vallejo [a student of Birri's in Santa Fé]), close to the still powerful underground peronist labor movement, began to make a film about labor and ended up making one of the most powerful and radical documentaries of the whole period –*La hora de los hornos* (Hour of the Furnaces, 1968).

The nearly four-hour-long film is a daring experimental and militant documentary. Drawing sounds and images from a variety of sources, the filmmakers constructed on the editing table a complex film essay in the tradition of both Jean-Luc Godard and the famous Cuban documentary filmmaker Santiago Alvarez. Bob Stam comments on the film's minimalism:

> Time and again one is struck by the contrast between the poverty of the original materials and the power of the final result. Unpromising footage is transmogrified into art, as the alchemy of montage transforms the base metals of titles, black frames and percussive sounds into the gold and silver of rhythmic virtuosity. Static two-dimensional images (photos, posters, ads, engravings) are dynamized by editing and camera movement.[17]

Courageous filmmakers continued to make films in Argentina up to the beginning of the so-called dirty war, a reign of terror conducted by the Argentine military from 1976 into the early 1980s, during which few films were made at all. In Argentina the New "New" Latin American Cinema emerges from and often comments on this terrible period in the country's history.[18]

The Rise and Fall of Brazil's Cinema Novo

The demise of the Vera Cruz studio experiment in 1954 led to two very important developments: first, an intense debate within the film community about what sort of cinema would be most appropriate in an underdeveloped, dependent country like Brazil (theory) and, second, the beginning of an independent filmmaking, based on the model of the Italian cinema, using actual urban and rural settings, nonprofessional actors, popular themes, and a straightforward cinematic realism (practice). The most influential of these was Nelson Pereira dos Santos, who commented:

> The influence of neo-realism was not that of a school or ideology but rather as a production system. Neo-realism taught us, in sum, that it was possible to make films in the streets; that we did not need studios; that we could film using average people rather than known actors; that the technique could be imperfect, as long as the film was truly linked to its national culture and expressed that culture.[19]

To give a sense of the range of Cinema Novo, I want briefly to discuss three films: *Barravento* (Glauber Rocha, 1962), and *Vidas Secas* (Barren Lives, Nelson Pereira dos Santos, 1963), two classics of the early period, and then *Antonio das Mortes* (Glauber Rocha, 1968), made in a very different style just during and after the rigorously censorious 1968 coup. *Barravento* and *Vidas Secas* both strongly reflect the influences of Italian Neorealism on these young Brazilian filmmakers. Both shot in poor rural areas of Brazil with nonprofessional actors, they focus on the lives of ordinary people: a community of fishermen in Bahia and an itinerant cowboy and his family in the barren

Northeast. Yet both films add a whole symbolic and ritualized element to the social realism of the Italian films.

As described early on by a narrator, Barravento means the time of change, the turn of the wind, the moment of storm and metamorphosis. The film concerns four outsiders in Buraquinho, a Brazilian Bahian fishing village: Firmino, who has been to the city, learned to steal and pimp to survive, dressed in white Panama suit with a city hat; Cota, the village whore who loves Firmino; Aruan, the future leader of the village, thought to be the son of the sea goddess, Iemanja; and finally, Naina, a white woman, who is also associated with the sea goddess and loves Aruan. Firmino returns from the city with the desire to change the villagers. He attacks their dependence and ignorance, dethrones their leader, Aruan, and cuts the white men's fishing net, forcing them to fish in the old way from boats.

At the end, Aruan, disgraced, commits himself to Naina, who has been initiated into an Afro-Brazilian religious sect called Condomblé, and leaves the village the same way Firmino came, saying to Naina he will be back in a year after making some money to help the village. The film is filled with loving images of the villagers at work on the beach and of the religious ceremonies the women perform. At the same time, an intense struggle is going on between the traditions of the village and the ever stronger influences coming from the city. Like many Latin American villages and small towns, this one balances uneasily between tradition and modernization, a balance Rocha and his colleagues seem unwilling or unable to resolve in this film.[20] Interestingly, this contradiction no longer underlies the more recent films, because, as the result of a massive internal migration, most Latin Americans now live in cities.

Based on Graciliano Ramos's famous realist novel of 1938, *Vidas secas* is one of the most famous early films of the Cinema Novo movement in Brazil. Ramos's novel bears considerable comparison to John Steinbeck's *The Grapes of Wrath*, written a year later in 1939. Both novels deal with

> an identical subject; drought and migration. The droughts of the dust bowl drive the Joads from Oklahoma to California, just as the droughts of the Brazilian northeast drive Fabiano and his family to the cities of the south. In both works the trajectory of a single family comes to encapsulate the destiny of thousands of oppressed people. In one case the oppressors are real-estate companies and agro-businessmen; in the other, landowners and their accomplices.[21]

Vidas Secas portrays the life of a peasant family –Fabiano, Vitoria, their children, and their dog, Baleia. They enter a new area, Fabiano gets a job working for a rancher, it rains, there is food. But then the dry season returns, Fabiano is fired and ordered off the land, and the family continues its wandering. The film opens on a bleak landscape through which the family drags itself, clearly exhausted in their search for food, water, and most important, work. These exquisitely stark, overexposed images are accompanied by an almost unbearable screeching sound. The source of this sound is not revealed in this sequence, and we only discover later that it comes from the enormous wheel of a wooden cart. This dislocation of sound and image clearly goes beyond anything we would see in Neorealism, and the wheel itself symbolizes the family's never-ending search for food, clothing, shelter, and work. The film shows both the enormous pride gained from finding and doing work and the desolation of losing it –which in the case of such poor people initiates a new life- and-death struggle. At the end of the film, a title informs us that this family has joined the steady stream of rural workers heading to the city in search of work and thus life.

Glauber Rocha made *Antonio das Mortes* (1968) after the coup within the coup in 1968 and within its climate of intense censorship. The film is a complex folkloric, operatic, and mythic film, drawing on actual historical people and incidents as well as myths, legends, and the various religions important in Brazil. Antonio is a hired killer, employed by the wealthy landowner to protect his property and kill the *cangaceiros* (bandits), who threaten him and his class. Antonio is a wanderer in Brazil's barren Northeast, a solitary figure, a romantic hero, not unlike the gunfighters of Hollywood Westerns. In terms of the social structure of the countryside, Antonio begins as a bad guy, but during the course of the film, in a series of richly photographed and highly ritualized encounters with Coirana, a leading bandit and peasant hero; la Santa, a woman who represents mass religious opposition; Antão, who represents both black rebellion and Brazilian religious expression; and finally the teacher or intellectual (and perhaps also representing the filmmaker), who is finally shaken out of his lethargic, drunken apathy and joins the revolt against the landowner; Antonio changes and ultimately takes up the cause of the oppressed.[22]

The Cuban Film Institute

Only a few months after the triumph of the Revolution, the Cuban government gathered its few filmmakers together in the Cuban Institute for Cinematographic Art and Industry (ICAIC). The Cubans, mostly quite young, had lots of enthusiasm and commitment, but very few resources. As a result they began making short, cheap documentaries about the revolutionary process itself. All Cuban filmmakers have begun their careers making documentary films, which perhaps explains to some extent their penchant for including documentary material in their fiction films.

Cuba's first great filmmaker, Santiago Alvarez, was able to turn this lack of resources into an expressive asset. He became head of and continues to head the documentary section and the weekly newsreel. Julianne Burton has written the following about Alvarez:

> Obliged to draw from existing film archives and such "second-hand" sources as news photos and television footage, he developed a methodology which circumvented the need for on-the-spot footage and elevated the film-collage to a high level of political and artistic quality.[23]

In one short film called *Now* (1965), Alvarez combines mostly still images, taken from magazines such as *Life*, about the civil rights movement in the U.S. On *Now*'s soundtrack Lena Horne sings the Jewish liberation song, Hava Nagillah, with new lyrics appropriate to the Civil Rights movement. [24]

Most of the early fiction films the Cubans made, were reminiscent of the Italian films that so influenced them. However, Santiago Alvarez, as a major leader in ICAIC, set an exuberantly experimental tone, thus encouraging the rest of the filmmakers to follow him in this direction. Many of the classic Cuban films of the late 1960s and early 1970s were experimental in form as the directors searched for ways to make distinctively Cuban films and also reach their highly politicized audience. Perhaps the most famous film of this period, certainly the most written about, is the late Tomás Gutiérrez Alea's *Memories of Underdevelopment* (1968).[25] In the film, Sergio, a middle-class man who owned and managed a furniture store, remains in Cuba after his parents, his wife, and most of his friends leave for Miami. He feels disgusted by them and by their values and expresses curiosity about what will happen in Cuba. Though his critique of his own class, of the Revolution, and of the Cuban people in general is often acute and cleverly expressed, his inability to connect in any positive way with the Revolution renders him superfluous and irrelevant. At one point Elena, a young woman he picks up, says that since he's not a revolutionary or a counterrevolutionary, he's nothing.

Gutiérrez Alea juxtaposes Sergio's wanderings around Havana with a series of documentary images, such as TV reports, documentary film images, censored clips from old entertainment films, and newspaper headlines, some of which originate from within the film, others of which do not. These inserts constantly remind us of the seriously escalating U.S. opposition to the Cuban Revolution and the Cuban's preparation to defend themselves (the film is set between the Bay of Pigs invasion in April, 1961, and the Cuban Missile Crisis in October, 1962). These images establish an objective pole in contrast to Sergio's subjective concerns expressed in the "fiction" parts of the film.

Sergio obsesses about sex –classic art images, pictures of women in magazines, fantasies, memories of previous love affairs, and one actual affair with Elena. We learn that Sergio harbors very negative attitudes toward dark Cuban women, finding them much inferior to blonde, blue-eyed Northern Europeans and North Americans. Some of these inserted documentary pieces suggest that Sergio's views come from European and North American media, from Cuba's long dependence on and exploitation by the United States. At the Cuban Film Institute, where Sergio has taken Elena, we meet a filmmaker, Gutiérrez Alea himself, who is also working with sexual images, the censored clips from European and Hollywood films. Here, another middle-class man, one who looks surprisingly like Sergio, uses sexual images to deconstruct their negative influences. He uses them as part of contributing to a revolutionary culture rather than for his own private fantasies. Thus, while Sergio disappears into the grain of the film (quite literally in one shot), essentially disappears as a significant character, we see that other middle-class intellectuals and artists have found ways to support and advance the revolution.

The three-part *Lucia* (Humberto Solás, 1968) represents another of Cuban cinema's great achievements during the classical period. The three parts, each shot in a different visual style, examine three key turning points in modern Cuban history through the lives of three women named Lucia. The first part takes place during the Cuban war of independence against Spain in 1898. Here the milieu is that of the landed Creole aristocracy. Lucia is approaching spinsterhood. Her sheltered world consists primarily of her family and other women of her class. Though her brother Felipe is involved in the war for independence and she sews bandages, the war is also distant. The charming Spanish agent, Rafael, takes advantage of Lucia's vulnerability to court her and find out where her brother and other rebels are hiding. The film shows how her social circumstances limit her ability to understand the world around her and how through bitter life experiences she slowly comes to greater awareness.

The second part takes place during the struggle against the dictator Machado in 1933. Here Lucia comes from a wealthy middle-class family and falls in love with and helps the revolutionary Aldo. To support him she works in a tobacco factory where she becomes involved in a strike that the police violently put down. Though the revolutionaries succeed in overthrowing Machado, many of them become corrupt opportunists, undermining the ideals Aldo and Lucia fought for. The third part begins shortly after the 1959 Cuban revolution. Lucia, a recently married peasant woman, fights against her husband's backwardness in order to work and learn to read. Each part of the film concerns history and its effect on human consciousness. Because of a changing world and their own altered circumstances, the people come to see things very differently. And an initial relative passivity and acceptance of the norm gives way to action.

Finally, I want to look at *One Way or Another* (Sara Gómez, 1974–1977), the only feature film directed by a woman in Cuba from the early 1960s to the late 1980s. Sara Gómez was a Cuban woman of African descent who, like most Cuban filmmakers, started making documentary films. She died of severe asthma before she finished the film; Gutiérrez Alea and Julio García Espinosa, both of whom worked as advisors on the film from the beginning, finished it, apparently according to her wishes. A Swedish lab severely damaged the negative and it took until 1977 to restore it.

The film concerns urban renewal and marginality in Havana and the deeply internalized culture that such marginality produces. Like *Memories of Underdevelopment*, but in a much more radical way, the film inserts documentary segments into its fiction. In fact, it does this to the extent that the viewer cannot always tell what is documentary and what is fiction. The narration over the documentary sections of the film tends to claim that the Cuban revolution has ended the problems of marginality by building new housing, training people, and giving them jobs. The film itself argues that while these material things may have indeed changed, that does not automatically end marginality and slum culture. Individual and social change are far more complex than that. Some people can change rapidly and others find it much more difficult.

Julia Lesage, in writing about the film, says that we, the audience, are being asked by the film "to create social meaning: about the characters, about the relation between fiction and documentary, about modes of discourse, about marginal life and culture, and about the relation of the personal and emotional to the political and public sphere." Then Lesage talks about the audience itself – about us.

> Historical reality is inside us as well as around us, and it is created by what goes on inside us emotionally as well as by our will. To grasp the idea or principle behind appearances is to be more involved in history than not to do so. When we see social and conceptual structures and their interconnection and their movement, we can fully see our own choices and areas of responsibility and can act in accordance with both reality and the potential of our own fullest being.[26]

The Cubans' more experimental fiction films are open-ended, concentrating on process rather than product. They want to stimulate their audience to think about what they see, to encourage a critical response and debate in the audience. As a result, many Cuban films have become centers of intense controversy and debate, with people going back many times to see the same film. The film becomes both the catalyst and the substance of the debate. Though Cuban films are no longer formally experimental, they often continue to have this kind of interaction with their audience, such as the considerable excitement created in Cuba by Gutiérrez Alea's internationally successful film, *Strawberry and Chocolate*. The film recounts the relationship between David, a young, straight-laced university student and communist youth member, and Diego, an openly gay male intellectual who continues to be persecuted by the authorities. While Diego decides to leave Cuba, the film leaves David's fate open. A macho and virulently homophobic fellow student has denounced David for this friendship with Diego. The film leaves it up to the audience to debate David's fate.[27]

Jorge Sanjinés

"New" Latin American Cinema spread well beyond its initial places of origin to most countries on the continent. I have space here for just one example: the Bolivian Jorge Sanjinés, who has been able to fashion a filmmaking career under the most difficult of circumstances. For thirty-plus years he has made films in cooperation with a variety of Andean peoples –Quechua, Aymará, and Guaraní speaking people– in his native Bolivia, as well as in Peru and Ecuador. He has consistently made films that dealt with topical, sensitive, political issues and that usually got him into trouble. He has had to flee all three of these countries at one time or another. He has struggled, in more detail than anyone I can think of, with the contradiction between using an elite medium to speak about, for, and to the masses, here the indigenous masses of the Andean countries.[28]

Yawar Malku (Blood of the Condor, 1969) became one of his most effective and thus most famous films. In this film he used non-professional actors and location shooting to reveal the social environment of a group of Quechua-speaking Indians. They figure out that a U.S.-sponsored clinic is sterilizing their women and attack it. In reprisal soldiers shoot two community leaders and wound the third, Ignacio, whose wife Paulina takes him to La Paz to get medical help. His assimilated brother, Sixto, searches unsuccessfully through La Paz for the blood plasma the doctors need in order to operate on Ignacio. He can't find any and his brother dies. At the end, Sixto, now dressed in traditional clothing, returns to the community with Paulina to continue the struggle.

Sanjinés's next feature film, *Courage of the People* (The Night of San Juan, 1971), dealt with the repression of a tin workers strike in 1967 at the Siglo XX mines, which ended in a massacre. The film continues Sanjinés's effort to make films with and for the indigenous peoples and to make films that actually promote revolution as a solution to people's problems. Critical of his own earlier work, in this film he turned away from historical reenactment with actors (even nonprofessional ones) representing characters to having the survivors of the massacre recreate the events in which they themselves participated. Sanjinés later expressed the view that filmmakers should simply record a creative process that belongs to the people, and he called this method reconstructive.

The Legacy of "New" Latin American Cinema

By 1975 military interventions and dictatorships had crushed most of New Latin American Cinema. At first it seemed that no hope existed, but then, toward the end of the 1970s, there began to appear fascinating work from small groups of mostly women film and video makers. Women's liberation came slowly to Latin America and particularly slowly in the rather privileged enclaves of film production. Nevertheless, in the early 1980s women's meetings were held within the Havana Film Festival and became very lively events. More important, the first Latin American women's film festival, called *Cocina de imágenes* (Kitchen of Images) took place in Mexico City in 1987. The festival was a major success not just for film and video makers, but as a continuation of the series of feminist meetings that had been held in prior years (e.g., Bogota in 1981, Lima in 1983, and São Paulo in 1985). In various countries women had come together to form film and video collectives to deal with women's issues. Two key examples are Lilith Video in Brazil and Cine Mujer in Colombia. Then in the early 1980s, the Sandinista revolution in Nicaragua and the insurgency in El Salvador created favorable circumstances for a new wave of film and video production, often using the most inexpensive equipment possible. For example, in Nicaragua women worked alongside men in the Taller Popular de Video (Popular Video Workshop) to make tapes about women's lives and the impact of the revolution on them.[29]

Conclusion

The political and cultural upheaval in Latin America in the late 1950s through the 1960s and into the early 1970s had as one important goal to throw off U.S.

influence and even dominance in the cultural as well as economic realms –what many have called cultural and economic imperialism. Thus Latin American filmmakers sought a style, a mode of production, and a relationship with the audience that was very different from that of Hollywood –an anti-show, if you will, derived partly from the example of Italian Neorealism. However, it seems impossible to avoid the conclusion that they lost this struggle on all fronts. The United States first isolated Cuba, forcing it to concentrate tremendous resources on its own defense rather than allowing it freely to develop in its own way – socially, culturally, and economically. This hostility forced Cuba to accept help from the Soviet Union, and this relationship distorted their own development and ultimately made them dependent on their benefactor. Furthermore, as is well known, our government encouraged and materially supported the militaries in Argentina, Bolivia, Brazil, and Chile, which one after another overthrew their democratically elected governments.[30] This support continued through years of brutal repression in which tens of thousands disappeared, died, or were forced into exile. Collaterally, the effort to create and develop national film industries collapsed under these circumstances.

In the early to mid-1980s, their own incompetence and courageous opposition by the citizenry, including massive street demonstrations, forced these military governments out of office. The democracies that emerged were and remain tenuous, with the military constantly looking over their shoulders. Moreover, neoliberal, market-driven economics dominate these new, fragile democracies, demanding austerity for most of the people, widening the gap between rich and poor, and causing severe poverty and disease.

In this context, developing a renewed national cinema is extremely difficult. In Latin America, cheap foreign (and some domestic) exploitation films – gangster and action films, sex comedies, soft-core pornography– dominate film screens; distributors and exhibitors have little sympathy for local products that are not equally cheap and profitable. Major videostores in Mexico that I visited recently had few if any Mexican or Latin American films at all. Thus, in order to compete in this context, feature fiction films with artistic and/or political aspirations must seek commercial popularity to survive, to even get an opportunity to be seen.

Thus Latin American art films exhibit two, apparently contradictory, characteristics –one coming from the early "New" Latin American Cinema and one coming from the economic and political reality of their contemporary context. In keeping with the earlier movement and the continuing desire to construct a *national* cinema, the films often focus on familiar aspects of national history, popular topical issues, and known national figures. They often realistically examine a place or region of the country. They are often about ordinary kinds of people. They also try to engage the audience in a conversation about their contemporary reality in addition to entertaining them. In this sense, they are not unlike European art films and alternative features in the United States.

At the same time the films strive to reach a broad, popular audience, not just an elite, art house audience. They do this primarily by borrowing heavily from the region's enormously popular television form –the telenovela or soap opera. The films usually concentrate on intimate family relationships, especially sexual interactions. In keeping with this melodramatic form they often use common stereotypes. They take place in limited settings and involve many intimate conversations among the characters. They often focus on the urban middle class. They often use popular musical forms and musicians to increase audience interest. Many times they adapt well-known literary works (e.g., the series of films made from García Márquez's novels and stories). Their politics are muted, often displaced into the past or, as usual in melodrama, into the family situation. The family substitutes for society as a whole.

Many of these filmmakers, in spite of their recent successes, must raise funds internationally. Thus many of these films are co-productions with European countries, often television stations and networks. It is not hard to see the contradiction between international funding and the desire to create a national cinema. What of the national must be sacrificed to please international patrons and audiences? What does the European television audience expect from a Latin American film? They want something exotic and probably don't want their stereotypes, preconceptions, and touristic experiences or fantasies challenged in any significant way.

Nonetheless, in spite of the overwhelming difficulties and certain weaknesses in the films, Latin American filmmakers, inspired by "New" Latin American Cinema, continue to create innovative and meaningful films. And we have more access to this fascinating and encouraging effort than ever before. With some understanding of the history of this cinema and the conditions in which these filmmakers work, we can have a much greater appreciation of these films.

Resources

Teachers and students will find it relatively easy to locate enough Latin American films for self-study and/or to teach a whole course, although they may not find all the specific films they want. What is available in the United States is spotty at best. Begin at your local videostore: many will have 15 to 25 films from the 1960s to the present. (Finding Latin American films made before 1960 is almost impossible.) You can also obtain films (rental or purchase) from many mail order houses. The most comprehensive is Facets Video (1–800–331–6197, sales@facets.org). The Center for Cuban Studies, 124 West 23rd Street, New York, NY, 10011, (212) 242–0559, sells video-tapes of many Cuban films. The Latin American Video Archive (LAVA), 124 Washington Place, New York, NY, 10014, (212) 463–0108, Fax: (212) 243-2007, imre@igc.apc.org also sells video-tapes of a great many hard to find Latin American films, including many documentaries and short films. Finally, get catalogues from these film and video distributors: Cinema Guild (1697 Broadway, N.Y, N.Y, 10019), Icarus Films (200 Park Ave., Suite 1319, NY, NY, 10003), Museum of Modern Art (115–53rd Street, New York, NY, 10019), Third World Newsreel (335 – 38th Street,

5th Floor, NY, NY, 10018), and Women Make Movies (462 Broadway, Suite 500, New York, NY, 10013).

Alphabetical list of the films mentioned in the essay, by country

Argentina
Camila (María Luisa Bemberg, 1984)
Kiss of the Spider Woman (Hector Babenco, 1985)
La hora de los hornos (Hour of the Furnaces, Fernando Solanas and Octavio Getino, 1968)
Los inundados (The Flood Victims, Fernando Birri, 1962)
Miss Mary (Maria Luisa Bemberg, 1986)
The Official Story (Luis Puenzo, 1985)
The Old Gringo (Luis Puenzo, 1989)
Tire dié (Throw Us a Dime, Fernando Birri, 1958)

Bolivia
Courage of the People (The Night of San Juan, Jorge Sanjinés, 1971)
Yawar Malku (Blood of the Condor, Jorge Sanjinés, 1969)

Brazil
Antonio das Mortes (Glauber Rocha, 1968)
Barravento (Glauber Rocha, 1962)
Hour of the Star (Suzana Amaral, 1986)
O Cangaceiro (Lima Barreto, 1953)
Vidas Secas (Barren Lives, Nelson Pereira dos Santos, 1963)

Colombia
Rodrigo D: No Futuro (Victor Gaviria, 1989)

Cuba
El Mégano (Julio García Espinosa and Tomás Gutiérrez Alea, 1954)
Lucia (Humberto Solás, 1968)
Memories of Underdevelopment (Tomás Gutiérrez Alea, 1968)
Now (Santiago Alvarez, 1965)
One Way or Another (Sara Gómez, 1974–77),
Strawberry and Chocolate (Tomás Gutiérrez Alea, 1993)

El Salvador
El Salvador: El pueblo vencerá (El Salvador: The People Will Win, Diego de la Texera and Têtê Vasconcelos, 1981)

Mexico
Danzón (María Navaro, 1991)
Like Water for Chocolate (Alfonso Arau, 1991)

U.S. Latino
The Ballad of Gregorio Cortés (Robert Young, 1984)
Born in East L.A. (Richard "Cheech" Marin, 1987)
El Norte (Gregory Nava and Anna Thomas, 1984)
La Bamba (Luis Valdes, 1987)
Zoot Suit (Luis Valdes, 1982)

Italian Neorealism
Bicycle Thief (Vittorio De Sica, 1948)
La Terra Trema (Luchino Visconti, 1947)
Miracle in Milan (Vittorio De Sica, 1950)
Paisan (Roberto Rossellini, 1946)
Rome, Open City (Roberto Rossellini, 1945

Alphabetical list of the films mentioned in the essay

Antonio das Mortes (Glauber Rocha, 1968)
The Ballad of Gregorio Cortes (Robert Young, 1984)
Barravento (Glauber Rocha, 1962)
Born in East L.A. (Richard "Cheech" Marin, 1987)
Camila (María Luisa Bemberg, 1984)
Courage of the People (The Night of San Juan, Jorge Sanjinés, 1971)
Danzón (María Navaro, 1991)
El Mégano (Julio García Espinosa and Tomás Gutiérrez Alea, 1954)
El Norte (Gregory Nava and Anna Thomas, 1984),
El Salvador: El Pueblo Vencera (El Salvador: The People Will Win, Diego de La Texera and Têtê Vasconcelos, 1981)
Hour of the Star (Suzana Amaral, 1986)
Kiss of the Spider Woman (Hector Babenco, 1985)
La Bamba (Luis Valdés, 1987)
La hora de los hornos (Hour of the Furnaces, Fernando Solanas and Octavio Getino, 1968).
La Terra Trema (Luchino Visconti, 1947)
Like Water for Chocolate (Alfonso Arau, 1991)
Los inundados (The Flood Victims, Fernando Birri, 1962)
Lucia (Humberto Solás, 1968)
Memories of Underdevelopment (Tomás Gutiérrez Alea, 1968)
Miracle in Milan (Vittorio De Sica, 1950)
Miss Mary (Maria Luisa Bemberg, 1986)
Now (Santiago Alvarez, 1965)
O Cangaceiro (Lima Barreto, 1953)
The Bicycle Thief (Vittorio De Sica, 1948)
The Official Story (Luis Puenzo, 1985)
The Old Gringo (Luis Puenzo, 1989)

One Way or Another (Sara Gómez, 1974–77)
Paisan (Roberto Rossellini, 1946)
Rodrigo D: No Futuro (Victor Gaviria, 1989)
Rome, Open City (Roberto Rossellini, 1945)
Strawberry and Chocolate (Tomás Gutiérrez Alea, 1993)
Tire dié (Throw us a Dime, Fernando Birri, 1958)
Vidas secas (Barren Lives, Nelson Pereira dos Santos, 1963)
Yawar Malku (*Blood of the Condor*, Jorge Sanjinés, 1969)
Zoot Suit (Luis Valdés, 1982)

Notes

1. For details of this event see the *New York Times* 26 March, 1972 : 62. See Van Gosse's interesting account of the early responses to the Cuban Revolution in the United States: *Where the Boys Are: Cuba, Cold War America and the Making of a New Left* (London: Verso, 1993).

2. For example, see Paul Austerlitz, *Merengue: Dominican Music and Dominican Identity* (Philadelphia: Temple University Press, 1997); Yvonne Daniel, *Rumba: Dance and Social Change in Contemporary Cuba* (Bloomington: Indiana University Press, 1995); Charles A. Perrone, *Masters of Contemporary Brazilian Song*: MPB, 1965–1985 (Austin: University of Texas Press, 1989); Marta E. Savigliano, *Tango and the Political Economy of Passion* (Boulder: Westview Press, 1995); and Thomas Turino, *Moving Away from Silence: Music of the Peruvian Altiplano and the Experience of Urban Migration* (Chicago: University of Chicago Press, 1993).

3. Pedro Meyer, *Truths & Fictions* (New York: Aperture, 1995) and Sebastião Salgado, *Workers* (New York: Aperture, 1993).

4. Numerous artists from the United States went to Mexico in the 1920s, amazed by the flowering of art there after the revolution. The huge murals of Orozco, Rivera, and Siqueiros became particularly well known around the world.

5. See Kathleen Newman, "Latin American Cinema in North American Film Scholarship," *Iris* 13 (Summer, 1991): 2.

6. See B. Ruby Rich, "An/Other View of "New" Latin American Cinema," Iris 13 (Summer, 1991): 5–28.

7. See Michael Chanan, "*El Salvador: The People Will Win*: Resistance," Jump Cut 26 (December, 1981): 21–23.

8. The best short history of recent Latin American cinema in English is John King, *Magical Reels* (London: Verso, 1990).

9. Most of these films are available on video and many school libraries own them. For more detailed accounts of this important cinematic movement see Roy Armes, *Patterns of Realism: A Study of Italian Neo-Realist Cinema* (New York: A.S. Barnes & Co., 1971), Peter Bondanella, *Italian Cinema: From Neorealism to the Present* (New York: Frederick Ungar, 1983), Mira Leihm, Passion and Defiance: Film in Italy from 1942 to the Present (Berkeley: University of

California Press, 1984), and P. Adams Sitney, Vital Crises in Italian Cinema: Iconography, Stylistics, Politics (Austin: University of Texas Press, 1995).

10. Robert Kolker, *The Altering Eye* (New York: Oxford University Press, 1983) 20.

11. See my article for more detail on this relationship between neorealism and "New" Latin American Cinema: "Neo-Realism and 'New' Latin American Cinema: The *Bicycle Thief* and *Blood of the Condor." Mediating Two Worlds: Cinematic Encounters in the Americas*, ed. John King, Ana López, and Manuel Alvarado. (London: British Film Institute, 1993) 104–18.

12. "Cinema Novo," meaning New Cinema, is the Brazilian name for their part of this continental movement. See Randal Johnson, *The Film Industry in Brazil* (Pittsburgh: University of Pittsburgh Press, 1987) and Randal Johnson and Robert Stam, *Brazilian Cinema* (Austin: University of Texas Press, 1982).

13. The Latin American Video Archive in New York sells video copies of this film.

14. See Michael Chanan, *The Cuban Image* (London: BFI, 1985).

15. Fernando Birri, "The Roots of Documentary Realism: An Interview with Julianne Burton," in *Argentine Cinema*, ed. Tim Barnard, trans. Julianne Burton (Toronto: Nightwood Editons, 1986) 68.

16. The Museum of Modern Art in New York distributes both of these Birri films.

17. "The Hour of the Furnaces and the Two Avent-Gardes," *in The Social Documentary in Latin America*, ed. Julianne Burton (Pittsburgh: University of Pittsburgh Press, 1990) 259.

18. A particularly interesting recent book on this period is Diana Taylor, *Disappearing Acts: Spectacles of Gender and Nationalism in Argentina's Dirty War* (Durham: Duke, 1997) .

19. King, *Magical Reels,* 107.

20. For more detail on this film and Rocha's other work see Randal Johnson, *Cinema Novo X 5* (Austin: University of Texas Press, 1984).

21. Johnson and Stam, *Brazilian Cinema* 120.

22. See Terence Carlson's discussion of the film in Johnson and Stam, *Brazilian Cinema* 169–77.

23. Julianne Burton, “Film and Revolution in Cuba: The First 25 Years,” *Jump Cut*, ed. Peter Steven (Toronto: Between the Lines, 1985) 348.

24. See my article for a description and analysis of this film: “Santiago Alvarez: Cine-Agitator of the Cuban Revolution and the Third World.” *"SHOW US LIFE": Toward a History and Aesthetics of the Committed Documentary*, ed. Tom Waugh (Metuchen, NJ: Scarecrow Press, 1984) 384–402.

25. For the film’s script, the original novella from which it came, and considerable commentary about it see *Memories of Underdevelopment*, ed. Michael Chanan (New Brunswick: Rutgers University Press, 1990). This film is also readily available on video.

26. Julia Lesage,“*One Way or Another*, Dialectical, Revolutionary, Feminist,” *Jump Cut* (May, 1979): 20.

27. See my article: “Melodrama, Sex and the Cuban Revolution: *Strawberry and Chocolate* (Tomás Gutiérrez Alea, 1993),” *Jump Cut* (May, 1997): 119–25.

28. Though out of print, an important collection of Sanjinés's writings remains: Jorge Sanjinés and the Ukumau Group, The Theory and Practice of a Cinema with the People, Art on the Line #6 (Willimantic, CT: Curbstone Press, 1989).

29. For an important discussion of women’s film and video work see Julia Lesage, “Women Make Media: Three Modes of Production.” in *The Social Documentary in Latin America*, ed. Julianne Burton. Pittsburgh: University of Pittsburgh Press, 1990: 315–47.

30. Almost any history of modern Latin America, as well as more specialized articles and books give the details of these counterrevolutions and our government’s support for them. See, for example, Tulio Halperín Donghi, *The Contemporary History of Latin America*, trans. John Charles Chasteen (Durham: Duke University Press, 1993).

Contributors

The Editors

Julio López-Arias is Associate Professor at Ithaca College where he teaches Spanish language, literature, culture, and civilization. He has published books and articles on Spanish, Portuguese, and Latin American historiography and literature. His primary interests include the cultures and civilizations of Spain, Portugal, and Latin America. He received his undergraduate degree in *Pedagogía* from the Universidad de Santiago de Compostela (Spain) and a graduate degree in *Filosofía y Letras* from the Universidad Pontificia de Salamanca (Spain). He received his M.A. and Ph.D. in Romance Languages and Literatures from the University of Michigan, where he taught for six years.

Gladys M. Varona-Lacey is Associate Professor and Chair of the Department of Modern Languages and Literatures at Ithaca College where she teaches Spanish and Latin American literature. Professor Varona-Lacey has published in the field of Latin American literature. *Introducción a la literatura hispanoamericana: de la conquista al siglo XX* (1997) is her most recent publication. She is currently writing a book on the Peruvian writer José María Arguedas. Dr. Varona-Lacey received a Certificate in Latin American Studies and a Ph.D. in Hispanic Languages and Literatures from the University of Pittsburgh and has taught at the Massachusetts Institute of Technology, Tufts University, and Harvard University.

The Contributors

Gustavo Alfaro is Professor of Romance Languages at Tufts University. He teaches Spanish literature of the Golden Age and Latin American fiction. His publications include *La estructura de la novela picaresca* and *Constante de la historia de Latinoamérica en García Márquez*. Articles he has written have appeared in journals in Europe, Latin America, and the United States. He holds a Ph.D. in Romance Languages from Harvard University and has taught at Stanford, Dalhouise, and Tufts Universities.

Sarah Brooks has an M.A. from Duke University and is currently a Ph.D. candidate in political science. She specializes in Latin American politics.

Carol Callaway was Assistant Curator of the Pre-Columbian collection at Dumbarton Oaks in Washington, D.C. Among Dr. Callaway's publications are

"Pre-Columbian and Colonial Mexican Images of the Cross: Christ's Sacrifice and the Fertile Earth" (1990) and "St. Michael and the Sudarium: A Christian Soldier and Human Sacrifice." With Susan Bergh she co-authored "Form & Rhythm: Ancient Andean Textiles at Dumbarton Oaks" (1996). Dr. Callaway recently completed a monograph about the Cross of Topiltepec and the early colonial history of the Yanhuitlan Valley in Oaxaca. Dr. Callaway received her Ph.D. from the University of Maryland. We are sad to report that Dr. Callaway passed away on January 8, 1998.

Miguel Angel Centeno is Associate Professor of Sociology and Master of Wilson College at Princeton University. He is the author of *Mexico in the 1990s* (1991) and *Democracy within Reason: Technocratic Revolution in Mexico* (2nd edition 1997). He is the editor of *Toward a New Cuba* (1997) and *The Politics of Expertise in Latin America* (1997). Professor Centeno's publications also include over a dozen journal articles and book chapters. His current work analyzes the roles of war and peace in Latin America. Professor Centeno has been the recipient of grants from the Harry Frank Guggenheim Foundation, the National Science Foundation, the National Endowment for the Humanities, and the Woodrow Wilson Foundation. He has also been a Fulbright scholar in Russia and Mexico. He holds a Ph.D. in Sociology from Yale University.

Walter Aaron Clark is Associate Professor of Musicology at the University of Kansas. His specialty is Spanish and Latin American music from 1800 to the present. His research has appeared in the *New Grove Dictionary of Opera, The Musical Quarterly, Inter-American Music Review, Revista de Musicología,* and the *Journal of the Lute Society of America.* Professor Clark is the author of *Isaac Albéniz: Portrait of a Romantic* (1997) and *Isaac Albéniz: A Guide to Research* (1997). He is also a contributing editor to the *Handbook of Latin American Studies.* Dr. Clark received his Ph.D. in historical musicology from the University of California at Los Angeles.

Sarah Chambers is Assistant Professor of History at the University of Minnesota. Her teaching interests within the field of Latin America include colonial and early republican history as well as women's history. Professor Chambers has published on the topic of domestic violence in Peru and has a book forthcoming entitled *From Subjects to Citizens: Honor, Culture and Politics in Arequipa, Peru, 1780–1854.* She is also researching and studying the issues of gender and colonialism in Gran Colombia circa 1780–1840. Professor Chambers received her Ph.D. from the University of Wisconsin at Madison.

G. Reginald Daniel is Assistant Professor of Sociology at the University of California at Santa Barbara. His teaching and research focus on comparative and ethnic relations, particularly as they relate to multiracial individuals of partial African descent in Brazil, South Africa, and the United States. His scholarly contributions have appeared in *Racially Mixed People in America* (1992) and in *The Multiracial Experience: Racial Borders as the New Frontier* (1996). He is co-author of "Being Different Together in the University Classroom: Multiracial Identity as Transgressive Education" and author of "Black and White Identity in the New Millennium: Unsevering the Ties That Bind." Professor Daniel is a member of the advisory boards of AMEA (Association of Multiethnic Americans) and Project RACE (Reclassify All Children Equally). He holds a Ph.D. in Latin American cultural studies from the University of California, Los Angeles.

C. Alejandra Elenes is Assistant Professor of Women's Studies at Arizona State University West and an affiliated faculty member of the Hispanic Research Center of Arizona State University. She specializes in Chicano/a and Mexican cultural studies, the formation of identity and national consciousness, and feminist and critical pedagogy. Her most recent publications include "New Directions in Feminist Curriculum Transformation Projects," which appeared in *Feminist Teacher,* and "Reclaiming the Borderlands: Chicana/o Identity, Difference, and Critical Pedagogy," published in *Educational Theory.* Professor Elenes received her Ph.D. in educational communications and technology from the Curriculum and Instruction Department at the University of Wisconsin at Madison.

Anita Herzfeld is Associate Professor of Linguistics at the Center of Latin American Studies at the University of Kansas. She is editor and co-author of several books. She has written numerous articles on the sociolinguistics of the anglophone creoles and the indigenous languages of Central America. Among her publications is "La auto imagen de los hablantes del criollo limonense" (1992). Professor Herzfeld is currently working on a book on Limonese Creole. She received her Ph.D. from the University of Kansas.

John Hess is co-founder of, and continues to co-edit, *Jump Cut, A Review of Contemporary Media.* He has taught film studies at California State University-Somona, San Francisco State University, and Ithaca College. His most recent publications include "Melodrama, Sex, and the Cuban Revolution: Tomás Gutiérrez Alea's *Strawberry and Chocolate,*" and "Neo-Realism and the New Latin American Cinema: *The Bicycle Thief* and *Blood of the Condor.*" With Patricia Zimmermann, Dr. Hess co-authored "Transnational Documentaries: A

Manifesto." He is currently writing a book on New Latin American Cinema. He obtained his Ph.D. from Indiana University at Bloomington.

Colleen Kattau is Assistant Professor of Spanish at Ithaca College, Ithaca, New York. She has published articles on the work of Isabel Allende and Julia de Burgos. Her most recent publications include first-time translations of articles by Diego Rivera in David Craven's *Diego Rivera as Epic Modernist* (1997). Professor Kattau is also a singer/songwriter of *Nueva canción* or New Song. She received her Ph.D. in Spanish language and culture from Syracuse University, with a concentration in Women's Studies.

Timothy D. Murphy is Associate Professor of Anthropology at Northern Kentucky University. He has carried out primary research in the Central Highlands of Mexico, mainly among Nahuatl-speakers. His publications include "Labor Migration and Family Structure in the Tlaxcala-Puebla Area of Mexico" and "Marriage and Family in a Nahuatl-speaking Community" which appeared in *Essays on Mexican Kinship,* edited by H. G. Nutini, Pedro Carrasco, and James M Taggart. Dr. Murphy received his Ph.D. in Anthropology from the University of Pittsburgh.

Satya R. Pattnayak is Associate Professor of Sociology at Villanova University in Pennsylvania. Dr. Pattnayak is the editor of *Globalization, Urbanization, and the State: Selected Studies on Contemporary Latin America* (1996). In addition, he has published articles in *The International Journal of Comparative Sociology*, *Journal of Developing Societies,* and *International Studies.* He received his Ph.D. from Vanderbilt University.

Blas Puente-Baldoceda is Associate Professor at Northern Kentucky University. He is the author of *Quechua Tarmeño, Textos I* and *Fonología del Quechua Tarmeño.* Professor Puente-Baldoceda has also published fiction and numerous articles on Latin American literature. His most recent fictional works are "Había una vez un reloj" and "Los orongos." His latest articles include "Itinerario de una poética narrativa en las obras de Ednodio Quintero," "La narrativa neoindigenista en el Perú," "Algunas ideas en torno al arte de narrativa en U.S." "Las estrategias narrativas en tres obras de Salvador Garmendia," and "Textualidad e ideología en *Crónica de San Gabriel*" in *Asedios a Julio Ramón Ribeyro*, edited by Ismael Márquez and César Ferreira. Professor Puente-Baldoceda received his Ph.D. from the University of Texas at Austin and has held teaching positions at the Universidad Nacional de San Marcos in Lima, Peru, Cornell University, the State University of New York at Buffalo, and the University of Illinois at Champaign-Urbana.

Susan Randolph is Associate Professor of Economics at the University of Connecticut and a faculty member in the Latin American and Caribbean Studies Program. Dr. Randolph also serves as an occasional short-term consultant for the World Bank and the United States Agency for International Development. Her recent publications include *Determinants of Public Expenditures on Infrastructures* (with Dennis Heffley and Zeljko Bogetic), *World Bank Policy Research Working Paper #661*, "Structural Adjustment and Family Policy in Africa: Lessons from Sudan" (with Fareed Hassan), and "Liquidity Constraints, Productivity, Employment and Output: Evidence from Nonagricultural Activities in Bangladesh" (with Habib Ahmed). Professor Randolph received her Ph.D. in economics from Cornell University, with a specialization in development economics.

Christian Smith is Assistant Professor of Sociology at the University of North Carolina, Chapel Hill. Dr. Smith specializes in religion, social movements, and Latin American social change. He has recently published *Resisting Reagan: The U.S. Central America Peace Movements* (1996), *Disruptive Religion: The Force of Faith in Social Movement Activism,* and *The Emergence of Liberation Theology.* He earned his Ph.D. in sociology from Harvard University.

Index

abertura democrática, 24
abolition, 20–21, 24, 28
Acatzingo, Puebla (Mexico), 219
Acolman, 217–218, 220–221, 224
Acosta, José de, 184
Affonso Arinos Law, 28
African Brazilian, 19, 21–36
African Brazilian women, 28
African influences in Latin American music, 233, 236, 239, 240, 243–244, 246, 247
Afro-Caribbean, 44, 61
Afro-Central America, 44, 49–50, 58
Afro-Costaricans, 49, 51
Afro-Limonese, 49–50
Agua, 206
águila y la serpiente, El, 187
Aleph, El, 189
Alegría, Ciro, 199
Allende, Salvador, 257–259
Alliance for Progress, 109
Altar of the Kings, 226
Amalia, 186
amarelo, 29
Amerindian, 44, 49–50, 60
amor en los tiempos del cólera, El, 192
Andean music, 241
Antonio das Mortes, 278
araucana, La, 184
arauco domado, El, 185
Araujo, Juan de, 237
Aréstegui, Narciso, 199
Argentina, 74, 77, 81, 82, 85
Argentinean music, 242
Arguedas, José María, 204
Army of National Liberation, 113
assimilation, 21, 25, 29
Asturias, Miguel Angel, 188, 191
Augustinian convent, 217
Augustinian monastery at Malinalco, Mexico, 220
Aura, 191
average income in Latin America, 165
Ayala, Ramón, 253
Aztec, 3–4, 7–8, 17, 94–95, 102, 217, 220–221, 224, 228
Aztec goddess, 94–95
Aztec music, 234
Azuela, Mariano, 187

balance of payments crises, 167, 169
Balbas, Jerónimo, 226
Balbuena, Bernardo de, 185
Ballad of Gregorio Cortés, The, 272, 288
ballet, 241
Bamba, La, 272, 288
baptismal fonts, 219
Baratta, María de, 241
Barravento, 278–279, 287–288
Barrios, Augustín, 244
Básilica de Guadalupe, 92
Battle for La Plata, 124
Bay Islands, 48, 54, 60
Belize, 3, 44, 53, 58, 217
Bello, Andrés, 186
Benavente, Toribio de, 184
Bezerra Tanco, Luis, 92
Blades, Rubén, 253, 265
Boff, Leonardo, 115
bolero, 246
Bolívar, Simón, 72, 123
Bolivia, 106
bomba, 242
Borges, Jorge Luis, 188
Born in East L.A., 272, 288
bossa nova, 244, 248
Bourbon reforms, 9
brancos, 19, 29, 34
Brazil, 19–37, 106–107, 114–115, 117
Brazilian cinema, 275
Brazilian Constitution of 1988, 28
Brazilian Institute of Geography and Statistics (IBGE), 29
Brazilian music, 244
Brazilian race relations, 20–21, 27, 29, 30

British West Indian culture, 50
Brown, Roy, 265
budget deficits, 171, 174
Bustamante, Fray Francisco, 92
Bustos, Salvador, 264

Cabrera Infante, Guillermo, 190, 192, 194
cachorros, Los, 192
Camila, 271, 287–288
canción protesta, 253
canciones rancheras, 240
candombé, 243
Cangaceiro, O, 275
Canto general, 190
Caribbean, 4, 16
Carpentier, Alejo, 188–189
Carrasco, Eduardo, 258
casa verde, La, 192
Catholic Church, Roman 69, 105, 107–116, 118
Catholic doctrine, 106
Catholic unions, 108, 109
Catholicism, 95
Central America, 3–5, 7, 10, 13, 16, 43–51, 53, 57–61, 63
Central American music, 240
Chaco War, 121, 122, 127, 135
Chamorro, Violeta de, 76
Charles IV, 228
Chávez, Carlos, 240
Chicana, 87, 90, 99, 101, 103
Chicano nationalism, 89
Chile, 110, 115, 118
chilena, 238
chiluca, 227
chinampa, 7
Cholula, 91, 228
Cholutecas, 91
choroes, 245
Christian Democracy, 109
chronicles, 87, 90
Chungara, Domitila Barrios de, 74, 78, 81
Cien años de soledad, 192
Cihuacóalt, 94–95
Cinema Novo, 276, 278–279, 291
Ciudad y los perros, La, 192
civil rights movement, 24
civil wars, 128–130
Coatlicue, fertility goddess, 224
Códice Aubin, 91
Códice Florentino, 91
Códice Ramírez, 91
Colchado Lucio, Oscar, 207
Colombia, 3
Colonial Era, 108
colonial law, 71
Colonial Mexican churches, 221
Coloreds, 20
Columbus, Christopher, 183
Comentarios reales, 185
commercial bank loans to Latin America, 171
common-law unions, 20
comparsa, 247
comunidades eclesiásticas de base (CEB), 110
concubinage, 20
congregaciones or *repúblicas de indios*, 8
conquest dances, 239
consagración de la primavera, La, 189
Conversación en la catedral, 192
Convite, 263
Copán, 48
Cordero, Roque, 241
Corn Mothers, 69, 80, 84
coronel no tiene quien le escriba, El, 192, 195
Correa the Elder, Juan, 226
corridos, 240
Cortázar, Julio, 191
Cortés, Hernán, 3, 70, 90–92, 97–98, 100, 183, 217
Costa Rica, 3, 43–44, 48–51, 53, 60–64
Creole, 88, 89, 92, 94, 95, 98, 228
creole languages, 45, 49, 51, 58
criollo, 3, 48
Cristóbal Nonato, 191
Crónica de una muerte anunciada, 192

Cruz, Sor Juana Inés de la, 71, 80, 86, 185
Cuba, 74, 76, 81, 86
Cuban feminist congresses, 74
Cuban literature, 185, 187, 189, 190–191, 194–195
Cuban music, 246
Cuban revolution, 109, 131
cueca chilena, 238
Cuentos andinos, 202
cumbia, 240
currency devaluation, 173–174, 176
Cuzco, 228, 232
danzón, 246, 271, 288
Darío, Rubén, 186
development and dependency patterns, 152
development strategies in Latin America, 167, 173
developmentalist ideology, 109
Diamantes y pedernales, 206
Díaz del Castillo, Bernal, 90, 96, 97, 183
Diego, Juan, 92–93, 220
Domínguez Navarro, Ofelia, 74, 81, 86
Dominican music, 247
Donoso, José, 190, 195

Echeverría, Esteban, 186
economic growth, 137, 139, 143–145, 152
Ecuador, 74
Ecuadorian music, 241
educational level in Latin America, 161
El Salvador, 3, 111, 115, 217
encomienda, 9, 106
Enrique, Luis, 264
Episcopal Conference of Latin America (CELAM), 110–111
Ercilla, Alonso de, 184
escape hatch, 21
Escorza, Manuel, 207
España en el corazón, 190
España, aparta de mi este cáliz, 190
Estigarribia, José Félix, 127
estrella del norte, La, 92

Facundo. Civilización y barbarie, 186
Family Code, 75
female education, 73
Ferdinand of Aragón, 105
Fernández de Lizardi, José Joaquín, 186
Fernández, Gaspar, 236
festejo, 242
Ficciones, 189
Fichte, Johann Gottlieb, 46
filo del agua, Al, 187
Flemish artists, 221
Florencia, Francisco de, 92
foreign capital, 169–170, 175–177
foreign debt, 170–174, 179–180
foreign investment, 138–139, 142, 144, 152, 155
foreign trade, 139, 145, 152
Francia, Dr. José, 125
Franciscan Mission of San Juan Evangelista, 219
Franciscans, 106, 217, 219, 220
Franco, Hernando, 235
Frente Negra, A, 28
Freyre, Gilberto, 20, 32, 36
Fuentes, Carlos, 188, 191, 192, 195

gachupín, 3
Gama, Antonio de, 92
Gante, Fray Pedro de, 217
García Calderón, Ventura, 190
García Márquez, Gabriel, 190–193, 195
General en su laberinto, El, 192
Gilberto, Joao, 245
Gillén, Nicolás, 260
Ginastera, Alberto, 243
Gómara, Francisco López de, 90–91

González, Sara, 261
González Prada, Manuel, 199

grandeza mexicana, La, 185
Gregorian chant, 236
Gringo viejo, 188, 271, 2 87, 289
Gross Domestic Product, 163–165, 174–175, 177
Gross National Product, 139
Guadalupe, Virgen of 87, 88–89, 92–93, 95–96, 99, 102–104
guajira, 246
Guaraní, 46, 59, 64
Guardabarranco, 264
Guatemala, 3–6, 8–11, 13–15, 17, 43–44, 46, 48–51, 53, 58, 60, 64, 111, 115, 217
guerra silenciosa, La, 207
Guzmán, Martín Luis, 187

Habana para un infante difunto, La, 191
Haitian music, 247
haupango, 238
health and life expectancy in Latin America, 159
heraldos negros, Los, 190
Herder, Johann Gottfried von, 46, 59
Hernández, José, 186
Hidalgo, Miguel, 123
hijos del sol, Los, 202
Historia de los indios de Nueva España, 184
Historia general y moral de las Indias, 184
Hojeda, Diego de, 185
Hombres de maíz, 188
Honduras, 3, 44, 48–49, 54, 60, 217
hora de los hornos, La, 278
Hour of the Star, 272, 287-288
Housewives Committee, 74–75
Huamán Cabrera, Félix, 207
Hue Tlamahuizaltica, 92
Huejotzingo, Puebla (Mexico), 221–223, 231
Huitzilopochtli, 69
Humboldt, Wilhelm von, 46

illiteracy rate, 161
Import Substituting Industrialization (ISI), 109, 140, 142
Inca music, 235
income inequality, 146–148, 165
Indígena, 3
Indigenismo, 6
indigenous literature, 199
indigenous peoples, 5
inflation, 168, 171, 174
Intermediate Area, 44, 58
International Monetary Fund, 169, 173
International Wars, 121–123
interracial marriages, 20
Inti-Illimani, 258–260, 263, 267–268
Instituto Brasileiro de Análisis Sociais e Económicas (IBASE), 29
inundados, Los, 276–277, 287–288
Isaacs, Jorge, 186
Isabella of Castille, 105
Italian artists, 221, 226
Italian Neorealism, 274–275, 277–278, 285, 288
Ixmiquilpan, Hidalgo (Mexico), 220, 230

Jamaican Creole, 50, 60, 61, 63
Jamaican music, 247
Jara, Víctor, 257, 258, 266, 267, 242
jarabe, 238
Jaramillo, Juan, 90
Jesús, Fray Felipe de, 224
Jim Crow, 19
Jobim, Antonio Carlos, 245
John XXIII, Pope, 110
joropo, 246
Juana of Spain, Princess, 70
Juárez, Benito, 128

Justice and Peace Movement, 115

Kennedy, John F., 109
Kiss of the Spider Woman, 272, 287, 288

laberinto de la soledad, El, 91
Lamia, 94
language and identity, 44–47, 58–59
las Casas, Bartolomé de, 106, 184
Latin American Catholic Church, 107–108, 110–113
Latin American cinema, 274
Latin American colonial music, 235
Latin American literature, 183–193
Lauro, Antonio, 246
Lecuona, Ernesto, 247
Lei Caó, 28
Ley, Salvador, 241
liberal-pluralist theory of development, 140
liberals, 107, 108
liberation theology, 76, 112
Libertad bajo palabra, 190
Like Water for Chocolate, 267
Lima, Peru, 106
Lillith, 94
Limonese Creole, 43–44, 49–51, 60–61
Llorona, La, 87–89, 94–96, 98–99, 102–103
López Albújar, Enrríquez, 199
López Solano, Francisco, 124, 125
Los de abajo, 187
Los hijos del sol, 202
lost tribes of Israel, 95
Loyola, Margot, 255
Luisi, Paulina, 74
Lutz, Bertha, 73

Maestro mayor, 224
Malinalxoch, 69
Malinche, La, 70, 87, 88–91, 94–100, 102
Malíntzin, 87, 90, 91, 96, 97, 98, 100, 101, 102
Malintzin Tenépal, 102
mambo, 248
Mannerism, 221, 224, 229
Manns, Patricio, 267
María, 186
mariachi, 248
Mariátegui, José Carlos, 201–202
marimba, 239
Marina, Doña, 87, 90–91, 96, 100
Marmol, José, 186
Martí, José, 187
Martín Fierro, 186
Mary, Virgin, 69–70, 92–95, 104, 106
Mary Magdalene, 224, 230
matadero, El, 186
Matto de Turner, Clorinda, 200
Mato Grosso, 125
Maya, 3–5, 7–18, 43–44, 48–51, 53–54, 58, 60–61, 64
Maya speakers, 50
Mayan languages, 48, 51, 58, 60
Medea, 94
Medellín, Colombia, 119
Mégano, El, 276
Mejía Godoy, Carlos, 264
mejoranera, 240
Memorias del subdesarrollo, 191
merengue, 248
Mesoamerica, 3–4, 6–8, 10–13, 17, 217, 220
Mesoamerican families of languages, 44
Mesoamerican religion, 220
mestizo, 3, 5–7, 9–11, 223, 228
Mestizo music, 235
Mexican Baroque, 221, 224
Mexican Colonial art and architecture, 217
Mexican literature, 187
Mexican music, 238
Mexican national identity, 95
Mexican nationalism, 88–89, 93, 95–97

Mexican nationalist consciousness, 87, 89, 92
Mexican revolution, 131
Mexican-American War, 127
Mexicas, 92, 97, 98
Mexico, 3–8, 10, 13, 15–18, 44, 64, 87, 89–95, 97–103, 106, 217, 219–220, 222–224, 226–228, 230–232
Mexico City, 71–72, 78, 80, 84, 92–93, 217, 224, 227
Mexico, Cathedral of, 221
Mexico, Conquest of, 87
Milanés, Pablo, 261–262, 268
military expenditure, 148, 151–152
military governments, 111, 113
military regimes, 76
Miss Mary, 271, 287–288
Mixtec, 3–4, 11
Montezuma, 217
Motecuhzoma, 91, 97
muerte de Artemio Cruz, La, 188, 191
mulato, 3, 20–23, 26–27, 30–31
mundo es ancho y ajeno, El, 203
música norteña, 238, 239

Nahualismo, 241
Náhuatl, 90, 92, 97, 100
Náhuatl-speaking communities, 10
Napoleonic invasions of Spain, 123
natural resources in Latin America, 139
negro, 3, 19, 29, 30, 31, 35, 236
Neo-Classicism, 228–229
neoliberal state, 143–145, 148
Neruda, Pablo, 189
Neves, Tancredo, 28
New Argentine Revolution, 277
New Christendom, 108
New Latin American Cinema, 272–276, 283–286, 290–291
New Song, 253–257, 259–266, 268
New Spain, 219–221, 228, 231
New World, 217, 220, 222–224, 228, 231
Nican Mopohua, 92
Nicaragua, 3, 44, 48–49, 54, 63, 69, 75–76, 81, 84–85, 109, 111
Nicaraguan Revolution, 69
North American Free Trade, 146
Nuestra Señora de la Soledad, Chruch of, 224, 231
Nueva canción, 253–254, 257, 259–260, 262–263, 265–266
Nueva España, music of, 235
Nueva trova, 253, 260–261, 268
Nuevo cancionero, 253, 262–263
Nuevo canto, 253, 260
Nuevos cuentos andinos, 202

Oaxaca, 11, 17, 224, 231
Official Story, The, 271
Old Gringo, 271, 287, 289
Olmedo, José Joaquín de, 186
Oña, Pedro de, 185
one-drop rule, 19–21
opera, 242
opera, Peruvian, 237
Origen Milagroso, 92
Orozco, José Clemente, 91
otoño del patriarca, El, 190–191

Padilla, Juan de, 236
padre Horán, El, 199
Panama, 3, 44, 48–49, 54, 58
Panamanian music, 240
Paradise Garden murals, 220
Paraguay, 109
Paraguayan music, 244
pardos, 19, 30, 34
Parra, Violeta, 254–257, 260, 267–268
pasos perdidos, Los, 189
Patria Potestad, 70, 73
patronato real, 105
Pávez, Héctor, 255
payada, 243
Paz, Octavio, 91, 190
Pedro Páramo, 188
peninsula, 3
Pentecostalism, 115
per capita income, 163–164, 165

Pérez Huaranca, Hildebrando, 207
Periquillo Sarniento, El, 186
Perón, Juan, 74
Peru, 46, 71, 81, 84, 106, 115
Peruvian music, 242
Peruvian-Bolivian Wars, 125
Piazzolla, Astor, 243
Pinochet, Augusto, 115
Pizarro, Gabriella, 255
Plateresque style, 218, 221–222, 228
Poemas humanos, 190
polca, 244
Ponce, Manuel, 239
populist governments, 109
Portuguese influences in Brazilian music, 244
post-colonial music, 237
poverty in Latin America, 165
pre-Columbian music, 233
pre-Hispanic culture, 6, 7
pretos, 19, 31, 34
progreso católico, 199
protestantism, 115, 117, 118
province of Limon, 49
public social expenditures, 148
Pueblo people, 69
pueblo vencerá, El, 273
Puerto Rican music, 247

Q'anjob'al, 4, 10–11, 15
Quetzacoatl, 228
Quiché, 4
Quilapayún, 258–260, 267
quotas on imports, 167, 174

racial discrimination, 23, 26–28
recurso del método, El, 189, 191
Redoble por Rancas, 207
reino de este mundo, El, 189
relación, 184
Renaissance, 218, 221, 226, 228
Renaissance and Baroque music, 236
repartimiento, 9
Republican period, 9
Rerum Novarum, 108
Residencia en la tierra, 189
Revueltas, Silvestre, 240
ríos profundos, Los, 204
Rodó, José Enrique, 187
Rodríguez, Lorenzo, 226, 232
Rodríguez, Osvaldo, 254, 258, 267
Rodríguez, Silvio, 257, 261, 268
Roman Catholic Church. See Franciscans; liberation theology; Vatican
Rulfo, Juan, 188

sagrario or parish church, 226
Saint Michael, Church of, 220
Sahagún, Bernardino de, 88, 92, 94, 103, 184
salsa, 248
samba, 244
Somoza, Anastasio, 109
San José de los Naturales, 217
San Martín, José de, 123
San Miguel, Church of, 224
Sánchez, Father Miguel, 92
Sandinistas, 76
sanjuan, 241
Santa Ana, 127
Santa Cruz de Tlatelolco, Colegio de, 92
Santa Cruz, Andrés, 125
Santa María Tonanzintla, Church of, 228
Santiago, Zoraida, 257–258, 265, 267, 268
São Paulo, Brazil, 28, 33, 35, 36
Sarmiento, Domingo Faustino, 186
Segovia, Andrés, 240
Señor Presidente, El, 188
Serlio, Sebastiano, 226
siglo de las luces, El, 189
Sigüenza y Góngora, Carlos de, 224
slavery, 20–22, 24, 27, 28, 31
social development, 137, 145, 147, 151
sombra del caudillo, La, 187

son, 238
son de marimba, 238
son guatemalteco, 240
Sosa, Mercedes, 260, 262–263, 268
Spain, 89, 90, 95, 100, 104
Spanish conquest, 87, 90, 94, 99
Spanish crown, 9, 106
Spanish, 43–44, 46, 48–49, 50–51, 53–55, 58–59, 64, 217, 219–223, 226, 228, 230, 232

stabilization and structural adjustment loans, 173
standard English, 49, 60
standard of living in Latin America, 159
Strawberry and Chocolate, 271, 283, 287, 289, 292
Stroessner, Alfredo, 109
Sumaya, Manuel de, 235
syncretism, 106
Tabasco, 70
Tales and Legend of the Q'anjob'al, 10, 15
tango, 243, 248
Tarascan (Purépecha), 3
tariffs on imports, 163, 167, 169
Tejano, 248
Tenochtitlan, 7, 91, 221
Tepeyac, 92–93
Tepeyacac, 220
Terra Nostra, 191
tezontl, 227
Tikal, 48
Tire dié, 276–277, 287, 289
Tlaxcala, 4–5, 15, 17
Tonántzin, 88, 95, 103, 220
Tonantzintla, 228
Torrejón y Velasco, Tomás, 237
Torres, Father Camilo, 113
Totonac, 3, 4
transracial/transcultural, 21
Treaty of Guadalupe Hidalgo, 128
Tres tristes tigres, 191
Tribunals of the Inquisition, 106
Trilce, 190
Unified Black Movement (*O Movimento Negro Unificado*, MNU), 24
United Fruit Co., 50
United Nations Women's Conference, 78
United States of America, 5, 69, 73, 76
 intervention in Latin America, 274

Uruguay, 74, 81, 85
Uruguayan music, 244

Valdelomar, Abraham, 202
Valdivia, María, 71, 80
Valeriano, Antonio, 92
Vallejo, César, 190
Vargas, Getúlio, 25
Vargas Llosa, Mario, 190–192, 197
Vargas Vicuña, Eleodoro, 204
Vatican, 107, 110–111, 115
Vatican Council II, 110
Vega, Garcilaso de la, 185
Vega, Lasso de la, 92
Veinte poemas de amor y una canción desesperada, 189
Venezuela, 110
Venezuelan music, 246
verdadera historia de la conquista de la Nueva España, La, 183
Viceregal Mexico, 227
viceroys, 221
Vidas secas, 278–279, 287, 289
Villa-Lobos, Heitor, 245
Villalpando, Cristóbal de, 226
villancico, 236
Virgin of Guadalupe, 92, 220, 224
Virgin of Ocotlan, 227

Wars of Independence, 121–122
War of the Triple Alliance, 124
Weisse Frau, Die, 94
West Indian, 48–50, 59, 61, 63
West Indian Creole, 48
West Indian English-based creole, 49

World Bank, 139, 144–145, 147, 154–156, 173, 179, 180
World War II, 137, 143, 144

Yánez, Agustín, 187
Yawar fiesta, 205
Yo el Supremo, 191
Yucatan peninsula, 3, 7, 8
Yupanqui, Atahualpa, 254

zambo, 3
Zapotec, 3–4, 11, 18
Zavaleta, Carlos Eduardo, 207
Zocalo, 228
Zoot Suit, 272, 288–289
Zumárraga, Fray Juan de, 92– 93